URSULINE NOVITIATE

THE CHARACTER OF MAN

Emmanuel Mounier

THE
CHARACTER
OF
MAN

by

Emmanuel Mounier

Translated into English by
CYNTHIA ROWLAND

HARPER & BROTHERS · PUBLISHERS
NEW YORK

PRINTED IN ENGLAND

TRANSLATOR'S PREFACE

To be asked to abridge any volume of some 800 pages to a third of its length is an invitation to a massacre. When the volume is a finely integrated, comprehensive yet peculiarly personal work such as THE CHARACTER OF MAN, the result will always be open, even if not to criticism, at least to regret.

The original, to which it is hoped many readers of this abridgment may be led, suggests nothing so much as a literary *mandala*, the symbol of integation and individuation, which, with its often detailed and elaborate patterns, will be familiar to readers of *The Secret of the Golden Flower*. In Jungian symbolism the *mandala* is also a healing symbol and it is appropriate to remember that this book was written in the shadow of a great defeat. From those to whom the original, with its lucid tolerance and unquenchable if tragic optimism, has something of this healing quality, the abridger can only hope for forgiveness if passages have been omitted which they would have preferred to keep, and others included which might seem to them less representative of Emmanuel Mounier's thinking.

The abridgment, however, has been prepared with the approval of Mounier's literary executors, including Madame Paulette Mounier, to whom the translator is particularly grateful for her ready help, advice and criticism.

On the whole it has been possible to follow certain clear-cut principles in this abridgment. The multiplicity of case histories has been reduced and where an account of certain developments, such as the growth of intelligence or the emotions in childhood, is readily available in any manual of psychology, these have been omitted. But a study of the development of religious feeling in childhood has been retained, as covering fresh ground. Passages relating too closely to French art, literature or politics to be readily understandable to English-speaking readers, have been excluded, also the majority of the references to Heymans' typology, with its rather baffling alphabetical nomenclature, on the grounds that it might be too confusing to readers brought up on other classifications. A short account of the theory is, however, given in an appendix.

Two further abridgments are perhaps more important. In the first

v

place, the second, third and fourth chapters have been omitted entirely. Dealing as they do with the physical human background, from the influence of climate and geography to that of the endocrine glands, they were inevitably a resumé of other men's work, of the state of knowledge on the subject at the time of writing. Given the limitations of space, and the fact that such subjects are naturally most liable to revision in the light of continuing research, it was decided to omit them in order to allow more space to Emmanuel Mounier's own original thought which, it was felt, would stand, and in fact has stood, the test of time.

But the result is certainly an unbalance on the side of the spiritual and metaphysical aspects of the human condition, which cannot be allowed to pass unmentioned, when Mounier himself was so deeply imbued with a sense of incarnation, of man's close conditioning by the three-dimensional world in which we move. Readers are advised to look at the list of the original contents, which is given at the end of the book, to see what real weight was attached to these factors.

This is particularly important with regard to Mounier's own attitude in the conflict between the objective and the subjective approach to psychology. In his first chapter, which begins with a theoretical discussion of this problem, also omitted as being too exclusively addressed to French psychologists, Mounier points out that no study of character can fail to be marked by the character of the author, and by his view of man, which is also partly the view of his epoch. He has tried to reconcile both the analytic and synthetic approach, the static and the dynamic, utilising the mosaic of data provided by research and showing the fundamental structures which give it meaning and purpose. He says himself: 'The psychological current which we have chosen to stress is the one in which the sense of the spiritual is united with the sense of the physical, to create a figure which is neither an automaton, nor a frail dreamer after vanished ideals, but complete and dramatic and a man.'

In conclusion my very sincere thanks are due to Dr. L. S. Stein and Dr. L. Paulsen, for many suggested renderings of technical terms, though neither is to be taken as necessarily endorsing any portion of the text: and to Miss E. Cox and Mrs. M. L. Longden for their help in the preparation of the manuscript.

CYNTHIA ROWLAND

FOREWORD

The Character of Man and not *The Characterology of Man.* The distinction is deliberate. It is true that this book is an attempt to fill a regrettable lacuna in French psychological literature, and is intended to be scientific. But the very date at which it was written is enough to reveal an even more immediate purpose. We have entered one of those periodic crises of humanity, in which man makes an agonised attempt to preserve the traits of a visage that is breaking up, or to recognise the semblance of man in the new countenance approaching. Then, in the confusion of all values, he must choose firmly all that it means to be a man, and a man of his time: then will it with daring, linking imagination with his fidelity. We have chosen. This study is not solely a study of man: it is a struggle for man. No one, incidentally, can deal objectively with man. It is so customary to disguise a particular standpoint by a show of science, that we prefer to declare openly that our science, though honest, is none the less a fighting science.

EMMANUEL MOUNIER

In umbris
Clermont-Ferrand—Lyon 1942
In loco quem Deus fecit
1943-1944.

CONTENTS

PUBLISHERS' NOTE

BREAKS within the chapters, indicated by four or five line spaces in the original French version, are here indicated by three five-pointed stars. Asterisks at the extreme left show where paragraphs or longer passages in the French have been omitted; an indication of the nature of such passages will be found at the foot of the page. The translator's footnotes are indicated by daggers. The superior figures in the text refer to Mounier's notes, a translation of which appears as Appendix III on p. 320.

I

TOWARDS THE MYSTERY OF THE PERSON

TYPICAL STRUCTURE AND PERSONAL STRUCTURE
*

IF science can only deal with generalities, if the individual is
ineffable, then the only understanding of the individual that can be
formulated and communicated is of a generic order. The spontaneous
psychology of language, folklore and literature is constantly building
up types out of the shifting sands of individuality. Types of attitude:
the vain, the jealous, the miserly; or types of action: the hero who
avenges weakness, the weak who spread discord. Jung has shown that
some of these are part of the universal folklore of humanity. And
indeed, for many people, the understanding of others is not a search
for a remote personal mystery, but the reduction of a confused
experience to typical forms. The novel, which is required to be both
penetrating and far-reaching, fluctuates between the portrayal of
types and the portrayal of individuals. Characterology partly follows
the line of common understanding. Mental pathology, endocrinology,
morphology, graphology, the study of temperaments, all conceal
behind their little monographs the desire to isolate types sufficiently
constant and comprehensive to cover a great number of cases.

This method presents no problems if man is only one object
amongst others in nature. It is the line of normal development in
natural science, which proceeds from collection to classification and
the establishment of a law. Difficulty arises, and acutely, when dealing
with a clearly metaphysical position: that which affirms the existence,
at the root of empirical personality, of a Person transcending the
given. If the purpose of characterology is only to record appearances
and define them by distinct concepts, it could be satisfied with partial
results and an ever increasing systematisation of these results: there is
nothing further to be considered. If, on the other hand, the ultimate
unity of the personal being is placed beyond all possible objective
determination, if it allots to each individual a value incommensurable

---

* The introduction deals with a preliminary exposition of principles, which are resumed
briefly in the translator's introduction, and with Heymans' typology, with is given in
outline in the Appendix.

with any other, if this inaccessible centre supplies the force and the intention which animate the essential manifestations of behaviour, then typical structures become an approximation which is basically inadequate to the individual, and to transcendent reality. If the person performs free and transcendental actions which escape determination by the empirical character, then the prime source of character eludes characterology, which can only deal with the external projection and the observed results of action. Any intermediate representation, at this level of projection, is liable to systematise only the traces left by vital action, to treat effects as causes and to lose sight of the true resources of the personality under the mask which it sometimes assumes.

However, even the strongest individuality is charged with some generality, which takes it out of itself but does not dominate it entirely, unless there is abdication of the self. This overlapping is a fundamental situation in our psychology, and is sufficient to justify typology, provided solely that typology does not claim to *fix* the description and the possibilities of the living person by its models.
*

We may state the following rules, which considerably soften the asperities of typology:

I.   There is no such thing as a pure type: we never find the 'proud man' or the 'hypocrite', the 'schizoid' or the 'paranoiac'. Certain schizophrenics had to answer a questionnaire bearing on 'schizophrenic' traits: only 50% corresponded to the type: normal individuals often showed more schizophrenic traits than those in mental hospitals: only the traits were compensated. One can say that no morphologist has ever seen a purely 'digestive' or 'respiratory' type, as defined by Sigaud. The typical syndromes are often intermingled and it is not uncommon to find the characteristics of opposing types, say the schizoid and the adapted, existing simultaneously in the same subject. The startling contradictions, the ambivalence of behaviour, the bitterness and boredom that reveal latent states in contradiction with the apparent type, bear witness to the complex structure of actual individuals. When the psychiatrist speaks of 'associated psychoses', 'complex psychoses' and 'polypsychopathic states' he admits the inability of typology to classify a great number of morbid psychic states under its chosen syndromes. The same is true in normal psychology. In fact, these ideal types are not given, but constructed, like scientific concepts, not from the very stuff of experience, but from the provisional suggestions prompted by experience, on the basis of

* Describes briefly the origin of the more flexible modern typology.

a priori intuitions, subjected to pre-established tests. We speak of the vain, the paranoiac, the emotive, because we have succeeded in finding a comprehensive link between several associated symptoms. It is not experience that imposes this connection: the pure type is rare, and the cases which we shall call 'mixed' are more frequent: a comprehensive intuition, on the contrary, provisionally imposes the type as a guiding line, and the evidence for this intuition, which we accept as a postulate, is composed of somewhat dubious material, including the prejudices and theories of the epoch, collective ways of thinking, and so on. In so far, therefore, as one describes or defines a type, one renounces perfect exactness with regard to experience. One cannot thenceforward 'apply' it, as it stands, to reality. Thus while it is useful to provide the concept of each type with a solid centre, it is wiser not to be too precise as to its frontiers; by allowing for a certain marginal fluidity one runs less risk of departing from reality. The type should be considered, like many scientific concepts, as a guiding principle with variable limits, and not as a strict model.

2. Types are realities of a statistical nature: the complete description is not valid for all the subjects in that category as individuals, but only for the mean. A psychologist (Brown) after twenty-six tests for suggestibility, declared that he could not find individuals with an index of suggestibility sufficiently constantly high or low to enable him to classify them as 'suggestible' or 'non-suggestible'. M. Poyer rightly remarks that there is a fundamental difference between 'species' of character and the animal species, since the former, unlike the latter, tolerate within their category every gradation down to zero, and every possible intermediary transition between neighbouring categories. It is not, strictly speaking, possible to describe 'an introvert' or 'an extravert' since the one fades imperceptibly into the other. Only the lateral interconnections at the two extreme poles make it possible to formulate portraits sufficiently accentuated to be contrasted.

3. Types are not stable crystallisations. Sometimes they are consolidated under the influence of suitable phenomena: an emotive type, having also little inclination to come to terms with the external world, will shut himself off in an increasing maladaptation at each successive defeat. Some may slide easily from one type to the other: a man who is on good terms with the external world (adapted) slips easily into extraversion, (an abundance of physical and verbal exteriorisation), and thus becomes liable to lose all emotivity. A primitive type may even, as we shall see, give rise to his exact opposite, as happens in the phenomenon of compensation: the weak, overcome

by life, become authoritarian and acquire the appearance of strength, to defend themselves against their weakness. Finally, there is the ambivalence which, at every turn, offers the possibility of divergent meanings for the same data. Psychological life resembles a landscape of driven sand, where the frail contours of the dunes are always forming and disappearing and piling up on each other, and here and there showing some rocky salients to mark the harder structure of abnormality.

Typology suffers from even graver weaknesses. Spranger has stressed the limitative character of all typology: it defines the individual by that which is not himself, just as a silhouette defines a body by its surrounding space and not by the internal plastic energy which shapes it. It defines the edges instead of revealing the origins, and those edges are in fact the stopping places, the limitations and sometimes the deviations of personal effort. Thus one might say that, in one sense, every type is a negative type. Character is, as it were, the pattern of the defeat of personality. We are only typical in so far as we have failed to become fully personal. So those wonderful typological portraits, so easy to read and memorise, are dangerous refuges from understanding, an adventure which is always open and inviting one beyond all limitation.

Further, as Klages remarks, types are built up by the calculation and subsumption of contents (behaviour, expression, etc.), but what is the genesis of these contents? If one pursues the enquiry, many types, far more elaborate than those of which science makes short shrift, will be exploded by a deeper analysis. To take up Spearman's metaphor, types are only touchstones designed to discover certain alloys frequent in nature: but any list one might make of them would fail to establish a systematic, continuous and exhaustive classification, such as Mendelieff has done for the chemical elements. Considering the infinite practical diversity of individual character, types are, in some great provinces of character, like the little sketches in tourist maps which indicate the particular feature of the province by a historical monument or a bunch of vegetables. For all these reasons we shall try, in the following pages, to distinguish the fundamental polarisations of character, its elementary orientations, taken as intentions, as directed movements, rather than to add any new typology to those which are already painfully labouring to classify acquired facts. Just as creative thought cannot dispense with a certain stability of words, nor action with certain permanent rules, so characterology cannot dispense with the help of typologies. But whilst utilising these solid handholds, without which it would dissolve into verbalisation and approximation, we must not forget that portraits of types are only a step on the road to the understanding of the individual being. The vocation of characterologist, though straddling that ambiguous divide which separates science from intuition, draws more towards the vocation of novelist than to that of naturalist, in so far as he never discovers man until he rediscovers or re-creates personal man.

* * *

Are there, then, beneath the type, structures proper to the personal being? This is the central problem of characterology. We have noted the shortcomings of systems which have represented the psyche by turns as a list of faculties, a coral reef of images, a system of functions. Faculties, images, functions: we are still dealing with an elementary psychology built on the model of mechanical realities, however complex or ingenious the mechanism may be. The movement of personality utilises a rich assortment of mechanisms, but it is precisely the task of the characterologist to determine in what way it is personal, that is to say, in what way it surpasses and dominates mechanism. Its proper object is therefore the total attitudes of the person. It matters little whether they are observed from 'without' or from 'within', through intention or through expression. There is no shade of thought which does not provoke a gesture of the body, nor of movement which is not the spatial pattern of a gesture of the mind. Let each one take the approach that he prefers. What is important is not the point of application, but the orientation of the research. When Pierre Janet defined his psychology of behaviour, as contrasted with the uncertainties and monotonies of introspection, he invited us to look *from* outside, but not *at* the outside: for this outside of active behaviour was only chosen by him as his point of application, because he considered it the most revealing of 'mental states',[1] that is to say, of the overall themes which define concrete personalities. The idea of 'attitude', the correlation between an inner disposition and objective information about the individual, is of growing importance in collective psychology and this development is itself significant.
*

Minkowski relates how, one day, during his long study of persecution mania, he had a peculiar feeling about one of his patients,

* Argues that psychology based on phenomenology leads to results not far different from behaviourist psychology.

whom he had already frequently questioned, which could be expressed thus: 'I know everything about him'. He was surprised to find the feeling disquieting, suggesting loss and not gain. Following this intuition, he saw the paranoiac in a light different from all the classic descriptions, as a man whose vital impulses were so blocked that his universe had become petrified into forms without a future, which, precisely because they were thus divorced from life, appeared to him as threatening shapes in a cloud of deadly fear. He had thus discovered, behind the ideo-affective content, and the various manifestations of psychosis, the *generating factor*, the original theme which, with its variations, generates all the contents perceptible to inner or outer observation.[2] In such a perspective the interest of the psychopathologist is no longer in seeking for particular disorders related to isolated functions, but in trying to observe a general modification of psychological structure: he tries to discover the basic form in which the self has chosen to present itself to life, a form which is only partially expressed in the discontinuous indications of expression. This attitude is as necessary in normal psychology as in psychopathology. It is no longer the generating disorder, but the *generating theme* of the individual psyche that we suggest as the final object of the characterologist.

There are common directive themes which define mental families: thus Minkowski was able to group a series of disorders under the heading of loss of affective contact with reality. But each individual contributes his own development of the theme. The greatness of Freud lies in having been the first to state unambiguously that in the final analysis every psychology must turn on a dramatic singularity, since psychological life is a life made up, not of verbal or physiological abstractions, but of connected events in which the agent is a concrete person.

*

Psychological explanation does not end, like physical explanation, in the establishment of a causal chain, of objective relationships between elements or functions observed from without. It is essentially a *comprehension*, the personal interpretation by the observer of a personal significance. The psychological contents are solid facts on which comprehension rests. But placing them in order or in a system does not reveal to us their specifically psychological reality. Since this reality is, for the object, a total act, it can only be understood by the observer through a total act at the same level. Though mechanistic or rational sequences may provide an approximate transcription of isolated forms

* Refers to the critical work of Georges Politzer, 1926.

of behaviour, only a person can adequately understand a person. The paradox of the understanding of an absolute individual by another absolute individual can only be resolved by this act of direct knowledge of one person by his like (Scheler). It is neither an 'alienation' nor an 'introjection', which would turn it into possession, dissolving into either a negation of the other or a negation of self. It is a communion, changing both the knower and the known.† Is this the reintroduction of that terrible thing, subjectivism? If it is 'subjective' to require an act of personal comprehension for acts deriving from a person, then either words have lost all meaning, or it is no less 'subjective' on the part of the clinical psychologist to affirm the necessity for unimpaired sense organs and a healthy perceptive judgment in order to receive the impression of things. Each reality demands an apparatus of the same order, and an act of the same order as itself, to become an object of knowledge.

The shortcomings of the laboratory are not alone at fault here. Just as misleading, perhaps, to all the deeper truths of man is a certain brilliant and subtle manner of taking an interest in others and oneself, which frequently passes for psychological awareness and discernment of spirit, whereas it is only an excitement of the mind, a sterile form of *libido sciendi*. The real awareness of man, which it simulates, is entirely different. One has only to think of the strange impression of absence given by Jules Romains' characters, however sharply etched they may be. The scientist must undergo a stringent 'subjective' ascesis before his work can be acceptable: he must shed all traces of undue haste or bias, and serve truth with a passion which can withstand all other passions. Is the understanding of man less exacting than the understanding of nature? This also is denied to anyone who refuses to pay the preliminary tribute of one person to another. It requires a much higher tension than the self-sacrifice of the scientist, though within the reach of more persons. We are constantly finding that we have lost it. We are perhaps deeply disappointed by someone we have known and deeply loved: has he suddenly become degraded? Indeed no, it is we who have allowed his face to be hidden by some mask: with a gesture he removes it, and we had never been aware of it because we had forgotten that understanding is a joint creation. Characterology, it has been said, is not a key to the interpretation of dreams. And may it never, in spite of pedants, lapse into comparative tabulations, like the flora and fauna of the textbooks, which invite you to follow them from

† In the French text, 'une co-naissance du connaissant avec le connu', a quotation from Claudel.

description to description until you reach the specimen in front of you. The Abbé de l'Epée has already demonstrated that the deaf and dumb can be educated by appealing to deep latent capacities and not by the imposition of external linguistic structures. Binet and all those who have had to deal with the abnormal, insist on the same: thus we find that practical psychology confirms a necessity of being.

*   *   *

When investigation reaches the verge of the ineffable, psychology approaches a metapsychology, without which it is inconsistent, but which it is incompetent to establish. A general psychology, like that of Freud, may finally shatter on its founder's metapsychological (or, if you like, metaphysical) weakness. This is a danger that cannot be dispelled by ignoring it: there is no psychology that does not require a metapsychology to define its horizon, its boundaries, its relationships. In the end, the structure of character can only find its perspective in a metapsychology.

The person, we have seen, is a significant unity, the character the generating and determining form of a structural theme. Given a certain psychological fact, in order to discover its full significance we must know what particular grouping of structural tendencies has led to its occurrence. According to these groupings the same material fact, to which the behaviourists cling, may reveal such diverse intentions that its real meaning may be totally transposed. If words have any meaning, then it is by grasping this totality of structure that we attain 'objectivity', that is to say, a knowledge fully adequate to its object.

*   *   *   *

The person is not an immobile architectural structure: it persists and establishes itself in the course of time: the structure is not so much architecture as a musical development, since it cannot be imagined outside time. Does this mean that it is a moving stream, not to be grasped by thought? No: as in counterpoint, it maintains its form through the permanent themes and strict rules of composition which underlie its constant mobility. Even time, in its three dimensions, provides its measures. It is inseparable from a personal present, and therefore every psychological initiative comprises choice, affirmation

---

* Analyses the characterology of Klages, with his theory of 'levels' or 'stages' of character.

and commitment; inseparable from a personal past, and thus no psychological situation can be understood apart from the history of the subject; inseparable from a personal future, and therefore present behaviour, charged with the past that prepared it, acquires its meaning, in the last resort, only through the future it envisages, that is to say, through the values it accepts.

*

But here we reach the turning that leads from characterology to ethics. We shall see if this is as abrupt as one might think.

CHARACTER AS GIVEN, AND CHARACTER AS WILLED

The word 'character'[3] possesses a happy ambiguity. It means both the set of conditions we are given, and which are more or less imposed on us, and the degree of strength with which we master these conditions. Thus it is possible to say 'a man of firm or soft character' and, without further definition, 'a man of character'. This in itself shows how arbitrary it is to try to define a character 'objectively'—and against all experience—as a purely given fact, as inalienable as the shape of our faces.

Popular literature has, however, done much to sanction this way of thinking. 'What is your character?' ask the intriguing little booklets in the shop windows. They offer the public a sort of key to the book of their lives, to be interpreted by the lobes of the ear, the set of the mouth, or the workings of the nervous system. Thus people become accustomed to regarding themselves as the plaything of a number of unchangeable fatalities, acquired like a winning or losing ticket in a lottery. 'I never had a chance', says the recidivist receiving his fourth sentence. 'What can I do? I'm like that', says the angry man when his bad temper has calmed down.

Psychological positivism, in the last century, created the famous problem 'Can we change our character?' a commonplace even in the schools, insidiously suggesting the answer by the way the question was framed. Indeed, the moment the psychologist trusts only to the dead facts of objectivisation, to the *character as seen*, as distinct from the *character as experienced*, the answer can only be in the negative. His method shows him only permanent or successive determinations, and never an inner disposition through which these determinations are received, rejected or modified. If you photograph a dancer in action, and show the photograph to someone, asking him 'Can you make this figure move?', of course he will say no. If we reduce our actions to

* Reference to the personalist attitude to psychology.

fixed states, and psychological life to a list of psychological commands, it is not astonishing that psychological positivism should only find a rigorously determinist explanation for them.

Attempts have been made to provide an ancestry for this 'fixity' of character, by making it hereditary.[4] Some psychologists, haunted by the success of the Mendelian theory, have tried to adapt characterology to its laws, which undoubtedly cover some of the physiological determinations which enter into the structure of temperament. Why should they not cover the whole psychological picture? Each trait would correspond to a 'gene' and be included in the chromosomes of the original cell just like somatic genes. Certain observable facts support this hypothesis. We have all observed striking psychological similarities between parents and children and between other relatives. Family psychologies have been studied: families of mathematicians, like the Bernouilli, musicians like the Bachs, families of vagabonds and prostitutes. Psychological correlations have been found to be twice as frequent in twins as in siblings: according to Galton, who liked strict mathematical precision in such matters, the correlation decreased in geometrical progression from the former to the latter. It seems that research has not yet gone sufficiently deeply into this question. Incidentally, Mendel's laws are statistical laws of great number, and human fertility is too low to allow them to be verified with accuracy. Some believe in an alternating heredity, in which each individual receives his characteristics from one parent, as against intermediate heredity, in which he receives them from both.[5] The inheritance of certain characteristics may, it is suggested, be linked with sex: the male, for instance, inheriting propensity to crime, nomadism, intellectual capacity; but the arguments adduced are doubtful. As to knowing whether this heredity is Mendelian or not,[6] we have insufficient evidence to reach a conclusion. We know few ascendants in each case studied, and these we know badly. Davenport tends to support divergence, the germinal elements pertaining to diverse chromosomes and inherited independently. Heymans and Wiersma believed they could distinguish characteristics that were always 'dominant': resolution, carelessness, chastity, practical ability. Generally speaking, character traits valuable to man would be favoured. Kosanoff set up a scale of predominance: the man of normal temperament, the anti-social, the cyclothymic, the autistic, the epileptic; the manifestation of each type being masked or inhibited by that which preceded it in the scale. But if the Mendelian theory can be applied to elementary dispositions not far removed from the physiological, it becomes extremely risky when applied to more complex traits of character. In the present state of characterology, it is very difficult to define the simple elements of character. And the observations made are often based on obsolete concepts of faculties and qualities which have no more psychological than physiological reality.

Boven has stated that to speak of 'polymorphous heredity' is only a cover for ignorance of facts, and the expression, which is still used, of a 'hereditary mosaic' in which the subject seems to be composed of pieces taken from his father and mother, describes an appearance, and not a structure or law. The heredity of acquired characteristics is still less understood, although we can postulate some intermediary channels, such as modifications of temperament. The whole problem of heredity should be re-examined, starting from a new and dynamic analysis of structures, such as Pfahler[7] has attempted. He considers certain central functions as congenital, notably those which affect the vitality and impact of activity, the expression of vital energy and of affectivity; they are certainly inborn, not in the sense that they cannot increase or regress, but that, if absent, they cannot be created by education. Kroh[8] says that certain superstructures that seem to arise in education apart from the influence of teachers or environment, are inborn and not inherited. Jaensch[9] has investigated the heredity of certain communal tendencies, fundamental collective forms and typical environmental influences. His work can be related to that of Jung[10] on the hereditary material in the forms and metamorphoses of the libido.

There is nothing in this assembly of facts to justify the systematic assertion of the heredity of personality. That there is a hereditary contribution to character is undeniable. That this hereditary or congenital factor imposes limits which cannot be indefinitely extended, and themes which, maybe transposed, will persist even in our transfigurations, is equally certain. Klages claims that, if character may vary, there is in each person a capacity for variation which remains constant, since it is, in the last resort, of metaphysical nature; he adds, incidentally, that this capacity is usually vast, except in morbid cases, and that it is rarely fully extended in normal persons. In any case, we cannot master our character except by being fully aware of its resistances in order to use them as a support if we cannot dissolve them. But even so, the only question that matters is to know whether this hereditary or congenital element is such that psychological and moral history is thereby strictly determined. If we accept as elements of character the results of partitioning psychological life into fixed materialistic states or functions, devoid of inner life, then the answer must be yes. But it will be quite different if we try to describe psychological life as it presents itself to experience, in terms of liberty and action.

A more careful scrutiny of all that has been classed as hereditary or congenital only reinforces this conclusion. The results of early 'training' have frequently been treated as congenital idiosyncrasies or incapacities: the child was taught at an early age that one thing was clever and another stupid, there was a misplaced laugh at some misfortune, and an affective kink was formed and persists even if the person concerned changes his attitude. Physiological habits that have become set and difficult to modify are still treated as constitutional. But even in psychiatry a reaction has set in against according too large a role to heredity. Often the psychoses which are considered constitutional originate from an acquired emotive sensitivity, whose onset was unconscious: it is, for instance, found in a childhood where every expansive tendency was repressed and every initiative thwarted by systematic distrust. This often appears to be the origin of the suspicion and the egocentricity of the paranoiac. The sometimes miraculous results obtained by treatment show that the majority of the perverse are not constitutionally but occasionally so.[11]

But we are still not being sufficiently exact if we oppose the idea of character as given, a sort of pure or complexly automatic obstacle, by the idea of a radically heterogeneous moral intention, which can enlarge or contradict what is given. Kant's opposition, restated by Schopenhauer, of intelligible character and empirical character has largely contributed to confining moral reflection too exclusively to this kind of psychological manichaeism. Even what is given in character participates intrinsically in moral life, if we refer to the structure of the person as already described. Freud, who might have been the first to introduce to psychology the concept of a personal dynamic, largely failed through a metapsychology which reduced this dynamic to a causal and retrospective one. If I am only the pawn of an inexorable and menacing past, what does it matter to me if this tyrant rules me by a refinement of procedure unknown elsewhere? How can one speak of the restitution of the individual by psychological explanation, if individual analysis only lays bare past determinations and unchangeable forces behind each individual history. Now determinism does not find such forces in experience because they are there, but because they have been put there. This was Adler's chief argument against his master. The self is not only an agent of compromise with reality, more or less sceptical as to the possibilities and value of its work: it is reaction against the given, a will to affirmation and to power, a capacity for devotion. The very core of Bergson's criticism, a criticism widened and deepened by every advance in contemporary thought, beyond its first approximations, is that determinism is only a language, the most suitable for expressing the negation of the experience of duration.

Monakow and Mourgues[12] have stressed the importance of the time factor even at the stage of elementary biological facts, and shown that the mechanistic theory has to make abstractions of the most characteristic forms of life, in order to overlook this element. Thus the visual act consists of a dozen stages from birth onwards, from pupillary reaction to light, in an eye that is still blind, to the incorporation of the visual world into the whole psychological field. At each of these stages it is *something other* than in the previous stages: how can one explain these successive creations by the immobile formulae of a liaison between a given process and a ready-made mechanism? Mechanistic theory has the same difficulty in explaining the progressive function of movement in the newly born child, as the myelinisation of the nerve cells and the organisation of the frontal lobes is completed. These developments in no way resemble a mechanical evolution in which the diverse stages of a determined programme are gradually completed. Each moment of development influences in its totality the moment that follows, according to a process which Monakow and Mourgues have likened to an avalanche, because it is enriched at each new stage by the acquisitions of the previous stage. If poison or trauma or some form of asthenia attacks these embryonic forms and obstructs their development, a mechanical process would be disturbed and fall short. The formative instinct, on the other hand, maintains the general programme of life by trying to correct the accidents or continuing the work in progress along new lines, instead of those unexpectedly blocked: thus we get the cerebral vicariances which sometimes occur after serious or extensive lesions. There is, as it were, an inner finality, a subordination of the obscurest workings of life to distant values and unknown purposes, which Monakow and Mourgues do not hesitate to describe as an embryonic form of moral consciousness. As the instincts become more and more complex, the immediate moment is subordinated to a more and more distant future. The effect of this extension of the sphere of finality or future is to create an increasingly important slowing up of reaction, and then the organisation of this delay by the complex personality.

Thus from the most modest beginnings of life, we can see the individual factor manifesting itself, not through the single complication of a maze of determinations, as Freud sees it, but by the *maintenance of a future* against wind and water, for the individual compromised by determination. Personal activity is of the same pattern, if not of the same order. It is, fundamentally—or duration has no meaning—the *maintenance and the organisation of a future, persisting through the rhythm of impulsions, inertia and crises.* Even in its most summary forms we see it, not as a picture but as an activity, and even its most clearly defined aspects seem to be more situations than silhouettes; nuclei of possibilities offered for resolution, laboratories of responses awaiting development. In a reality so essentially prospective there is little place for the techniques elaborated from a study of the past and the immobile. 'Those who hold the key to the future', said Nietzsche, 'are alone qualified to decipher the mysteries of the past.' He was talking of history. But the psychology of an enduring being is inseparable from history: only those who envisage man's future are qualified to decipher the mysteries of living man. There is no understanding of man without a humanism conformable to man's essence. For thirty years dynamic psychology has tirelessly fathomed the abysses of 'vital man' and of the organic and collective Unconscious which arises to torment us with a tumult of obscure and impersonal forces. But if this unconscious self lends a dramatic quality to personality, it is only, to the personality, matter to be shaped, and the shape is the decision of the person who imposes it. This decision is not always fully conscious in its origin, for the inner transcendence of the person has its own abysses, antithetical to the abysses of the unconscious self, which sometimes escape our gaze and often our control. But decision is always assumed, and it is this *choice of position* which defines the personal being, and locates him at every moment of time in the scale of values he has chosen.[13]

Thus we cannot define the person without a future, nor a future without a *valuation*, a desired finality. Here again the most elementary forms of the psyche foreshadow its superior forms. A patient suffering from total aphasia after severe lesions, seemed incapable of reading a word in the newspapers. One day his eye fell on an obituary notice. He read it at a glance: it concerned his best friend. Another patient, suffering from motor aphasia, was incapable of pronouncing a single syllable but, being very religious, could recite his prayers impeccably. It seems therefore that many disorders which were explained by lesions should be attributed to a considerable lowering of the threshold of interest. What is only indicated at a low level becomes clearer higher up. This has led Spranger [14] to differentiate characters according to the 'typical attitudes' adopted by the person towards the different values presented to him. We might extend the remark he makes about the romantic period, and say that the only reality for the person, is that which can become the object of creative interest. These vital attitudes are none other than the structures of individual consciousness, as they come to light whenever a value is placed in the centre of an individual life. He distinguishes six, which correspond to six fundamental viewpoints: aesthetic man, inclined towards an interest in the expressive character of symbols; economic man, inclined towards the useful, through the interplay of his psycho-physical energies and his real vital purposes; theoretical man, possessed by an interest in the objective and impersonal; religious man, moved by an aspiration to totality and the reference of all particular experiences of value to the all-embracing value of personal life; the man of power, inclined towards positions of command, in all their historical aspects; social man, concerned above all with love and sympathy. The first four types might, if they wished, be hermits, the last two are specifically social.[15] There is probably no reality which does not touch on these six values. But the 'vital attitudes' are each distinguished by a dominant value. Petermann remarks relevantly that this 'typology from above', starting from the highest forms of life, courts failure in concrete cases where a certain level, below which such characteristics have no content, is not attained. But if there is a mental drive and a civilisation at work in the diversity of individual constellations, such a characterology is as much true to reality as others, and its place is more essential.

Now character has been restored to its metapsychological background, it transfers the stress from the given to the willed, or more exactly, from determination, to a personally directed choice. My character is not what I am in the sense of a snapshot registering all past determinations, all the features already formed. It is the form of a movement directed towards the future, and concerned with greater fullness of being. It is what I can be rather than what I am, my availability rather than my possessions, the hope that is still open rather than the achievements I have left behind. 'What is truest of an individual, and the most himself, is his possibility, that is only shown indistinctly in his history.'[16] To know a character is to know and love its promise and not to imprison it in a carapace. Thus this knowledge is never exhaustive, and always attracted towards the depths which sink away beneath our grasp. Thus nothing is more odious than the peremptory way in which some persons despair of a man when describing him: it is even a way of driving him to desperation, which is extremely common amongst those who have become resigned to being used to each other. The given character, if indeed it can be separated from the forward movement of the willed character, is not the reply which the characterologist seeks when he approaches the mysteries of the person. Either he is the *caput mortuum*,† or he is himself a *question asked* of the person, the Sphinx across his path: in his weaknesses he represents the resistance to be overcome, without which spiritual effort is anaemic: in his qualities the talent to be multiplied, without which the workman loses his dignity as creator.

★   ★   ★

We are beginning to see the relationships between the psychological and the moral aspect of characterology, to which we shall revert later. A static and so-called 'objective' characterology is radically detached from ethical considerations and not, as it believes, through the requirements of its subject, but rather the contrary. It has replaced its real object, prospective personal activity, by a mosaic of inert objects; it is not astonishing that there should no longer be any possible connection between this mosaic and the effort at the heart of personal life, which makes both the 'psychological' and the 'moral' appear secondary distinctions. If, as we have said, the given in character is integrated in the moral effort, the whole field of character has a moral quality.

Here again we must be precise. Moral effort is not identical with the ethical pseudo-typology which allocates vice and virtue at the dictates of prejudice and ready-made social categories. The intrusion of a certain moralism and an untimely attribution of coefficients of goodness and badness would do untold harm to the study of characterological traits. There are no 'good' or 'bad' data, but data that are more or less difficult, and a good or ill will: the poorer the soil, the greater the victory. We should not, incidentally, extend the definition of character to include the whole content of psychological life. It is not a trait of character, for instance, to be a musician. We agree with Dessoir, [17] that 'the character includes all that which, if it were suppressed, would destroy the permanent identity of the individual', or better,

† *Caput mortuum* (Lat. dead head). An alchemist's term, used to designate the residuum left after exhaustive distillation or sublimation; hence anything from which all that rendered it valuable has been taken away. Thus a learned scholar paralysed is a mere *caput mortuum* of his former self. The French Directory, towards its close, was a mere *caput mortuum* of a governing body. Brewer, E. C., *A Dictionary of Phrase and Fable*, Cassell and Co., London, 1923.

this identity being the continuous creation of a free activity and not the immobility of death, 'anything that *may* become the object of moral judgment is a part of character.' This implied moral judgment is not within the competence of the characterologist, but it defines his object. Even the apparent absence of all ethical initiative, and an acceptance of all the hazards of empirical character, is itself an ethical attitude: even the worst form of all, an unconscious moral abdication. Character, finally, seems to be not a given fact, but something like the link between a bundle of questions and a bundle of answers, between a provocation and mobilisation of forces, which both compete and collaborate, as we see in any state of collapse. Conflict appears, not as the essence, but as the distinguishing mark of this rivalry between the self as received and the self as desired.[18] Reich,[19] following the same line of thought, has identified character with the resistance which the self opposes to instincts and spontaneous tendencies, in order to contain and repress them. For him it is the 'armour of the self' which forms character in the course of its development. Each link in the armour corresponds to an effort which has been made to deal with an instinctive or affective problem. Even psychoanalysis, so divorced by its founder from ethical considerations, makes a distinction between a relaxed complex and a repressed complex.

It is therefore not enough to say that character is the product of the given and the willed, if by that one supposes a more or less automatic equilibrium: facts of maturation, fluctuation, determination, training, reinforcement, orientation, inhibition, suggestion, repression, sublimation, etc. . . . What does it matter if M. Delmas tells us that the five aspirations he has analysed, combined with the three aspects of intelligence produce 5,764,801 possible combinations? What do all these possibilities matter to me if I happen not to like them, if I am not able to choose the one that shall be mine? *Character is not a fact, but an act.* The synthetic unity of character is not a product, it is a living effort and this effort may be effective far beyond what the majority of men consider possible. Descartes claimed to be the master of his dreams: modern medicine states that this is not impossible. Even structures bordering on pathological degeneration are, according to psychiatrists, amenable to a heroic effort of self-defence; 'Few individuals', writes Kretschmer '(and this is naturally true of every category) are exclusively schizothymic or cyclothymic to the extent of being incapable, with goodwill, effort and a little talent, of adopting a mental outlook quite at variance with their structure, if external conditions make it necessary.' This dominion of the person over the

instruments of its destiny extends so far that even the events of our life
seem sometimes to group themselves around us in the very image of
our character: to a large extent we may say that everyone receives the
events he deserves.

BEYOND CHARACTER

This intrinsically ethical nature of character sets a bound to the
science of the characterologist, which may become a dangerous
implement in the hands of rogues. It is time to remember the necessity
of modesty. Even what seem, under analysis, the simplest and most
obvious formulae are most uncertain of application without a
sympathy derived from much human experience. Often, in practice,
says M. Bovet, 'a deficiency in technique must be replaced by
cordiality'. This approximation by a practitioner should not be
misunderstood. It certainly does not imply an abandoning of
intellectual effort, but is simply a tribute to the complexity of the
concrete case, the spontaneity of life, and the miracles of the human
spirit. Between voluntary effort and conscious successes, and the
gratuitous miracles which the believer accepts as supernatural
intervention, extends an immeasurable field of human mystery.
Somewhat too accustomed to working by dissociation and
recomposition, our rationalist psychology tends to eliminate this from
its study. From time to time there are visionaries to arise and challenge
us. 'Who am I? If for once I apply the proverb, it should be enough to
know whom I frequent. Yet I must admit this confuses me, as it
establishes between me and others relationships much more peculiar,
unavoidable and disturbing than I thought. It says more than it seems,
it turns me into a phantom during my own lifetime, and evidently it
alludes to all that I have ceased to be in order to be what I am. It is
hardly exaggerating its meaning to say that what I take to be the more
or less deliberate objective manifestations of my life are only traces
that appear in this life of an activity whose real field is quite unknown
to me.'[20] The writings of Dostoyevsky echo to the same note. Even
psychology in its analyses is moving in this direction and, like the
positive sciences, revealing the ambivalence and contradiction, the
interplay of influences and the unforeseen underlying the unitary
concept and the rational equilibrium.

Duhamel makes Salavin say: 'Anyone who tried to explain in ten fat
volumes what goes on in the heart of man in a single minute, would
be undertaking a superhuman task.' No system will ever account for
the infinite combinations which stream forth in an inexhaustible yet

never entirely comprehensive coinage issuing from this inner, inaccessible sanctuary of the individual psyche. This hidden self is fed by two great streams arising from outside consciousness, the abysses of the organic and collective Unconscious and the abysses of personal transcendence. The world is full of obscure persons who never succeed in deciphering the enigma that is their destiny. They are embarrassed by themselves until their death, and their dialogue is with shadows in a language which isolates them by its harshness. Hamlet pursues a perplexity which is not solely impotence, and Adolphe will never find the voice of his desires. *Vere tu es homo absconditus.*

Complexity is not the only obstacle. Every movement encounters a contradiction. The most obvious of these contradictions results in a simple disintegration, with liberation of the divergent energies, as with impulsive types. Others are complicated by an attempt at reintegration which is defective, partial or composite: the gaps are filled, as in some organic disorders, as best they may be, with faulty links and defective gearing. The material substituted is sometimes anachronistic, borrowed from another age of life: or inappropriate, because introduced too late into an organism in which there is a time for everything and everything must come at its right time: hence you find the wisest scientist uttering puerilities when a journalist is rash enough to put him metaphysical questions: or an extreme romantic, like Delacroix, proving entirely classical in politics; the war hero intimidated by his *concierge*; the militant revolutionary dreaming of retiring to private life in the suburbs, and the last of the *poètes maudits* spending his time between the brothel and the cloister. There are few attitudes that are truly general to the extent of dominating the whole register of our activity.[21] An incomprehensible action, an unexpected suicide come and upset the convenient pictures we had made of men without history, after having abandoned them to an isolation which we soon find indecipherable.
*

Yet even in the pattern of contradictions there is a minimum of clarity, if not of explanation. But what of the compound and indistinct contradiction of ambivalence? Since Bleuler established its existence, since Freud considered he had found the root of all later ambivalence in the affective ambivalence of childhood, particularly in infantile sexual ambivalence, psychologists have been discovering it everywhere.[22]

It may happen to be an effect of perspective and not a phenomenon

* Contradictions of character sometimes valuable, as in cases of artistic genius.

of structure. Every desire is strong, not only in its own right, but from the weakness of antagonistic desires: chastity, calm, goodness, as well as positive behaviour, may only be the overrated result of the absence of energetic passions. At this level the ambiguity is still easily resolved: a direct, deeply seated drive can be recognised by its richness, its originality, the breadth of its expression and effects; the pseudo-strength by its lustreless, banal and inexpressive aspect or, when the simulation is strong, by its forced and fragile nature.[23] It is not enough to explain these ambivalences, as Klages does, by a difference of level and of vital force. In the majority of cases a profound difference of values is at work, which excludes a simple empirical description. Thus every psychological indication may represent radically opposed psychological itineraries, although confused by a similarity of expression. Thus susceptibility to influence may betray, in a minor key, personal inconsistency and psychic debility, or, in a major key, a great capacity for assimilation and transformation. A liking for privacy may, in a minor key, express dissimulation or maladjustment, an artificial protection of an inner emptiness, or in a major key, the reserve that is connected with an acute sense of inwardness. The sciences of expression (graphology, morphology, etc.) are well aware of this ambiguity which makes a final interpretation so delicate a matter. We should note here that ambivalence, behind its apparent determinations, denotes the field of spiritual liberty.

A more involved ambivalence is due to a fundamental psychic law: every psychological intention provokes a contrary tendency, every psychological force creates an antagonistic force at its very core. There is ambivalence where one aspect of consciousness is superimposed on the other without fusion, or when the two forces are incompletely merged. Ambivalence then narrowly approaches ambiguity, and interpretation is often inextricably confused. Some lives, contrary to reason, maintain the two tendencies more or less intermingled: we are compelled to allow for these dual states, so scandalous to logic, which unite sadism and masochism, timidity and pride, a sense of inferiority with an assertion of superiority, certainty and doubt, the one inducing, exasperating or cloaking the other. One may both consciously love and unconsciously hate the same person, or vice versa, and men have been known to kill, like Julien Sorel, through a mixture of love and hate for the same object.[24] At other times the secondary tendency overthrows the original, by some disorder of the process of compensation: then there occurs a state which has to be interpreted in a way opposed to its immediate significance: that display of indifference conceals a fierce and morbid sensitivity; this brutality, a great tenderness disappointed and rebuffed; that prudishness, a tumult of the senses; this act of courage, a panic running ahead of itself. In children who always fall ill before an examination[25] there is a blend of the desire to succeed and the fear of failure: they avoid the possibility of failure by their illness, but only by foregoing the possibility of success. Thus the scrupulous person may yield to the very obsession he abominates, his force of resistance being low; another, who accuses himself of contemplating suicide, is violently attached to life; another, who dreams of nothing but robbery and violence, detests injustice; and a deeply religious man may plunge into sacrilege. The subject has still some awareness of his oddity, and suffers from it.[26] It is not always so, and the most difficult cases are those in whom this ambivalence arouses no reaction, and is only apparent to others. Take, for instance, an ethical denial of brutal instincts or of a character trait considered inferior; these are not always, as in the previous cases, given a more subtle expression by their contraries, but are more or less disguised, as explained by Freud, by processes not accessible to consciousness. There is sometimes a simple expression, as in those adolescents who seem to display an astonishing naïvety with regard to sex, but in whom psychoanalysis reveals extremely precise and deeply engraved concepts: or again, those women who try to prove to themselves that they are frigid, by denying any pleasure they may really feel. This is a symbolic representation or satisfaction, as with the person who, to evade an incestuous desire he cannot avow, mimes his repulsion by a fugue or a mania for travelling;[27] another, obsessed by an insatiable craving for social advancement, and, inwardly unhappy at this ambition, will mime his unhappiness by mountain sickness: ambivalence is here introduced into objective behaviour. It is a rationalisation, another way of dramatising the problem, like the sadists, who cover themselves by a political theory of brutal power, or the exhibitionists who develop theories of dilettantism or snobbishness. Or it may be a simple displacement, the most difficult to detect, for the subject develops a violent and thenceforward absurd interest in anything that comes to hand, to conceal an interest he will not admit, even to himself: then one has to find the slender link which has determined this substitution! Numerous irrational likes and dislikes can be explained in this way. Similarly there are scruples in which a strong sense of guilt is alleviated by an attention to peccadilloes. Sometimes, by lateral infiltration, one sentiment slips into another: this too lively fraternal affection hovers on the verge of incest, this loving friendship keeps its frontiers undefined, this burning mysticism borrows its ardours from two conflicting sources, this liking for ideas is also a flight from social effort.[28]

Ambivalence is often due to the curious phenomenon of *introjection*. The subject and the object of a tendency tend not only to combine, but to be identified with each other; if the object is inaccessible or appears to be, which, psychologically speaking, is the same, the identification takes place through a process of mimicry. Thus the one who loves tends to imitate the loved object. Further, the child who has lost an adored mother tends to identify with her. It does not matter if the object is hostile: one imitates one's enemy by fighting him, by the very fact that one fights him. Hence such astonishing reversals of behaviour as the sadist becoming a masochist[29] (as aggressor, he identifies with the object of aggression); the passive man, an authoritarian; the traveller, an exhibitionist. Or one behaviour may be superimposed on the other.

Under the influence of these ambivalences, most of our feelings and actions have a multiple determination, and both in faith and crime one may find the best and the worst inseparably entangled at the same moment, without the best being an excuse for the worst, or the worst depreciating the best, in the eyes of the moralist. There is both a kind of sincerity and a kind of bad faith in such a fusion that it is equally mistaken for the immoralist to plead sincerity, or for the moralist to attack the bad faith, so delicate is the fluctuation between the two poles.[30] On this frontier between the psychological and the ethical, the parable of the tares and the wheat takes on a new light, and leads us towards the troubled zones of action, where Lear cries: 'Not one has offended, not one. . . .' And Prince Muyskin, his lament weary and charged with forgiveness: 'Oh, if Aglaia only knew everything. It must be absolutely everything, for in such a case it is essential to know everything. And we can never know everything about another precisely when it is most necessary, when the other is guilty.' Every attempt to know another finds this warning on its path: 'Judge not', a warning that psychology has already noted on its own level.

Complexities, contradictions, ambivalences, spring from the Unconscious and often escape the control of the subject himself. As if the confusion were not already sufficient, conscious elaborations, personal effort, education or social influences and culture still further complicate individual characterological formulae. Essential traits are masked by social inhibitions, which have so many ways of burying elementary feelings, drives and spontaneities that it is often difficult to trace them later through their indirect effects. The dominant formulae are flexible and acquire great elasticity according to time, place and mood. Secondary characteristics of replacement, compensation or stabilisation, sometimes just of playfulness, spread out in depth behind the principal structure, and any one who believes he has caught his man in a net, will find him suddenly reappearing a hundred feet away. With culture a thousand traits are there to correct a defect, attenuate an excess, create a contrast, suggest a phantasy or underline a value, all alien to the primitive outline of basic character, sometimes integrated with it, like the ornaments which form a logical, integral part of a building, sometimes clumsily and obviously added to the façade, parasites or failures of taste in the psychic make-up. In addition to these well-defined zones, there are traits in the course of development. All this adds to the difficulty of defining the 'character' of a man whose civilisation, social life and self-control have made a composite work, with many approaches, out of the original psychic material. This has led certain characterologists, like Dr. Vermeylen, Jacques Lefrancq and José Brunfaut to distinguish a *basic character*, a primary temperament, from the superstructures added by later influences. The first work of Lefrancq and Brunfaut[31] had the merit of describing the conscious means of character-building over and above a given nucleus. This nucleus is constituted by the different ways of handling primitive emotions, either by extraversion-introversion, adjustment-maladjustment, operating in an emotive or inemotive field. These six primary sectors correspond to six groupings of intellectual or social behaviour, which accentuate or attenuate the excesses of the basic sectors. The authors present these attitudes not as static components, but as forces either for education or destruction, which we must learn to handle in order to create a work of art and of liberty out of the original material given to each of us.

The geology of such a system is not calculated to simplify characterology, but it states a rule of capital importance. A trait or a syndrome of character must always be considered as the constant of a curve which may affect every qualitative value from the richest to the poorest. To be 'phlegmatic' may, in different cases, indicate either mediocre indifference or superb self-mastery. The emotive may be a silly, excitable person, or one who is capable of heroic passions. Only an *evaluation* can here complete the objective description.

The explanation of these misfortunes of psychology lies outside psychology. Outside, and yet at its heart. It is not necessary in this difficulty to appeal to magic or duplicate this universe of unfortunate experience by postulating a further universe behind it to make substance of our embarrassments. But this contradiction, this ambiguity is a living indication in the heart of experience, of transcendental existence and personal existence. They are the disquieting signs of a reality which cannot express itself in a simpler way. They provide the profoundest background to the experience of subjectivity. They suggest to the philosophy of the psychologist the same type of deduction as is suggested to the philosophy of the mathematician by irrational, imaginary and immeasurable quantities. Only the constructions of the brain, or its more superficial grasp of the existent, offer to the lazy and the utilitarian the broad, reassuring light of clear ideas. Existence finds no direct language of communication with us, either through reason or through the sense perceptions. It can only transmit itself indirectly and inadequately, through a cipher which is never fully interpreted, whose secret is always elusive. And further, we are not dealing with objects, but with ourselves, these men here. If there were a science, very complicated perhaps, but complete, which could explain us, we should have to admit that liberty was a phantom of the imagination. The powers of the world would not fail to illustrate this conclusion by annexing the science of character to their arsenal of techniques of domination. But the person is a source of liberty, and therefore as obscure as the heart of a flame. By refusing to be a system of clear concepts, it reveals itself the more strongly as a source of creation and the unforeseeable. By evading objective knowledge, it compels me to drop my tourist camera, and if I wish to communicate, to share an adventurous destiny, whose data are obscure, whose routes uncertain, and encounters disconcerting.

Thus the very object of the study of character is incapable of being known objectively, but not of being known. Characterology is to the knowledge of man what theology is to the knowledge of God: an intermediary science between the experience of mystery and the rational elucidation to which the manifestations of this mystery may be subjected. The analogy may be pushed further. Positive characterology, which treats types and structures as approaches to the mystery of the person, stands out against a dark background of negative psychology, like positive theology and the theology of unknowing. Only personal engagement in the total adventure of man, and widely active comprehension will give the candidate to knowledge of his fellow that prudent ignorance which is the beginning of wisdom. In spite of its emphasis on moral decision and the metaphysics of the person, characterology is none the less a psychological science. It is located in the zone of contact between objective psychology and metapsychology. It ranks as one of those frontier sciences which link two different planes, and which can never be placed in any purely positive classification, but which keep the scientific spirit in contact with true wisdom, and wisdom in contact with the scientific method.

This intermediary position should not discourage methodical research and the elaboration of concepts which must include a fourth dimension, the quality of that 'projective universe' described by M. Bachelard as a universal, poetic presence underlying our solid, lucid world. The fundamental question in characterology is much the same as the one he uses in different fields: 'What are the elements of characterological form that can be distorted with impunity by irrational intrusions and yet allow a structural, characterological coherence to persist?' Thus neither mystery nor science is excluded. But a psychology which carries its positive investigations sufficiently far, is for ever cured of the illusion that man is a mechanism which can be built up, taken to pieces and reassembled as one pleases. The elements of character are the cipher of a secret language which arises, not behind phenomena, but out of their inexhaustible fertility, and without which the whole of anthropology would be incomprehensible. To eliminate the attempts at determination would be to abandon the science of character to confusion, and the future of every character to the weaknesses which arise when mental control is relaxed. To eliminate the mystery would be to condemn oneself to the suppression of our experience of irrational actions, the incursions of liberty and grace, crises and encounters, and the dramatic divides which give life its savour and its price.
*

Fluctuating thus between clarity and mystery, we must be sufficiently flexible when we are trying to understand and shape our own characters, to maintain two attitudes, attentive yet relaxed, controlled yet available, circumspect yet spontaneous. This is the essential principle of education and the understanding of others, of which Rousseau wrote: 'All that one can do, with a great deal of trouble, is to approach as closely as possible to one's purpose: but one must be lucky to attain it.'

We have to employ the same flexibility in our method of investigation. It will no doubt be long before we can unify not only the results but also the methods of characterology. Those which we called the most important are even so not applicable in every sector. When we

* The vocation of French genius to humanise mystery.

examine the appearances presented by others, the search for descriptive correlations will be our chief instrument of analysis. The more deeply we go into structures and conflicts, the more we shall have to use the direct description of the forces at work, whether expressed in pathological statements, or in the inner dialogue of personal experience. But few are the deeper regions sufficiently explored by the experimental method: in more than one chapter we shall have to be content with introspective analysis, or the description of symptoms, just as, not so long ago, the geographers could only describe the heart of Africa on the basis of travellers' tales. The reader will observe these variations in the following chapters. It is enough for him to remember this in order to attribute to each conclusion its own degree of maturation.

2

THE FORCES OF DISTURBANCE

A BODY momentarily at rest in a certain state of equilibrium may be invited to a new equilibrium either by some inner spontaneity, as often happens with living beings, or by an external force. This invitation to change always provokes a crisis of transformation, followed by mobilisation of energy, which matter resists with the force of inertia. The same phenomena occur repeatedly in the much more unstable states of equilibrium which are always forming in the psyche.

Generally speaking, the sensitivity of the individual psyche to disturbance is measured by the emotions, whether the source of disturbance be external or internal. We could also speak of psychological irritability, by analogy with the properties of living matter. J. Lefrancq uses the word 'attackability' in order to avoid the special associations of the word emotion. The intention is good, but we shall continue to use the words emotion or emotivity which are not only strictly accurate, but better style.

By a process of limitation, emotivity, which can be used to cover every degree, strong or weak, positive or negative, of vulnerability to disturbance, has come, in the vocabulary of contemporary psychology, to mean only the excessive forms of this vulnerability. Thus Dupré[1] defines an emotional constitution as 'a form of disequilibrium of the nervous system, characterised by a diffused erethism of the sensibility and a deficiency of the reflex or voluntary motor inhibitions, as a result of which the reactions of the organism are excessively violent and prolonged, thus rendering it more or less incapable of adapting itself to sudden changes, unforeseen situations and new surroundings.' Since this linguistic habit is now widespread, we shall not speak, as we should, of varying degrees of emotivity, but of emotivity and inemotivity, it being understood that by these terms we are only implying varying degrees of one continuous function of emotion.

EMOTIVE DUALITY

This limited sense of the word which is now current inevitably compels us to associate emotivity, which is a fundamental function of the psyche, with emotional crises. The emotive type is, in fact, characterised not only by the sensitivity of his affective reactions, but also by their intensity and violence. He is not merely sensitive to the slightest stimulus, like a perfectly round ball on a perfectly plane surface; he is explosive. He reacts more quickly than the majority of men to any event, whether important or, even in his own eyes, insignificant. He is not emotive because he has emotions, like all of us: he is emotive because his emotional states recur with remarkable frequency and under trivial stimuli. Further, the emotion lingers and is diffused in many ways, it re-echoes after the event that occasioned it, it ricochets off the original object on to others, and seeps through into neighbouring spheres. Far from becoming immune through repetition, the emotive are rendered more sensitive by each new emotion, by a sort of psychological anaphylaxis. Above all, if he is unable to discharge his emotion outwardly, he becomes in time a prey to a real need for emotion, a toxicomania similar to many others: some satisfy this need by going to the Grand Guignol or to boxing matches; others pursue the macabre and the horrible with Edgar Allan Poe, or perversity with Baudelaire, scandal with Dada, or with Lélia the sorrow that is in love with itself. Just as the child likes to give itself a fright, the adult likes to make his own blood run cold, sometimes even by a dramatic form of moral severity.

This predisposition to emotion is usually precocious. The infant and child are normally hyperemotive, and one should avoid diagnosing a constitutional predisposition from such evidence as they provide. But the constitutionally emotive show some departure from this common ground: it is almost unquestionably present in the abnormally fearful or timid child, whose feelings have a quality of violence, exclusiveness or passion, either in joy or grief. But this constitutional emotivity is not necessarily congenital. Infectious diseases, physical or physiological trauma, particularly when repeated, may often induce an emotive predisposition, even in subjects in whom it was not previously apparent: it has appeared after an alarming accident,[2] as the result of war, etc. Life in the big cities, with their brutal or exquisitely contrived sensations, the noise and agitation, have been developing this emotivity for more than a century in our urban populations. We should not overlook, either, the effect of the cinema, particularly when the child's mind is exposed to its influence too frequently.

The inner duality of the emotional factor sets a problem in the study of character. The emotive appear sometimes as crude personalities, dominated by a primitive psychic constitution; sometimes as endowed with the most exquisite and refined personality. If they were just

erratic barometers, the importance we attribute to emotivity would be disproportionate. If their explosive irritability were, on the other hand, the inevitable compensation for some higher quality, we should be justified in ascribing to emotivity a central position at the root of character.
*

Everything happens, to use the language of Freud, as if 'affective charges' were distributed like electric charges, over the whole surface and depth of the psychic field. They are capable of variation and can be described both in physiological and psychological terms. They are centrifugal by nature: if there should be an excessive concentration, the organism endeavours to secure its discharge, through primary or derived processes, securing a sensation of relief. But we are still only using the language of description. The effect, at least, appears clear: in this upheaval, creating incoherence, inadaptation of movement, effervescence and clouding of the perceptions, emotion appears as a real crisis of spasmodic weakness. The nervous person is glued to the spot, the timid stammer, the liar is at a loss, the anxious collapse into impotence. The expressions 'psychic ataxia' or 'haemorrhage of the feelings' have been used. The more the emotive, in the sense of the words used by Heymans, is primary and inactive, the more the disorder is visible and expressive. After the crisis the subject is exhausted. But we should ask if he is not much more so at its beginning: and whether the emotional crisis is not so much an effect as a cause of a certain depression of the organism: like fatigue, emotion disorganises mental syntheses, modifies psychological tensions and creates mental conditions more favourable to the dissociation and separate development of inferior tendencies.[3]

In fact, the emotional crisis occurs (Wallon) when either automatism or representation, that is to say, the response to the psycho-organic stimulus, is slow in appearing: thus when the reflex fails the learner on the bicycle, the liar is at a loss for an alibi, the angry man feels impotent and the nervous encircled. This delay is a failure in adaptation, either from a state of psycho-organic weakness emerging into character—the exhausted man starts up at every moment, fails to find the words or gestures he requires—or from a state of inferiority relative to the urgency, the difficulty of the strength of the reaction required. The tension produced by the stimulus tends to resolve itself, but not being able to link up with the external provocation, becomes embedded and static in the given situation, producing not a positive gesture, but as it

* Physical symptoms attendant on emotion.

were a reaction-tumour, global, confused and unadapted, which gradually overclouds all clear concepts of reality by a sort of 'progressive earthquake' of the sensory and motor systems.
*

But this primitive and disordered aspect of emotion is not the only one. It may happen that fear intensifies the effort, that the angry man replies with the precision and intensity of gesture necessary. The gestures of the emotive are not entirely without significance or use. For emotivity keeps psychic and nervous energy in a state of supermobilisation. In so far as the emotional disorder is partially dominated by the subject's discipline or richness of personality, the intensity, sensitivity, and vigilance of this permanently mobilised energy may add not only to the intensity, quality and efficacy of the act undertaken, but also to the sensitivity of the subject himself. We must never forget that, apart perhaps from the more rudimentary crises, emotional disorder covers a phenomenon more primitive than itself, an exceptional sensitivity to stimuli and impulses, an aptitude for initiative and hence a repugnance to automatisms, a trigger-quick attention and a sort of organic generosity which is manifested by a prodigality of the emotions. If certain temperaments, weighed down by a vegetative existence, are riveted to their own inertia, the emotive have the advantage at the start of a sort of inner liberality, a state of being always ready, which is not yet sympathy or goodwill, but which smoothes the path for them. In the act of isolating itself from the outer world, the emotional reaction turns part of its energy into contemplation of itself, into a dramatisation of its peripatetics, thus it is a natural education of sensitivity and an inner life: it keeps the subject in a state of permanent vibration. By making him vulnerable, it makes him attentive. More than any other factor it exposes him to the abysses of organic life, to the obscure influences of the Unconscious, and to the heavy structures of that elemental personality which continually threatens to undermine spiritual effort, but without which spiritual effort deviates into subtleties. It colours all sensation, clothes the instincts, emboldens tendencies, orchestrates the inner harmony. At the same time it keeps the organism attentive to the external landscape, and by the intensity and the finesse which it lends to the sensations, it perfects the keenness of the mind. It not only opens the mind to the outer world, it drives it towards the outer world. We have seen that there is a centrifugal force in the emotive charge. Emotion is the need to express oneself, and if this is often thwarted,

* Janet's definition of emotion as recoil and simplification.

permanent trouble results.[4] The emotive person is someone who is 'always open'. He calls to mind the 'psychasthesia' or capacity for experience described by Kretschmer. He produces the 'retracted type' described by Sigaud, Corvan, Monod-Herzen, who retracts in order to reduce hostile contacts, simply because he is hyperexcitable and exaggeratedly sensitive to his surroundings; but so deeply and painfully multiplying the contacts he still retains, that he knows the world infinitely better than his opposite number, the 'dilated type' who is indifferent to shocks and who expands easily in his environment, but allows it to slip over him without affecting him. If, in thus exposing himself to external stimuli, the emotive is forearmed against the effect of habit, it is a proof that emotivity is not only a factor of psychic disorder: only the abnormal manifest attackability in its crude state.[5] Taken all in all, emotivity contains a considerable promise of psychological richness. In a primitive nature, close to the instincts, it arouses only a faint tremor. But apart from its cruder products, it is the trait the most likely to extract the maximum of resources from a given character. It has the same relation to that passion for inwardness which marks the highest lives, as a certain natural liberality has to generosity, an easiness and a sensitivity which are not yet virtue, but which lend an inestimable grace to its beginning.

PORTRAIT OF THE EMOTIVE

If one groups under the heading of emotive those individuals nearest the pole of maximum emotivity, the prolonged duration of their emotions, particularly of the unhappy ones, is the dominant trait of this group. Pity and cruelty are specially intense. This affinity renders the emotive susceptible even to trifles: they take everything to heart. Their friendship thereby acquires a timbre and a warmth which sometimes lend an unparalleled charm to their company. But their way of giving rein to every feeling, of putting the full weight of their affective capacity behind each one, of becoming enthusiastic about almost anything, of remaining wounded or ecstatic for a long while after a single moment of fervour, all this exhausts them and renders them infinitely vulnerable.

Habitual anxiety is, in fact, a frequent result of this affective over-sensitivity. It is found to some extent in every emotive. When it dominates the psychological picture, one should perhaps speak, as has already been done, of the anxious constitution, a variety of the emotive constitution.[6] Anguish is generally depicted as one of the secret emotions, a lonely terror which gnaws away at the sufferer from within and thus drives him back, as it were, upon this hidden evil. But no one is more located, surrounded, than he. Anxiety is above all the perception of the environment as menace. One understands that Freud should have made anguish the centre of mental pathology, and almost the centre of psychology: the Freudian universe is essentially a menacing universe: from within, hidden complexes,[7] latent conflicts; from without, a hostile mass;[8] and above, a formidable Superego: the very world of the anxious. The anxious are literally drowned by their insecurity. Their anguish, in its primitive form, is a 'free floating anguish' (Freud) which slips from one's grasp and reappears immediately in a hundred diverse forms, passes from scruple to hypochondria, from whim to obsession, from uncertainty as to the morrow, to metaphysical torture. We have all some experience of anxiety. A banal anxiety is born of the knowledge of real danger: we fight, and it disappears with its cause. The constitutionally anxious person anticipates anxiety, even though it torture him. He is anxiety, before being anything else, he reflects it upon the world and sees advancing against him the very phantoms he has himself produced. A 'permanent and paroxysmal state of insecurity' pre-exists, independent of any cause, and attaches itself even to the most insignificant provocation. His generalised fear is never fixed to any one object, but slips from fear to fear, from presentiment to presentiment. Overwhelmed by the sense of his incapacity, hypersuggestible, always regretful, doubting, an obsessional self-analyst, scrupulous, irresolute, the anxious person struggles obstinately but without confidence against bad luck. Delays, separations, journeys, excursions, plans for the future, bilious attacks, surprises, are all pretexts for an attack of anxiety. He is worn out by the unequal struggle against unknown Titans. He perceives that he is so obviously bound to lose that he builds up a series of childish defences in a vain attempt to reduce the alarming impact of his fear: insurance policies, locks and spyholes in his door, superstitions, crazes, fetiches, vows, consultations with astrologers, sometimes fugues and repeated changes of domicile.

The physiological accompaniments of anxiety are varied: the most characteristic symptom is a sensation of physical constriction of the respiratory organs, of the pit of the stomach, the heart or the head. The feeling of constriction of the stomach comes from a muscular spasm due to contraction, as opposed to the dilatation caused by laughter (the mask of anxiety is the antithesis of the smiling mask). These basic symptoms may be connected with other spasmodic troubles: aerophagy, respiratory difficulties, colic, hay fever, genital disorders and, in the state of gross anxiety, nervous breakdowns, vertigo, asphyxia, syncope. These physiological and psychological disorders of constitutional anxiety are at their worst in the morning. The physical symptoms are so marked that for a long time attempts were made to explain anxiety by its purely organic symptoms. But each of them may occur independently of anxiety; it is the anxiety which brings them together into a significant psychological mixture.

The life of the anxious person is a painful and unceasing state of alarm. As a child he is a prey to nocturnal terrors: timid, nervous, impressionable to excess, he fears solitude as much as he fears society. He needs, from early childhood, a protective tenderness: this need will remain, making him in this respect a perpetual child. At puberty he is consumed by scruples of modesty, and sexual misgivings. Then he has to decide on a job, get married, extend his risks on either side: no sooner has he left the family nest than his life begins a tormented drift. Fear of growing old, fear of dying, fear of being left without means (the 'false avarice' of Rogues de Fursac) all overwhelm him as the years go by. He lives driven back upon his own sufferings, pursued even into his unhappy solitude. 'The whole order of things fills me with a sense of anguish, from the gnat to the mysteries of incarnation; all is entirely unintelligible to me', writes Kierkegaard,[9] 'and particularly my own person. Great is my sorrow, without limits. None knows of it, except God in Heaven, and He will not console me. None will console me, except God in Heaven, and He cannot have pity.' His destiny is one of those described by Minkowski,[10] to be bewildered by a 'capacity for conflict' which results from being so deeply immersed in the ideo-affective sphere. Should one ascribe it to a hereditary disposition? Or, with Freud, to an accumulation of excessive sexual energy which has been violently repressed? But it is difficult to explain fear, at the level of paroxysm, by anything other than fear, and whatever may be the displaced energy utilised by anguish, it is first of all a neurosis of fear, and perhaps, in the Freudian hypothesis, the fear of a fear. Fear, far from being reducible to a strictly localised formula, covers the whole psychic register. On the one hand, it springs from organic disturbances of the most primitive kind. At the other extreme, its victims become sensitive, even to the marrow of their bones, to the vertigo caused by a precarious balance between being and non-being.[11] Goldstein has described the 'reaction of catastrophe' which grips us, and emotives more than most, every time we face, or believe we face, the threat of total disintegration, which seems to exceed the threat of death itself. Its content is vague, but it is this imprecision which is so terrifying (consider the world of Kafka) enveloping us, as it were, in an infinite hostility. This state, exceptional in most people, is chronic in the anxious. The ultimate fears of the mind, and the primitive fears of the flesh, join forces to create the most formidable ordeal to which man is exposed.

If the emotive do not always experience this painful, chronic anxiety, they are sufficiently anxious and unbalanced by the unforeseen or by danger to be entirely lacking in the natural courage given by physical equilibrium and a certain coldness of mind. Emotion reduces the awareness of danger to a sort of frantic hallucination of the dangerous object, which separates them from any chance of escape, and from all the protective reactions which occur to the emotionally normal. Hence arise, collectively or individually, emotional panics, to which the more emotional Southern peoples are more easily subject than the Northern.

Emotivity gives too much power to each momentary sensation for the emotive to be able to control them in the light of wider considerations. A reduction in the field of consciousness is one of the dominant effects of the emotional habitus, and at the same time, by a circular process, this reduction of consciousness creates greater emotivity.

Emotivity is also linked with an inconstancy of humour, and the need for alternation of feeling. It is the natural background of the dilettante. One may observe the emotive individual swinging backwards and forwards from one impulse to its opposite in the same crisis. This variation of humour is at its maximum in the inactive emotive, who is free from the checks of an external control. It leads to a great instability of affection and friendships, which blaze up in an instant and then one day disappear into apparently total oblivion. It leads some to be always changing their profession or their residence, a habit which is described, according to their social status, as a taste for travel or vagabondage, fantasy or instability. This inclination is, however, modified by a fear of the unknown and of the decisions entailed by these constant adaptations. Emotivity appears to be a kind of denial of duration: it leaves no time for the theme of an action to work itself out, so great is the haste with which one element is thrust upon the other. When the affective sphere is so mobile, the will, defined as the capacity for continuous effort, is considerably weakened. The emotive man acts, when moved by a lively impulse, but the fire burnt out, his action is exhausted and collapses of its own accord. Emotivity may create heroes, but few men of action. Continuity of action is sacrificed to the immediate satisfaction of an impulse, to the detriment of future considerations. There is a form of unreflecting generosity in this impulsiveness which expresses a psycho-organic prodigality. The emotive man abandons himself entirely, more than any other type, to the inclinations of his heart. When exhausted, he seems unfaithful, and in fact he is so, but it would be harsh to interpret this inconstancy, which is more organic than conscious, as a lucid betrayal. Where anxiety is weak, the force of his impulsiveness leads him to a liking for sport, which he follows recklessly. This recklessness reappears in many a detail of his life. Finally, this same incapacity to sacrifice the immediate to the more distant, gives him a very low coefficient of punctuality: he will never abandon a fascinating interview, an attractive friend, a piece of work which enthralls him, for the abstract duty of keeping an appointment.

The general tone of the emotive is violence and passion, for he can never entirely contain the fire inside him. Impatient of obstacles and contradiction, easily insulted, given to brief and violent anger,[12] to impulsive gestures, nervous laughter, to political and religious fanaticism, he is endowed with an infinite capacity for hyperbole and explosion. Education may reduce these excesses but it will be rare if they do not break through occasionally even in the most cultured and contemplative character. At the very least, they will cause inner upheavals which are none the less tempestuous for being controlled. Sometimes they will be discharged in the form of bad temper, which is often a symptom of a repressed crisis of the emotions.

Vibrating to all stimuli, always feeling exposed, the emotive are particularly sensitive to the presence of other persons. They are the rank and file of the great army of the timid. They need to share a feeling of emotional warmth with their companions, and accept such a feeling with alacrity. Emotivity, says Wallon, is 'an antenna between the inner world and the stranger', a factor of unity: even its frictions are used in primitive societies as a means of collective communion. Perhaps, he adds, this rather vulgar facility of communication can be explained by the fact that a non-repressed emotion offers an appearance of exhibitionism, and almost of insincerity. 'It is made for incitement'.[13] This need to attract inclines the emotive to great suggestibility, particularly coming from those on the fringes of his acceptance, whereas he frequently abruptly and often unjustly rejects others after some initial dissonance, which was perhaps accidental. His very ingenuous vanity is founded on the same desire for approval. Unlike satisfied vanity, it is due to personal insecurity. Nor, when he is tyrannical, is this from lack of respect for others, but because of the irresistible drive of his own emotion which he imposes on others whilst believing that he is communicating it: the narrowing of his field of vision makes him overlook the vital requirements of the other person, through the very intensity of the affective intercourse, in which, in spite of himself, he plays the leading role. There is an egocentricity in the hypersensitive, rivalling their natural generosity, and a sort of dullness induced by a fervour of giving, which explain their partialities, their irritating forgetfulness, their passionate blind spots. The emotional lie must be attributed to this same intensity of feeling and narrowing of the field of consciousness. The emotive, under the stress of affectivity, always exaggerate. They are artistic in their sensitivity, and one of their most frequent exaggerations is the lie of embellishment, which arises spontaneously out of a need to make reality more expressive or more moving: the story cannot be told or the happening related without some improvement on it. The result is not always a Chateaubriand. Emotivity is also the root cause of the panic lie.[14] The narrowing of the field excludes any consideration other than that of the dreaded avowal: objectivity, never a close friend, disappears entirely under the shock of surprise: a lie appears the only salvation, as brutal and uncontrolled as the panic: the emotional lie is often an ingenuous lie, running counter to all the evidence. It is not, however, inevitable to slip from emotivity into lying. The emotion is often resolved still more quickly and crudely than by verbal invention: the child, pressed for a confession, flies into a tantrum and hits out at his questioners, the woman has an attack of nerves, the man gets into a rage. Emotivity, in characters of high quality, may also lead to frankness, which is the affective form of veracity.[15] In fact, however swift the emotional drive may be, it always leaves time for a lightning reflection, a violent application of the brakes, to anyone who wishes to take the trouble. Some emotive persons have trained themselves to a first reaction of silence, in order to let their temperament run free for a moment in a vacuum, before common sense gains the upper hand.

Emotivity does not lead to any weakening of the intelligence: on the contrary, the feeble-minded are very seldom hyperemotive. It only creates obstacles to the proper functioning of the mind by its secondary effects, particularly in the narrowing of the field. Memory is powerfully affected[16] and the failures of memory mark the site of affective lesions. It seems that repeated emotions act on the memory not only in this selective manner but also by disintegrating mental synthesis by their impact.[17] The principal handicap of the emotive on the plane of intellectual activity is the difficulty with which he adjusts himself to objective attitudes, shakes himself free of immediate reactions and prejudices of feeling, and distributes his attention amongst various objects. Thus he usually dislikes abstractions, or plunges into them—with a rigidity of mind which is a form of passion—only as a form of self-protection; he has only a mediocre capacity for mathematics; he is weak at scientific observation,[18] since he completely neglects all that does not interest him or, in a subject that does interest him, the aspects that interest him least, and thus spontaneously deforms the information he extracts. On the other hand, he is remarkably gifted in intuitive intelligence and concrete imagination, in all operations which require penetration rather than breadth and careful setting out. Emotivity, so susceptible to the shock of feeling, to strength of desire and to tragic conflict, is above all favourable to artistic effort: Heymans, in his biographical research, found that the number of artists in each characterological group diminished strictly in proportion to the reduction of emotivity. The sense for the living flavour of words, and the feeling tones of expression usually endow the emotive with a special facility for languages.

They cannot live in an atmosphere of suspicion, which disconcerts them. And they lack the patience and the forethought which make the cunning combination of falsehood and intrigue more attractive to some than even the actual results obtained. Thus it is not unusual to find in them the honesty and kindred virtues which attract confidence. This confidence is sometimes destroyed by their inconstancy, although it is understood that it is without malice. Their fantasies are a menace in business and in mechanical fields, but they are aware of this difficulty themselves, and by preference abstain from such activities.

Their deep need for communion and for inner fervour predispose them to religious feelings. They know the glow of faith, and being fairly independent and little inclined to dogmatism, often verge on heresy, being too inclined to religious sentimentalism or to the fanaticism of sects. But even allowing for all their vagaries they are perhaps those without whom the fires of religion would grow cold and the bright flame of heroism flicker.

Heymans' figures reveal two further correlations of emotivity: manual dexterity and the frequency of nervous disorders. The first is linked to the delicacy of their perceptions: the hand of the emotive type is one that gives the greatest impression of intelligence. This may be reduced by the paralysing effect of the emotions on the motor centres: a re-education in precision of gesture may then be one means of combating this emotional intimidation. The second quality is connected with their state of permanent psychic strain and the fragility of their nervous constitution.[19]

The constitutional predominance of emotivity in women should be noted. Heymans' research has given every confirmation of the findings of everyday experience. A woman is practically never indifferent. The concomitants of emotivity are point for point the same as for femininity. Psychoses of affective origin are much more frequent in women than in men. Her desires are usually so violent, that a waiting state, with its fluctuations between uncertainties, exhausts her. Disappointments upset her more than a man. Her feelings, compared with those of most men, develop more quickly and last longer. Her versatility of temper is greater, and she is more vulnerable to fear and mockery: Maier has already remarked that irony, 'an act of cold aggression', is distasteful to her warmer nature. Her emotivity tends to attract her towards religious or aesthetic feeling, and handicaps her for abstract studies. Her decisions proceed from emotional grounds far more often than in a man. Hence the frequently impulsive quality of her actions, her extreme, apparently fantastic mobility from the serious to the frivolous: the mother who is at home a miracle of patience, becomes the bad-tempered saleswoman outside, because her work fails to attract her.

*   *   *

It is unnecessary to deal at length with the portrait of the inemotive, after having described the emotive. No one is totally inemotive, there are only more or less emotive persons: those who are at the bottom of the scale are normally called inemotive. But a good educator will always look for the germs of emotivity even there, and try to develop them, in order to prevent an excessive hardening of the character.

This is all the more necessary when the inemotive is perhaps a repressed and barricaded emotive, with very little access to his emotions. Vermeylen, in particular, has distinguished very rightly between the expansive emotives—sociable, influenceable, given to dramatisation, who might be called the visibly emotive—and those we shall call the inhibited or cryptemotive, who clamp down on their emotions with a brutality equal to the force with which they emerge, and who overcompensate their inner vulnerability by an excessive coolness or even stiffness. Every other impassive, haughty or formal countenance conceals a delicate, irritable sensitivity. The physical expression, when it can be caught, the tapping of the foot, the twitching of an eyelid, the nervous contortions of the fingers, a quaver in the voice, a sudden pallor, a lost, vaguely anxious glance, are furtive denials of a superficial appearance. This habitual inhibition often has its origin in the repressions, ill-treatment or emotional shocks of childhood, or in a severe education which creates, as with a Robespierre or a Guizot, an abnormally harsh moral judgment. We know those quiet, sad, timid, solitary children, whose inner fever is only betrayed by their excessive preoccupations or dislikes. The inhibition may affect only the surface gesture and remain a mask. But it may also take root and gradually lead into an affective and motor apathy and to total inemotivity: it is then necessary to recover the original emotional process by anamnesis.

In the inemotive, as opposed to the emotive, any internal or external excitation immediately calls into play a system of reflexes or ideo-motor adaptations which displace the disturbance and prevent it from being resolved on the spot. The resulting picture is the exact complement of the picture of the emotive we have just given. First there is a greater or lesser degree of impassivity, which can range from gentleness and self-control to coldness and phlegm. This is a natural gift, like emotional sensitivity. Just as the latter tends to a liberality of heart and mind, so the relative invulnerability of the inemotive protects him overmuch from the drama of events and persons. He thereby loses in drive and in warmth of sympathy, in breadth of view, in constancy. One degree too much and he tends to egoism and coldness. But that spiritual love which the theologians call benevolence, is not exclusive to any one humour, and finds its own way and its own undertones, in one as well as in another. The inemotive is calm, and if devoted, it is with a deep, long enduring devotion; he easily resists suggestion and intimidation. Inclined to objectivity, unlike the emotive, he succeeds best in intellectual work of an abstract or technical nature, whereas he is unfavourably placed with regard to intuition and artistic sense. It is good to correct this inadequacy by trying to encourage in him an acceptance of reality (Lefrancq). Cynicism and wile can be found in his company. His aggressiveness is limited, intractable and coldly elaborate, or else primitive, according to his intelligence. When he is moral, he is dogmatic on principle. Fairly often he is irreligious, but when he is a believer, he follows less a God speaking to the heart, than a God acceptable to reason. He attaches himself to the apparatus of religion as much or even more than to the inspiration it provides. But he may also aspire to reach the upper limits of this type, towards 'a loftier and clearer humanity' whose virtues are 'mastery, solitude and lucidity'. Then he shares the rational wisdom of those who think with Nietzsche, that the heroes, the martyrs, the geniuses, the enthusiasts are not 'sufficiently tranquil, sufficiently patient, sufficiently subtle, cold and slow.'[20]

It will be seen that this portrait bears a marked relationship to the phlegmatic type of the early classifications.

*   *   *

Apart from hereditary or acquired factors, emotivity is closely linked with environment. It is more easily found in urban, mechanical civilisations, with their rapid rhythms, and multiple sensations, than in peasant civilisations: it creates both the richness and the fragility of the townsman. Southern peoples are more subject to it than the Northern: the negroes are the most emotional of races. Further, these oppositions, which are valid for European longitudes, are distributed, no doubt in different ways, over other continents. Culture and the refinements of living are favourable to the higher forms of emotivity, by differentiating and sensitising affectivity, but we should not forget that primitive life, with its rougher conditions, its adventures, its surprises, its cruder instincts, develops a primary emotivity, different from the other, but no less essential. The too sheltered and enervating type of education, practised in certain families and at certain periods, was largely responsible for the formation of the excessively frail personalities found at the beginning of this century. A healthy life, with a balance between the discipline of the mind and the discipline of sport, should aim at neutralising the poison of over-complicated civilisations, avid for violent excitement.

It would be impossible not to speak of the collective forms of emotivity. When instinctive and powerful collective energies cannot find an outlet in normal political activity, in an order which satisfies what is essential in the forces at work, an emotional explosion occurs, similar to the individual emotional outburst, with a return to primitive and often violent forms of behaviour. Revolutions and their excesses, reaction and White Terror, are typical manifestations of such crises. Collective psychotherapy is not very unlike individual psychotherapy: these periodic accidents show the necessity of providing channels or alternative outlets for the social forces, thus preserving the state from such dangerous accumulations of unstable and destructive power.

*   *   *

Can one overstress the difficulties of the emotive temperament? Certainly. Experience has shown that, save in extreme cases, constitutional emotivity can be mastered, provided that the will accepts the particular style imposed on it by the emotive constitution. Highly emotive persons have been known to make excellent motorists: their actions retain from their basic emotivity a precision and a subtlety that are very rare.

The best prophylaxis, whether or not one is dealing with predisposition, is to avoid emotional intoxication. Nowadays we recognise the decisive effect on emotional balance of the shocks of early childhood, and even, at pre-puberty, of feelings transmitted through the mother. We must avoid catastrophic developments from these early shocks of birth, weaning, the first sexual revelations, the first social contacts. The crisis of puberty is difficult: here it is above all important to avoid withdrawal, scruples, false shame and superfluous suffering. The systematic use of terror in education, particularly at tricky periods of transition—first social adjustment, first sexual weakness, can immobilise someone for life in the painful, lacerated affectivity of the emotive. With sensitive natures, to threaten with bogus and obscure menaces (particularly with imaginary sexual mutilation, even as a joke), with fantastic stories, shouts, blows or threats of blows, may have the same result by creating a real cult of fear in the child[21] or, similarly, by using too brutal methods of accustoming the child to fear. Inversely, an education which is too soft, a hothouse cultivation of sensitivity under the disquieting and timorous solicitude of an exclusively feminine environment, under artificial conditions (consider the childhood of Proust, Wilde, Amiel), stimulates a sensitivity which will always rebel against adult disciplines. The same effect is sometimes produced by a solitary childhood, where the children are either deprived of, or rejected by, their natural environment.

Here we must be more than ever on our guard against the imperialism of mental health. Often a great life has drawn its richness and vital energy from an unhappy childhood. Though here, however, it is essential that the resilience of the nervous system should not have been destroyed by an accumulation of affective shocks. The emotive child will always suffer so much conflict that one does him no harm in providing a certain discipline for his emotive life. One must first reduce the number of emotions. Those which remain (for to remove them all would be to deprive him of his daily bread) should not be interrupted or aggravated by excessive harshness, humiliation, mockery or bullying. They must be understood, and the emotive must know that they are understood. But at the same time one should take care not to be too conciliatory, but gradually to accustom his hypersensitivity to a sharper climate, where it can face surprise without dismay. It is no use appealing to the 'will' of the emotive, or to his 'energy'. These cold, cruel words mean nothing to him. Every forced effort he makes in this direction arouses a painful tension, mingled with revolt, and therefore useless. Neither is reasoning any more effective. The worst of teachers for the emotive is another emotive, who only increases his sensitivity, or the strong-willed, or the high-minded intellectual, who only antagonise him. He needs a well-balanced and sensitive person at his side, on whose firmness and security he can lean, but such a person must above all be friendly, so that his understanding is felt even through his strictness: for the emotive's first need is to be understood, and the simple, irrational fact of another's presence can give him this rare joy, even without a word being spoken. With this understanding he is capable of considerable effort. The person who has his confidence can lead him to cultivate self-control, continuity of thinking and of affection, to become more accustomed to risk, to objectivity, even to a certain insensitivity, in so far as these help to correct any excesses, without trying to run counter to his nature or to blunt the fine point of his perceptions, which is the recompense for so much anxiety. Dr. Paul-Emile Lévy claims to have obtained excellent results by teaching his patients to tranquillise their impressionability by details: he encourages minor emotions, which are easily controllable. A good state of health and particularly of the endocrine system, is essential.[22] The abuse of alcohol, toxins and drugs is strongly contra-indicated, although their moderate use is sometimes a necessity for the emotive. Everything that facilitates external activity at the expense of dangerous inner turmoil is desirable: observation, artistic creation, which objectivises the emotion in work, instead of abandoning it to itself, a minimum of activity which directs the emotions into external interests, critical analysis, the presentation of varied points of view, the equilibration of reaction: if the budding emotion is thus offered channels of expansion into the external world, the massive force of the incipiently pathological drives is shattered. Analysis of the emotion itself is a particularly good way of controlling it. Experience has shown that attempts to divorce emotion from consciousness will fail: the emotion persists and wreaks its will in blindness: a concentration of the mind on the emotion in order to intellectualise it[23] will, however, diminish it. Pascal was able to cure his toothache by calculating the surface of the cycloid: more ordinary folk can sometimes quieten their suffering by analysing its physical manifestations. Those who are predisposed to the cruder forms of emotion may be advised to practise reverie, which is the beginning of exteriorisation, a working out of the primitive emotion. The simple introduction of a rhythm is sufficient to disarm it. Thus Saul used David's harp, and Theodosius had young children taught music in order to calm his rage when necessary. Music stimulates vitality and raises psychological tension. Janet has two good stories on the subject: Suleiman II, having been sent a troupe of musicians by Francis I, perceived with annoyance that his character was becoming softer: but instead of becoming a saint, he sent back the musicians. It is said that at the wedding of Joyeuse in 1561 it was enough for the musician Claudius to change the mode, to divert a dagger thrust aimed at the king.

In any case, the emotive child must be dealt with early, otherwise he will exercise a veritable tyranny of weakness and susceptibility over his surroundings, for egocentricity can turn everything to its own advantage, even the qualities most likely to appeal to one's heart.
*

* Section on emotivity as the root of character, describing the forms of expression of emotion in Heymans' categories.

3

THE VITAL RESPONSE

LET us place ourselves for a moment at the level where personal life is just emerging from the life stream. It is still vibrant with organic impulses, still mingled with the enchantments that arise from earth, race and centuries, even in the blood that pulses in our veins. Here we are thinking in terms well below the higher psychic syntheses and complex forms presented by the personality shaped by the interplay of physical and social environment, in which it has more or less affirmed or abdicated its dominance, mastered or abandoned its intercourse. But we have already crossed the vast gulf which separates purely organic from personal life. We must expect to meet, from the very beginning, certain attitudes which, however merged with organic influences, cannot be reduced to the sole pressure of the body. It is this group of rudimentary attitudes, considered at the level of the life stream, which it is proposed to call 'the vital response'. 'Vital' because consciousness is still not always sufficiently autonomous, nor activity sufficiently mental, for it to be considered a purely personal decision.

This group of responses is global and primitive, capable only of a confused vital awareness, and hardly at all of appraising the current which moves it, whether breath of the spirit or biological flux. It determines, however, the manner of a person's being, even if it is the first most elementary orientation, shaped in the raw clay of the human aggregate. It expresses not only a force emerging from life itself to be transmitted without a break from organic effervescence to purely human activities. It is already a statement of the person in the face of matter, a response to provocation, heavily weighted by our particular humour, but which we can progressively disentangle from the action of humours by our own intervention: like those deeply buried rocks whose structure can be altered down to the molecule by the action of their superficial masses. This is why we speak of responses, as the word suggests our own share of authority and responsibility in this fundamental polarisation. These responses will remain primitive in their vast structure and their kinship with organic drives, even in the adult personality. But they can be rendered infinitely flexible and valuable by the influence exercised on them by the upper levels of the psyche. Although they define the fundamental limitations of the psyche, they are capable of infinite complexity and their angle of sight covers the whole range of human existence.

PSYCHOLOGICAL FORCE AND WEAKNESS

To speak of psychological force is not to abuse the use of a term borrowed from physics. The concept of force, as Leibniz has shown, was in its early form a psychological concept, and only acquires its full meaning when applied to the activity of a subject.

Psychologists and doctors began to speak of psychic energy at a time when mechanistic theories proved unable to explain life fully in terms of the operation of reflexes, even of the most complex kind. It often happens that the reflex mechanisms are intact, but do not function, or function too rapidly, in virtue of a factor independent of their sole control. These facts entailed the hypothesis, already familiar in physics, of a capital of psychic force, variable in quantity, availability and tension, according to the time and the individual, and capable of reconstituting itself more or less rapidly when impaired.

Is it a physical or psychological reality? Both the one and the other, since it is a capitalisation of the human aggregate. On the one hand the force is derived from physiological sources, from the basic vitality of the individual. Its quantity and potential, even sometimes its rhythm, are maintained by the anabolic function of the sympathetic nervous system, which must be considered the directing system of the dynamic function. This function draws its energy from two kinds of source: the one external, heat, light, food, stimulants; the other endogenous, such as sleep and all the economies of nervous expenditure achieved by the organism, from habitual automatisms to psychological processes. Psychological force is thus conditioned by good nutrition, equilibrium of the sympathetic nervous system and, as a result, of the metabolism, and finally by the absence of abnormal sources of expenditure. There are incessant transformations from the force called physical to the force called moral: anger, the fear of ridicule, can give us unaccustomed muscular strength; fear or emotion 'make your knees tremble', timidity makes one's gestures heavy, moral depression affects the articulation of one's words: inversely, good health confers assurance, strength of mind, stubbornness, and there is, as we know, a psychological picture for every disease. In addition, this psychic force is connected solely with the general metabolic system, without any differentiation. It can pass from one activity to another without changing its nature (the 'drainage' of Janet and the 'displacement' of

Freud). Once one has observed the multiple ambivalence of psychological force, one has to admit, with Janet, that we observe its effects without knowing anything of its nature.[1]

What are these effects? First of all, particular feelings, the feeling of plenitude, of ease, of exaltation, or again of need, of change, of improvement, of abasement. But these feelings are not an infallible guide, any more than the effectiveness of action, which may depend in part on external circumstances. We shall appreciate the nature of force more positively by drawing an overall picture of the quantitative and qualitative modifications of behaviour which differentiate the two great subdivisions of character: the strong and the asthenic.

*   *   *

We can distinguish the psychically strong character primarily by the power, rapidity and duration of his movements and of his work. He is usually, according to Heymans, an active-emotive, the pressure of emotivity reinforcing the power of his activity. Primary psychic force is particularly associated with the elemental, primeval drives (fear, anger, hunger, sexuality). It is always attended by a powerful assertion of the vital instincts, a strong temperament usually having to carry the weight of a heavy sensuality. It is a support to other tendencies only in the sense that the foundations of a building support the fabric, but the whole tone of psychic life is thereby modified. The strong character engages in action right away, without being waylaid by any initial difficulties; he is, before he asks himself if he is; he lives before reflecting on his life. He sets death aside by forgetting it, illness by not listening to it.

The surface of his life is wide and marked by the volume of his actions and initiative. Unlike the child and the weaker person, he is particularly adapted to multiplicity: he is capable of embracing at one and the same time several actions, several conversations, several projects, and several moments of time, even if all are divergent. His thinking is panoramic and complex and includes many points of view. He is not only rich in his capital of energy, but also by his great capacity for recuperation, and by the graduated rhythm of this recuperation, demonstrated externally by his calm and self-control. His behaviour is marked by a sense of balance, continuity, flexibility and solidity, which is certainly of inestimable advantage to him. But it is a matter of experience that a too well adjusted psycho-organic balance entails the risk, like too great physiological distress, of impairing a more spiritual life: there is a sort of rough blindness of excessive health which closes the mind to consideration of others and of the human condition. The strong temperament is the less vulnerable to that fundamental compassion of man for man in that he himself has a solid resistance to shock and uncertainty, and has no vital need for the presence of others. In this force is also a kind of weakness, if he pursues the advantages of his privileges. Force can harden into brutality, psychic health creates a florid, smiling, self-possessed egoism as unconscious of itself as of the misery of the world: a splendid animal, tough as a bull and thinking with his fists, or supple as a cat, and living on his insouciance. Force is only great when one can see, through its strength, the suffering compassed, the latent weakness and the continuous effort.

We have already said that the system specific to the dynamic function was the sympathetic nervous system: the central nervous system is not, in fact, an organ of production; it is concerned only with transformations of quality and with the distribution of loads. But psychic force is not crude organic force: its qualities, power, flexibility and polyvalence are those of the cortex. The integrity of the central nervous system is therefore essential.

Force is not always in action. In a latent state it maintains psychological reserves. There are persons with great reserves of energy who can indulge in all forms of wastage: others, without being ill, have very small reserves and have to resign themselves, once and for all, to not exceeding a certain level of expenditure. Yet this psychic energy has hidden strengths which we often underestimate, just as we overlook a host of secret expenditures which unknowingly drain our life away. This capital and its capacity for recuperation depend in the first place on heredity and ancestral wastages; a healthy stock of recent peasant origin produces stronger subjects than several generations of urban overstrain. And reserves are not always accessible to the same degree; one may be able to mobilise a high degree of energy at a given moment, and yet have few reserves, like those subjects who are capable of a sudden nervous effort, which leaves them exhausted for many days; or great reserves, little of which can be actually mobilised, either because they are otherwise occupied or because a certain vital impulse is lacking.

Psychic force is not defined solely in terms of quantity. Two factors are essential to it: impetus and degree of organisation. We shall deal with the latter further on, under the concept of psychological tension. The former has been isolated by Pfahler as the percussive force of activity. It is a permanent index of individual energy; it can be increased, but cannot be awakened below a certain level. With all its overtones and undertones, it becomes a dominant quality in emotional impetuosity. In the eager impatience of passionate types it would seem that an overabundance of all their powers unites with a vital basic impulse, to create a hypertension preparatory to action. This tension is also found, with its tonic and motor accompaniments, in the nervous, the restless and the obsessional, but whilst it stirs up infinite possibilities in the colourful personality of the passionate type, in the more impoverished personality it becomes exhausted in hopeless contradictions.

★ ★ ★

Psychological weakness has it origin either in the inheritance of a mediocre capital of energy or in an accumulation of burdensome expenditures:[2] illness, chronic physiological disorders (particularly of the endocrines and the intestines), emotions, prostration from an excess of too rapid, complicated, difficult or novel actions, or of actions which appear so to an impoverished organism (such as the great decisions at the great crossroads of life), the complications and struggles of social life, moral scars, the weight of the past, overstrain, and so on.

We have all experienced states of temporary weakness. We should only speak of asthenia when dealing with a habitual weakness, which affects the whole behaviour. And even then we should distinguish between constitutional asthenia, which borders on neurosis, and the slight asthenia which is so common among the 'normal' particularly in the population of our cities.

Constitutional asthenia starts in childhood with a habitual laziness. These lazy children, susceptible to all childish ailments, particularly digestive weakness, are hypothyroid children, whose general and sexual development is extremely slow. They are not incapable of difficult intellectual operations, but they lack the force to carry them through,[3] which shows them to be asthenic and not atonic, lacking psychological force but not tension. Thus they are inclined to lie from economy, in a quite different way from the emotional or hysterical. They are always slow. Janet compares them to the animal that, left to itself, does not work. They are quite disposed, from time to time, to do something that pleases them, but they are totally incapable of effort against their inclinations: punishment only serves to inculcate a morbid terror. They are considered sweet-tempered, for they are not prone to complain, as this would be overtiring. Being unable to finish anything, they are ineffectual, unfaithful, unstable. They always end by falling ill, particularly with gastric and cutaneous diseases.[4]

Acquired asthenia is usually the result of infectious diseases, mental depression, or long periods of physiological or emotional overstrain. Under the heading of *accidie, morositas, mentis enervatio, animi remissio*, this was denounced by theologians as the gravest illness of monastic life.

The slightly asthenic are very numerous and very solitary, for no one is more difficult to know or to accept than an asthenic, to one who is not. Nothing that they do is abnormal, but they seem to display such ill will in doing things that others consider normal. We reproach them for not making an effort, and they are incapable of effort; we reproach them for being swallowed up in details, and their misfortune itself is made up of details. The unconscious egoism of the healthy man accepts a madman more easily than a near neighbour who seems a perpetual challenge to the normality of his own conduct. The world of the asthenic is, paradoxically, both close to and remote from our own. Every day he comes up against its boundaries, seeing it, as it were, within his grasp and yet inaccessible, this world of the well-adjusted, the paradise lost he strives to regain. It is difficult for the healthy to make the necessary effort of comprehension, to understand and to help the citizens of this tired world.[5] One can never fully appreciate what may cause them fatigue. On the other hand, it is difficult for the asthenic to realise how depressing are the checks they impose on the vitality of the stronger person living in their vicinity.

*

Asthenia is, in part, open to medical treatment, which is outside our scope.[6] The normal regime of the asthenic should, above all, allow for economy of effort: in severe cases, total repose: in milder forms, their effort should stop as soon as fatigue sets in, which is not always easy, as they often do not experience fatigue immediately; in a general way, they should keep the rhythm of their lives at a level determined by their own experience. They should avoid the most costly expenditures of effort: complex situations, psychological impasses, exhausting deliberations, the element of risk and social overstrain. If inclined to rumination, self-doubting and scruple, one should not reason with them but simply induce them to abandon the rumination by absorption in their daily work. They need not only repose, but sufficient solitude and silence to prevent them frittering away their

* Gives three indications of a state of asthenia, according to Dr. Deschamps, *Les maladies de l'énergie*, Alcan, 1908.

reserves through the friction of fatigues due to noise, agitation, presence of many persons. From time to time they need an oasis of complete silence and solitude in order to reconstitute their strength: holidays, which are for some a period of release and expansion, should be for them, at least partially, a period of retreat, during which they can detach themselves even from the closest personal ties, for a certain number of days.

When handled with skill, some forms of stimulation may tend to promote a renewal of energy. If, in this general weakness, one tendency can be singled out and animated, its activation may communicate itself to the rest, by irradiation and syntony. It has often been observed that the asthenic become suddenly capable of an action contrary to their usual habits under the influence of strong emotion (for instance, flight from danger), or positive feelings (for instance, an act of devotion). It is incorrect to assume from this, like Dubois of Berne, the previous non-existence of fatigue. Improving the morale of a depressed person often simply means making an empirical appeal to such stimuli.

The helpful presence of a psychologically strong person can be one of these stimuli, if he knows how to contain his strength, and prevent it overpowering the asthenic by being too obvious. The asthenic should be made more aware of his capacity for calm and self-control than of the surge of his creative capacities. Otherwise he disconcerts the asthenic rather than helps him. A disciplined environment may have the same salutary effect: the difficulties of the asthenic are often found to disappear during military service or in a monastery. They often love and respect the discipline which provides support for their weakness. Some psychotherapists have even attempted to apply direct discipline, not of effort and perseverance, which are no use, but by the control of attitudes and muscular tone.[7]
*

*   *   *

We owe to Pierre Janet the invaluable distinction between *psychological force* and *tension*.[8] Psychological force refers to the potential quantity of tendencies and their effects: power, rapidity, duration. But certain paradoxical facts show that the quantity of force engaged is not enough to explain psychic activity. It may be that by increasing the force of an asthenic, one creates only disorders: agitation,

* Details of physical exercises prescribed by Camuz and Pagniez, and Déjérine Glaucker.

convulsions, anguish, brooding, etc. In acute cases, this is often the result of rest or sleep. Inversely, the psychologically depressed may often be considerably revived by the exhaustion of an illness. Here we have subjects impoverished by an addition, and enriched by a withdrawal. In others the extreme limits of fatigue will never produce a psychological depression. This is because, in man, psychological force never operates in its crude state, but is transformed by more or less superior mechanisms of the psyche. In the zone of elementary and instinctive tendencies, it remains qualitatively gross and massive: one might say that these are the zones of low tension or of low psychic level. In the sphere of the higher tendencies, it has to adapt to a quite different situation: it meets functions with a high degree of evolution, it must sustain complex unities and fragile states of equilibrium, and actions of extreme diversity covering a wide range of space and time: we will call these the zones of high tension or of high psychic level.[9] In ordinary life there is infinite variation from the first to the second. Psychic potential is rather like electric potential, not only in its intensity but in its location, by its concentration at a higher or lower level. Janet compares the force F to an army's combat potential, and tension T to the strategic employment of this potential and to the military qualities exhibited in its use. He makes it clear that tension is not only defined by a higher mental synthesis, but by the mental richness, the psychic mass, which go to form this synthesis: the psyche of the low-tensioned type is not only characterised by dispersion but also by simplification and impoverishment.

The paradox mentioned earlier can now be explained. Force is a source of disorder when tension is low: it then overflows in an excess of elementary activities and throws them into disorder: those whose tension is low do better with a small supply of energy. But in the normal person tension increases at the same time as force: as Janet put it, you seldom keep a million pounds in threepenny bits.

Acts of high tension must count as the most exhausting of all, for they require not only an enormous mobilisation of capital on the part of the psychic force, but also many difficult operations in setting it to work. Such acts include all complex actions, painful delays, adjustments to new situations, important decisions, brusque or rapid actions, long-term activities, overwork, conflicts, the great events of life, such as the first communion, the first mixing with society, examinations, choice of occupation, engagement, marriage, setting up house, bereavements, separations, removals, change of work, the bringing up of children, even leisure and the social and family problems entailed. In other words, the sum of activities involved in adjustment to reality, in being present in the here and now. Below these is a scale of decreasing tension, such as free, purposeless action, detached thought, reverie and abandonment to diffused emotion. High-tension acts mobilise a hundred times more force than acts of low tension. This does not mean that in normal circumstances they dissipate our reserves, since their purpose is to achieve an overall economy of effort by their fecundity. But they exhaust the low-tensioned, for the mental effort cannot be maintained at the height required, and the force mobilised is squandered on secondary agitations, agitations of all kinds, tiffs, incessant reasoning and questioning, and so on.

The strong and the weak present two types of behaviour in a complex situation. The strong character is a better exploiter than any capitalist of his psychic force. He can easily and repeatedly perform the actions which require the use of the higher tendencies. Inversely, the low-tensioned are obliged to content themselves with actions that require only a moderate employment of the lower tendencies.

Acts of high tension are marked, in the normal person, by those feelings of calm, joy, interest, confidence, independence, triumph, which Janet has grouped under the heading of 'feelings of elation' which are the various modes of expression of what is generally called the optimistic temperament. In persons of high quality, this optimism is calm, measured, as if it were a basic strength and confidence in a goodness and order at the heart of things, which excludes neither warmth of heart nor an awareness of the dramatic element in life. The optimism of the 'good sort' is of a lesser quality. His primarity makes him superficial, equally forgetful of the sufferings of others and of his own, of the world's misfortunes as of the injuries which slide off his own back. If his happy disposition is partly due to the feelings stimulated by a powerful emotivity, it is also due to his faculty of forgetfulness, and the superficial turn of his mind. Then it appears somewhat vulgar. Neither is the excitement which Janet finally decided to call 'elation' always a state of strength. It is often the effect of a depression trying by means of 'multiple, small, limited' actions[10] to find an equivalent for the small number of superior and extensive actions which are the virtue of the strong. Action on a high level is always condensed: a fall in the psychic level, on the other hand, always increases the volume of action.[11] In the cemeteries of psychological life, those unhappy madmen whose minds are shattered, or simply in a state of deficiency, like the epileptic aura, certain morbid ecstasies, or in narcotic intoxication, we find a state of expansive 'beatitude'[12]

which is far from being equalled by an expansion of psychological force. The happy imbecile is in this sense happier than the saint. We see that feeling is always ambiguous, and that its significance can only be assessed in relation to the whole of conduct.
*

We cannot deal directly here with the pathological outcome of certain psychological wastages. These cases are to be sought in the convalescent home and mental hospital. But on the other hand the measures for dealing with ordinary atony are part of the psychotherapy of daily life.

The most important preventive measure is to proportion the accumulation of psychological force to the tension available, and not to increase the one without trying to raise the other. Otherwise nature reacts by diverse symptoms of intolerance, of which the most frequent is discharge: 'an excessively rapid expenditure, in a very short period, of accumulated forces which have become intolerable';[13] thus the laughter that follows a disappointment, the epileptic or hysterical crisis which answers the need to exhaust oneself by muscular action. Thus absolute rest must be used with caution in cases of acute depression: some low-tension types are more agitated and fretful when they have slept well, and total inactivity leads them into exhausting mental agitation. The most effective treatment is the same as for the asthenic, but still more strictly applied, that is, a restricted life with well-chosen economies. Left to themselves the depressed and psychasthenic know how to build up the life that suits them, modest bureaucratic or subordinate functions, few relationships, few struggles. If they have suffered in love, they renounce love; tormented by religious scruples, they abandon faith. If they do not succeed in moving on after a crisis, they sometimes have to be pushed on, even abruptly, so that they do not lose themselves in interminable liquidations. They sometimes succeed in carrying on fairly well if they have someone at their side who removes obstacles, shelters them from defeats and recurring hold-ups, which drain them little by little of their energy. Janet sums up their therapy as: simplification of life. So regular and monotonous a way of living may not seem particularly attractive to the strong, but it is the only one that permits the weak to exist: it leaves them in the rearguard of the struggle for existence, with a sensitivity sharpened by ordeal and a capacity for devotion which are enough to make them feel that, though diminished, they are no longer disgraced.

★　　　★　　　★

* Asthenia only a state of general weakness: depression can by degrees lead to neurosis and psychasthenia. Description of psychasthenia.

There is therefore a complex problem of the equilibrium of forces at the base of human behaviour. A man in a state of good health is always having to rebuild a threatened equation: but he has sufficient capital of energy to do so, and by clever administration he sets up successive states of equilibrium with the same flexibility as an athlete moving from one position to another. In those whose energies are impaired, the new states of equilibrium are discovered with difficulty, and are unstable, interrupted, shaky, as in the manic depressives we shall come to later: or the equilibrium is partial, as in the hysterical, who can only maintain one section of their psychic life, isolated from the rest, which they ignore. The most unfortunate establish a balance almost at zero: these are the totally demented. The asthenic and the depressed form a numerous group, with uncertain boundaries, between powerful temperaments and descending degrees of neurosis. The miseries of a troubled epoch, fatal to the fragile sensitivity, can only increase their number and now, more than ever, they must not be abandoned.

We should, incidentally, be careful not to try to explain too many things by weakness. Like the former theory of degeneration in mental pathology, the explanation is too easy and often inadequate; it accounts for certain deficiencies which condition certain psychological states: in normal circumstances it is not capable of explaining the attitudes adopted and their psychic content.

THE ACT OF CONSCIOUSNESS

Of all the assertions of the modern world, the claim to consciousness is one of the most vehement. After Descartes, and particularly after the eighteenth century, to be conscious seemed an ideal all the more absolute in that it was identified with being reasonable. At the time consciousness and reason appeared to be, if not the most common faculties of mankind, at least the most communicable. Then came the philosophies, followed by the psychologies of the Unconscious. It is accepted today that consciousness is far from covering the whole of psychological life. Consciousness is one aspect of conduct amongst others, and not the spontaneous phosphorescence of all psychic activity. It is practically absent from the simple actions of the organism: the motor reaction follows promptly upon the sensory stimulus, following settled rules of vital adaptation. Then comes a moment in the development of life when a hitch occurs in the circuit. The first act of consciousness, notes W. Stern, is a halt: the child stops repeating the same gesture indefinitely, such as shaking his rattle, in a sort of motor frenzy, in order to look at his fingers or at the object he holds. This halt is not an aim in itself. It conditions reflection, which makes the action more perfect in quality but poorer in execution. It offers to temperaments fearful of action the temptation to dwell dreamily on the proposed act. But in such cases it is displaced from its natural function. The act of consciousness is in purpose an active halt. It requires the subject to summon up all his energy to overcome the pull of impulse: he must quickly examine a complex situation, overcome multiple resistances, form an opinion, take a decision and set it in operation. If consciousness appears at first glance a halt, it is above all a summons and an act. It is not a vague reflection of something on the surface of our perceptions, it is the initiator of action and intensive action. This inner reflection is only its secondary and partially borrowed light, part of the regulatory feelings which accompany its functioning.

We should therefore no longer speak, in the terms of a static psychology, of 'states' of consciousness, nor in the terms of a dynamic psychology which is still too impersonal, of a 'flux' of consciousness, but of an *act* of consciousness. The act of consciousness is not a giving way to reverie; it is a combat, the severest combat of man as spirit, the constant struggle against the torpor of life and against that intoxication of life which is torpor of spirit. An adventurous consciousness is always trying to give meaning to its own activity. The act of consciousness is a taking possession of a value which, once apprehended, delivers an ultimatum; once possessing, is immediately possessed by the necessity of choice, being thus made captive by its captive. And this drama is the true vibration of psychological life, still known as life even to those psychologists who are only weighing out, like so many apothecaries, the dust of a corpse.

Such being the case, we can understand that 'we only become conscious of a limited number of things, and in fact each of us has his own particular way of becoming conscious.'[14]

Let us leave aside the sickness of consciousness, either through excess or absence. This has abounded ever since the crisis of Western consciousness which followed the rationalist optimism of the eighteenth century and the progress in the understanding of the Unconscious.

It seems that consciousness impairs its own functioning when too occupied with itself. The halt which precedes the act of consciousness has been, for many of our contemporaries, a pretext for evading action. Like Zeno's runner, they lose the capacity to achieve their goal by too much meditation on the route. The philosopher, instead of extending his reason, discourses inexhaustibly about reason. The historian forgets

Napoleon in writing about Napoleon's historians. Inner life serves as an excuse for deserting external life. Introspection becomes a substitute for action instead of an illumination of action, a dream becomes reality instead of transfiguring it. Politics are lost in speeches, public spirit in opinions, spirituality in effusions of the spirit, thought in prolegomena, energy in vague ambitions. This *cancer of consciousness* employs the processes of consciousness to reverse its true function; a creative consciousness is action and command; an effort towards higher forms of action, more effective command: the cancer of consciousness is retreat from action and abdication. Creative consciousness is a process of commitment, its cancer a means of evasion. Creative consciousness is an instrument of truth and clarity, its cancer the creator of mystification. Nothing would be more mistaken or dangerous than to reproach the one because the other leads life and thought into defeat. It is possible that at the root of all consciousness there lurks a secret evil, a power destructive both to itself and to the world, at least in our human condition. But this sickness of consciousness is not its essence. The impotence of an Amiel no more condemns the awareness of the self than the delirium of intellectuals condemns intelligence, contrary to what modern anti-intellectuals may think, as much as the rationalism they oppose. Thus one cannot ask for a full development of consciousness without requiring a fullness of commitment.

Active consciousness is capable of a greater or lesser degree of openness to the field of experience. Generally speaking, its narrowness is remarkable in comparison with the accumulated memories and experiences of any average educated person.[15] If one adds a cloudy marginal awareness to the lucid consciousness, the total field varies greatly according to the individual. There are persons in whom consciousness is broad and powerful; the amplitude and mobility of their range allows them to base action on a diversity of data and flexibility of concept which greatly increases its effect. These are the persons with a highly organised psyche, not disconcerted by the unforeseen, sure in judgment, masters of themselves; the obstacle loses half its difficulty when placed in the perspective of the whole field. A wide range of consciousness may even mask inemotivity under a cover of animation. But it reduces the percussive strength of action by introducing complexities and hesitation.

*

However rich the field of lucid consciousness, it is far from exhausting

---

* Morbid forms of narrowing of the field of consciousness: describes and enlarges Dessoir's three types, the man who is, the man who lives and the man who produces.

the whole domain of the psyche. From the depths of the body, the depths of the universe and the depths of inner life, the mighty waters of unknown worlds rise to the surface of its shores. Three such areas have already been well defined: the repressed sexual desires of childhood (Freud), the disappointed power drives of childhood (Adler), the residues of archaic and collective instincts (Jung). These discoveries are still only preliminary soundings in vast, unknown seas. A scientific attitude suggests that one should not overestimate or underestimate, in advance, the importance of the treasures that one may be drawn to seek there. However, the discovery of the Unconscious has decentralised our understanding of man. Jung notes that the tendency of Western man to locate consciousness in the brain is significant. The brain is above all the organ of perception for the outer world. Primitive peoples, however, locate the 'soul' or thought sometimes in the heart or, in the most primitive, in the belly. Whatever reaches their consciousness must first, in the old phrase, 'have moved their bowels', like the aphasic, who could not read a newspaper until one day his eye fell on the obituary notice of a friend. Jung also tells the story of a negro messenger in the heart of Africa, to whom he once gave some letters to post. No verbal explanation could arouse him from his immobility until another negro, by mimicry and blows, recalled to his consciousness his function as a messenger: then he set off immediately.

It is impossible to divide men into conscious or unconscious. No one can escape from the Unconscious: it flows in an unending stream, in sleep and half-sleep, in the intervals of lucid awareness. It enfolds our most conscious thoughts and most well-defined feelings with a silent orchestration, of which we register only a few notes and the total effect.

But our ears are more or less sensitive to this murmur from the deep. The richness of personal life depends to a large extent on our accessibility to the Unconscious. It is at its greatest in the poet, not necessarily the man who writes verses, but who lives poetically. We should not confuse glows arising in the obscurity with the somnolent consciousness. The latter is a decrease, the former an increase of being. It is more common to women, who generally live closer to these subliminal zones than men, and also it seems, in the present state of civilisation, to Eastern than to Western man. This is understandable, for the main factors in reducing marginal attention to the Unconscious are action, particularly when practical, critical analysis, routine and a

disciplined existence, and inattention to the body as a mystery of and a witness to the spirit.
*

But the Unconscious, if neglected, will not leave you in peace. It erupts into the established order of lucid consciousness in more or less brutal forms: sudden and irrational feelings, vagaries, abortive actions, whose purpose and violence and origin we find inexplicable. Sometimes it explodes and overwhelms the personality like a tidal wave, in the form of a great crisis which amazes both the subject and those around him. But more often it is like a spider's web of mute anxiety pervading conscious assurance, and betraying itself by irrational, oddly situated fears, by superstitions and the grotesque intrusion of magic into lives normally as regulated as a public administration.

This does not mean that we should believe, as some would have it, that the Unconscious is productive of nothing but monstrosities and perversions. The depths within us are not exclusively infernal. We shall see later that there is an ultimate regulator of the Unconscious.

PSYCHIC RHYTHMS

Between absolute change, which would never allow a person to revert to the same state, and absolute identity, which would keep him always equal to himself, rhythm assumes some form of reversion, and thus a certain stability in change. The rhythmic structure of the universe, in spite of all seasonal and astronomical phenomena, has impressed the mind of man from of old. The importance of biological rhythms was only appreciated much later. If spirit is duration, and duration, by definition, can never return upon itself, can we speak of psychological rhythm? The human aggregate is, however, not pure spirit, and in the space-time complex in which it moves, there is place for a rhythm which demonstrates the composite nature of its activity.

Elementary psychic rhythms are differentiated by their speed (slowness-rapidity), by their flexibility (elasticity-rigidity) and by the law of their oscillation or alternation. They can be distinguished from instability. They answer to an inner law of periodicity: they are dependent on variations of the sympathetic nervous system and basal metabolism (and the effects of this on the endocrines), on the sub-cortical centres, and the activity of the frontal pyramid with its fronto-thalamic connections (Gourevitch). Instability, on the other hand, is usually provoked by external and not internal factors, and, like all strong and irregular emotional upheavals, is due to lesions of the brain.

* Reference to Heymans' categories.

Foullée and Ostwald have already tried to regroup the early classification of temperaments into humours, along the lines of fast and slow, the former being the sanguine and the bilious, the latter the phlegmatic and the melancholic. There is a general reduction of reaction time in the rapid, thus allowing a greater number of gestures in a given time. Binet[16] has shown that these variations are independent of attention. In pathological states of mania or flight of ideas the rapidity sometimes assumes an infernal rhythm. The mind seizes with disconcerting rapidity on its surroundings, leaping from one object to another like a grasshopper. Is this psychic rapidity or motor rapidity? Kraepelin considers that, at any rate in the case of mechanical acceleration, thought and ideation are no quicker than usual. The transmission to the motor apparatus of every image that emerges into consciousness is, however, facilitated by the abeyance of the controlling function of the damaged frontal zones. In addition, the impoverished mind of the maniac provides more primitive circuits for ideation and thus reduces reaction and transmission time. It seems, however, that maniacal excitement has as its basis a generalised psycho-motor erethism. Normal psychology, on the other hand, provides types whose overall activity, ideation, sensitivity and motor functions have a coefficient of rapidity which Kretschmer has shown to be constant.
*

As a positive value, rapidity is connected with presence of mind, activity, initiative, ardour, intellectual agility, vivacity and flexibility of affective reactions. When negative, it often leads to instability, impatience, dispersion, affective over-excitement, suggestibility.

The slow show a general reduction of spontaneity of reaction, combined with a phlegmatic temperament. Their efficiency may appear to be thereby compromised, but they often produce excellent long-term results. The physiological root of their psycho-motor slowness may generally be attributed to thyroid deficiency (heaviness, torpor, somnolence, infrequent ideation), sometimes to kidney trouble (the fatigability of the asthenic), liver trouble or motor debility.
* *

All forms of laziness—and there are many—are in one sense a disease of the vital rhythm. We have spoken of asthenic laziness, due to pituitary deficiency, which results in extremely slow general and sexual development: this is slowness due to incapacity for effort. The

---

* Physical and clinical descriptions of rapidity and slowness of psychic rhythm.
** Slowness induced by psychasthenia and melancholia. The slowness of the timid and the heavy types.

torpor of the unstable hypertonic is quite different. The explosive instability of his actions creates a form of torpor in the organism as the effect of repeated shock (Wallon), and impairs the flexible continuity of the psyche; hence his inability to modulate an idea, to introduce a choice, to compare data, work out connections, which slows down the psychic process. Here effort can be used effectively to combat sluggishness. The perverse also present a systematic attitude of defence and opposition to external stimuli, which plunges them into profound intellectual lethargy which is only deepened by any effort. In education, as in psychotechnics, it is essential to seek the original causes of this laziness or slowness for they are not all amenable to the same treatment. Only the second of the three types described is capable of direct cure, but endocrine treatment may improve the condition of the first.[17]

Finally, it may be that slowness expresses, particularly with approaching puberty, a refusal to move forward in life, to accept maturation and the future, a way of making others hold one's hand, of withdrawing from the game, which is compensated by an inner activity of reflection and reverie.

Slowness promotes calm, self-control, a sense of responsibility, the weighing of words, meditation and contemplation, consideration and perseverance in action, and emotional serenity. But it often leads to indolence, indecision, apathy, rigidity, heaviness of mind, timidity and melancholy.

These variations in the rapidity of the psychic rhythm are only normal within certain limits. Like all other creatures, man has his average tempo. He needs a certain speed without which that which is necessary at each age and moment is slow to emerge, cannot develop properly, and dislocates the whole personality by its delay, such as, for instance, delayed puberty. He also needs to be able to wait patiently on time, for maturation cannot be forced.

*   *   *

Well-adjusted conduct offers the image of elasticity. The inner controls are flexible, allocating energy with the necessary exactitude to the points where it is required, responding promptly to external modifications and requirements, starting again without fuss, and making connections without collisions. Psychic elasticity is conditioned by a basic psycho-plasticity due to a good state of liaison between the various layers of the brain and the diverse cortical fields, and a healthy balance of the sympathetic nervous system. These conditions do not exclude a particular quality of intelligence or of active tone, since every corporal disposition is only the aspect, taken at a certain level, of some more comprehensive psychic intention. Psychic elasticity proper is due, above all, to the perfection of the dialogue between the self and reality, a happy combination of the authority of the self over its initiatives and its availability to the needs of reality, of consent and resistance. Dialectical virtuosity for instance, in ideas or feelings, supposes the maintenance of personal consciousness at various levels, united and contrasted by the interplay of multiple illuminations and the complex reflections of irony. This should not be confused with the mental lability of the unstable or demented, enslaved by deficiencies to external provocations, or with the plasticity without resilience of the suggestible.

Rigidity has several causes. It can be born of a spasm, of a contraction of psychic activity. Pende has described a spasmophilic temperament, predisposed to muscular and psychic contractions, the latter appearing in the form of obsessional thinking, perseveration and stereotyping. The outward expression of a spasmophile is serious and contracted, a 'Beethoven' mask, with a stiffness of movement, a cold, calm character, but subject to crises of excitement and depression, the intelligence usually good, but always polarised and unilateral, without flexibility and often fanatical. His whole attitude seems welded into a massive defence against his surroundings and against life. This rigidity of approach, which is the rigidity of refusal, converts the subject into a solid wall on the threshold of action. The rigidities of tension present a quite different aspect, in that they achieve the action embarked on. The term 'anal eroticism' is used by the psychoanalysts, to describe an attitude of obstinate concentration which far exceeds the importance of the action in question. Although the term and the origin of the attitude may be disputed, it indicates an extraordinary perseverance which persists when even experience has shown that the undertaking no longer has the value originally attached to it. This adherence to the past, this psychic 'perseveration' of habits, memories, will be described later under the heading 'secondary', but does not cover this peculiarly pent-up attitude. In obsessions and *idées fixes* the contraction is of an emotional character, and is accompanied by a narrowing of the field of consciousness. Analysis can, in fact, reveal an emotional state behind the fixed idea or ideas, which is permanent and renews the obsession indefinitely in one sphere or another, until it is itself reduced.

In other cases rigidity betrays a poverty of psychic content. The flexibility of the psyche, like a flexibility of manner or speech, is

maintained by a profusion of inner richness and a constant adaptation
to the environment. Ideas that are few and poor are inevitably rigid.
Hence the rigidity of the apathetic, who is often obstinate; of the
primary type; or of the imbecile; and the temporary rigidity of the
timid, whose mind is clouded by emotion to the exclusion of conscious
thought. Rigidity in a sense negative, evoking both the rigidity of the
body attacked by a vertigo of height, and the rectilineal trajectory of
the primary reflex, before intelligence has introduced a capacity for
modification. It leads to a serious, sometimes starchy and dry
deportment, sometimes solemn and portentous.[18] The maximum
effect is seen in a psyche approaching an absolute void, as in the
schizophrenic. It rejects moderation and discrimination as weakness:
one person will declare his intention 'to free himself entirely from the
material, look at men impersonally, and draw near to the absolute'.
To do a little gardening to help his parents would be against his
principles, time stolen from spiritual preoccupations. He gives up
reading to avoid being influenced. His whole conduct is dominated by
antitheses and system mongering. Before sitting down to a meal he
draws up a list of subjects to occupy his mind, in order not to waste
his time. All spontaneity is excluded from his life, simply because he is
no longer capable of spontaneity.[19] The symptoms of this illness are a
perfect caricature of the stubborn and doctrinaire minds we are
constantly meeting in daily life. The consciousness of the perverse type
is of the same family. He suffers from excessive liaison between the
thalamus-opticus and the *corpus striatum* and stiffens into three degrees
of contraction. In the first he maintains the attitude adopted at the
beginning of the required act, through a partial adaptation of the
postural muscles to the message transmitted. In the second he resists by
movement the change requested by another: his difficulty lies in
changing his situation and in passing from a static to a dynamic
attitude. In the third he becomes antagonistic to his environment, to
discipline and the established order. This is his struggle against the
inadequacies of his personal consciousness, compensating his lack of
stability by such excitements. Then he withdraws into a permanent
churlishness, quite insensitive to encouragement, promises or threats,
to a suspicious unsociability, veiled or ostentatious, interrupted by
explosions of brutality. Bravado, insolence, derision, threats are all
signs of his incapacity to accommodate himself psychologically by
attuning his life to reality. Many quite ordinary fits of bad temper
show the same pattern in a milder form; they are always an admission

of an inner weakness. The narrowing of the field of consciousness has the same effect as its rarefaction.
*

The various aspects of psychic elasticity offer more complicated rhythms.

Gentleness is a combination of extreme flexibility of psychic and affective liaisons with a low incidence of impulsive drives, particularly from the emotions, either because emotivity is low or has been controlled by training. The result is an extreme lability of psychic rhythm (one speaks of 'fluid' characters), and a fresh, velvety surface which suggests the tranquil mirror of calm waters. When gentleness is not solely of temperament, but of grace and virtue, then an inner light steadily and tranquilly illuminates this psychic facility. It implies then a high control of affectivity, offering others the gift of patience and infinite comprehension. But it is not always stuff of such quality. For one gracious or heroic type of gentleness, there will be a hundred born of supineness and insignificance. Even true gentleness has the weakness of its own perfection, a too flexible adaptation that deprives it of reaction, variety, combativity, fantasy or great passion.

Calm is less a sign of an easy flow of psychic energy than of static equilibrium and a power of stability. It is of very diverse quality. In the mentally weak it is only the uprooting of all personal energies. In the phlegmatic it expresses the predominance of mechanism over impulse (secondarity). The danger here lies in a form of dullness due to a too systematic dispersal of mental energies; calm then becomes coldness and egocentric instability. In higher types there is a fortunate harmony betweeen emotional check and drive; each may be powerful and passionate, but the outcome seems a product of moderation and sometimes even of indifference. All impairment of the psyche, in great fatigue or great emotion, compromises this superior calm, which requires a high psychic tension.[20]
**

Side by side with these continuous rhythms we also find alternating rhythms.

The most common is the *constitutionally cyclothymic rhythm*, which is normal in the man who suffers from 'ups and downs', and exasperated in manic-depressive psychosis. There is an alternation without apparent reason, of two absolutely contrasting humours: a phase of excitement, when the mind works with vertiginous rapidity, all perceptions are alert, gesture and speech are turbulent and unstable:

* Describes various forms of rigidity.   ** Describes epileptoid types.

and a phase of depression, in which ideation is poor or infrequent, movements slowed down, the expression restricted to a shade of painful sadness. The rhythm allows no free intervals and appears to be highly capricious, but perhaps only so because of our ignorance. This circular process is definitely more frequent in women than in men, and it has been suggested that it is due to the rhythm of their sexual life. But even in 1902 Ballet was asking whether we were not all, to some extent, circular, 'lunatics' in the sense of the old astronomical characterology, which attributed these fluctuations to the influence of the moon. We all, in fact, display unjustified variations of humour, which are only very attenuated forms of cycloidism.

*

. . . All higher forms of life have a characteristic duration, made up of growth, followed by crisis, death and renaissance. Living nature, unlike the rigid duration of matter, seems to offer us a distant analogy in its rhythm of seasons and generations. Nothing that is human: neither love nor intelligence, nor moral ascesis nor civilisation, develops continuously by indefinite accumulation. Here we touch on the error common to early analyses of progress: only technical and scientific progress, which deals with material forces, follows the linear pattern assigned to it by Coutrot. And even then this pattern is more one of outline and end-product than its living history, which is made up of a succession of eclipses and new beginnings. Purely human affairs would fall into mechanism and banality were it not for the periodic and redeeming intervention of death. In order to endure eternally, even the highest values must accept a periodic death.

PERSISTENCE: PERSEVERATION AND REBOUND
(Primarity and Secondarity)

I meet a friend. He speaks to me rather sharply. I retort, and the conversation continues on its chosen theme. But when we have parted I feel a sense of growing uneasiness. I discover a peculiar sort of activity going on underground around my friend's remarks. They are joining up with others, recalling furtive attitudes, snatches of gossip, and for several days I feel ripening within me the distress of a friendship going adrift.

One can say of my first response that it corresponds to the primary function of representation, an action instigated by factors in the psyche which are still conscious. My subsequent rumination is born of the secondary function of representation, the sum of the effects of such

* Describes various types of rhythm.

factors at work below the actual field of consciousness. These two functions have been described by Otto Gross[21] under the name of persistence (*Nachwirkung*). They are, as it were, two indispensable branches of actuality and continuity. Without the first, we might lose our attention to life, and become submerged by our dreams. Without the second, we should be unable to understand lengthy sentences, follow a complete demonstration, enrich our mental or affective life, or undertake any long-term activity. If the balance is broken in favour of the first, psychic life gains in intensity, but tends to superficiality, to incoherence and the avoidance of abstractions. If it is broken in favour of the second, psychic life gains in associations, but loses in flexibility of adaptation, and frequently in breadth; abstractions outweigh practical abilities, introversion predominates, except in those individuals who succeed in grasping their surroundings as a whole, and in forming a *Weltanschauung*.

Both Gross, and later Heymans and Wiersma,[22] have distinguished two types according to whether the first or the second function predominates: the primary and the secondary.

When Gross calls the primary a 'broad and superficial' type we must understand by this a breadth of range which lends great mobility to consciousness, which can, in any case, only project a thin beam of attention on any one thing at each moment. Poor 'insistence' of comprehension, short duration of impression, are the more dynamic terms used by Kroh and Pfahler[23] for types whose make-up is labile, whose capacity for experience flexible but fragile. The primary type apprehends quickly and can immediately utilise external impressions, which pass out of his mind as abruptly as their entrance was lively. His emotions are strong and shortlived. After an outburst of anger the primary is immediately reconciled and thinks no more about the motive of his anger. He is relatively quickly consoled after trouble or bereavement and soon returns to his business or his amusements. He displays a great aptitude for oblivion. Somewhat of a 'milksop', his vengeance is usually purely verbal abuse, without consequence. Primarity thus tends to atomise conscious duration.

*

In action, the appeal of the immediate is always more attractive than the long-term prospect, which is helpful to direct interests such as money or profits, as against more remote and complex interests. The primaries have the gift of immediate response to the needs or emergencies of action, which sometimes makes them conspicuous for

* Further description of the 'broad and superficial' type.

audacity and courage. But this activity is not sustained. They are unconcerned at discrepancies between their principles, their words and their deeds, being always for an immediate and effective solution, whatever the means employed. Their impulsiveness is the compensation for their presence of mind. For the same reason they hold a record for mendacity, since speaking the truth implies passing over the immediate benefit procurable by a lie in favour of some deeper preoccupation. They are emotive and little capable of distributing their emotion, which makes them impatient: a primary seldom opens a book without soon taking a glance at the end.

Primarity does not favour objective intellectual activity. It sets a premium on vitality, the enjoyment of good food, good living and sex, whose demands are imperious and peremptory, also on emotional mobility. It pulverises judgment into ephemeral impressions, and even destroys the awareness of contradiction, which requires that the terms to be compared should remain alive in consciousness. When the mind has a strongly objective tendency, it escapes this emotional dispersal but tends to the fragmentary acquisition of knowledge of a technical or practical nature. But it is above all the predestined background for the cultivation of the artistic sense. It ensures that the mind is spellbound by the immediate image (which shows that it is not necessarily synonymous with superficiality); it reinforces present emotion and facilitates its brilliant elaboration. One might say that a primary of high quality is infallibly an artist. Save in very amorphous and barren natures, primarity also encourages wit and vivacity of conversation. It often hinders the creation of great continuous works: one meets authors who are incapable of constructing a connected work, and who can only produce aphorisms, sketches or notes.

By keeping the subject at the surface of himself and of things, it promotes extraversion, the centrifugal energy of personality. The primary is demonstrative, a man of unseasonable confidences, the perpetual purveyor of news and opinions. He reacts quickly to the presence of others, gives his sympathy with great facility and distributes it with flexibility amongst very varying circles. He is too attached to intercourse with the public not to be extremely susceptible to vanity.

*   *   *   *

The secondary, according to Gross, is a 'deep and narrow' type. Such a person, he says, has difficulty in the immediate apprehension

* Quotation from Rousseau to illustrate the secondary type.

and elaboration of external stimuli, particularly if they are numerous and disjointed. Often there is a delay in perception: he says 'What?' and hears a few seconds later. There is a strong 'insistence' of excitation, great duration of impressions, for the secondary is a type of strong and rigid calibre. Emotivity, which would lead to immediate registration of impressions, is inhibited; ideation is therefore slower to establish itself and to fade. Impressions[24] with their effects last a long while before disappearing: one of Proust's characters keeps discovering fresh sources of grief in the disappearance of Albertine. The secondary is incapable of experiencing pleasure through direct perception, but he possesses a more or less remarkable aptitude for savouring it in memory.[25] The whole of Proust's work, this search for time past in the field of inner reflection, is a poem of secondarity. The survival of impression is here of cardinal importance. The secondary remains under the influence of bereavement, suffering or emotional injury longer than the primary emotive. He also persists in his bad temper or rancour, and perseveres in affection and devotion. He is subject to remorse (and doubly so, for he respects the law). Impressions accumulate for a long while, and explode suddenly in actions which those around him find difficult to understand. This survival, which makes the past more present than the present itself, explains his attachment to memory. He keeps his childhood friends, likes to revisit the village where he was born, the graves of his dead. This deeper harmony of life enriches his whole being, particularly if he has the good luck also to be emotive.

In action this disposition adds perspective, continuity and substance. It inhibits immediate action and even tends to distract the subject from action by turning his gaze inward. But at the same time the richness of past impressions which converge upon the present give subsistence, power, depth and persistence to action. It resists the pressure of immediate interest, it allows when necessary for foresight, is patient, and knows how to assemble material for later use. Goethe's father had a mania for collecting and keeping small objects. He encouraged his son to finish whatever he had begun, less from interest in the thing itself, than from a meticulous love of order. This left in Goethe traces of an irritating orderliness and circumspection. The secondary errs, in fact, by circumspection, prudence, calculation, *Sachlichkeit*, where the primary sins by impulsivity. This brings us to the chapter of his weaknesses. To invoke a love of the past is to invoke the danger of automatism. The secondary is a man of habit, attached to the invariable routine of his days, the repetition of his entertainments, the retention of old furniture, old documents, old suits, the arrangement of his house, and the cut of his clothes. He is stubborn of humour, particularly if he is highly inactive, recalcitrant to argument, and inaccessible to advice, holding to decisions once made, even if his information invalidates them. He resists change and rapid adaptation and adjusts with difficulty to a diversity of surroundings, or a change of circumstance. On the other hand, he acts in strict, sometimes even rigid conformity with his principles and thus creates confidence.

*

Unlike the primary, the secondary is a man of abstract thought. His ideas, like his impressions, have the persistence which allows for perspective and correlation. He often likes the long, architectural phrases which quickly tire the primary reader. If he is an artist, he is a skilful employer of allusion and short cut. The turbulence of instinct and emotion is abated and the tendency to contemplation and the unity of knowledge encouraged. But if he is gifted for abstract thinking the secondary pays for his inertia of ideas by stiffness, fads, all the forms of intellectual rigidity: obstinacy, partiality, fanaticism. Or even, hesitating over his impressions and handling too many well-conceived ideas at the same time with the same strength, he cannot make up his mind at all. Secondarity is unfavourable to the artistic sense: in Heymans' statistics the number of artists decreases with the increase in secondarity. Secondaries with strong emotivity then try to discover satisfactions of a deeper quality in moral and religious preoccupations (Amiel, Maine de Biran): they become artistic philosophers, moralist writers and persons with a lively religious conscience. Generally speaking their brilliance is of the mind. They slip easily from the serious to the solemn, which is their form of excess, as display is the extravagance of the primary. They like law and order. The persistence of habit favours the specialisation and professionalisation of the personality. It also favours the separation of the personality into watertight compartments, which Leo Ferrero considers the key to the English character. For this secondary systemisation is not without rigidity: Gross has already noted that if each of the systems it creates is closely structured, well developed and deeply rooted, there is poor association between them, owing to a lack of fluidity in their frontiers.

Secondarity inclines to introversion and to the development of subjectivity.[26] Temperamental hesitation before action, like the delay in receiving impressions, often causes a miscarriage of the great projects conceived by the mental processes. Manifestation of ideas and

* Further description of the secondary type.

impressions is inhibited: as a result there is a certain withdrawal at least into reserve, if not into taciturnity. Consideration for others may even be affected, unless it is restored at the instigation of reason, or some requirement of the inner life: in any case the secondary vibrates less intensely to the presence of others, or to any presence: he tends to objectivise every drama he witnesses by standing a little aloof, and thus has to struggle against a certain unconsciously haughty insensitivity. At other times he is painfully conscious of the inertia underlying his will to love and to suffer, with the anguish of Bernanos' country priest: 'Oh God, if I should cease to love!' In return, he is little liable to vanity and adulation.

Primitive peoples are more primary than maturer cultures and, generally speaking, the Southern peoples more than the Northern. Secondarity normally increases with age. At first sight the affective mobility of woman would make her appear less secondary than man. Heymans has shown that this appearance is only justified where the emotions are concerned: for women provide unique examples of emotional fidelity, intuition and tact, which require the overall mastery of great internal resources.

However precisely we may try to define primarity and secondarity, it is impossible to eliminate all ambiguity on the fringes of these concepts. In some of these more complex aspects they resemble Jung's introversion and extraversion. Spearman has remarked that secondarity is often wrongly applied to cover both perseveration, which is psychological inertia, and strength of purpose, which is quite the opposite, since it requires an unceasing struggle against all forms of inertia, and a lively alertness to external impediments. He considered that when secondarity had been carefully isolated from all forms of perseveration-inertia, it would be found to be one of the essential elements of the psyche. It would perhaps therefore be an advantage to modify a vocabulary which tends to ambiguity and to speak, at this particular level, not of primarity or secondarity, but of *rebound* and *perseveration* or *psychological inertia*.

THE EXPERIENCE OF SPACE AND DURATION: THE 'ME-HERE-NOW'

Utopia and Uchronia are the two countries through which we try to escape from our condition by cloaking ourselves in the abstract appearances of eternity. But our destiny is spatial and temporal. Not a single one of our actions but is cut from this strong broadcloth, which modern thinking tends to accept as being the same thing seen under

two different lights. To accept this double reality, to come to terms
with it, to locate ourselves in our own space and time, is to assure both
our mental stamina and our primary orientation. Any attempt at
evading this basic issue throws us into some form of psychological
disequilibrium. It is so difficult to speak of the self apart from the
spatial and temporal conditions of its existence, so that German
psychologists sometimes describe the incarnated self by the composite
and indissociable expression 'me-here-now'.

The 'here' of this vital complex is the act by which I accept and take
possession of the richness of my experience of space.[27] The concept of
the experience of space is fairly new. It has been stifled between the
primitive concept of space, which has crept so subtly into our
common-sense imagination of space, and Bergson's brilliant rehabilitation of our experience of duration which seems to reason space out of
life altogether. When St. Paul, speaking of the profundities of the
spirit, speaks of height, width and depth, when we speak of a sense of
greatness, are we using a superficial metaphor of geometric space, or
are we trying rather to express an intuition of pure quality, of which
the geometric dimensions are only an aspect? Pathology points clearly
in the latter direction: the patient suffering from general paralysis is
'disorientated' in the clinical space that surrounds him, yet he retains
his perception of the 'me-here-now'. This is because the space we
experience is not a quantitative and as it were external area, but the
very special mode of being of our activity, the inner experience of an
outer expansion. There is a way of conceiving it as purely external
and of locating ourselves as *outside* space, which, however, put us on a
footing of exteriority, a thing amongst things. We may, however,
conceive of it *from within*. It is not without reason that we speak of
from within to describe the deepest form of spiritual intuition. This
within is that inner place where obedience and mastery, the ingoing
and the outgoing of the soul, are at one. In the full sense of the words,
it is true to say of space as of duration: *in eo vivimus, movemur et sumus.*
Our existence is made of it, and thus it has its share both of fulfilment
and of anguish. Once again the contempt for 'matter' in the name of
'spirit' seems a simple refusal to live and locate oneself. The best of
Balzac's descriptions, which the modern reader, accustomed to the
short cuts of the cinema, finds so slow, are amongst the most striking
initiations into this condition of the mind. Balzac's characters are not
pure consciousnesses wrapped up in their own inner thoughts. They
form a single world and a single destiny with the objects that surround
them. Almost imperceptibly, a character detaches itself from a

background of faded wallpaper in an old pension, and when the first conversation is launched amidst the hurly-burly of a bazaar, one hardly knows whether it is two men, or two *bibelots* that have begun to speak.

Progress in the apperception of space, moreover, follows on progress in preoccupation with, and knowledge of, the self. Reduced to his digestive preoccupations, the space known to the newly-born child is purely oral, so that he puts everything he touches into his mouth. Then hands and feet explore the space around, which is still limited by the restriction on his movements. Anatole France as a child situated China behind the gates of the Luxembourg which he was not allowed to enter. The child is for a long time even uncertain of the location of the pain he feels, and his concepts of interior and exterior are by no means as clear as in the adult. Tell me where you are to be found, and I will tell you who you are. Each personality has its own very different way of describing the dimensions of the space it experiences.

I do not perceive my living space from some distant star. I am held in its heart, as in the centre of a sphere, the sphere of my activity, everything being disposed around me along a radius. The world being there, quite close, up against me. Normally I feel there is a certain free space around me in which I 'breathe'. I am bound up with the life that surrounds me, but also 'I feel to some degree independent, and there seems to be a quality of space in this independence; there is, as it were, a quality of distance which separates me from or, rather, unites me with life. There is always something like a *free space* ahead of me, in which my life and activity can develop without impediment. I feel *at my ease*, I feel free in this space in front of me; there is no *immediate contact* in the psychological sense of the word, between me and the possibilities around me' (Minkowski). The sense is clear: space is liberty, or the promise of liberty. This is shown by agoraphobia (the fear of open spaces) which is an unconscious reaction, inhibited by anxiety, of the striving for emancipation. The fact that it disappears when the sufferer is accompanied by someone, shows that it is a repressed anxiety at 'going out alone'. Thus a 'sphere of ease' is developed around me, which is not liberty, but very close to it; we have experienced the exact opposite when going out on a moonless night in the blackout, the sense of being hemmed in by a solid obscurity, against which we lurched at every step, our eyes tense with the strain imposed by objects too close to us. When activity develops normally, life has a certain fortunate distance and breadth into which our acts are projected. We have seen this sense of 'vital space' transmitted with obsessional fervour from the psychology of individuals to that of nations and peoples.

Some persons are particularly scrupulous about maintaining their distance: they feel perhaps that it is vaguely menaced by some secret weakness. They cannot bear to be too crowded; they are exasperated by a room that is too small or overfurnished, by railway compartments or the cabin of an aircraft (claustrophobia). When personality is disintegrated, particularly when contact with reality is impaired, it seems that this invisible tension, which wards off the indiscretion of the outer world, collapses. The few happenings and the few thoughts that persist in the impoverished psyche of the schizophrenic, crowd together and are confused into a 'single bundle' instead of being projected into the wide world around. The paranoiac has the impression that the outer world is insolently accosting him on every hand; the posters he passes, words caught at random, the gestures he intercepts, all seem to refer to him personally, and he interprets their incongruity as hostility; hence come the persecution manias. One can trace a similar tendency in jealousy and susceptibility. The first, a feeling of situation and of its difficulties, is closely linked with the feeling of privacy. For a spatial, temporal being, privacy can never be the entirely mystical secret garden of spiritual solitude; like any other spiritual power, it extends into a minimum of symbolic space, my clothes, my flat, my gestures. A solid personality does not tremble at every sound, fearing the violation of this privacy, of whose elasticity he is assured. A weak or morbid personality feels it is always being threatened and defends it jealously.

It may be that this weakness is betrayed by an exactly contrary feeling. Some psychasthenics feel that the world evades them. They perceive objects both at a sort of 'moral' distance and also physically reduced. The sphere of ease becomes so absurdly enlarged that they are overcome by the sensation of having lost their centre. They speak of 'cosmic isolation', of 'floating in interplanetary space' far from the earth.[28] This 'space opera' is only the text of their own fear of living. It is the same with the patient who complained every day that everyone was leaving the institution, leaving the town, leaving her alone and abandoned. The sense of distress that follows a defeat, a bereavement or a separation is partly a feeling that the world is withdrawing from us, and this is particularly painful. This feeling can, however, be encouraged, or even provoked, by 'distant' or 'haughty' mannerisms or tone of voice, which explicitly repulse the presence, the sympathy or the demands of others, and always betray some flight from reality.

Within the sphere of my ease I am master of all I survey. But some masters like to stay at home, and others to voyage abroad. These two ways of feeling space introduce a new experience, that of being 'centred' in the space experienced. Some are strongly centred and need to feel centred. This need is usually more strongly felt by women, at any rate in our sedentary civilisations. She is root and stock, the pivot of fidelity. It is perhaps from this vocation that she derives her need for stability, to which men usually pay less heed. Sometimes a mistaken attempt has been made to limit her exclusively to this instinct. Nevertheless woman, more than man, is creative of the home, of the hearth and of the household gods. She can ill tolerate an uprooting. But we find similar temperaments in men also. They cannot leave their home town or village without dismay, and the loss of an estate which means much to them, of a family home[29] which brings with every season a rhythm of constancy into their lives, is more painful to them than chance misfortunes or the ingratitude of events. This passion for being rooted may betray a lazy attitude to life, a sort of vegetative inertia. Yet in the liking for the fixed point, there is a valuable element of civilisation and culture: the fixed point is the unshakeable promise, loyalty under fire, the oath or vow: it is the seriousness of contemplation which never wearies of returning to the same spot and of plumbing the depths of its inexhaustible monotony; it is orthodoxy, conviction, faith. 'What are we worth when we are immobile?'[30] This is indeed the final criterion of human value.

Some, on the other hand, only feel safe in mobility. 'When I am at ease, then I begin to feel unsafe,' said Newman. Their mysticism is not of taking root, but of uprooting; not of commitment, but of detachment. This spatial disquiet may take on a morbid or vagabond form which is due to lack of inner balance; hence the need to move about, to be somewhere else, which is so frequent in the paranoiac, pursued by his imaginary persecutors. Hence morbid fugues, and compulsive walking. But it may also be the expression of a way of living little attached to places or stability: the French, who are still peasant and stay-at-home at heart, tend to consider this disposition somewhat immoral: not so long ago many families considered a liking for travel as almost a sin, or at least an expensive prodigality and a sign of frivolity: to leave one's town seemed treachery and a stranger was greeted with deep and lasting suspicion. A short-term and unilateral morality. It is true that agitation of the body may betray an uneasiness of mind that escapes into entertainment, but the liking for stability of existence may be only a flight from life into retreats of tranquillity.

St. Benedict was right to compel his wandering monks to a vow of stability. But in other times, and for other times and characters, rest and deep rooting mean crystallisation, a refusal of risk and generosity. A spiritual detachment is the indispensable complement of a spiritual commitment. However ambiguous the many voices of Gide, one should not forget that they preach haltingly but with fervour the gospel of detachment that is so akin to the Sermon on the Mount.

At the limits of the sphere of our ease takes place the *vital contact with reality*. It is so important that we must return to it in detail later. It develops over a *vital area* which varies with the extent of the sphere of ease, the accessibility of the field of consciousness and the continuity of contact between self and reality.

The experience of space would be considerably diminished and become imperceptibly equated with geometric space, if it were described solely in terms of immobility. It is animated, to use the bold image employed by the Stoics, by a periodic respiration, a recurrent wave of expansion and contraction, which is the very pulsation of the self. We have already met expanded and contracted natures. These shapes symbolise a fundamental orientation. The expanded personality is moved by a superabundance of inner energy which feels the need to exercise itself in space, utilising, if necessary, the most immediate symbolism, perhaps a commanding view of the landscape, where distance promises a fulfilment to the eye that is denied to the physically limited gesture. When he is happy, his first need is often to go for a long walk. His psychological complexity, his excellent adjustment allow him to accept a volume of activity and influences that would shatter a less powerful personality. This breadth of activity pushes the sphere of ease back to the limits of the personal universe. For this type the space that surrounds him with possible activities has the same miraculous plasticity as that which surrounds the athlete. Just as nothing that is human is alien to him, he feels at home in conditions utterly removed from his normal circumstances. He is truly the possessor of the world. This radiating energy was called by Nietzsche the love of what is distant, which he contrasted with the narrower liking for what is too close and too easy.

There are pathological forms of the expansive mood to be found in patients whose actions have gained abnormal facility not through flexibility but through impoverishment. Like the happy fellow who believed he was generalissimo of the Allied armies from 1914-18 and won a battle every day on every front, they believe they affect the whole world by the least inflection of their thoughts, and can be everywhere at once by a flick of the imagination, without being in the least amazed at the importance they attribute to themselves. But whereas the expansiveness of the one craves for realisation and real efficacy, the phantom productivity of the other finds a falser expansion: there is a vague breath of action, enough to stir a feather. It is the same with the 'greatness' of the megalomaniac. The quality of action is to include the future, with all its charm and infinite possibility, in the present action. The greatness of the maniac is all decided, defined and achieved. It offers no hope to a psyche which has been, as it were, 'flattened and reduced to single dimension'[31] which holds neither secret nor promise. He knows everything about everyone, everything is known about him. This is not a human greatness but an inert, monolithic massiveness.

Others are aware of a voluminous expansion, but with a feeling of disquiet, which Dr. Dide has called a 'sense of cumbersomeness'.[32] One person feels he fills a whole room, another, on his bicycle, has the sun for his front wheel and the moon for the rear. Normal states provide examples of a similar feeling, which the English call, very aptly, self-consciousness, an excess of consciousness embarrassed by the amount of space occupied by body and by presence: it grips the late-comer entering an attentive audience, the timid in any form of social gathering. This feeling of disagreeable or merely confusing volume is already a sign of a certain insecurity about the place one occupies in the world, or of a certain withdrawal from action. Similar feelings, although more diffused, are attached to bodily structure. Large persons have often a sort of suppleness and goodwill which is like a free gift of their energy; small persons, who always feel more exposed and diminished than others, react by a livelier sensitivity and by greater self-regard and tenacity.

In some people the experience of space is stunted. They detest being too visible, having conspicuous seats in the theatre, anything that one might call an affirmation of position. They dream of living in small valleys, a low-roofed house hidden between its neighbours, and do live there if they can. They 'make themselves small', both literally and figuratively, in public places and in social activities. One sees them trying to slip by, effacing themselves by a minimum of gesture and movement, as if apologising for the amount of public ground they still occupy. Contrary to the types we mentioned earlier, they have no ambition to attain through conquest the limits of the possible, or to make the world smaller by the adventures of civilisation. But they are possessed by a mania to reduce everything to the dimensions of their own indecisive, petty or pusillanimous natures. They like a reassuring proximity, even to the point of promiscuity, in family or social life. They confuse it with intimacy, they look for the exclusive circle, the obscure sect, the so-called family atmosphere which stifles taste and intelligence: they are the persons of whom Nietzsche wrote that their love of their neighbours is their uncertainty of themselves. This disposition has its morbid forms. The schizophrenics and the depressed huddle up under their blankets, refusing all contact with reality: we may note that the transition from foetal to adult life in the human being is marked by passing from a crouching to a completely extended position, and that a bending of the limbs, particularly of the legs, can be found in several mental or cerebral disorders. Other patients 'lose' little by little all that they possess: possessions, relatives and friends— or at least, so they think. They convert their inner suffering into a delirium of separation, like the patient who was always seeing the people around her leaving to take the train home. After having thus massacred their own vital space, they end up by denying their own existence, which they find too burdensome for whatever psychic energy is left to them.

*

Like all other psychological facts, space is not imposed on us, as our lot: like all the rest, it is an adventure offered to our grasp. In order to possess space, we have to dominate it.

**

On the borders of space and duration we find a feeling of *presence* and *absence*, where our location in space and our experience of time are closely intermingled. Something is present if I can attain it now, absent if it is out of the range of my present perception. But this spatio-sensory criterion is not precise: does one consult one's sense of smell, touch or taste? Can I say that the star I am looking at is present in my room? Or the symphony orchestra I can hear by twisting a plastic knob? Strictly speaking, perhaps yes. Perhaps the whole world is made present at each of its points by waves, known or unknown, to be grasped by my senses supplemented by such aids as I can provide. But there is often a gulf between the physical presence and the sense of presence. In the experience of perception, presence and absence seem to depend on a certain strength of affirmation and communication in the realities at stake: this is above all true of persons. There are persons who create the impression of 'not being there', either through a

---

* Gives details of the perception of space. Describes clear and dark space and the importance of positions.   ** Space not entirely objective.

dispersal of their personality, or through a cold aloofness which they use as a defence, or through absentmindedness due to inner fantasies, or simply through a sort of poverty of being, which deprives not only their conversation but also their actual presence both of quality and of any strength of affirmation. Others, on the contrary, impose themselves almost insolently as soon as they appear, some by a kind of vulgar assault or indiscretion of appearance, others by an imperious authority, and yet others, who leave one much freer of their presence, however fascinating it may be, by an invincible personal radiance. This presence is not solely affirmation: those who are most strongly present are often the least conscious of it; but they communicate immediately by the warmth of their sympathy and understanding. We are aware by introspection that we are not always equally present to our friends and to things: that our physical vigour decreases, and that we no longer feel solidly anchored to the situation in which we find ourselves; our minds are elsewhere, or 'absent'. Some sick persons deny the presence of those around them, even to the point of denying the reality of the relatives who are with them every day. The equilibrium between presence and absence is maintained by a form of psychic tension: if this is lowered, the sudden narrowing of the field of consciousness considerably reduces the number of presences, loosens one's grip, and may also confuse the sense of presence: the 'mystics' of the mental hospital feel surrounded by the presence of objects created by the imagination. If psychic tension rises again, space is once more coloured, so to speak, at its own density, situations are affirmed in a few seconds, like soldiers coming suddenly to attention. The presence of others is not solely an empirical fact, but a more or less colourful reconstruction according to the contribution of the persons present.

*   *   *

A discovery that is too exciting often restrains attention within exclusive channels. By restoring the dignity of the experience of duration, Bergson consciously or unconsciously prevented justice being done to the zones where duration touches on space both in extension and in the measurement of time.
*

It is not possible to represent this creative movement, whose dual polarity is so exactly rendered by the term expansion, outside the concept of spatial abundance. We have had enough of the romantic

* Minkowski on Bergson.

concepts of pure duration, which suggest impossible evasions into a further dimension, in which we should lose both body and significance. Time recovered is also space recovered. Duration has certainly more affinities with what we have called obscure space than with clear space, but nowhere can a precise dividing line be established between these basic realities.[33] Duration, like space, is accepted by a positive movement towards the future. The Englishman and the German tell the time by reference to the hour to come, and not that which has passed. So time goes, and life with it: Dr. Mourgues describes this forward looking as one of the primary qualities of instinct. We often think of the future as of something unreal, that does not exist: but it is no paradox to say that the future is the most immediate fact in our consciousness of duration. A healthy perception of duration does not require some peculiar subtlety of consciousness, but rather an earthy, almost animal solidity as well as a vision that goes beyond duration. Kierkegaard said of women that they had a good understanding with Time, and knew how to pass it better than men. Perhaps it is because they are both closer to the earth and to the divine. In addition, this future is not just some sort of future: it is *my* future. Awareness of full, forceful duration is due to a choice at a deep level, the acceptance or refusal of the burden and the greatness of personal existence. 'Time and memory are created', wrote Guyau.[34] Some succeed and others fail in this creation.

How to succeed? My duration is not a spectacle slowly unfolding itself before me; it would only be so if I were no longer present to myself and to the world. A vital awareness of time is, in this sense, an aggressive awareness.[35] But it is also a perceptive awareness: the future, since it is the future, only yields to me and takes on reality to the extent that I give it credit, and accept it for what it wishes to be, a future: the gospel of the lilies of the field is also a short treatise on mental health. Inspired by my future, my duration is no longer a kaleidoscopic succession, but a full and tense duration, a continuous deployment: it is composed of movements and articulations, but they are organically connected the one with the other.[36] I can make it a dramatic biography. All such conduct, which seems so simple from within, is a higher form of conduct. Janet remarks that primitive peoples, children and the mentally retarded, cannot formulate a biography: the child, for instance, attaches an event to someone in the third person: a lady came and brought something, and then he jumps to another set of events, and so on. It is very difficult to make simple people recount their life story: all is muddled up. Furthermore, as we

descend the steps of life, duration becomes steadily weaker. The reflex, the purely instinctive action, has hardly any duration, the response is immediately switched on, everything is given at the moment of discharge. Duration is the contrary, a perseverance which responds, perhaps, to some invisible patience outside me. It asks for a special effort, the 'effort of continuation' covering a thousand incidents on the way, starting up, changes of speed or direction, halts and fresh beginnings.
*

Our behaviour in each of the three dimensions of duration varies completely according to our fundamental attitude towards this dynamic of time.

Life presents itself to us as a creative future: memory is knowledge of the past in the service of the future; the present, the place from which action starts towards its future.[37] The future is not alien to space; we speak of it being 'wide open' before us, as offering wider or narrower horizons. Starting from desire, I move towards it in a series of attitudes which express my fundamental attitude to duration.

Waiting always causes uneasiness, since it suspends life and threatens the future. It snatches us from the wonderful automatism of instinct and throws us into a new world, whose promise is paid for by security. Instinct is antagonistic to delay: the child does not know how to wait, his desires insist on immediate satisfaction. From this point of view, all education is learning how to wait. If I am normally confident in duration, because I trust its good intentions, or possess an abundance of vitality, indefinite waiting may be more cheerful than anxious, and even an uneasy delay will not disturb my balance. It casts the shadow of the obstacle over duration, stimulates me, attaches me to reality by dictating a limit to hopeful impetuosity. If, however, I float passively in duration, waiting becomes intolerable, throwing the whole psyche into disorder. Sometimes there is a premature explosion; it has been shown experimentally[33] that delay is a source of emotional discharge. Or it takes possession of a whole life, like those who drift through the years, waiting for a marriage, a happy chance, the miraculous change of condition which will at last help them to get on their feet and make the new start they are always talking about. Sometimes it simulates a real love of the future, like an enthusiastic movement towards Utopia or success, but then I only love the future against its nature, with the secret hope of nailing it down into a past which holds no more surprises and allows me to rest: pseudo-believers, pseudo-conquerors,

* Gives details of inadequate perception of duration.

pseudo-revolutionaries are all candidates for a static paradise. For those in whom the psyche is still further relaxed, waiting becomes clouded with misfortune and catastrophe, and even more exhausting than activity. Although every day confounds their anxieties, they are, in fact, no longer capable of establishing the bond of living experience between the diverse moments of time. This same transmutation into a massive hostility, of a time from which nothing further is expected, is the source of persecution mania.

Hope is more generous than waiting, since it renounces uneasy calculations and the satisfaction of immediate expectations by placing unconditional confidence in a future which is accepted as basically good. It implies an act of metaphysical faith in the quality and significance of time, and therefore an inner disarmament, a pacifying, active abandon. The schizophrenic builds up an inexhaustible terminology as his experience of duration. 'Something that can be inventoried is a source of despair.'[39] At the summit of hope the believer discovers prayer that is not, as some believe and practise, an exposition of particular intentions, but an identification with the full intention of the future: FIAT *voluntas* TUA. It is beyond the scope of this psychological enquiry to go deeper into the spiritual essence of hope.[40] Trial has shown what a powerful force it is for the alleviation of anxiety, agitation, dispersal, and cowardice; in one word, for unification and inner peace.

If the drive towards the future lapses, duration itself collapses, disperses or becomes crystallised. The aged present, in so far as is normally possible, the picture of persons without a future. The first awareness of old age causes confusion and distress. Then an adjustment is made: the old live in a present without motive power, which little by little becomes turned in upon itself; their memories crystallise into allegory and idealism; into ill-tempered criticism of the present which eludes them. Only a living faith in a future beyond life's delays, whether expected from the memory of man, or from a promise of eternity, is capable of a successful struggle against this slackening down of life. The road to the future is completely closed in the schizophrenic. 'I have a sort of routine which prevents me considering the future', declared Minkowski's patient. 'My creative power has been destroyed. I see the future as a repetition of the past.' One day he tried to do nothing all day, not moving, not even passing water, in order to put a plug between past and future. He wanted to stop time from passing.[41]

In the full experience of duration the present is not an instantaneous, mathematical point. Such a narrow present is the present of maniacal excitement, a tempest of actions without development, a vivacity discharged on the spot. The living present is experienced as spread out, heavy with living memory and future promise. It is affirmation of the 'I' in its actuality, and at the same time a reminder of its weight of experience and its creative capacity. It is even more than the point of impact of mental energy on reality. It disposes of a 'temporal horizon'[42] extending, as it were, as far as one can see. This horizon is very restricted in primitive and retarded natures; in the weak-minded it does not exceed twenty days in all, and they live with what is immediately present to consciousness, without being able to foresee, or to organise themselves (De Greeff).[43] In the child, eight days' holiday is an infinity and there 'is nothing of himself to be encountered' at a distance of several weeks or months. For the present is not only the passage of time: in order to acquire meaning it requires from us a complex behaviour and an aggressive attitude. Without this formative act, or 'presentification' as Janet calls it,[44] the passing moment never achieves reality, it slips beneath the somnolent consciousness and is lost to the future which we are forging. Those who have no memory, those with grave psychic weakness, have no present. 'The present seems to me an intruder' one of them declared. It is, in fact, an exacting intruder. It requires to be, wishes to be, an activity reinforced by the whole weight of personality. It is the living bridge by which the eternal is incarnated in historical existence, where the act of choice makes us man, and changes a world. If the response wavers or is delayed, then we get the illusion of the *déjà vu*, or, more exactly, of the 'already experienced', which begins to form as a shadow of reality. Perhaps Janet is more correct in calling it the 'sense of non-presence'. At its morbid extreme, it ends in feelings of unreality, of nullity and of self negation.

*

The past is not only a sector of time, it is a certain way of living in the past. Carried by the movement of creative time, the past has several functions. Either it appears as the home of the renunciations necessary to the growth of the living tree, protected by a voluntary oblivion from the profusion of experience; or I can grasp it as something I have moved beyond, or something that has to be 'outstripped'[45] in the sense that it does not rivet my attention, or act as a support, except to save me from repeating it without renewal, and from becoming spellbound in its leaden grip. Or, again, I may savour it as an unity, as a film of experience in duration, tinged with the slightly dramatic

* Describes Paulhan's 'presentisme'.

charm added by regret, when regret is not clouded by despair; but what this regret regrets, is not that which is finished and done with, but the rich flood of hope which ran like sap, and which I now rediscover in memory, free from the inertia of the present. Remorse is a variant of the second attitude, nourished by the past, through an unhappy awareness of faults and a resolution to do better, or simply the remorse that is a second, ill-tempered death, adding to the first sin the sin against the grace of time. Thus the creative past is always experienced in a motion to the future, the moving sentiment in the past is moving, not overwhelming. The objective memory, memory of things learnt, is hardly the same as time experienced. It neither moves nor overwhelms, it is only utility. Beyond this dead zone we find consciousness overcome by the past. Some are overcome to their satisfaction, taking pleasure in maintaining it close to the present for as long as possible, and in living in its desolation more than in the present, either the actual or the subjective present.

*

The slavery of time is such that consciousness tries obstinately to overcome it, to cling to it or to evade it, like an animal in a cage looking vainly for a way out. But the moment we escape from the rhythm of duration, hammered out on the keyboard of space and time, we fall into anxiety. Stern has observed the phenomenon of alarm registered by children at a prolonged note, even if at the end it becomes an agreeable melody. The adult feels a similar distress at a sound which continues indefinitely, like the whistle of a train in the distance: it maintains us in a state of expectation without a future, an expanse of meaningless present: we feel a tremor of vertigo at the death of time. Monotony has a similar effect on weak spirits. The strong can tolerate it, even rejoice in it when they recognise the infinitely generous repetition of an act of love or welcome. If we think of a monk's life, the value, to a man of a faith, of the rosary, the litanies, the Gregorian chant; of the lover, endlessly repeating the elementary words of love; of the beauty of the desert, the plain or the sea. Contemplation is never wearied of returning again and again upon itself, for it never repeats itself but only becomes deeper.[46] But if nothing sustains this apparent return to the same theme or stimulus, the whole psyche becomes numb: consciousness enters into boredom. It scents, in this repetition, the void and the absolute levelling of death. 'Sickness of duration which is too long, and existence which is too empty':[47] regrets and unformulated aspirations in a present without presence,

* Extreme forms of living in the past.

this boredom is a general weakening of duration without collapse, the dead weight of existence no longer kindled by creativity, but not yet disintegrated. Halfway between action and despair, it is not yet the loss of all hope; it is the absence of hope, with a blind, distraught sense of this emptiness. It may hover like a ghost over a superabundance of activities, if these activities proceed from a cold heart. It is the death of receptive awareness, which can be filled with joy by a blade of grass, a passing glance, a spring morning, for its own generosity enlivens and multiplies the generosity of things. A mournful reflection of eternity on a lake of death, boredom achieves extension without history, without existence, without promise: not yet the damming up or refusal of being, but its interminable and disquieting eclipse. Does this suggest a special trait of character? Although active persons condemned to inactivity seem more subject to it than others, it does not seem peculiar to any one temperament.[48] It is significant that it does not appear in states of grave depression: the melancholic are not bored, they just sit on their chairs and expect nothing. Renan said of the Bretons that they dreamed too much ever to get bored. Boredom is to be found in an intermediate zone, close to that slight agitation which betrays the first dispersal of the mind, when instead of tightening up duration and action, it starts on a thousand things none of which is concluded.[49] It would then be the perception of duration which is hamstrung by a still practically healthy consciousness: hence its very acute and painful character.

An utilitarian awareness of duration is another way, as we so rightly and so unconsciously say, of 'killing time'. It sterilises personal life at its root in order to be free from the anguish of time. Its keynote is an intolerance of leisure, that is to say of time experienced in full freedom and relaxation. Some find it only 'vacant time' and absolute boredom, and have only one passion, to escape such enforced unemployment by cramming the smallest intervals of duration with objective ends and occupations. They have, in fact, to occupy time with details, in order to stifle its protest, and their consciousness is overburdened and breathlessly preoccupied with itself, yet fearful of any hold-up which might leave it alone with itself. To this is due a certain Americanisation of life, urban agitation and the addicts of the cinema who flee from the last chance of solitude. It is peculiarly Western.[50]

It is for metaphysics to establish whether time can be transcended by a conquest and a reception of eternity. Here we need only deal with the psychological incidence of the belief in eternity, or better, with what one might call the behaviour of eternity. This is not the same as an indefinite schedule, or an inflation of time in the direction of eternity, as happens with the mental patient. The so-called 'Cotard' syndrome is found in some melancholics, who accuse themselves of having committed all the crimes and caused all the misfortunes of the world, so that their misdeeds have brought about the end of the world: the universe has now disappeared, and they are condemned to suffer always and everywhere, throughout the centuries, an eternal damnation. Sufferers from general paralysis enjoy the massive but happier belief in which every affirmation of existence is swollen to an enormous size. In both cases time is not transcended, but inflated to monstrous forms in one dimension alone, that of the dead past which then becomes pan-catastrophic or statically enormous. Neither does a perpetual negation of the present introduce eternity into time, as some morose believers would have it,[51] fearful of the life they are trying to transcend by degrading all its generosities. Those who believe, on the contrary, in a living eternity, feel it like the transcendent but never distant presence of positive and infinite promise. It is no longer the future which attracts creative time towards it, it is the supra-temporal which is pulling the whole of time towards a fourth dimension. It is not commensurate with the other dimensions, but if it must be compared, it is closer to the future than to the present. For the man who pays rational homage to this element beyond time, the past is transfigured into alternate recollection and detachment, his present is rich with absolute commitments and invisible succour, his future bright with unconditional hope and maturations which will not be ineffective. Eternity is not an object somewhere above, or beyond his death as a man: in it he lives and moves and has his being. By the future which it offers to all his past, by the infinite responsibility it entrusts to the present, by the immensity of its transfiguration of the future, it opens up the mind to the powerful subjectivity of time. The whole of a man's conduct acquires a continuity, a drive, a firmness which the psychologist has to accept, for just as Christians say of the use of extreme unction for the maladies of the body, it is a way of experiencing time which counteracts the maladies of the soul just as it claims to purify the sins of the heart.

In temperaments particularly open to emotional perceptions, this experience of the eternal may occur through a sudden, lively sensation; the little miracle of the sudden fusion of memory and an apparently related perception, which detaches us from the degrading servitude of time. There are the celebrated examples given by Proust; the taste of a madeleine dipped in a spoonful of tea, a teaspoon clinking against a plate, the feet standing on two unequal flagstones; this is enough to open up the inner paradise: 'one minute free from the discipline of time has re-created in us a man set free from its discipline in order to experience it.'[52] Disquiet about the future, fear of death, lack of self-confidence, all disappear in this instantaneous and delightful certainty.

But men as sensitive as this must be capable of being deeply wounded by the immediate language of things, if suffering, however trivial its original cause, is thus to open a gate into the very heart of spiritual life. This capacity for transcending even the most banal sensation is the mark of the artist. Those whose emotions are slower or more superficial care little for these colourful and transient flashes of eternity. They will seek a more secondary version of eternity, broader, more persistent, and if it is not too paradoxical to say so, more extended in time.

GENEROSITY—AVARICE

In this dual concept we touch, perhaps, upon the most essential of psychological determinations. Matter is exactitude itself, at least at our level. Its almost immutable laws establish that basic economy which is the foundation of good housekeeping. Life introduces the first practice of abundance: where matter levels down, life throws up again: where matter manoeuvres with a capital which is gradually being used up without reconstituting itself, life is the first to create, accumulate and throw away. But it still does this blindly. Only with the person is there a beginning of meaning in this superabundance, when it is enlightened by a generous intention. The person creates and gives without calculation, because the person has, if not the capacity always to give more, at least a movement to go further. But at the same time the person knows why it gives, to whom it gives, and why it should give more abundantly. Generosity is the most representative virtue of the person, appearing like the image of a creative Infinity. One might be tempted to say that generosity was more essential than affirmation to the locating of man, if conscious affirmation were not necessary to provide a solid root to its activity.

Psychology comes across generosity even before it is a virtue, when it is still only a very great docility of temperament with regard to the spontaneity of personal life. There are some who seem to have received it as a gift from heaven, an act of grace on the part of life. It begins with kindness, this little thoroughbred virtue so lost in the modern world. Egocentricity is at a minimum in such temperaments. They have an innate liberality which is like the ease with which a fruit falls from the tree, the possession from the possessor, the act from the agent. Confronted with a choice, they proceed with the certainty of a thoroughbred and the simplicity of a child, to the course of action which costs them the most and gives the most to others. After so many tense, ill-favoured virtues, so many taut forms of heroism and ascesis, they seem the unassuming ambassadors of a truer world, no less exacting, but youthful and natural even to the point of immolation. Their action shows us, as it were, the real presence of fecundity. They are not just incompetent stocktakers, wandering between possibilities, rushing breathlessly after a fullness they will never achieve. 'Thou art careful and troubled about many things' said Christ to Martha, bustling with hospitality. The generous do not prefer the intoxication of the indefinite to the modesty of reality, neither are they, on the pretext of realism, closed to all that is most beautiful in reality. They like to grasp things, real things, with both hands, and when they consider the world, are never tired of savouring its luxuriance of detail: think of Péguy, his prodigious detail, his delight in treasuring the finest shade, the smallest object, the least word in his overflowing Paradise. Klages contrasts this vital abundance with a dryness of spirit and will. But it cannot thus be reduced to a psychic profusion not yet differentiated from the first plethora of instinct. We have seen that instinct, in man, tends to slip into egocentricity and the poverty of repetition. Generosity receives from instinct an element of its sap. But its movement implies a mastery of instinct, a victory over its egoism and rigidity of impulse. It is inexhaustibly multiple, perpetually inventive and adventurous. Thus the generous detest the calculations on which our rules of good behaviour are based: the giving and the giving back, the strict regulation of movements from the heart, of hospitality and human relationships. These customs were originally a discipline of homage to a certain grace of living, a technique for controlling egoism. With bourgeois avarice they have become the perfect way to spiritual death. The generous man is a poor proprietor and a bad economist: he prefers to give rather than to possess, to distribute rather than to accumulate, to let things live instead of conserving them. Seeing how self-satisfied mediocrity and sordid economy are honoured around him, he is often tempted to make virtues of extravagance and prodigality. Generosity shapes the world in its own image or, more exactly, it reveals the latent image of itself within it. Not that it falls into the illusions of the impulsive, of whom it is said that they give themselves quickly, whereas one should say that they deliver themselves quickly, a sort of surface lightness and not from an abounding inner richness. Generosity sees beneath a poor world a generous world, sees it transparently behind the wretchedness of daily life, trusts in it, will deal only with it, knowing that by behaving generously one awakens generosity.

The avarice we are dealing with here is more fundamental than the avarice of money. It is a narrowness of heart, a 'vital poverty' (Prinzhorn), an absence of spontaneity and liberality, a basic parsimony in the communication of the self. Often these fundamental misers are the weak, the malingerers, the 'little lives': if they expend little it is because they have little; hence their moroseness, 'little sadnesses, a lasting petty avarice of morality and physique', which Janet finds to be a frequent characteristic of asthenia. They depreciate everything around them, making themselves a petty world, in order not to be overcome by the overwhelming power of the real world. There are some anxiety states which should be classed separately. They display every appearance of parsimony, but they are thrown into it by a sickly fear of risk and uncertainty and not by a basic narrowness of heart; even the awkward punctiliousness of their practical behaviour contrasts with a life of generosity and devotion. Hypersensitive and not indifferent, irresolute even in their calculations, their pusillanimity is more often attached to a concern for others than designed to aid their own tranquillity.[53] Apart from such cases there is the basic avarice we are considering here. Countless beings, not ill-favoured by fortune, have such a radical distrust of men and events that they reveal an attitude of refusal towards any being anywhere: more than a refusal, a protest: more than a protest, a resentment against creative generosity. They reserve their feelings, they withhold their actions, they compress their thoughts. Only faintly emotive, for emotivity exposes one and carries one away, they are usually inactive and of secondary type. They live not only in reverse as to their spiritual life, but against the grain of life itself, for life is the first outline of the movement of spirit, by putting a premium on the risks of generosity. It is one of the merits of the Freudian school to have shown that throughout all the crises of growth, from weaning onwards, life can only expand when there is a courageous abandon, which accepts the sacrifice of acquired systems for the adventure of moving forward or, if you prefer it—it is the very formula of generosity—for the adventure of greater being through the sacrifice of having. When a vital avarice refuses this jump forward there arise the manifold forms of affective involution: egocentric withdrawal, narcissism, rigidity, demandingness and so on.

The avarice of money is an exception, a sort of monstrosity. Life offers us a much more banal picture of essential avarice, the parsimonious type, of whom M. Toulemonde has given us a vivid portrait.[54] He has a passion for order, tidying, polishing, putting corks back in bottles, straightening pictures, making everything symmetrical. He employs a fertile imagination in inventing new adaptations, which are not exactly inventions, but arrangements which reduce risk and increase returns: this object might be better placed there, this instrument used a better way, that arrangement perfected. He is always careful not to spend any capital uselessly: frugal with candle ends and bits of string, attentive only to the immediate economy which satisfies his narrowness, even if a longer term economy should thereby suffer. He is equally pained by social waste; he turns out the light in hotel corridors, and if a dish is unfinished in a restaurant, he prefers to pester his fellow customers to eat it, rather than lose it in any case, but see it unused. He could not be more serious in the way he tries to make use of worn-out objects, he frequents the sales, even if the pleasure of buying something cheaply should involve him in useless expenditure. He is the abomination of saleswomen, a tireless haggler, always afraid of being robbed, the typical customer of the one-price stores, which allow no scope either to surprise or to folly. Even his fantasies are governed by the same pattern, he is so possessed by his fear of the unforeseen: an insufferable traveller, overburdened with information, timetables, tariffs and guidebooks, insolently checking his money, arguing with taxi-drivers, waiters, his travelling companions, always on guard against the imposition of an expense or a neglect of his rights.

Many just men and men of order would be much astonished if under their so noble masks one showed them the terrible face of this avarice. They consider they treat life correctly because they expect nothing from it, and ask for no extraordinary privileges. This reasonable moderation is real madness in a world made up of promise and superabundance. Its mystery is whispering around them, with unhoped for advances, miraculous propositions, but in order to find their way they keep their eyes glued to the railway bye-laws. Their system of strictly equivalent relationships with others, their constant guard against spontaneity, surprises, enigmas, adventures, against the mad gesture which would break up their world of calculations, makes them worse than unhealthy: it makes them the most odious product of the complications of the death instinct in a civilisation which has raised it, under false names, to a level with the will to live.

4

THE STRUGGLE FOR REALITY

'TO know is to "explode towards", to tear oneself away from a moist gastric intimacy in order to hurry over there, beyond oneself, towards what is not oneself, close to that tree and yet not in it, for it escapes me and rebuffs me and I can no more lose myself in it than it can dilute itself in me.'
*

These lines, by Jean-Paul Sartre,[1] date from 1939. What a distance we have travelled from that lyrical sincerity with oneself which enchanted the last romantics of twenty years before.

One would think that after a century of incorrigible subjectivity, the twentieth century would be dominated by a quest for realism on a grand scale. We looked first at the human aggregate from this wide approach,† looking at it fully submerged in the universe, moist with the milk of things and not yet interested in questioning itself. But we immediately found that face to face with things, there developed an initiative under pressure, with its own way of accepting the stimuli of things and offering a response. I feel that I live through the air on my cheek, and the muscles pressing against it, through the world under my gaze and the heart expanding in joy of it. The sense of reality is born of our contact with the resistance of things, when we advance towards them and confront them with the solid drive of our combined mental and physical effort. It is this welding together of the two drives, or rather the struggle between them, the endless wrestling with the angel, that alone assures this double presence, ourselves with the world and the world with us. This encounter would never take place if the universe rolled on, indifferent to the destiny of its tenants, like Aristotle's first sphere, or the monastic conception of the indifference of matter. It does not happen when the tenant tries to be self-sufficient by withdrawal into the charm of solitude. A man 'bursting out' towards the world, a world dynamiting man into the limits of his invention, and tempestuous with its demands upon him: such is our vital equilibrium.

* Omits part of long quotation from Sartre.
† The author refers to chaps. 2, 3, 4 which have been omitted.

*
    A clear psychological distance is first established between myself and reality, with the beginning of intentional activity. On the side of objects it introduces the possibility of choice; on the side of the subject, reflection; and the meeting of the two produces the free act. This distance, which gives play to my activity, can cut me off from the universe. And yet, on the contrary, it is made to unite me to it by a tighter yet more flexible bond. To fasten the bond, I have to project myself ceaselessly towards the world, and the world must never cease to exercise its stimulating pressure through all the intermediaries which complicate our relationship.

    But we must not unjustifiably restrict from the beginning the field of 'reality'. Reality surrounds me from without, in the message of objects, and from within, in the experience of commitment. It is part of the human condition that I can only grasp reality completely by combining these two ways of approach. The predominance of one or the other approach is the basis of the characterology of our relationship to reality.

EXTRAVERSION—INTROVERSION
**
    We are indebted to Jung[2] for his clear definition of the two primordial movements of the dynamic self (libido) with regard to the environment, by the terms extraversion and introversion.

    The *extravert* moves spontaneously towards the object and towards others. His emotions, whatever may be the cause—noises, events, insults, surprises, lively joy or acute sorrow—are regularly discharged through these centrifugal channels (Lefrancq–Brunfaut). They release a flood of words, gestures, affirmations and activity, by which the trouble is eliminated. 'It must come out', says the extravert, and the provocation of a dangerous moment is swept away in a tumultuous stream. Using this primitive nucleus, Jung has described a rather more complex behaviour. The extravert, with his attractive and open manner, adapts easily to every situation, he is quick to make new acquaintances, and often plunges into the unknown without care or suspicion. His physique itself suggests this adaptation by the roundness of its gestures, curves predominate in his handwriting, which slopes to the right (towards the future, the conscious, virile activity). He has a positive relationship to external objects and is, as it were, attracted to them. He is a merchant, an engineer, a naturalist. He acts before reflecting, more decisive than uneasy, more a lover of solid pleasures

---

* Studies the elementary consciousness of the amoeba.
** Quotes Goldstein and Klages on forms of exteriorisation.

than of inner harmonies. He is more than well-adjusted: new or unknown situations attract him. He can hardly wait for them, sensing whatever is germinating, whatever is to come, hence his taste for novelty and his cavalier disregard for the past. Extraversion tends easily to aggressiveness, in which case it fosters a sectarian and tyrannical disposition: often there are none so intolerant as the child of fantasy or the apostle of free thought. It produces a type of intelligence which is more social than concentrated. In a rather unemotional temperament it leads to a bustling indifference, as in the type of man who is always there, and always active, but whose insensitivity freezes every approach. Too great a docility to the environment makes his sociability unstable. It melts with the environment and produces beings without frontiers.

The *introvert* is characterised, on the other hand, by the predominance of his subjective life. The primary introvert, described by Lefrancq–Brunfaut, instead of exteriorising his emotion, keeps it captive, chews it over, recapitulates and savours it, differentiates and augments it on the spot, without showing any outward sign, at any rate for the moment. A tension results which may be liquidated by a nervous crisis, but this catharsis, which is permanent in the extravert, is here only an occasional accident. Jung describes a more complex behaviour pattern which, as with his extravert, draws its traits from every level of psychic life. Hesitant, reserved, meditative in character, he does not easily betray himself, is held up by a certain distrust of objects, and always withdraws behind the defensive barrier of observation. He weighs the pros and cons before acting, which slows up his acts. His timidity and hesitation make adjustment to the external world difficult. His gestures also are often angular and staccato: his handwriting is angular and sloping to the left (return to the past, the Unconscious, the mother, tradition). With little self-confidence, he is irresolute in action. His thinking, which is entirely subjective, is more comprehensive than that of the extravert; but he may perhaps become coldly indifferent to all that is non-self; his intelligence is then theoretical, fantasy-bound, or mystical. He lacks common sense, and fails to achieve his purposes. Stiff and stubborn, he is liable to fanaticism. Easily wounded, bitter and caustic, he bolts and bars his solitude. His affectivity is 'locked to the self', all inward-turning, undemonstrative. He seeks intensity, not extension. Withdrawn, indifferent to others, his coldness is sometimes offensive, although he can show to intimate friends a warmth that is sometimes ardent. He likes to be secret and isolated. The outer world only exists for him as an interpretation of himself, hence his great capacity for illusion. He runs all the risks of his weakness, and those around him frequently take advantage of it, but he reacts periodically by an aggressive and vindictive anger out of proportion to its immediate object. Often an artist and a dreamer, the rich reserves of his unconscious grant him a lively faculty of intuition: introversion is in no sense an inner spirituality; it may dissipate personal life into mist, instead of strengthening it in depth, but it is obviously a disposition which favours the inner life, if the calibre of the subject is appropriate. Maladjusted to reality, the introvert lives with an inner sense of insecurity revealed by his frequent timidity. His interminable consideration before acting paralyses his power of decision. If he is endowed with an excess of emotivity he suffers all the more from the least act of presence required by the world, and turns in upon himself, consoling a painful susceptibility by his dreams. His psyche then tends to regress more and more, first towards infantile forms, then towards the archaic collective psyche. When his satisfaction with his own inner life is associated with a violent disharmony with his environment, he tends to unsociability. Spearman regards introversion as a high degree of inner perseveration. This is confirmed by some findings of J. W. Pinard; the introvert does not give up easily, he adjusts himself slowly to changes of lighting, finds it difficult to do two things at once, suffers a persistence of the same temptations, and once he has made up his mind, never abandons an unsolved problem.

It would falsify Jung's theory if we were to set these two types in opposition, as if we had necessarily to choose one or the other in a diagnosis. Introversion and extraversion are not two inborn temperaments, but two powerful mechanisms, both of which exist in each of us, and can be brought into operation by us, in turn. They only become characteristic through the acquired habit of developing only the one, in accordance with which, it must be said, we usually act. And we can never free ourselves entirely from the tendency we have passed over. Each of us lives on two levels at once: below the manifest psyche stirs a latent psyche, unconscious and repressed. According to Jung, he who is introverted on the first level, is extraverted on the second, and the reverse: the timid person 'puts his foot in it' on every possible occasion, drops bricks, upsets all the things and persons around him. There is no inevitability about extraversion or introversion: 'One is not born extravert or introvert, one becomes the one or the other.'[3] For the time being, let us leave the still unsubstantiated theories which explain the origin of these mechanisms. They are not exclusively confined to the individual. The introduction of the mirror in its modern form into Europe in the sixteenth century coincides with the birth of an introspective and narcissistic literature. Certain historical rhythms may well coincide here with the accidents of biography and the pressure of vocations. It is agreed that if the subject is too exclusively limited to one or the other disposition, the results may be serious: the extravert loses touch with himself, the introvert with the world.

*

The extravert tends to dissolve all disturbances by a theatrical motor agitation, short circuiting his feelings by verbal or mimetic gesture, thus blocking any inner response to the demands of the world. Thwarted as it forms, his spiritual life tends to be nullified by the suppression of that inwardness in which personality gathers itself together and ripens. It is constantly being diffused amongst the impersonality of the world of things. One should not therefore thwart the need for expression which he feels more acutely than others, but restore to him that inner concern which will sustain his very active presence in the external world.

Lefrancq–Brunfaut stress the need to develop imagination in order to inhibit agitation and develop the deeper faculties, if, by imagination, we understand 'the capacity to see things in the round, the spontaneous and generous evocation of images, persons and events, the invention of stories and the complication of anecdotes, the love of playing with ideas like children'. The dramatic mimicry of emotion is indeed accompanied by imagery, but this imagery is subordinated to visceral and muscular reaction, and only illustrates the emotion concerned, which they both reflect and stimulate. But if imagination begins to take its own course and to simulate psychic activity, it then diverts emotion from its primary manifestations, by intraverting and spiritualising it, in a world of feeling, aesthetic pleasure, or reflection. A literary or aesthetic education, a religious conviction, rich or painful human experiences are the necessary corrections of a temperament too constantly driven by its own nature outside itself.

Extraversion is shown on the physical level by an excess of centrifugal movements, which can be reduced by systematic forms of motor inhibition. Training can eliminate spontaneous gestures that are incongruous and useless, provided that there is no attempt to impose perpetual restraint on an emotional type, to which he would only react by withdrawal and maladjustment; one should aim at a voluntary self-control which should not be contrary to the very core of the personality, lest in the name of order one provokes a profound

* Quotes Lefrancq and Brunfaut.

disorganisation; his natural attentiveness must be educated by deliberately discordant exercises, such as tapping something with the left hand whilst doing additions with the right: the too spontaneous gesture will be held up by inviting attention to attitudes.

Socially, a deaf, chilly environment is a useful obstacle to extraversion. The extravert is obliged to fall back on his own resources if the environment lets his rowdiness echo in a void, and refuses to provide a complacent audience.

If, in fact, an 'inner life' is for some a rather dangerous *gourmandise*, it is the very thing that is lacking to the extravert to give him the deeper perspectives necessary to a rounded life. He should be offered everything that will encourage it, within the framework of his own disposition, and to the extent that he can tolerate it.

Thus, by compensation, the slapdash, theatrical disorder to which extraversion sometimes leads, even the bonhomie, the rather too facile charms of its milder forms, can be replaced by a sort of easy psycho-organic availability and liberality, which will blend happily with the reserve introduced by introverting influences.

Excessive introversion may well develop into an egoistic enjoyment of the self, into complicated delights and sterile reverie: imaginary romances tarnish the joyful appreciation of everyday life, self-defeating subtleties lower the sense of reality and of concern for others. If it is not strengthened by the effort of engaging with reality, the inner life founders into a sort of wishful asthenia which perpetually retreats from action. Lefrancq and Brunfaut called the compensatory power which should be developed by mental training '*sthenia*', the 'psychic capacity for effective effort tenaciously directed towards an end to be achieved'. The value of mental struggle against obstacles has been dangerously underestimated in the early years of the twentieth century, in reaction against the rationalism and formalism of earlier years: the appeal to an inconsistent intuition, the wayward fantasy of spontaneous imagination, to an entire liberty of the mind. This seriously endangers the virile virtues of the intelligence and thus of character. Here we have both a disease and a remedy on which, in our epoch, it is appropriate to dwell. By retaining the subject on the hither side of action and even of expression, introversion tends to develop a rigid immobility of behaviour, which may turn into obtuseness and a drowsy stupidity. The introvert may come to find it too much trouble even to articulate or terminate his words: his speech is turned inwards, for he is in fact indifferent to whether one listens to him or not: just as once his ideas are worked out, his dreams dreamed, he does not care whether they are realised or not. Without expression, inactive, stilted, the introvert is therefore only too much inclined to withdraw into his shell, wrapping himself in a silence which may easily turn into the progressive psychic lethargy known to the sick, the prisoner and the inactive. It is necessary therefore to force him as it were, into space, through gesture, by developing his psycho-motor activity. He must move, go for walks, take exercise, practise verbal expression, dancing, violent sports, anything that will stimulate his rhythm. The effect will be twofold: movement progressively awakens the slumbering consciousness, and makes the withdrawn consciousness engage with reality and confront the obstacle. With emotive persons, one must proceed gradually and with caution, for they are liable to display violently inhibitory reactions to the first efforts at exteriorisation. Socially the introvert, as opposed to the extravert, requires a stimulating, understanding background. This again will have a twofold effect: on the one hand it will offer the introvert a friendly echo, without which he may harden into maladjustment, but on the other hand it will excite him, through a variety of interests in the persons and possibilities that surround him, to come out of himself, and to require the world, and require to be in the world. Amongst non-understanding people who mock or rebuff him, or in a colourless environment which bores him, the results are fatal. Any mental training which forces the introvert outside himself is good. 'To lose oneself in order to find oneself' should be his motto. He must act, create, devote himself, forget himself amongst things and amongst man.

A compensated introversion produces that reserve, that real distinction without mannerisms or haughtiness, which makes for a charming discretion and allows the necessary pause before action. It can then lead to the higher forms of life and thought of which, in the history of ideas, Plotinus is the most characteristic type.[4]

It is a commonplace that extraversion predominates amongst southern Europeans. Childhood, from seven to ten, is generally speaking extraverted, and puberty introverted. Conditions of life, the basic sensitivity or philosophy of an epoch, may encourage the one or the other disposition. The men who cut the clearings in the Celtic forests were not inclined to complications of feeling any more than workers struggling to make a living, or a people fighting for its existence under hostile conditions. Wealthy epochs that are too comfortable, civilisations at their peak and above all in their decadence, encourage, on the other hand, a disequilibrium in favour of reflection which quickly becomes a vacuum if there is no maintenance of the vital contact with reality. There appear then the romantics, the relativist philosophers, pasturing on hollow nourishment, thoughts without objects, dreams without consistence, loves without aim, gratuitous actions and a universe without direction.

THE ACCEPTANCE OF REALITY

Inevitable are the conflicts between life within us and life outside us. Manifold discords arising from the universe and from other persons assail the conscious purposes of man, the purposes of the species. The 'pleasure principle', which demands the complete and immediate satisfaction of our egoistic tendencies, is not the only reason. The 'reality principle' is often, in fact, a self-centred renunciation, which is a moratorium conceded by egoism: it is then, as has been said, only a principle of 'improved pleasure', an arithmetic of enjoyment. This has already been perfectly defined by the English utilitarian philosophers, and in spite of some over-pretentious language, nothing of consequence has been added to their system. But egocentricity is not our only source of impulse. The triple universe of men and things and values may appeal to us as strongly as the instinct of self-preservation, possession or aggression. Freud and Marx have swept away the empty magniloquence of a decadent spirituality. It is now time to move a step further. It is the whole personality in movement, in partnership with its surroundings, which seeks for spheres of expansion in the entire universe, and not purely a few moments of satisfaction. A sense of reality is much more than the sullen resignation of an instinct repressed by society, and asserting itself brutally and without justification. It is a desire to live with the world, not lost in it, nor merely parallel with it, but in a discipline of exchange and interpenetration which is ever expanding the personal richness of life. It contains also a competent assessment of limits and possibilities, which at all times adds range and flexibility and wisdom to our action. It contains moreover an eager sense of communication, a desire for harmony and breadth which corrects whatever tendency the former might have to be too easily resigned and passive. It says: 'So be it', and it says: 'Further'. A great part of our psychic energy is employed in reaching this agreement between concession and advance, with every unforeseeable event of daily life. With the 'function of the real' of Janet, the 'attention to life' of Bergson, and the 'affective contact with reality' of Bleuler and Minkowski, this cardinal function has slowly attained the importance in contemporary psychology that it deserves.

We must never overlook its ceaseless dual action: movement

towards things to achieve a positive harmony with them, movement of withdrawal before forces superior in number or requirements, so that we do not shatter ourselves uselessly against them, but withdraw to gain new strength by the consolidation of our vital energy. Continuing and completing Kretschmer's work, Bleuler has stressed the unison of these two rhythms with the reality function. *Syntony* and *schizoidy*, the faculty of vibrating in unison with the surroundings, and the faculty of detaching ourselves from them; flexibility in shaping our behaviour to the requirements of reality and capacity to abstract ourselves from the play of external forces, are the two complementary principles of normal life, and complete the equilibrium of action. When they alternate and support each other, like systole and diastole, they produce a way of living that is remarkably harmonious and effective. But generally one or the other predominates and marks the character accordingly.

*

The first condition of adaptation to reality is a relative forgetfulness of self. One must lose oneself to find it, and to find oneself in it. This rule, both of biology and of spirituality, can be observed in the simplest form of adapted movement. My consciousness of this movement is projected entirely forward, towards the end of the spoken phrase, the theme played, the initiative launched. If my attention is arrested by any intermediate phase of its development, it is held up and confused. Ribot noted that the reflex sense of personality is abolished in the expert rifleman as he shoots, in the surgeon as he operates. His whole personality is gathered together to converge on the whole of the action; he is transformed into the action itself, alienated from self in the supreme realisation of self. The creative mind feels a similar sense of alienation at the moment of creation, which has often been described. Should we consider it the cruellest trick of nature to annihilate us at the precise moment of fulfilment? This would make an absurdity of the slow birth of personal awareness. The sense of effective achievement which distinguishes this terminal state, completely separates it from the depersonalisation which, at the other extreme, accompanies states of separation from reality.[5] In the latter state the subject feels literally distant from, or outside himself; far from being concentrated on an intentional action, he does not succeed in making contact with the outer world. The reduced consciousness of the adjusted agent is not an enfeebled consciousness, but one working

* Describes the growth of adaptation in childhood and a false adaptation which is only mimicry.

with a lighter rhythm and a broader aim, which tends to pass beyond egocentric consciousness. This experience helps us to understand the vital function of work, which compels egocentricity to confront the conditions of reality, to relax in the thing done, to expand in the task achieved.
*

All work works to make a man, as well as to make a thing. The modern experience of the machine and, more generally, of technics, has been invaluable in recalling a too verbose civilisation to a sense of necessities and resistances, to a liking for solidity; the world can no longer be subjected to our desires, our sorceries, our verbal intimidations. It would, however, be a mistake to believe that intellectual work requires less severity than that which exercises hands and muscles. But men are less sensitive to accidents and lapses which have an immediate effect on the mind only. This is why manual work is essential to a complete culture. It is designed to correct any tendency to flee from reality into woolliness of mind and reverie without object.[6]

A successful sexual adaptation is no less essential to the maturation of the function of reality. It is an exaggeration to identify one with the other. Jung, who did so at the beginning, admitted that there is more in the second than in the first.[7] But they are closely intermingled and almost coincident in origin, and the closeness of the link, due to this original confusion, is clearly evident in the course of development.

By forcing egocentric sloth to pass outside itself, the contact with reality restrains the turbulence of unformed desire, and compels it to choose precise and limited ambitions, to pass from the luxuriant welter of possibilities to the strong and naked reality of the achievable. Some, either through inability to introduce their dreams into life, or because they are overburdened by an over-fertility of inner life, never succeed in freeing themselves from this inner abundance, in order to choose amongst it all that is not yet, or to resign themselves to what will never be. They remain perpetual day-dreamers, encumbered by unrealisable ideas, at the mercy of stray impulses and wandering dreams. Sometimes a great poet emerges from their ranks: the majority lead an impotent life, not without its own attraction, but always incomplete.

There is, therefore, in action a sort of reductive capacity indispensable to the building up of personality. It alone frees the road to personalisation from this too-much of ourselves and from the necessary but indiscreet presence of ourselves to ourselves. We do not know reality,

* Gives an example from Henry de Montherlant.

either external reality or our own reality, by waiting for it to be delivered at our door. We receive the one and the other solely by the effort we make to metamorphose them.

*

We all bring a greater or lesser degree of energy[8] to this struggle for reality, and its achievement is more or less difficult according to the reality in question.

**

The cyclothymic constitution described by Kretschmer[9] is a complex temperament, centred on adaptability, and equally likely to include the floating plasticity of the hyperadjustable, as the vital equilibrium of flexible self-mastery. As a social attitude it is marked by openness: charm and cordiality, gaiety, calm tranquillity, the cyclothymic has all these qualities that can be summed up, on first approach, as warmth and simplicity. But this attitude is more than a social attitude, it is a way of living with the world, with things and with events, as well as with men. One can analyse various elements, the adaptability of the sympathetic nervous system, hyperemotivity, and deficiency of the regulating frontal zone, but the psychic picture is homogeneous. Cyclothymes, hence their name, have in common brusque fluctuations of humour, in which periods of hyperactive well-being, irritable, brilliant and a trifle eccentric (hypomanic pole) alternate with periods of morose depression and acute despair (depressive pole).[10] More often than not, one of these humours achieves predominance and the subject becomes fixed as an excited or depressed type. But although the turn of their behaviour may appear in different colours, in both types there is the same affective disposition, the same fundamental vital tone. They seem to offer their love and gratitude to the whole world. They ignore conflicts and negative attitudes on principle, and also the desire to improve the world according to certain immutable formulae. When they have any marked feeling of themselves, it is not in the opposition of their personality to the world, but in a kind of sense of well-being at living in the world: towards the hypomanic extreme, this communion with the world makes them bustling, suggestible, flighty, anxious to enjoy all the good things of life: towards the depressive extreme it takes on an ethical flavour; they do not moralise, but show understanding to all, with a charming modesty. Their intelligence is governed by instability in the hypomanics, and by the spirit of concession in the depressive. Of a practical nature, they

* Criticises Janet's and Bergson's concept of the function of reality.
** Further details from Janet of the struggle for reality.

are more sensitive to the real possibilities of an individual than to integrity of principles: they like neither systems nor dogmatisms. All the qualities derived from acute psychic tension, all opinions or beliefs that are bitter or fanatical, are foreign to them. They set to work with energy and warmth, but without the power of persistence of the schizoid. The hypomanic are restless, busy, enterprising; the depressive, capable, economical, serious. Those who carry these qualities to the highest level become first class business men, speakers, journalists. The depressive cannot become organisers or leaders: they provide the type of 'old and faithful servant, conscientious and liked by everyone'. Finding themselves in abnormal circumstances they lose their heads and become discouraged. Their sexual life is normally without incident, simple, natural and lively, with a force of temperament beyond the average. Their psychological rhythm is accelerated, their thoughts flow easily, with a tendency to blossom in all directions, and a liability to a 'compulsive flight of ideas'. Their attitudes are continuous, unaccented, their gestures rounded. Bleuler speaks of them as living a life 'in waves'. One should not imagine this particular psychic structure as being open to every wind. Their syntony is often selective, and the subject adheres to a world modelled by himself, so true it is that one cannot live without taking up a position and affirming oneself.[11] What is specific to this syntony is that he spontaneously adapts the perspectives he has chosen, to his surroundings. If he could be summed up in two words, they would be goodwill and ease.

Kretschmer is the first to admit that this type, like all the others, is never met in a pure state. He prefers to expand his description by the addition of various sub-types, rather than to make it too exclusive. Ordinary life provides us with innumerable examples of 'medium' cycloids. The 'alert hypomanic' is prompt and talkative: he sees everything at a glance, he is never at a loss in any situation: if he has the means he loves to surround himself with pictures and *bibelots*: as a child he is inclined to fantasy. The 'quietly contented' type is peaceful, sober and liked by all: he does not, incidentally, achieve very much. Satisfied with his lot and disliking difficulties, he often remains a bachelor, or leads the life of a benevolent recluse in some retired corner. The 'heavy-blooded' type is markedly depressive, studious but slow, timid, easily put out of his stride. The 'happy gossip' is heard afar off: always present at any entertainment, talkative, loving sport and wine, he is a factor of animation in society, amiable, superficial, without self-love, often overpowering in his verbosity and exhibitionism. The 'quiet humorist' observes men and things in silence, interjecting here and there a perfect sally: a born storyteller, he grows animated in society, where he becomes gently witty: the only things that irritate him are 'high principles': for the rest he is a faithful and indulgent friend: he chooses for preference what is natural and popular. The 'quietly sentimental' weeps easily, has a serious manner, loves the country and appeals at once to anyone who does not react violently against his sentimentality. The man 'who enjoys life and likes his comforts', not particularly well-educated, petty bourgeois frequenting commercial hotels, reproduces the two previous types, but on a more trivial level, crudely cordial and facetious: the love of comfort predominates over all other preoccupations: his life is without drive, the background typically *Prudhomme*. The 'active and practical', always overworked, like being overworked, are tireless, and perpetual committee members: they prefer, above all, concrete activities, medicine, politics, social work: from this activity they derive a healthy self-satisfaction. One can see the relationship between all these types and the 'sanguine' temperament of the old school, to Heymans' 'choleric' and the morphologists' 'round' type.

But the cycloid type should not be confined to the 'fat, good-tempered fellow', as we should find this rather simplified pattern unsuited to deeper diagnosis. Kretschmer has shown that this disposition can produce types of genius or, at least, of great quality. Cyclothymic artists display a blend of realism and humour. A good contemporary example would be Georges Duhamel, who has projected his depressive side in *Salavin*. The cyclothymic writer is humanitarian, modest and natural, and candidly honest: he loves all beings and all things with a childlike tenderness, particularly human beings and humble people. He is full of common sense, which sometimes leads him into somewhat shallow judgments on new and disconcerting realities. He knows nothing of aggressive irony. Cyclothymes produce little lyric or dramatic talent: they have a predilection for an unstylised prose and simple narration: their poetry is exquisitely coloured, warm in feeling, but their work lacks great tension of feeling, the drama of will, the force of problems, the hierarchy of the essential and the secondary. This is sometimes replaced by a rather too banal good humour. At the hypomanic extreme they are salty, with a spontaneous good humour, sparkling, sometimes a little too crude and uninhibited, with a vigorous popular style in which each word takes on an indefinably fresh and comic quality (Marcel Aymé, for instance, in the lighter vein; Luther in the more caustic). At the depressive extreme, they are contemplative, letting everything come to them, fingering things tenderly, describing them in natural, simple language, with a predilection for simple folk and the painting of details. Their temper is always benevolent, even in distress. Kretschmer gives Franz Hals as a typical example in the plastic arts. Simple objectivity, or spontaneous freshness or adventurous living. One could also cite Chardin and Rubens. Cyclothymic scientists prefer the concrete, natural and descriptive sciences: Pasteur and Darwin. They have three traits in common: enormous range of the area of work, with great mental universality and mobility; empirical and visual methods of working ('He fingers things too much', said Schiller of Goethe); aversion for system, theory and metaphysics. Cyclothymic leaders and heroes (except for the heavy-blooded type) are active. At the hypomanic extreme, they are carried forward by a happy impetus, hardy, optimistic, quick-witted, amiable, supple; in more modest careers they display good humour, tact, practical ability. On the other hand, they lack firmness and idealism. 'Cyclothymic metal' said Kretschmer, 'is rather soft of temper.' The great leaders they produce are therefore often strengthened by a schizoid alloy. Here we find the popular dare-devils, the great pioneering industrialists, the large-scale organisers, who are more interested in founding an empire than in organising it systematically: supple politicians, conciliatory negotiators. Mirabeau is a magnificent example of a combination of the two extremes: drive and flexibility, brilliance and a popular manner. So is Luther, 'heroic and childlike, prophet and hard drinker.'

Our whole behaviour, is capable of two different fundamental dispositions, according to whether it is directed by a constant of egocentricity or by an objective attitude which puts the self at the service of the world. These two attitudes cannot be defined without implying a final assertion of value. We are for or against the world, and choice here is compounded with instinct.

*

The egocentric clings to the image of himself or to the purpose in life which he has formed: if these elude him, his balance is upset; he hardens into a refusal to accept this defeat, or falls into panic. The objective man, if defeated, adjusts himself and continues to develop or modify his purposes, without becoming a slave to their provisional formulae. This ease of adjustment gives him a vast capacity for modification. Being convinced that that which is, is always justified as against that which could not be, he finds even in the surprises of reality scope for imagination, invention and fresh conquests. The

* Künkel on egocentricity-objectivity.

egocentric is a preserver of his cherished, irritable self, which is always on the defensive against a world whose every approach endangers his fixed and jealously guarded ideal. The objective man is expendable, sensitive, always 'for' any advances on the side of the world, for he knows that the richness of his values is infinite and their capacity for metamorphosis inexhaustible. He does not feel the checks imposed by reality as any loss of integrity, but as a new revelation and an opportunity for new expansion. He is happy to undertake something unforeseen, to be something he had not imagined himself to be, of dying and being transfigured every hour, whilst remaining faithful to a faithful world. For he is faithful. His philosophy of living, as Künkel says, is not yes, or no, but 'however', a synthesis of renunciation and continuity, inspired by a confident vitality of invincible generosity.

As we see, the adjustments of the 'objective' man are only possible by a perpetual self-negation in order to rise again out of the ashes. Once acquired, the adjustment of the moment enters the field of egocentricity and becomes automatic and thus rebel to new adjustment. If this automatism remains flexible, it tends to turn a man into a distributor of ready-made reactions which, however finely calibrated, stifle that source of indefinite, disquieting possibilities that animate a personality. Thus an objective disposition is only favourable to personal life thanks to the disquiet provoked by the daemon within. Engineers and pedagogues, rationalists and well-intentioned technocrats sometimes think they can satisfy the demands of personality by planning a city in which the masses are no longer treated like sheep, but each individual neatly adjusted to his living conditions and his own temperament, by the widespread use of eugenics, health records, hygiene, vocational guidance and psycho-technical laboratories. These utilities may indeed contribute something to order and happiness, but we must insist that the portrait of the perfectly adjusted person, muscular and satisfied, without disquiet, without the unpredictable, the type sometimes advocated by the more candid enthusiasts for new education and human rationalisation, this type is not the best equipped to deal with the higher tasks of humanity. We must first decide—and neither psychologist nor educationalist can evade the question—whether man is made to be adjusted in this sense, becoming static, acquiring a balance he does not utilise, or whether he should not be permanently maladjusted, or rather 'under-adjusted', finding in this 'under-adjustment' the urge to advance always a little further, thus keeping his future open. This salutary under-adjustment is obviously not to be sought by artificial anxieties, or by systematically refusing the benefits offered by civilisation. It depends on the height at which we fix our guiding values, and the creative opportunities which they propose as a result. It may therefore be indefinitely sustained, without creating an ill-placed resentment against health and life. But this level of harmony is easier to define than to realise amidst the surprises of human evolution. Now that we may at least hope that the blood-stained crises of development in western Europe may be followed by an unparalleled rise in standards of living and in the control of the uncertainties of fate, we should realise that we are about to reach this, the gravest of all spiritual problems. Doubtless no one wishes to break up civilisation, as the first workers in modern industry broke the machines. But left to its own resources civilisation is a machine for making robots, it is not a machine for making gods. It is for man to decide or to refuse to be a god, and if so, what sort of god. If by happiness we understand a well-adjusted slumber enfolding 'the best of all possible men' in 'the best of all possible worlds', the paths of happiness are not the paths of man. The passion for reality is a devouring passion: we can anchor ourselves neither in an objective adjustment which mechanises us, although it is useful at its own level and necessary to our mental well-being; nor in the refusal of reality, although this sometimes has the quality of metaphysical necessity. The conflict of reality is the conflict of an insoluble tension.

THE REFUSAL OF REALITY

There are many ways of refusing reality. One almost always finds their origin in some emotional shock, more precisely, some emotional shock in childhood. The child presents to the world both a powerful egocentricity and inexhaustible reserves of acceptance and affection. For him there is no cold and objective perception of reality. All knowledge comes to him through his affections. If these are rebuffed by contempt or malice, ill-treatment or habitual indifference, or if one day they are violently wounded by some disgrace or disappointment which strikes a vital spot, he is liable to throw the whole world overboard, in order to build up a life of his own, withdrawn and self-sufficient. He becomes wild, dreamy, 'moonstruck', absentminded, jumping when spoken to, sometimes irritable and sulky over nothing, avoiding initiative and conflict. He is seen to seek solitude, peaceful games, or passive roles in group games, preferring the company of books to that of children of his own age. The danger of such behaviour is often overlooked, for he is studious in so far as study favours withdrawal. He is said to be 'thoughtful' passing over the fact that his thoughts are a constant re-hashing of worn-out themes. He is well on the way to becoming 'autistic', a word coined by Bleuler to define being 'detached from reality, with an absolute or relative predominance of the inner life'. Infantile narcissism, which should have been overcome by the reality principle, will finally get the better of him.

*

Withdrawal may take place in any direction in any of the varying degress of maladjustment: indifference to environment, opposition to environment, destruction of the environment.

The field of perception of reality is considerably reduced: the subject is absentminded or unaware of half the things or persons present: he limits his relationships, his concerns, banishes all thought of expansion, takes pleasure in subordinate positions, 'makes himself small', retires into his shell as soon as he is approached: in its extreme form he offers large areas devoid of interest or perception (hysteria).

At the same time as he narrows the range of consciousness, he retires into the past, into his own past, his childhood memories, deep rooted beliefs, regrets, puerile and egocentric affective reactions: his behaviour regresses to the squalor, the disorder of early childhood: these symptoms reveal not only the wish to remain a child, but a sort of nostalgia for the mother's breast, a longing to be curled up in a corner, in an adult's arms. This retreat leads the subject back not only to his own past, but to the past of humanity; for it seems that we cannot retrace our steps without bringing with us all that has come to us from the collective; the errant imagination borrows the majority of its forms and symbols from primitive thought (Jung).

Just as reality, once perceived, immediately acquires a value, so this withdrawal is perceived as a tremendous reduction in the value of the world.

**

Reality is not delivered to your door. It is to be found by going to look for it, and the sense of reality is born of the very endeavour to discover it.

***

There are several forms of retreat from reality which do not present the same structures or the same gravity.

The simple asthenic withdraws to the extent that his energy is diminished: but there is no friction between him and his surroundings.

---

* Relates the refusal of reality to Heymans' categories.
** Clinical examples of the refusal of reality provided by Janet's patients.
*** Further clinical examples.

When too heavily charged, reality exhausts him, and he reduces the pressure by a more or less evident retreat. He is generally perfectly aware of the maladjustment produced, in spite of this lowering of the tension, and it does not become permanent.

In the really severe cases of psychasthenia, with the obsessional and morbidly scrupulous, the paralysis of action may become subjectively very painful.

*

Slowness, irresolution, scruples, obsession, incoherence, absence of mind, are only secondary effects of the reduction of the function of reality. Prolonged crises of scruple can lead to a true precocious senility which sterilises intelligence and perception. The state of diffused scruple, the constitutional perplexity which, with the best will in the world, is produced by some forms of moral education, leads to hardly less lamentable results. The disease is so widespread in cultured circles, particularly in those where the development of the inner life is specially cultivated, that one can hardly go to too great a length to prevent it, if one wishes civilised education to remain virile: a flexible education is required, without excessive strictness or inquisitorial supervision, using active methods from earliest childhood, very great frankness on sex questions, training in exact, practical tasks, which combat what Vittoz has rightly called the 'mental vagrancy' of the psychasthenic, also found in many other unanchored lives. What differentiates the psychasthenic from the types we are going to discuss, and particularly from the schizoid, is that he is not altogether affectively alienated from the surrounding world, nor from an adjusted life. On the contrary, he considers them as ideals, and suffers because he cannot attain them. He is weak, he has not abdicated from combat with reality: even his troubles (obsessions, etc.) are due to a frantic effort to achieve reality.

In the paranoiac of the persecuted type, the great misunderstood, the cleavage is no longer felt as despair, as with the psychasthenic, but as friction, in an aggressive discordance. He can neither do without the world nor adapt himself to it. Often, as the result of a humiliation, or a series of humiliations, he has turned away, affectively, from the world, but without breaking contact: he even becomes hallucinated by this contact, which is obsessional through failing to be intimate, and he interprets its constant indiscretion as systematic hostility. It is untrue to say that this is only a pseudo-rupture with reality, since the paranoiac is haunted by his surroundings and deliberately tries to exercise an influence on them. Behind the obsession the rupture is so

* Further clinical examples.

real that no change of surroundings ever cures the persecuted: they reconstruct a new delirium in the new background. It is, however, true to say that he does not turn his back on truth, he withdraws from it by moving as it were backwards and pushing it away with both hands. It is as if he could never break contact with a reality which has suddenly become hostile, and burns him up instead of warming him. The affective discordance is the same, but here the individual reacts with a basic aggressiveness, instead of reacting by retreat and cacatony. He builds up his autistic world within reality, instead of above it, in the empyrean, but he knows reality only to combat it, break it to pieces, drive it out in favour of his own system.[12]

It is in the schizoid states that autism is most clearly marked and has the most formidable consequences. However reluctant one may be to approach normal psychology through the medium of pathology, it would be lacking in the appreciation due from the psychologist to the psychiatrist not to give such an outstanding example of the way in which psychological explanations of everyday life can be derived from the findings of the mental hospital.

At the beginning of the century Kraepelin, before Minkowski[13] wrote of 'the rupture of affective contact with reality' as one of the most terrible disintegrations of personality it is given to man to know. This disintegration had already been noted, particularly by Bleuler, under the name of schizophrenia.
*

The psychosis is in fact characterised by two traits:

1. All the elementary functions of the psyche; memory, intelligence, etc., are intact, although their incoherence resembles mania.

2. But they function according to a curious psychic mechanism which Bleuler has called *autism*, a broken circuit with the environment.[14] This detachment may be selective, the contact being maintained in other zones. It is expressed by mimicry: the patient turns his head away, wears a veil. 'Autistic', as compared with 'realistic' thinking, is no longer determined by the demands of reality, no longer tries to communicate intelligibly or to direct activity towards real ends.
**

. . . The schizophrenic is active, and as often extraverted as introverted. The woman who has the *idée fixe* that she must buy a piano, useless, and disastrous to her modest budget, is not content with acting or dreaming her ambition, she goes out and buys it. There is therefore an

* Describes earlier efforts to define schizophrenia.
** Clinical symptoms of schizophrenia.

autistic activity just as much as autistic affectivity or thinking: this makes one appreciate the difference between introversion and maladjustment. I can shut myself up in an action just as much as in a reverie: like the patient who is driving in a nail and never wavers an instant from his little preoccupation even when someone shouts 'Help' just behind him. Normal activity starts from a personal impetus, but expands into a real environment in order to integrate it. In the schizophrenic there is a brutal cleavage between the one and the other. His actions are 'actions without a future', 'petrified reactions' (Minkowski), and not a medium of communication with the world. They stiffen into absolutes, blindfold the future. In extreme cases they do not expect a result. An icy void surrounds them. Even the patient feels a sense of vertigo which drives him restlessly onward, trying to fill all his time, without the shortest interval, as if he feared that peaceful relaxation amongst things and happenings, that vital confidence which is the element of contemplation and ease even in activity.[15]

*

This rupture of affective contact gives a stereotyped effect to behaviour, with a predominance of immobility or of rigid and sterile gestures. This stereotyping affects thought and feeling also.

Normal reverie is still only partly detached; sometimes it works more or less on behalf of reality; schizophrenic reverie expels reality; the repetition of one or two poor quality ideas creates a void all around. The schizophrenic lives solely in the past (the sulky morbidity of Borel, morbid regrets). But this past is a crude past, detached from any sense of time: reproaches and regrets stand out against a background of what has been, without liaison with the present, as if time were stationary. The schizophrenic feels neither anguish nor emotion: he lives in the objective; one of them, writing what he called his biography, mentioned objects only.

When he thinks, he gives way to a frantic rationalisation. Life is everywhere replaced by abstract formulae. One of his most constant attitudes is antithesis: yes or no, all or nothing, useful or harmful, good or evil, allowed or forbidden. One patient, for instance, submits himself for some time to a 'strict' military discipline, then switches over to the other extreme, refuses to work and advocates the principle of 'absolute' indulgence. There is the same rigidity in everything, which is betrayed by a propensity to a morbid geometry. The only criterion of value is geometric or quantitative: one of them, at sixteen, was already doubtful of the solidity and verticality of every wall. Or he

* More clinical examples of schizophrenia.

is overcome by a mania for symmetry: he takes care to walk exactly in the middle of the street, or is always trying to achieve a perfectly symmetrical pose in front of a mirror. 'The pattern', said one, 'is everything in life to me. Life displays neither symmetry nor regularity, and that is why I have to create reality.'

*

We have dealt particularly with this picture of a psychosis, because even its minor structures shed light on a number of traits found in normal behaviour or on its immediate fringes. As the portrait of the schizophrenic grew clearer, Kretschmer and Bleuler were able to describe a schizoid constitution and a schizothymic character, in which the principal traits corresponded almost point for point with clinical findings.

**

Just as the majority of cycloids are 'warm' so the majority of schizoids are 'dry' and 'cold'. They are not at all aware of this, living in the radiance of their inner hypersensitivity which does not, however, permeate their relationships with others. Unsociable and timid, they turn to the outer world only an icy countenance, and create the impression of being impenetrable, inaccessible or sullen. They may produce geniuses like Frederick II or types of bestial cruelty like the last Caesars. If they are also slightly hypomanic they are improvisers, founders of sects, prophets of humanitarian ideas, bizarre religions, minority doctrines, nature cults and nudism, or perhaps loquacious popularisers of ideas. If the dominant schizoid trait is more marked, they fall into vague, obscure exaltation on mystical or metaphysical themes, with a tendency to systematisation or schematisation. Jung has clearly shown that the majority of intellectual systematisations are instruments fabricated by a fear of living, to protect us from living experience. Schizoids carry to a high degree disinterestedness and contempt for money, which serve as an alibi for a contempt for action and conflict. In every cause they support, they aspire to a sublime purity, which authorises them not to compromise themselves. They would like to make man happy, but only in dreams, by means of one or two fixed ideas which admit no modification: for they are also fanatics of the sterile antithesis which extracts from the living and continuing richness of the universe only an all or a nothing: utopians or nihilists, the human in-between is alien to them. Rigid doctrinaires or neurotic revolutionaries, they will preach the improvement of humanity, model education, the abolition of the death penalty, the

* Further schizophrenic attitudes.   ** Clinical examples of schizoid types.

city of the future, but in a sort of visionary trance. They are recruits to that sometimes touching, sometimes irritating army of 'idealists' who persist in 'sublimating' problems until they are more orchestrated with sighs than with arguments; or who seek in realms as remote as possible, through Buddhist, theosophist or occult initiations, authority for being confused, ineffective and precious. They love adorning their projects with schemas, plans and mathematical demonstrations. Their blend of mysticism, and their union of woolly ideology and systematic thinking is one of the most typical syndromes of the intellectual schizoid type. The types quoted are the inferior forms. But a Kant or a Kierkegaard approaches genius, the one at its fiery, the other at its frigid pole, the marriage of a rather tense mysticism with an astonishing capacity for dialectic. Poe raised this blend of mysticism and calculation to a form of aesthetics. Often, instead of dreaming of humanitarian utopias, schizoids simply turn away from men and take refuge in the silent world of things: if they have a cyclothymic element in their character they love things with tenderness, the affective rupture which has led them to this choice being only apparent in the rather tense or affected quality of their feelings: for, after all, they love things as against men, and not as almost inseparably mingled with the human presence: if this cyclothymic element is absent, a schizoid rationalism intervenes and develops geometric patterns: mania for collecting, avarice, etc.

Schizoid action and expression are marked by an absence of immediate relationship between psychological stimulus and motor reaction. Transmission is obstructed by barrages, parasitical impulses, and cacatonic mechanisms. Bleuler has described their 'affective rigidity' which leaves an impression of affectation, formality, solemnity or pedantry. Kretschmer speaks of their 'aristocratism', preciosity of language, affectation in bodily hygiene or in dress, mannerisms.[16] In minor forms they are recognisable by a slight styling, giving them an elegance of appearance which usually lacks the roundness of the cycloid. The word distinction was coined for them, and indicates both the deeper source and the nature of their way of living. At their best, they display qualities of tact, good taste and delicacy. Sometimes their restraint turns into military stiffness.

Their psychic rhythm is a zigzag, their temper versatile yet rigid, moving in a series of withdrawals and discharges, long periods of latency and sudden flare-ups. They deflect conversation at right angles, suddenly becoming ironic, cold or disagreeable. According to whichever extreme they approach they are remarkable either for their tenacity or their excessive instability, often swinging from the one to the other. The cycloid is accommodating; they are often intransigent, for lack of a normal affective level. Here also they are all or nothing, suddenly delighted, suddenly offended, by trifles. Kretschmer says of them that they do not pitch and toss like the cycloid, but leap forward and then huddle back upon themselves, leaping from one extreme to the other, over the middle way.

Their religion tends to a blend of vague, obscure mysticism, and a rigid or doctrinaire phariseeism. If the former predominates they found esoteric sects outside the Church. If the latter, they entrench the soul of their Church behind the barricades of fanaticism and the scaffolding of aggressive apologetics.

Their sexual life is complicated, particularly by the schizoid cleavage between a turbulent genital sexuality and an infantile psychic sexuality.
*

The treatment of such maladjustment is directed towards the imagination and the discipline of the inner life. It begins with the earliest education. The child with such predispositions must find an understanding background, otherwise he will withdraw still further. Nothing is more fatal to him than an aggressive severity or even indifference to his fervours. But whilst accepting his inner life and without forcing it too much, for it is rebellious, he must be helped to keep it within normal limits, the normal for him being higher than for others. He must acquire through self-discipline a form of sublimation, a training in flexibility, so that he is not tempted by his natural rigidity into abrupt repressions. Lefrancq–Brunfaut introduce variations into their teaching, according to whether the maladjustment is only an inner discord (inner maladjustment), or whether it violently conflicts with the environment (maladjusted behaviour). Here are the main lines of the treatment.

As an intellectual corrective they suggest, in cases of inner maladjustment, the development of the intuitive way of thinking, which puts him in direct touch with some value or reality, even if only one, which he can experience as actually present in the world outside himself. The warmth of this experience should render him capable of communication and human flexibility. When he is religious, he will dogmatise with rigidity and fanaticism: he will be directed towards the mystical, historical, psychological aspects of his faith. As an intellectual he is a born systematiser: he will be directed away from abstract techniques which are all too favourable to his own rigidity,

* Further examples of schizoid types.

towards the experimental sciences, history, literary and artistic culture. As a man of action, he indulges in *a priori* planning, utopian strategies: he will be launched into the modest yet vital tasks of everyday tactics and adaptations. When his maladjustment leads to behaviour problems, which are more offensive, he will be met by the resistance of obstacles which in their turn disorganise his aggression. Intellectual measures will never be more than secondary here, but an understanding of the concrete is sometimes useful as an apprenticeship to the inevitable, which shatters the pretensions of a way of thinking that despises reality: it compels the schizoid to recognise objects that do not depend on him and constrains him to accept compromise and collaboration with other existences than his own.

The acquisition of muscular control is needed to replace the schizoid in an environment he has deserted. Those with an inner maladjustment have consummated the divorce between their bodies and reality, just as between their thoughts and reality. The capacity for physical adjustment, like sensitivity, works at haphazard, sometimes retarding muscular behaviour (gestures that come too late), sometimes causing excessively avid or staccato gestures, inhibitions (fixed postures), perseveration, condensations and slurring of speech (clumsiness, stammering, verbal confusion). The painful sense of being gauche and clumsy, awkward, stiff and therefore ridiculous, which they have suffered from early childhood, only deepens the maladjustment. It is essential to restore the capacity for related action, which has gone to pieces. The sufferer must recover a normal resilience: sports, dancing, athletics are fundamental to his psychological health, whereas adults, too proud of his seriousness or too concerned for his fragility, often try to keep him from them, as not being 'for him'. He finds all too many supporters in his first repugnance to exteriorisation, which has to be overcome gently and progressively. Those with behaviour problems have not only a disorganised motor system: motor adaptation is thwarted by systems of movement formed in a closed circle, repeating the rigidity of ideas which, at the other extreme of personality, strengthen his resistance to reality: tics, mannerisms, stereotyped attitudes. None of them has any meaning, or fulfils the purpose of movement, which is to locate and connect. Motor relationships must be restored by starting from the very beginning. These morbid crystallisations must be countered by practising primitive automatic movements, such as breathing, sucking, swallowing, walking, speech and mime, which are the preliminary apparatus of a related life. The extraverted type will be taught to breathe deeply and regularly, to eat and swallow calmly, to walk steadily without jerks, to speak in a calm, quiet voice, to overcome, if necessary, his stammering and stuttering, to sing in order to gain confidence in his vocal system, to repress his grimaces, his affectations and preciousness, and to develop a natural manner and a frank expression, without reserve and without excess of feeling.

It is dangerous to place the introverted type too early in an exposed or leading social role, such as a command or a post of visible authority: he would find there fresh grounds for intimidation, and a too humiliating breakdown might complete his overthrow: it is better to give him a subordinate position, where, without any problems of prestige, he may work in confidence and friendship with a guide (Lefrancq–Brunfaut). We should, however, add that it is useful to accustom him little by little to a responsibility which will give him assurance, a minimum of authority which will rehabilitate him in his own eyes, and of responsibility which will compel him to impress his will on the external world. The active type can be trained to collaboration by working with a team where he will be kept in check by ragging and where a rather primitive form of camaraderie will teach him, better than any expression of tenderness to which he is still inaccessible, to accept the existence of external wills and resistances.

IMAGINARY REFUGES

In simple cases the weak react to a failure of adaptation purely and simply by emotional discharge. 'He who is discontented with himself', wrote Nietzsche, 'is always seeking for revenge: we shall be his victims.' He vents his irritation at his defeat indiscriminately on his surroundings. His bad temper, if repressed, turns into recrimination against society or the authorities, with a hatred of happiness and of others' success. But resentment implies a certain conflict and does not suit every temperament. The schizoid usually re-establishes his equilibrium at his own level of weakness, which allows him to acquire a serenity within his powers. He does not flee from reality into nothingness, the hideous void that surrounds the schizophrenic patient, but into an inner universe which he substitutes for the real world, and which he enjoys more than reality. These constructions of the imagination take on a great many forms, but all have in common the fact that they replace a difficult adaptation by an easier one.
*

These worlds of escape may remain purely internal, and replace

* Examples from Rousseau and Janet and from literature, of escapes from reality.

action adjusted to the world by subjective satisfactions which have strayed beyond its confines. They may also intrude into everyday life and permeate even the substance of the dreamer with their fantastic divagations. In either case the tendency to objectivisation continues to function, since even unreality is composed of objects which oppose one: there is not, strictly speaking, any 'passive imagination'. But instead of finding an outlet in the realities that confront it, this objectivisation overflows the margin of the real, where it occupies a phantom space, real space having been banished, and is isolated from the vital relationships which would give it location.

*   *   *

Defeat or delay is usually at the root of the propriofective activity of the imagination. The desires which have not been able to find their way into reality are not relieved of tension. There is energy available which must be released on some desert island of consciousness, and the creative self is faced with a false situation which must be redressed.

The unspent energy is used up in the creation of imaginary satisfactions. The schoolboy struggling with a problem instead of going fishing sees nothing but streams and fishing rods on the ceiling of his classroom. The adolescent, whose love is not yet fixed, beguiles his romantic soul with countless fictitious and incompatible romances. In the average man this catharsis often lacks material; he seeks it in the theatre, in novels or in history, which sometimes provide him with a second life more glowing than the first. The more creative, instead of borrowing from without, draw it from the depths of their own being.

We must, however, avoid an erroneous simplification. Even from the purely biological angle, this fantasy activity has a far more complex function than simply to provide a safety valve for the incompetent at action. It contributes to our vital living room by extending it into a space beyond space, in which we can dissipate our ill-fortuned desires, without entirely renouncing their promise. It seems to be not only a liquidation of defeat, but the reaction of life to its defeats, a refusal of defeat, a byway of the essential 'however'. We have so deplored the destructive influence of the withdrawn imagination, that we neglect its temporising function. It releases tension pleasantly when an aspiration has been thwarted, it stimulates by a taste of satisfaction, precise enough to whet the appetite, deceptive enough to leave one still hungry and driven to action. It allows one to wait and mature a renewal of the frustrated action. It offers a symbolic, tranquillising expression to the thwarted tendency: for instance, fear of a father is diverted into a phobia of watch dogs—or a sublimation which carries it further: the same fear transformed into ambition or emulation of one's superiors. Thus the compensating activity of the imagination balances on an ambivalent tightrope, always in danger of slipping over into autism, but perhaps also maintaining a certain practical resilience in the less happy intervals of action. So long as it maintains this delicate, flexible role, it is proof of vitality and not of debility.

Fichte and Hegel reconstructed a world when Germany was lying in ruins, and Péguy admitted that it was in a state of sombre despair that he wrote his trilogy of hope. The future gave them what had been the ardent desire of their dreams.

However, this inner succour is a perpetual danger to the exteriorisation of action. Even its charms are likely to make us prefer the facile to the solid, imperceptibly colouring reality with the hues of unreality. Thus the enduring, vital lie creeps invisibly into the tissue of our days. We know its morbid forms; the mother distracted at the loss of her son, imagines for years that he is not dead but travelling, and elaborates each day the details of his life, without ever wearying. For Freud, the immense psychic field which includes dream and psychosis is built up on this ideo-affective compensation for the wishes repressed by the reality principle. The living lie is also everyday experience. The beginnings of dream and the first draft of psychosis, it sometimes takes root even in childhood, particularly as children love playing at identification, spending whole weeks being an animal or a flower, like the child Bettina, who had herself watered by her playmates. Children who suffer from being ill-treated or illegitimate, or from scenes of family violence, are apt to imagine that they come from an unknown family of rich or illustrious descent: this myth, more or less formulated in many children's minds, explains the success of the theme of the lost or abandoned child in literature (*Sans Famille*, *Oliver Twist*, etc.).[17]
*

But it may invade the whole of life and falsify its symphony. Jules de Gaultier has described as '*bovarysme*'[18] the power given to certain persons to see themselves as other than they are, and to distort their vision of their surroundings, both things and persons, to make them conform to the will of the imagination.
**

* Rank on the myth of the hero in childhood.
** Further examples of the type of Madame Bovary.

The adjustment to reality is generally admitted to be a value in life. Thus defeat not only releases a stock of unemployed energy, it also unleashes processes of justification and simulation destined to conceal this defeat from the eyes of its victim. To these the bypaths of the imagination open a way. Having failed to achieve a real objective, consciousness provides itself with a substitute with which it is content, or persuades itself to be content. Tartarin's baobab grows in a great many of our gardens. And some fragments of a fallen greatness form a more precious universe to some victims of life than the most enviable promises of a reconquered existence. Sometimes these unsatisfied desires, having failed to find an outcome in their true colours, take on a disguise, without its being always clear whether they hope to smuggle themselves through as contraband, or are merely trying to make a cruel travesty of their misfortune.[19] The myth is formed at the point of convergence of these two attempts. A people, sick with intolerable anxiety, builds a fable around the Jew or the Jesuit. Or they idealise their past in song, to console themselves and to re-establish themselves in their own eyes. A diffused remorse often engenders the most violent myths, the explosive energy of a bad conscience being always the most inflammable. Finally it often happens that the imaginary world derived from a failure of adaptation establishes itself directly as a judge of the defeated consciousness. This is one of the mechanisms of the 'Superego' to which psychoanalysts have drawn attention. By surrounding myself with a fictitious world in which some malevolent power pursues me with its hatred, whether I call it destiny, misfortune, chance, public malice, or turn it into a vengeful deity shaped in the image of man's resentment, I thereby acquit myself of responsibility for my defeat.

*   *   *

Instead of withdrawing slowly and progressively upon a steadily diminishing substance, as in the fantasies of schizoid type, the imaginary world may explode around me, mingling actively with my outer life, stimulating it to a rich and sometimes overflowing activity. Claude, Borel and Robin have pointed out, even more clearly than Dupré, this opposition between constitutional mythomaniacs and schizoids. The schizoid, far from trying to realise his fantasies in the external world, elaborates them in order to escape it: the mythomaniac is alert, active, communicative, something of a gay dog. The schizoid, tense behind his barriers, is the least suggestible, the mythomaniac the most suggestible of men. The fictions of the former are restricted to set themes, which vary little once they have taken hold: the fictions of the mythomaniac are constantly modified on the spur of inspiration or the stimuli of the moment. Finally the schizoid does not try to draw them into reality, the mythomaniac finds it difficult to distinguish his fiction from reality and, like a child, is constantly mixing them up in a vague, general belief.

*

His lies are seldom isolated. They proliferate, without system, in perverse or puerile fabrications, according to whether affective abnormalities or intellectual weakness predominate in the personality. The subject invents romances and adventures in which he himself believes, with one reservation which we shall deal with later, and his audience is almost always taken in by his tone of sincerity and assurance. There was a little girl who was longing for a black frock promised her for her birthday. She told her schoolfellows that her mother was dead and did, in fact, appear in black: a little later she talked of her father's remarriage and gave as many details of the wedding as she had done of the funeral: it was only discovered later by accident that her mother was still living and at home. The fertility of invention and aplomb of the storyteller increase with the interest aroused. They seem possessed by what Dupré calls 'a drive to narration', or 'inventive pruritus'. The psychological basis of such a personality is an extraordinary appetite for notoriety, lacking an adequate intellectual instrument. This deviation lends a complicated, bizarre and pretentious turn to the constructs of imagination.

Simulation is always associated with fabrication. It is a lie acted, even more difficult and complex to maintain, since it brings multiple physical and psychological activities into play. It sometimes attains prodigious ability when aided by a great aptitude for imitation (this aptitude, which makes the good actor, is always indicative of mental hyperplasticity); by acute presence of mind, and exceptional tenacity (some even go to the extremes of self-mutilation or to undergoing operations); and finally by an unusual degree of muscular control.

When these traits are accentuated, mythomania becomes frankly abnormal. It is found particularly in younger subjects, and usually amongst women: when occurring in men, it is a sign of infantilism or feminism.

**

Is it possible . . . to discover the original disorder at the root of this mythomania, which would provide us with a comprehensive formula?

* Dupré on the mythomaniac lie.   ** Further types of mythomania.

There is clearly hyperemotivity, combined with hyperaesthesia of the sympathetic nervous system. Suggestibility is a no less important factor, and more generally speaking psycho-plasticity (following Dupré's terminology) which is based on a certain deficiency of perception and an abnormal absence of self-critical faculties. But a still more important factor seems to be the need to attract attention, whatever the means or the cost. It is an aberration of the need 'to be seen' which we shall study later. The mythomaniac personality is a depressed personality, which feels the need to counteract the depression, but only along the lines of least resistance. The half-lie, particularly when it is unconscious, thus evading responsibility, is the weak man's way of dominating others. 'To make other people accept a lie is a victory: it imposes on them a belief and a conduct they would never have had but for us; it means we make them move at our pleasure.'[20] The difficulty lies in reconciling the affective passivity revealed by such attitudes and the intellectual poverty of the mythomaniac invention, with the profusion of inventiveness which carries him even into the most hazardous undertakings.

*

. . . It is a question of strong interests or instincts which insist on some form of representation, although vitality is too impaired to integrate them into broadly objective behaviour. The need for representation, lacking adequate foundation, is subjected to a sort of contraction, or psychic hypochondria, and becomes from then onwards, over a large sector of behaviour, an obsessive compulsion to action. The subject is disintegrated by his need to simulate, and concentrates the limited energy at his disposal on this restricted interest. The vital purpose of exteriorisation is our objectivisation *amongst* men: representation crystallised in oneself becomes a spectacle *before* men; it makes us exclusively dependent on our audience, instead of throwing us into the free community of a common destiny. Thus the activity of the mythomaniac, this exteriorisation which seemed to set him apart from the evasions of the schizoid, is only apparent. It isolates him in a glittering world, without foundations, and completely sealed off from reality. Here he loses not only, as we shall see, his own consistency, but all sense of, and liking for, reality.

We have several times stumbled on this difficulty of tracing the frontiers between the constitutional and the acquired. Heredity can easily turn into a facile solution for the problems of psychotherapy. But Niemeyer has already shown that it is not so much the

* Comparison between mythomania and hysteria.

constitutional factor which predisposes to hysteria, as education and style of living, and that external conditions are less important than the manner in which the individual reacts to them. The dispositions which range from hysteria to mythomania seem to be grafted on to a precocious habit of losing direct contact with the real world and of abandoning control of the psyche to an undisciplined affectivity. They are fostered by any circumstance which excessively develops imagination and romanticism. They are tenacious, partly because they can develop so easily, even in early childhood: someone who has once reacted by flight to an important situation in childhood is very likely to react in a similar way all his life. Mythomania, which is natural in children, should disappear between the age of ten and fifteen. If it is slow to do so, or even if the child has already, before then, begun to display the symptoms mentioned earlier, he should be drawn away from games which are too favourable to his affective egocentricity: he should be accustomed to being open and direct, and offered a background in which feelings are expressed sincerely and restrainedly, and which does not overstimulate his emotivity by constant scenes and distractions, nor provoke a reaction into mannerisms by an excess of brutality. If his display of feeling is already spectacular and tyrannical—immoderate outbursts of despair, anger or gaiety, affectation, sulks, falsehood and invention—it is inadvisable to exacerbate them by punishment or public reproof, which would only pander to the love of excitement and strong emotion; the best way is to display a complete indifference, which touches him on a vital spot: one should not listen indulgently to his storytelling, and mannerisms should be met by coldness. These subjects lose their sense of the familiar and natural because they are not sufficiently occupied by practical realities: one should promote contact with things, opportunities of objective activity, particularly of humble activity, useful without being glorious, and manual activity where trickery brings its own physical punishment. Their need for the extraordinary and the marvellous must, however, be satisfied, though disciplined and sublimated, or it will become, by compensation, more disordered than ever.[21] In reading, or the cinema, which can be a particular poison to these easily moved natures, one must be most careful to avoid sentimentality, passion, exaltation and the conventional: a solid store of the marvellous, linked with action and the difficulties of conquest, can be found in history, in the scientific or heroic aspects of Christian culture. Through the poets and writers of schizoid type they can learn the marvels hidden in each ordinary hour of life. The strict intellectual disciplines of logic, mathematics, languages, exercise a useful pressure on the imagination. The exceptional plasticity of the hysterical personality, if treated at the outset, can be sublimated into fineness of perception, skill in operation and flexibility of action. In a paroxysm, anything that will provide the effect of a cold shower is to be recommended, from the icy comment that punctures exaltation, to an abrupt, unambiguous correction. Nervous crises are frequent in the adult and should be treated by violent physical shock (cold water), and particularly by immediate isolation.

THE REAL, THE UNREAL AND THE SUPRA-REAL

We have now dealt with the imagination as mistress of lies and error. But is this all experience can teach us of the imagination? Two centuries of 'cartesian' psychology, given a fresh life by too much sickly romanticism, would be enough to close the chapter here and now, if greater voices had not spoken with authority above the noise of prejudice and statistics. When Novalis writes; 'Poetry is the absolute reality. The more poetic, the more true', or again: 'Genius is the faculty of speaking of imaginary objects as if they were real objects, and of treating them as such'; or Nietzsche, 'I have a horror of reality. To tell the truth, I see nothing real there any more, it is only a phantasmagoria'; or Rimbaud: 'Real life is absent. We are not in the world', shall we call it a disintegrating escapism, or a morbid divagation? Their experience, like that of a hundred other seers, has never been plotted or graphed, but if we cannot all enter into it as deeply as they did, it is open to us, as Aragon suggests, to practise it in the same way as one might practise the spiritual life. The experience of the poet is of the same value to the psychologist as the experience of the mystic in the life of religion. He is the prophet of a universe which is accessible only to experience. And between the spinners of impotent fantasies and the poet-seers, we find the same ambiguities and the same essential differences as between the mystics of the mental hospital and those who are justified by their spiritual fecundity. The former are in exaltation over ruins, the latter bring in a new life.

What is this life, more real than life itself? A whole line of philosophers, poets, mystics and wise men speak of it, from Kepler and Paracelsus to Cusa, Bruno and Boehme; from Master Eckhart, St. John of the Cross, Poverello, the Jesuit humanists described by the Abbé Bremond, to the great romantics of the last century. A profound kinship unites us with nature. We lost it through a historic (or trans-historic) fall, which favoured the movement towards individuation and separation from the universal sympathetic participation in the One. Further and further removed from the fullness of the world, we lead the withered lives of a plant half severed from its stem. The world that we call 'objective' is a convenient convention, but a poor convention, the least real of all our fictions. But our state is not entirely hopeless. We retain obscure memories of the lost unity; a presentiment, a face, a branch in blossom, allow us to catch a glimpse; it permeates the immense, enveloping, unconscious areas of life, it appears nightly in our dreams in veiled, uncertain forms, it slips even into our hallucinations and madness. But we have lost the key to life integrated in the All. The poet is its custodian. From time to time he opens for us this mysterious door. He teaches us to use imagination as a vision of the world in its profound reality, showing us each being in its kinship with the unity of the All. Here poetic meditation does not isolate us from the world. 'Every descent into the self, every glance within, is at the same time ascent—assumption—a glance at the true external reality' (Novalis). He who in wonderment at the imagery within stops there, stops halfway on the path to reconciliation. The role of the imagination, far from withdrawing or isolating us, is to restore us to that state of prophetic naïveté which, beyond consciousness and beyond perceptions, brings us into relationship with total reality, by a richer, more certain way than that of the closed perception and the isolated concept. Internal, external, the closer we approach reality, the imagination that reveals the soul of the world no longer makes a clear distinction between the two. It draws us back into the heart of all things, where we meet the vastness of the universe, so that one may speak of a vision, a hearing, a touching which move from the inner to the outer, and even of taking root in the world by the very fact of self-communion. 'Shut your eyes and you will see' (Joubert). The awareness directed solely to the external is short and blind. By withdrawing temporarily from the knowledge produced by the intellect and the senses, the self is not detached from its own body or the body of the world; on the contrary, it gathers itself together, both in order to know and to be, and to act with the whole of itself.[22]

*

* Realism and surrealism in art and literature.

5

THE MASTERY OF ACTION

ACTIVE AND INACTIVE

THE sole proof of a man lies in his deeds. They are the only irrefutable confirmation of the value of his words, and the authenticity of his thoughts. This is because we are thrown into action before we can reflect on action, compelled by urgency before we can deliberate. Our actions, moreover, reflect the smallest detail of our psycho-organic equilibrium. The study of character culminates in the study of action, the nature of which dominates all other aspects. It is even liable to engulf them, so we must first limit the scope of our subject, and isolate the definition of activity which we shall use as a criterion, from any allied concept.

A first crude differentiation may perhaps be established between the *active* and the *inactive*. Unless we enlarge the concept to cover a vast and vague opposition between strength and weakness of vitality, activity can only be measured by the extent of movement expended on a given act, all other things, incidentally, being equal. We use the word *extent*, where Heymans, who classes activity as one of the three fundamental elements of character, speaks of *quantity* of movement. There is more here than a shade of meaning. We shall see, in fact, that a basic inactivity may lead to considerable motor agitation, which should not be confused with a normal inclination to activity. In addition, even in normal conditions, human activity takes on a form which cannot be defined by the simple volume of gesture. The child who resists making a movement does not necessarily refuse physical effort: he will undertake ten long and painful contortions to avoid the simple gesture of obedience or adjustment: he refuses a certain form of movement, for instance the imagination, the adjustment, the obedience that it requires. Here again quantity and quality, space and tempo are closely linked. Just as we have seen that psychological tension always implies a certain richness of content, so activity is defined both by the abundance of movement, its range in time, its extension in space, and the ease with which it is performed. All these diverse data are covered by the notion of extension, and in doubtful cases, it will be the ease of performance, revealing the basic disposition, which will indicate the diagnosis. We shall say, therefore, modifying Heymans' formula:

If two men have the same esteem for the same object, if one is capable of action to an extent A in order to acquire it, and the other to the extent 2A, we shall say of the second that he is more active than the first.

Or again:

An active man is one who needs only slight motives for action, and an inactive man, one with the opposite temperament, their emotivity being equal (for emotivity favours certain motives, particularly in primary types).

Thus we isolate the motor drive of a psychological situation from an affective interest other than the sole desire to act: for one may also enjoy action for reasons other than the performance of action, such as the pleasure of dominating others, the pride of success, the pleasure of handling or mastering a large body of men. There are some empirical tokens: the mobile, busy types, the man who gesticulates, jumps from his seat, comes and goes on the least pretext, always busy at his work, particularly when it is fresh work, always occupied even when he could do nothing, does not know how to postpone a task, starts on it as soon as it is conceived and completes it without delay. Physical education favours activity by developing muscular initiative: debility, or simply lack of exercise, slows it down.

*

This active disposition must be distinguished from the *capacity to work* which brings into play a basic capacity for resistance which is not available to every active person. Neither are the active always active without stopping. Some have need of respite, physical relaxation or meditation, which others can do very well without.

According to Heymans' correlations, activity in this sense promotes the control of impulsiveness and hence the predominance of long-term indirect interests over immediate interests: the active are less dilettante, more punctual, have greater practical sense and are more economical than their counterparts. But although it helps these secondary traits, it also promotes presence of mind and quickness of reaction by a disinclination to fantasy and a preference for effective achievement as against art and the forms of inner life. It adds considerably to demonstrativeness, patience, the acceptance of tasks incurred, to loyalty, to dexterity. It attenuates the manifestations of sexual interest, disarms fear (soldiers exposed to panic must be given something to do):

* Biological basis of activity and inactivity.

it encourages a disposition to subordinate others to oneself and to despise the ineffective. Above all the active person can only find his real fulfilment, even the fulfilment of his inner life, if he has one, in action: cut off from action or even from his habitual field of action, his means are considerably diminished and he may come to be judged far below his true worth. Inaction fatigues him more than action.
*

There are no 'inactive' persons, only the less active. Inactivity tends to degrade emotivity by weakening the dynamics of affective discharges in favour of passive, inner enjoyment. At the same time it encourages mental secondarity and inertia. However, in spite of what this last correlation might lead us to expect, it leads to a predominance of immediate interests over long-term or indirect ones: if the inactive are still to some extent emotive, they have in fact only their emotivity to drive them to action, and emotivity encourages primarity; if they are inemotive they are at the mercy of random happenings: thus they are often found to be extravagant, dilettante, sensual, unpunctual, and lacking common sense. Inactivity promotes egoism and the deterioration (not only the quantitative reduction) of action into imaginary action, or into the purely imaginative performance of action. It tends to discouragement, to discrepancy between words and deeds, to falsehoods: an inactive person when required to make an effort to master a concrete situation, prefers to distort it or deny its existence rather than to produce the required initiative.
**

Language is our first line of retreat. Originally it was an integral part of action. Instead of the heavy, limited repertory of gestures, it provides a system of minute, more analytical gestures, which are capable of perfecting the duties performed by the other muscles. The savage shouts as he goes into battle, the civilised demoralise their adversaries by speeches so that their weapons may have more effect: the method is the same. But we are always caught between the rival temptation of blind agitation and passive contemplation. We make boats in order to be able to cross rivers, then to enjoy being on the water, then to show off to our friends. Language regresses in the same way. It can become so subtle and imperious as to lead another to act in my stead, or even to the point of persuading me that it still contains some reality, even when it issues upon a void. After having been action, then an agent of action, it has become cut off from action and

* Relates the concepts of activity and inactivity to Heymans' categories.
** Clinical symptoms of inactivity.

a substitute for it. The inactive use words as a form of half-naïve, half-calculated magic. Language is very close to gesture, and this magic begins with gesture itself, which is nearer to the act than the articulated word. The child, as Piaget[1] has shown, is impregnated with magic, which is reabsorbed by the normal man through the effect of action, except for a few grains of superstition left in the dark crannies of his behaviour. Traces remain in the inactive, much less openly admitted. They behave as if they believed in the effectiveness of gesture, or of the accompanying words which are not followed by decisive actions. See what happens when someone drops a pencil: either they show no reaction, or they sketch the outline of a movement to pick it up: they look busy, but someone always happens to complete the operation before they do, and they only have time to utter a word of regret or excuse which, with the abortive gesture, reassures them of their goodwill. Vapid in word and gesture, the inactive type idolises, more or less consciously, the verbal formula: where he should help, he sympathises; where run to the rescue, he exhorts; decide, he discourses. Once he has spoken, he believes all is done. When he has masked a reality by a pleasing interpretation, or even by setting it in a reassuring light, by some noble or conciliatory formula, or wisecrack, provided they dispense with the necessity of seeing clearly and intervening, he feels his duty is satisfied. The illusion is generally carried to great lengths: lacking retrospective irony, he is really convinced that he acted through having spoken. Thus one meets a great many kindhearted people whose goodwill is not particularly alert, or whose noble sentiments are fed more on eloquence than on intent to action: they are permanently unaware of their practical egoism and ineffectiveness. This talkative egoism is one of the weaknesses of the southern European, and a constant source of scandalised astonishment to serious and laconic Northerners.[2]

Even communication by language leads to too many objective consequences for some inactive persons. Why compromise oneself when one can have thoughts that commit one to nothing, that no one will know, or that none will take seriously, so quintessential, so inefficacious they can be? Faced with a provocation to action, they react by secreting a system, or a plan without a future, which occupies them entirely; some get as far as the project, an enthusiastically detailed project, that will never progress beyond this state of fervour. Periods of crisis, in which the individual, the collectivity, the nation are struggling temporarily in an impasse, are particularly subject to this ideological parasitism. It not only proliferates on the printed page;

each individual conscience avoids the burden of precise responsibility which awaits him, by pretentious reflections. It blocks the administration and government offices, where one plan of reconstruction succeeds another, reports pile on reports, estimates on estimates, and intelligence runs riot with all the profusion of decadence, creating innumerable bottlenecks in the transmission of authority. And scepticism installs itself amongst the hurly-burly, sometimes organised as agitations, sometimes as professional automatism. And to add to the confusion come the conciliators at any price, the inventors of well-argued imbecilities.

Such phenomena on a grand scale are very similar to those that occur in the feverish brain of some depressed types. At the very heart of their incapacity to act, there flows a torrent of mental rumination, which has been given the name 'mentism'.[3] Limited themes, without creative dynamic, yet lively and disturbing, impose themselves almost automatically, revolve and repeat themselves against a background of anxiety and anguished doubt. The phenomenon is analogous to that of the 'compulsive flight of ideas', but it is a circular flight, a mad turning around the same spot. In an inactive but normal person this inner agitation is tolerated, even entertained with pleasure. But it evokes too much possibility of action for the depressed: they are bowed down by a kind of insensate productivity. 'I get myself into a panic', said one patient to Janet,[4] 'by imagining an enormous amount of work I shall certainly never have to do: I am afraid of the people I meet and I wonder what they will ask me to do. I get upset beforehand and I try to do a quantity of things that no one has asked for: this is what tires and depresses me.' The fact is well known in certain states of overwork, fever or intoxication. It lies at the basis of obsessions.[5] Now an obsession is an inferior form of thinking which takes the place of effective thought when activity is weakening. The obsessional person tries to act, but does not succeed in performing a real action; he recommences this substitute for action indefinitely, without achieving the peace of knowing something performed. One can establish the equation: inactivity $+$ weakness $=$ mental or motor agitation. But this agitation is the contrary of action: the agitated person performs many little panic actions which cannot be resumed into a whole; acts of poor quality or devoid of significance, tics, gesticulations, etc. without real meaning, acts lacking that extension which, we have seen, characterises normal action.[6] The consciousness of the obsessional person is curious; his obsession is painful, he knows that his mind is concentrating on a purposeless activity, without advantage or real motive, and he feels driven to it, although sometimes he himself provides the pretexts for continuing it. Yet he does pursue it, changing if need be the content of his obsession, but never its exhausting rhythm. This content is incidentally less interesting in its material than in its forms: the obsession creates precisely those mechanisms of thought which are best capable of obstructing action: to reach an impossible precision in a given task, to strive indefinitely to recall some inaccessible memory, or to find some absurd solution; to ponder over a remorse which paralyses spiritual life, always to be perfecting something, even if it is only a way of sneezing, unsuccessfully explaining an insoluble problem, vainly pursuing a project foredoomed to failure. Obsession is indeed an effort grafted on to a state of weakness, as Janet admitted in his later work, and thus a reaction against inactivity. But this reaction follows the very processes of inaction; as the inactive are not free from the fear of action, they make a poor effort, systematising too much, applying it at a single point, instead of spreading it over the whole psychic field: they carry on too long and the means used are absurd. Many inactive persons, without having pathological obsessions, have 'little obsessions' and are the casualties of action, who have taken the first step towards recovery which throws them back again into their weakness, as if they had hoped to fail at the first attempt, so that they need not try to go forward any more.

The evasion of action remains possible by retreat into the obscurity of imagination and dream, something less than thought, which having a stricter discipline may perhaps by accident recall the requirements of reality. Not that we would thereby depreciate a life of imagination and contemplation. A constitutional inactivity may be a fortunate accident for the great artist or the great contemplative, but it is the source neither of the genius of the one nor of the spirituality of the other. It inclines them to turn their gaze inward, there to effect a conquest which is *another* activity. We recall, for instance, the escape into unreality which is connected with poetic action. 'I have a horror of everything that is petty and material,' one of Janet's patients declared haughtily, 'housework, collections, photographs, travel, of everything, in fact', and here she ingenuously reveals the cause of her horror, 'which means something to be done'.
*

The fear of action leads not only to these diverse forms of retreat from commitment, but intervenes in the remaining forms of behaviour to cause disorders ranging from simple embarrassments to total paralysis.

* Examples of inactive behaviour.

In the weakest form it occurs as a sort of general restriction of life. One is often deceived as to the nature of some 'simple' and austere lives; such asceticisms are due less to the virtue they claim to be, than to an inability to master a wider destiny. Desires, adventures, luxury, ambition cost as much in care and trouble as in money. How many good, continent, modest folk there are, who have indeed known the stirrings of passion, but who have never had the energy to cross their Rubicon.

*

Others are not content with such defensive action, but as a precaution oppose the activity of others, which might later entail their own. They prevent any activity taking place around them, whether by tyrannising everyone on the pretext of protecting them and taking care of their health, or by attacking whatever happens around them from a systematic hatred of action.[7] Lying, the lying which diverts the necessity of action is, finally, a common weapon of the inactive.

Timidity covers at least three aspects: a psychological and emotive aspect,[8] a social aspect which we shall meet again later, and a factor of inactivity. Janet remarks truly that if the timid person 'suffers from a disease of social behaviour' his timidity disappears with familiar friends, who have already classified him, or with anonymous groups who are not concerned with classifying him. He is particularly afraid of actions which entail a positive or negative social judgment, and which involve gaining the approval of others. He is thus, in this sense, a 'social asthenic' who is afraid, not of men, but of the possibilities of action they occasion.[9] His behaviour is disintegrated each time this act of conquest is required of him: he is seized by a sort of psycho-motor ataxia, casting all his reactions, ideas or gestures into disorder, out of harmony with himself and his surroundings. Anything that promotes action and social status, such as money, good clothes, a title, reduces timidity, but poverty and defeat are its greatest ally.

The fear of action can itself be active enough to create artificial obstacles which may perhaps one day be overcome, but which at least postpone the feared undertaking. Sometimes a great deal of trouble is spent on this manoeuvre, but the activity expended is only apparent. It consists of automatisms, habits, even of suggested substitutes which will be easier than the task so unwillingly accepted. The pleasure, the favour, the position one requires, may perhaps demand an effort complicated by decision, perseverance and realisation: one provides a verbal substitute by raising objections or by elementary acts of

* Quotes an anecdote by Landsberg.

obstruction. A stick is enough to derail a train. Or a torrent of initiative is produced when it is too late and the subject knows more or less consciously that this pseudo-activity will never be transformed into real activity. Proust's hero embarks on endless investigations of Albertine's conduct, when Albertine is dead and the investigation pointless: if she had been alive he would never have had the courage to pursue them. When the demon of action stirs in an inactive person, it is in retrospect.

The crisis of melancholic depression shows us the complete disintegration of action through fear of action. In order to avoid the least initiative, the sick person persuades himself in advance that all will fail. It is this anticipation which lends his universe the unvarying hue of pessimism and catastrophe. Nothing is beautiful. Every catastrophe is about to happen and he will share in every catastrophe. Concepts of catastrophe mingle with concepts of guilt, like the patient who foretold that the stars would be in collision, adding that it was all his fault for having given way to evil. These victims of despair seem to fear the whole universe but, basically speaking, it is of their own action that they are afraid.[10] The taste for action is stifled at its very root, the sources of desire. Even their frequent fugues are only a flight from themselves.[11] On this side of melancholia, but reflecting its faded hues, is boredom, with its similar tendency towards disintegrating impotence.

The flight from action is most active when it is not only a retreat from commitment, but an aggressive protest against the environment. It is already to be seen in some forms of childish 'laziness', without physiological cause, which usually appear suddenly after a normal period, or are restricted to one teacher, to one matter, to one sector of life. The link between inertia of behaviour and a process of opposition is naturally unconscious: it is therefore all the more difficult to discover and to dissolve.

*

THE MASTERY OF ACTION: THE CONSCIOUSNESS OF ACTION

The action that has been mastered is an adjusted action. It requires presence and extension of consciousness and flexibility in differentiation: normally these qualities are developed during one's apprenticeship. They are, however, of no value without the authority of decision.

We have seen that the awareness of action, and the language that articulates it, tend to develop anarchically, even to the extent of

* The degrees of action. (Whole section cut.)

turning against themselves and arresting action. Some persons have therefore rather summarily insisted on the superiority of the blind, unmotivated action: like Gide's Lafcadio, they relish its almost divine gratuitousness or its poetic absurdity: or they are intoxicated by its irrational, authoritarian brutality. Such eccentricity has an obvious purpose, to deliver action from one of its most pernicious contemporary ailments, the disease of purposeless rumination, the disintegrating fever of playing with ideas, or the rigidity of high thinking. But they have only jumped out of the frying pan into the fire. An action severed from reflection has no outcome but to degenerate into an instinctive or emotional explosion, or to give place to primary mechanisms. When Lafcadio threw out of his house a gentleman whose decorations offended his sense of the fitting, he was obeying not so much a divine inspiration as the uncertainty of his own humour. It is none the less true that the merits of reflection are not available to action on the formal administrative principles worked out by psychologists too overburdened by a systematising and ill-conceived cartesianism: primo, a notification; secundo, a deliberation: tertio, a decision; quarto, an executive process.

*

The quality of the action produced is not necessarily governed, as many persons consider, by the duration and concentration of preliminary deliberation: it can be gauged rather by the volume, or better, the breadth of the consciousness engaged in the action, even if it should be, as with certain rapid thinkers of high quality, only for the flash of a second. Tact, wit, repartee, acquired skills, heroic decisions, generous impulses, are not embarrassed by lengthy preliminaries, but are none the less based on a high degree of awareness. Yet they are only successful through earlier reflection, with all the difficulty, all the patience it involved. The advantage of a lightning awareness over an embarrassed awareness has nothing to do with any superiority of a somnolent consciousness or a blind unconsciousness over active consciousness. If it be true that one has sometimes to withdraw from action to achieve greater depth, to suspend initiative in order to uncover some vital centre in harmony with unknown forces, if it be true that our most successful actions are often those for which we feel the least responsible, this surpassing of action is something that can only be understood and achieved as something beyond and further than action or deliberation. It is the highest form of choice and not the rejection of choice.

* Describes a promethean type.

Flexibility of adaptation depends above all on the breadth of consciousness. Where consciousness is narrow, the agent is too concerned with the immediate stimulus. This may lead to a high degree of motive power and efficiency, and promote both concentration and application. On the other hand, it aggravates impulsiveness. It imprisons the agent in a disconnected rigidity, so that he throws himself upon the objective without looking to right or to left, his reactions often becoming ponderous, inferior and discontinuous. He is irritated by actions that are in the least complicated, does not notice changes in the environment obvious to others, and adapts himself to them badly or too late. He becomes the slave of mechanical stimuli, crazes and fads; he generalises his own experiences too hastily, particularly if they have been painful; his judgment of men and things is summary and rigid: he is often naïve through failure to appreciate promptly cunning, irony or complication: if cold by temperament he is obstinate or fanatical, if passionate, his passions lead him to triumph with intrepidity over every obstacle, for he just does not see them. A broad field of consciousness, on the other hand, enlarges the capacity for reflection, and provides that total grasp of the facts of a situation, that ease and ingenuity which bear the same relation to action as a broad education does to intelligence. Needs, interests, aptitudes, external reality are the four essential points of reference, which it is not easy to place at any given moment in a correct relationship. The only persons who can succeed in this are those whose angle of vision is sufficiently wide to embrace them all.
*

THE POWERS OF DECISION

The heart of action is to be found neither in deliberation, as the intellectualists would have it, nor in the movements of the body, as the behaviourists would have it, but in decision, the expression of the free, creative act. The distance between response and stimulus has been slowly widened only to allow the possibility of several avenues of action where only one existed before. 'The man of action', writes a man of action, 'is only interested in that which can be changed.'[12] The moment of decision, like the divine *fiat*, does not reveal its secrets to the psychologist, who can only pronounce on the manner of its appearance. From within the active consciousness, faced with the enigmatic appeal of reality, there flow a stream of 'motivations' and incitements, of plural origin, some of which are illuminated by

* A reference to Heymans.

intelligence, others due to the promptings of the senses. There results a confused and sometimes disturbing stimulus, which may lead to two opposing lines of conduct.

The irresolute are, first of all, the weak. They are bowed down by the weight of the conflict; the divergence and the multiplicity of the motivations in question are almost as fatiguing to them as the concentration necessary to reach a choice:[13] here we find the scrupulous. But weakness itself is not enough to create irresolution. There are asthenics who evade an exhausting decision as much as possible, but who can decide normally when there is no escape. Other factors intervene in typical cases of indecision.

*

The nervous are afraid of decisions because they are afraid of living, of changing, of risking anything. The timid lose their grip when confronted by the need for decision, particularly if it is urgent. The more sensitive suffer with peculiar intensity the drama of possible alternatives. They are overcome by the richness of all the possible actions, and to decide is to choose, to choose is to sacrifice and renounce, something that the primary emotive feel more as a reduction of emotional possibilities than as a narrowing of perspective.[14]

**

The sentimental are more complex. They are first of all torn between the affective drives coming from their emotivity, and the rational motivations due to their secondary: their lack of activity slows down the transition into action, and keeps the conflict on the plane of abstract possibility, with a further lag due to the inertia of the past coming from their secondary. The irresolution of the emotional, which we have just mentioned, is here replaced by the irresolution of the reasoners, who always postpone the letter to be written, the business to be transacted, the job to be started, through fear of not having sufficiently weighed up all the motives involved. They are not afraid of loss of emotional glow by embarking on action, but of being unreasonable: they are less afraid of sinning against abundance than against good order. Their emotivity, which is in any case reduced by its secondary, is sufficiently blunted to allow the factors in the conflict to be reduced to a colourless objective uniformity: their secondary increases the differentiation of these factors but crystallises them into opposing blocks of equal strength.

Thus we find at the root of both forms of irresolution not, as might have been thought, a lack of affectivity (even the abulic are usually

* A reference to Heymans' categories.   ** Further details of the nervous.

emotive) but a deficiency of the activity factor, leading cumulatively to a vital deficiency—typical abulia is accompanied by symptoms of devitalisation—and a deep personality disorder, which has so far only been described by calling it, like Janet, a deficiency of mental synthesis.[15] In extreme cases of abulia, there is a narrowing of the field of consciousness and a poverty of concept, 'simple, narrow, composed of few psychological elements', and thus an incapacity to elaborate a concrete decision. The normally undecided person often, like the abulic, plays the same poor tune on the notes of yes and no. There is also a richer indecision, common amongst intellectuals: they are encumbered by a sterile abundance of reflections which recalls in its rhythm other deficiency phenomena, such as mental or motor agitation. This deficiency, however, is not solely endogenous. The indecisive person is self-intoxicated, because he has no window open on reality, because he has never confronted the sun, the wind and the rain on the great highways of life, to strengthen the muscles of his thinking like the muscles of his body. We should, finally, allow for the lasting effect of certain infantile inhibitions: thus a characteristic irresolution has been found in persons whose affections had to be divided between a mother and a nurse, or where sexual curiosity has been repressed to the point of remaining a perpetual interrogation.

It is because there is this weakened vitality or affective lesion at the core of irresolution that it is quite useless to try to cure it by rational means. The indecisive person suffers from a psychic anaemia and should be brought out into the fresh air of action. In serious cases he should even avoid reflection, as far as possible: his reflection will be faulty, in any case, and will only increase his indecision. The best thing is to confront him at the last moment with the action to be taken, and to persuade him as quickly as possible to agreement.[16] In less serious cases he should be introduced by degrees to all the different situations which can eliminate pointless ruminations, particularly by making him assume responsibilities which entail irreversible decisions. We shall come back to the problem of character in the intellectual, but it is already clear that an apprenticeship to ideas must be combined with a parallel apprenticeship to action. A touch of instinct, of passion, of heavy responsibility and the handling of other men, far from impairing the disinterested activity of the mind, give it that vital weight without which it turns against life, against humanity and against the mind itself.[17]

We should not go to the other extreme and confuse resolution with rigidity of decision such as is found, for instance, in the impulsive.

Impulsiveness has two characteristic traits: action is very rapid, almost instantaneous: the gesture is no sooner conceived than performed, like a shot: 'No sooner said than done': from this follows brusqueness, inadvertence, impatience. Further, the motivation of the act is always the immediate impression, never the consideration of future consequences: hence we find carelessness and dispersal. We can recognise the product of a narrow field of consciousness and the primarity of the emotions. One should add a great readiness to lie, the instantaneous lie, and violently emotional colouring of thought. Is emotivity again the cause? Perhaps sometimes it is. But emotivity is usually inhibitory of action and its effects are almost exclusively propriofective. Impulsiveness, on the other hand, is active and discharges its effects into the outer world. Finally, emotivity is reactive, it is set in action by an external stimulus; impulsiveness is endogenous, a kind of spontaneous spasm.[18]
*

True resolution seems to be the product of a mental chemistry operating only at high tension. It is an equilibrium which must be supported on every side by all the elements of action: automatic mechanisms must be sufficiently controlled, as also spontaneous impulsiveness: instinct must be vigorous, the mind stable and enlightened, consciousness alert and accessible to reality, the vision not too easily nor too little satisfied: if too diffident, reality offers no hold for action, if too close, it is burdensome. Decision is an act of synthesis and of well-being: it tends to the greatest well-being of the greatest number of internal and external factors. Thus it is not, as some believe, akin to rigidity, to authoritarian dogmatism, to a blind and heedless arbitrariness. It implies a kind of profound universality, which makes it possible to take sides, whilst being still completely the contrary of partiality. It implies prudence: not the slow narrow calculation of circumspection, which hampers the secondary, but a wisdom which is often implicit and sometimes startling.
**

But if decision involves an equilibrium, it is infinitely more than an equilibrium, it is a commencement of being and the affirmation of an 'I'. No accumulation of motives and incitements, influences and forces can exclude the transcendental reality of this act. It was the error of both idealist and behaviourist psychology to try to eliminate this act, together with the first person singular that performed it. Decision is

* Clinical symptoms of over-impulsiveness.
** Quotes examples described by J. Daireaux.

not, in fact, an act inside a person, it is the person in action, exclusively concentrated on an affirmation creating either good or evil, truth or error: it is the person replying 'Present' to the call of the world, and committed both to life and death in the response that is given. At least, such is the only decision that is worthy of the name. Resolution of character is a habitual capacity for decision: it is the central force of personality. It escapes all psychological analysis. It is known by its practice, is tested, acquired and corrected in responsible action in contact with reality, in contact with men. We are again at the tangential point mentioned in the first chapter, where characterology borders on morality, and in practice, even if not in the analysis of its essential qualities, is merged in it almost to the point of being indistinguishable.

Thus the secret of action lies in the acceptance or non-acceptance of risk. A purely intellectual discussion will never lead to a decision: the more intelligently the motives are appreciated, the more their force is equalised, for the world is complex and there is no *for* which is not clouded by a great deal *against*, no motive that cannot boast, even without sophistry, a deal of wisdom. Thus the intellectual who is solely intellectual, an assessor of ideas, nearly always strikes a balance close to the dead point. The effect of action is, in fact, to cross this dead point, in a wager that is not necessarily irrational, yet not always entirely rational. The 'instinct' of security and repetition, the death 'instinct' is opposed to it with the whole dead weight of vital inertia. Its great argument, the argument of all the conservatisms, is summed up in two words: integrity, continuity. But the integrity of being it defends is the integrity of past being, which it defends against the lures of potential being, that is to say against the only worthwhile continuity, a creative continuity, the credit given to the future. The psychoanalysts are right to point out that to *decide* means to *cut* and that each decision is a repetition of the severing of the umbilical cord which kept the human being in a state of receiving life, and casts him out into the adventure of living.[19] The fear of mutilation and the fear of the unknown are always at the root of the fear of action. Descartes called generosity the highest virtue. He was right. If it can be defined as the wager without justification, the incalculable credit, it is the very behaviour that makes man.

To form a decision is to form the whole personality: it requires vitality so that the execution shall be incisive; sufficient primarity to make the act relevant and prompt, sufficient secondarity to strengthen it by the richness of experience, rapidity to brush aside faltering, slowness so that wisdom is not obscured, acceptance of reality to lighten reflection and yet sufficient aggressiveness not to veer with every breeze. The resolute man, the committed man, is not the authoritarian martinet who believes in the electric power of the eye or of the muscle: he has achieved what is both the most solid and the most complex of human constructions. It is mistaken to believe that intelligence complicates things artificially, or to persuade oneself that the man who wills achieves more than the man who knows. All the controlled forces of instinct converge in the resolute man with all the strength of culture and of courage. He is as rare a product as the man with a really fine mind.

DEALING WITH THE OBSTACLE, AND THE CONTROLS OF ACTION

Decision brings into play a series of functions—behaviour and feelings —whose role is to modify action by co-ordinating its purposes with the possibilities of reality. It rallies all the forces of the self against the tendency to let things slide.

Each of us is constantly, permanently tempted by the fascination of things and by the weight of inertia, to become a passive element, a 'one'. Be nameless, irresponsive, not mingling too much with others, miserly in initiative, parsimonious of risk, and a peaceful existence is assured. But one is driven by an inner fire that cannot always be quenched by an exhortation to tranquillity—the human person is a movement forward, and the broad promise of salvation for the whole world—once on this path there is no rest, no frontier, but ceaseless confrontation, conquest, sublimation. The slow decay of matter is a perpetual threat that, unless care is taken, it will infect and permeate us. Life, for the real personality, is a perpetual struggle against a perpetual menace, a war against obstacles, a drama whose plot is never finally straightened out. Resistance is not only outside, it springs from the heart itself, in the doubts born of every affirmation, in the scruple clinging to the finest intention, the sour taste that mars happiness, the spite that contaminates virtue, the sickness of living that blights the joy of living, and in the warring gods that harass reflection. The story of action is the story of our struggle against resistance.[20]

There are four basic forms of behaviour in the face of an obstacle: impatience, aggressive application, withdrawal and perseverance.

*   *   *

1. Desire is not pure intention. It has already seized hold of the organism, mobilised every preliminary gesture, set body and psyche on the alert for realisation, before we are conscious of it as feeling. If an obstacle thwarts this drive, desire must provisionally call a halt, giving rise to a specific emotion: *impatience*. The two principal factors in impatience are emotivity and primarity. Thus the most impatient are the primary emotives. Those in whom there is a swift, immediate transition from thought to action cannot wait for the execution of the orders given. Impatience is discharged in emotional manifestations: trembling, vertigo, insults, convulsions, etc. The strength of the forces destined to action is disarmed by this premature expenditure. He who waits badly, acts badly, the secret of any war of nerves.
*

The emotional may often plunge into real trouble to escape the sense of apprehension they suffer.
**

Such are the murderers who kill their relatives in order to avoid evils generally much less serious, or the anxiety-ridden who commit suicide to escape the limited risks of war and revolution. Rousseau would circulate criticisms of each of his books as it was published, that he would never have tolerated from another. For the emotive anything is better than waiting. Maine de Biran, after hiding from the police for two days, goes and gives himself up. Kierkegaard, unable to resolve the contradictions and complexities of the engagement he wishes to break off, suddenly went and suggested marriage to the girl he did not want: thus the impatient often flee from existing complications by loading themselves with additional ones.

*   *   *

2. The active behave quite differently. The obstacle arouses an attitude of suspense: a halt, followed by waiting. There is an inactive waiting, for which French politicians have coined the barbarous name of '*attentisme*', which consists of passing the time in a state of pure passivity with regard to the obstacle, either hoping that some undeserved miracle will eliminate it, or because the need to engage in hand to hand conflict with events is perpetually postponed. There are persons who spend their lives waiting, like a girl waiting to find a husband, interminably inactive. The waiting of the active person is quite different. A superior action is not immediately available, the

* Refers to Heymans' categories.   ** Refers to Heymans' categories.

path must be cleared, the necessary force mobilised and all possible methods of overcoming or sidestepping the obstacle discovered. During this preparatory work the drives which have been activated must be kept from lapsing into passivity. Primitive psyches, children, the backward, and in some cases the emotional, do not know how to wait. The forces aroused by the stimulus are prematurely discharged in the emotional explosion.[21] The inactive are overwhelmed by the obstacle, even by the thought of the obstacle. But resistance stimulates the active person; he looks for it, sometimes only taking up certain causes because of the conflicts it will bring him. It has been noted that a particular weakness is sometimes the stimulus in the choice of a career; the stammerer becomes an orator (Demosthenes), the emotional man a doctor. It would be a short-sighted psychology that refused, on the grounds of vocational guidance, to provide scope for these heroic successes which are also practical successes. The desire to conquer, to persuade, is perfectly healthy as an instinct. It always tends to exceed its rights and abuse its successes, but it is not in itself bad form, as weaker characters would have it. The passion it arouses is called *courage*. There are many forms of courage, not equally honourable. In its pure form it is greatest in the inemotive (Heymans), and most noticeably so in the poorest temperament, the amorphous. But it can be richer, integrating several elements; a spiritual drive, over-excited by the difficulty to be overcome or the cause to be furthered: an instinctive urge nearly always closely correlated or connected with sexuality; a more or less voluntary and complete contempt for the obstacle. True courage does not normally entail an absurd ignorance of the obstacle, unless there is some instinctive assurance of victory: but the man of courage is sometimes only a presumptuous man who has succeeded. The most modest action entails its risk and the psychological quality of risk is that it is an improbability rather than a probability. There is no action without a grain of folly, a sovereign unreason that laughs at reason. Never argue with the pusillanimous— all their reasons are reasonable, for reason foresees everything, except the miracle of the creative act.

It does not follow that all folly is creative. Success in action goes to him who unites the maximum of audacity with the maximum of preparation. Thus the controlling factors are of prime importance, provided they are handled with courage.

Just as decision is the outcome of desire, initiative is the origin of execution. There is, we know, an illness which kills desire—melancholy; and disorders that weaken it—the morose inertia of the inactive. There are also illnesses that kill initiative, the triggering phase of melancholia and particularly schizophrenia. If no one speaks to these patients they will stand motionless for hours, even under the pressure of need. Without reaching such extremes, the most obtuse, apathetic types and the amorphous present a similar, if modified, picture. What do they lack? Janet noted that mad persons never reacted to a general order such as 'Get dressed'. They had to be given specific detailed instructions, 'Put it on your right arm', 'Put it on your left arm', and so on. The absence of spontaneity seems to follow a collapse of mental synthesis. It seems, in fact, that initiative is bound up with the psychological unification achieved through the frontal lobe, which reduces or eliminates reactions competing with the reaction required. It increases with the power of mental synthesis and the breadth of imagination: it is diminished by inactivity or there may be antagonism between these two factors. Men of high intelligence, daring when the moment of decision occurs, may be affected by a kind of poverty of *impetus*. If one examined the record of their most fertile and sustained activities, one would always find that the initial spur was given by some other person: the spiritual quality of an encounter has always a singular importance for them. Poorer personalities, on the other hand, may render their maximum through the constantly alert flexibility of their impulses, and may thus stimulate richer personalities without whose aid they would be unable to take advantage of their power of initiative: of such quality are the 'givers of ideas', ideas half wise, half foolish, with always a pinch of genius even at their most grotesque: or the persons who can inspire the whole conduct of a business, but who would merely create confusion if they were allowed to administer it: or those innovators, of socratic temper, who can launch ideas or movements, and then abandon them in their mature shape, either because their imagination was too short-winded to persist (as with the emotive), or because they are solely interested in beginnings: the handy fellow, the jack of all trades, the small inventor, are of this primary type, characterised by the abundance, rather than the breadths, of their initiatives. There is a link here with the highly active, in their energy, the spontaneity with which they anticipate needs and the relevance of the satisfactions obtained. We see the close connection between initiative and creativity; unless there is a strong inhibition through inactivity, initiative is the elasticity of creativity. As with every elasticity, its limits are not rigid. It can be educated by the exercise of responsibility and the encounter with obstacles, in a post of solitary command, where victory must be secured through intelligent anticipation. And it can be obliterated by the habit of passive obedience as inculcated by some teachers, some regimes, some social situations.[22] Teachers can never be too careful not to confuse authority with a kind of monopoly of initiative and a constant intervention in the children's activities. From his earliest years the child must be progressively encouraged to this spontaneous vivacity of action. This form of education requires the adult to be more interested in the quality of the activity than in the upsets it may entail. The mistaken systematisations of 'free education' conceal an important truth, that initiative is learned by initiative, and that there is more educational value to the child in the discovery of the fortunate or unfortunate consequences of his attempts than in all the warnings he may be given. How many parents turn their children into valetudinarians or nincompoops in order to avoid a bruise or a broken leg.

As with decision, initiative as a guide to action must come to terms with the *solicitations and the limitations of reality*. These lend it an infinite flexibility. Our body itself is an instrument marvellously docile to all the possibilities of action. It has been observed that the insect, with its rigid members, seems limited to a geometric world: the bees' cells, the spiders' webs. But the human body masters an infinity of planes. Every instinct, however, every drive, every passion, every idea, tends to rush straight ahead, blind both to the objective and to its surroundings, under the exclusive control of its propulsive energy. All rigidity is derived from this and expresses itself in gesture. It is the controls represented by the object which shatter this rigidity and reduce our inner anarchy. Man is compacted by things as much as he himself compacts them. Reality has not only the function of flexing, bending and combining our initiatives. It prunes the profusion of our desires, so that they produce not a worthless shrubbery of latent wishes, but trees with defined branches and selected fruit. Freud has shown the humble forms and the capital importance of sacrifice in the formation of character. He has shown a successive 'weaning' in the course of individual development, on the success of which normal maturation depends. The first of these is the separation from the mother at weaning: the more painful it is, the less tolerable will be the later renunciations. Then comes the liquidation of infantile affective complexes, then that of the polygamy of desire, which sociologists as little religious as Proudhon have stressed as essential to the virilisation of character. To this progressive discipline of the instincts must be added the apprenticeship to dispossession and the double detachment from parental warmth which occurs on first going to school and then at adolescence. The manner in which these various renunciations are achieved leaves permanent marks on the structure of personality: they will be repeated in essence on every occasion which requires the sacrifice of the multiplicity of possibility to the solidity of the achieved, the whole meaning of adult action. With an impotence explained by their psychological history, some perpetual adolescents can never will anything sufficiently intensely to shake off the distracting chorus of all that is possible and shape their first renunciations and definitive loyalties by concrete acts: eclectics of knowledge or of love, amateurs and dilettantes for life, incompetents believing themselves *condottieri*, impotents who confuse their vital indecision with universality. The strong man, on the contrary, prefers the plenitude of accomplishment to the mirage of potentialities; the sense of sacrifice is identical, in its origin, with the liking for reality.

Initiative and objectivity regulate the intensity of the effort furnished at the beginning of action.
*

We overlook the purely human quality of effort. Animals do not work unless men make them work. Primitive peoples work very little. To work does not mean to allow the mechanism of desire to proceed as far as the satisfaction of need, however complicated. It is to prolong and adjust the effort, by stimulating certain tendencies, economising others and compensating for the weakness of some by the energy of the others. Work is thus a high-tension activity, which requires the collaboration of the most complex ideas: purpose, means, causality, production, technique. One can speak of 'effort behaviour', a specifically human reaction of augmentation or acceleration.[23] There are deficiencies, as in apathy, exaggerations of impulse, as tics, spasms and a sort of hyperbolic contraction, ridiculously exaggerated on insignificant grounds, which has already been described (mania for perfection, precision, insistence, underlining words, indefinite explanation, etc.). When it embraces the spiritual life as well, it culminates in that reflection which is the strength of the true man of action, and by that excitement of spirit which goes to swell the abundance of action.[24] But excitement is free and easy. Action is not enhanced by becoming tenser, and an irritant does not always lead to improvement. It is therefore dangerous to stress the training of effort, as some teachers are inclined to do: the effort may succeed in stifling the action it was designed to assist.

Some natures, in whom instinct is weak or psychic energy deficient, suffer from a permanent need to heighten psychological tension, which,

* Attention not a special faculty as described by earlier psychology.

left to itself, would slip imperceptibly towards depression. They achieve this by varying forms of *excitation*.
*

This systematic search for excitation betrays a narrowing of consciousness by its unreflecting and frenzied obstinacy. But one cannot deny that, up to a certain point, it may benefit its victims. It increases the potential which, by induction, and at certain privileged moments, benefits the whole psychic activity, or the group of tendencies which are particularly avid in the given case. A permanent depression would be worse than the inconvenience of this constant discharge. 'For lack of anything better', Bremond was already saying in 1893[25] to such persons, 'have at least an exciting hobby: it is much better to do even the most futile things than to spend a quarter of an hour doing nothing: cultivate rare tulips, collect autographs, breed rabbits, go fishing, make pots, cut out silhouettes for children, chase butterflies or collect postage stamps. The important thing is to be enthusiastic about something.' You may feel that these are mediocre occupations, but the quality of excitation must be adjusted to the qualitative possibilities of the subject. One may start as a fisherman and end as an apostle. Modest beginnings do not, of course, exclude a progressive education of excitation: the caprice should, on the other hand, be disciplined by trying to attach it to tendencies or actions which are the weakest in that particular person, but with due regard to fatigue; when this is persistent and progressive, it is a counter-indication.

*   *   *

Concentration and effort create a tension resolved by action.
**

Perseverance is a regulating factor in duration. It presupposes a minimum of force and resistance to fatigue. But it is much more a psychological virtue. A mental patient has only to be attached by a sort of hypochondria of duration for him to become incapable of further effort, like the man who complained to Janet: 'I could work a long time if I felt I could always break off and go away when I wanted to. It's horrible to think that whatever happens I have to go on working until mid-day.' Or another: 'I am capable of effort on condition that it is instantaneous and, above all, definitive. I can take action, provided it is short and easy and one can forget it.'[26] Here there is a sort of

---

* Further details of methods of excitement.
** A study of the movements immediately preceding action.

intimidation of action by action itself, which blocks the issue. Inconstancy, in fact, is due to causes similar in part to those which produce timidity.

*

Psycho-motor instability seems due to complex causes, or causes which can be observed at several levels.

**

These various forms of instability appear in childhood:[27] the unstable child, touching everything, always fidgeting, is often rowdy and combative, or at least mischievous and a tease, sometimes mildly delinquent. He should not be confused with the perverse. His self-control must be re-educated by habituating him to rhythmic movement, to collecting his thoughts, taking decisions in simple matters, and complete rest. Adolescence seems to be the time of the greatest instability and discordance. Tastes, projects, conversions, disaffections, enthusiasms, betrayals, follow jostling upon each other. The frequency of suicides shows how susceptible this age is to the slightest shock. But this instability is normal: it expresses the turbulence of desires attempting satisfaction in every direction: it is not an established state but a critical situation. The adolescent resembles the unstable person who wants to try everything, attempting to possess persons and things in order to belie some inner adequacy, but his inadequacy is only relative to the breadth of his aspiration.

***

Perseverance should not be confused with perseveration, of which we shall speak later. It is not inertia, a mere continuation, but a higher direction, an active intervention of a superior psyche, imposing on the discontinuity of elementary activities, the broader theme of duration provided by wider mental experience. In other words, it is not a function of maintenance but of synthesis; not conservative but creative. If its essential character is misunderstood it becomes impossible to understand its highest form, fidelity. Fidelity does not consist, as the unfaithful believe, in maintaining in the face of reason and actual feeling, a dead and past state, which we wish to prolong for reasons foreign to our contentment. Fidelity, or at least the only form that deserves the name, is the extension given to a creative impulse, always present, always tending towards an immediate promise and

* Refers to Heymans' categories and quotes a type of instability described by Kraepelin.
** Quotes clinical symptoms given by Dr. Leopold Levi.
*** Refers to Heymans' categories and a purely psychological distraction described by Dr. Robin.

void, as far as is possible, of a dead past; an extension given by an increasingly comprehensive duration, tinged with a flavour of eternity. It is the fullness of contentment and the fervour of hope, always the same and always different: it is both complete homage to reality and a preference for a durable existence over the pursuit of chimæras. In all these aspects it is the very summit of action.

We have still to consider two final controlling factors, one antagonistic, the other restorative.

Compensation is a very general form of natural activity. It is found both in the physical and physiological processes as well as in the psychological. It opposes any active force by an antagonistic one which restrains its effect. It is a constant phenomenon in psychology: a weak person harbours ideas of pride and domination, a timid person dreams of adventure and social success. Feelings artificially suppressed or compressed produce particularly violent compensatory activities: if a weak person has been long and maliciously goaded, he may become a monster of cruelty: a timid person, provoked, is capable of an outburst of audacity which astonishes everyone. This permanent and excessive fixation of a controlling function gives rise to over-compensated types, which Adler has so successfully described.

Rest, like sleep, is now no longer considered as a simple cessation of activity. It is an act of positive defence against an excess of fatigue. This is proved by the fact that there are persons who do not know how to rest: they are always working or moving about; always sitting on the edge of their chair instead of leaning back comfortably; they need to fill every slightest gap in their day by some sort of activity. With due exception for the hyperactivity and diabolic rhythm of the powerful, hyperthyroid type, there is a form of organic weakness in this intolerance of rest: it is often the same persons who cannot sleep, whose drowsy states, or the beginnings of relaxation, are invaded by the feverish rumination characteristic of states of low tension. But in many cases there is a still deeper poverty of mind, the vertigo of an empty head and an unfeeling heart; or even the inability to endure an inner silence, the dialogue with oneself, the enduring and meditative monologue.

*　　　*　　　*

*

3. When effort encounters an obstacle and cannot overcome it, there is a hold-up. We are held up in this way a hundred times a day. Normally we pass on, after a temporary vexation. There are extremes of temperament to be found on either side of this average behaviour.

---

* The effect of urban life on rest.

Some, as soon as they perceive the obstacle and the impossibility of surmounting it, have an exceptional facility in forgetting it and in passing on without crisis.
*

They behave in the same way with men who might become their adversaries. Their life is hardly dramatic, even if rich in associations and in work; little troubles them, and they simply cut out without difficulty anything that might disturb them. At least, they act thus when they are not attached to higher values; a religious outlook on life, a concern for others, leads to an extension of the area of vulnerability. Even then the shocks to which they expose themselves are inevitably less painful than to others.

On the other hand, the weak are held up by the slightest asperity, without being able to detach themselves from the incident concerned. Some spend whole months blocked by an insurmountable obstacle, wearing themselves out in a fruitless struggle. The obstacle may be a fact encountered in real life; it may be a disturbing and clinging memory, an idea that torments the mind. We shall deal with these delayed action natures when we come to the phenomena of liquidation.
**

The person who abandons the struggle recalls his energies and looks for shelter. The normal refuge of a man who fears the difficulties of the future, is the past. The most common reaction of the man frightened or hurt by an obstacle is withdrawal into his own past. We all suffer a little from this dismay, when we find ourselves running in search of our childhood memories.
***

Repression is a withdrawal which occurs unknown to the subject. According to Freud, it is due specifically to wishes of an infantile origin and of a sexual character, repressed by the 'reality principle', that is to say by social adaptation. But the mechanism described by Freud may operate at any time that a powerful wish is rejected or severely wounded by an external shock. It withdraws silently, allows itself to be forgotten. But here the retreat is not a renunciation. The disappointed desire accumulates in the shadow of the self an emotional charge, the 'affect' which remains available and aggressive, ready to discharge itself on other objects and a threat to the foundations of affective life; 'complexes' crystallise over the scars and give rise to the majority of the disturbances of consciousness. Psychoanalysis

---

* Refers to Heymans' categories.   ** Refers to Heymans' categories.
*** Examples of withdrawal into the past.

endeavoured to bring the nucleus of the repression to consciousness, and persuade the subject to admit it as such, in order to free him from this internal prison. The experience of psychoanalysts shows that the cure for repression, though it has had marked successes, is far from being generally infallible. In some characters the whole picture is dominated by their repressions. These are often sexual repressions; they underly that lack of modesty expressed in the intellectual sphere, by incontinence of secrets, of language or gesture: they also explain, by over-compensation, some excessive modesty and strictness. Apart from the sexual sphere, there are social repressions, which produce timid, silent, asocial characters or, by compensation, the ambitious and wildly authoritarian.

*   *   *

4. In addition to those who are impatient of an obstacle, those who face it and those who avoid it, there are those who are stiffened and hardened by its encounter. They will not give up and they will not adapt: they harden into the position which led to the obstacle and which the obstacle frustrates. This is stubbornness, radically different from perseverance, which is creation, and even from stubbornness, which is only a rather tense form of perseverance. Like an attack of cramp, stubbornness mobilises all the mind's capacity for systematisation in favour of primitive, perseverative drives. It is the advanced, symmetrical expression of rigidity just as fidelity is of adjusted continuity. It hamstrings the strongly secondary types, lacking a strong counterbalancing emotivity or activity, and diverts them from the vital activity that their breadth of character should facilitate. Sometimes it indicates a hysterical narrowing of the field of consciousness; in the openly hysterical it may lead to a sort of 'delirium of resistance' an inexplicable, involuntary, psychological contraction which can never be relaxed.[28] There are so many states of transition between stubbornness and true perseverance that it is not always easy to determine the part played by each in any reasonably firm behaviour.
*
**

THE LIQUIDATION OF ACTION

The liquidation or termination of an action has also been described by Janet,[29] and not only the disorders of action. An action carried through to completion should normally fall away from us, like a fruit

---

* The autonomy of commitment in action. (Whole section cut.)
** The globalisation of action. (Whole section cut.)

from a tree, and pursue its own course, leaving us to pursue ours. It would be error to assume that this detachment takes place without our help. Hardly is the action performed than we have to demobilise the forces which have been assembled without being used, and re-deploy them for fresh tasks. Even more difficult, we must reorganise the whole psyche to adapt it to the new situation resulting from the completed action. We must shape the story that will survive the action and represent it in future behaviour, adapt this story to the social background and communicate it (confidence or admission). 'Although it may seem strange, there *must be an action*, and often an energetic action, *to stop action*.'[30] It needs as much positive work as sleep or rest. It is cloaked by the sense of triumph caused by the dissemination of free energy, joy in the act achieved, like a troop of schoolboys rushing out after a long detention. But it is nevertheless an act of considerable difficulty.

The proof is that the asthenic and the depressed do not succeed in solving it correctly: 'I do everything by halves', declared one, 'and it is very tiring to do everything by halves.' Another: 'At the moment I can't do anything properly, either to be properly honest, or properly dishonest.'
*

The weak person clings to this moment that will not culminate, these efforts without conclusion: his regrets are interminable, he exhausts himself in apprehensions and fresh beginnings. He bows his head beneath the reproaches of all the unborn children who stand by the side of his path through life, stretching towards him their handless arms, overwhelming him by their monotonous despair.
**

No one is so dismayed as such persons when suffering a bereavement:[31] they cannot succeed in detaching themselves from the links with the loved object, or in doing what everyone is compelled to do, in order to live, accepting and organising this disappearance, without loss of fidelity. Some even clutch at the reality of yesterday to the point of psychotic hallucination. Janet considers that a great number of mental disorders are nothing but this continuation of an action for which grounds are no longer present.[32] Such persons must at all costs be made to achieve complete actions, not many, but carried through to the end, so as to obtain a clear and conscious modification of the actual situation.[33] For instance, after a bereavement, it may be necessary to use authority to put them in an environment which, by the nature

* Further examples of failure to liquidate action.   ** Another example.

of things, will oblige them to change their behaviour with regard to the past situation or action: to leave their flat, their town, to travel, etc. In short to teach them to forget, to make the best of things, to resign themselves, to forgive, renounce, let slide. These acts are difficult not only to the weak, but also to secondary temperaments. More aware of the extent of what they would achieve than of the actual form of what they are doing, they always have the feeling of running after a task which is slipping away from them, and they are little apt to forget suffering or insult. They cling to their actions and suffer embarrassment at their persistence, unlike the asthenic who fail to liquidate their actions through weakness.

Other types can liquidate their actions successfully, but with a meticulous application that itself requires explanation. Desire for perfection, it has been said, but desire for approximation would be more correct, for they are not so much interested in the completed act as in the exceptions to the completion: they want to find, as one says, the fly in the ointment. 'Perfection is not enough', said one such, 'I need the more than perfect.'[34] They make those political or military chiefs, who supervise the smallest details in the execution of their orders; those housewives tormented by the thought of dust in hidden crannies,[35] who excavate even the graining in the floorboards: they stay to the end of a show that bores them, are perpetually cleaning up their plate, and are haunted by the idea that they might have left a pea in the saucepan they were supposed to empty. This trait may have considerable utilitarian value, but is irritating to opposing temperaments, such as the emotive, only interested in the wide dramatic outline of a situation, indifferent to its objective realisation and, incidentally, soon recaptured by other enthusiasms; to the unstable, incapable of continuous, complete execution and to the easily tired, exhausted by such meticulous care.

*

The liquidations of action are not only longer or shorter, more or less voluntary. They have a qualitative significance in the sense of victory or defeat.

Success sets up a reaction of triumph, extremely tonic for the whole psychic organism. This is shown by the joyful agitation, the gay lightheartedness directly opposed to the constriction and narrowing of consciousness which follow defeat. The demobilised energy cheerfully unloads itself on to other activities, which are thus rejuvenated. A sense of fulfilment, partly excessive and illusory, invades the subject,

* Examples of meticulous type and the passion for perfection in art and literature.

the reverse of the emptiness which accompanies depression. What the moralists call pride is a fixation of this illusion which temporarily overflows from each state of triumph.

Some forms of delirium (grandeur, exhilaration) resemble a tetanus of the triumphal reaction, which becomes permanent without any support from action.[36] The mechanism is already rather too prompt in the primary active type, which is sometimes more sustained by this than by real results. It is laborious and infrequent in the asthenic and totally lost in the depressed.

Success depends, indeed, on external conditions, but some persons seem made for success as others for misfortune and defeat. Perhaps the appearances conceal a secret of destiny. Psychological laws can explain, however, many simple causes. Defeat is born of rigidity and preventive discouragement. Success favours the flexible, it loves those who love it, who prefer to dwell on it rather than on their defeats, who expect it in advance, confident in their star. All the manuals of success psychology which Anglo-Saxon literature has been dispensing to the world for the last hundred years, are based on this primary truth. It is one thing to appreciate the spiritual value of success, which experience tends to treat as mediocre, and another to evaluate the psycho-energetic value of success behaviour cultivated and exercised for its own sake. It is certainly a precious tonic and stimulant. But its quality is often abused. No one, we have seen, has an easier triumph than the mentally weak, seeing the effort he expends. The onset of the delirium of grandeur, which is the delirium of success, marks the final onset of mania. The beaming expression and manner of the happy imbecile are proverbial. When the vast enthusiasms of youth are over, with the exaltation and the sheen of the young, vital animal, a too carefree reaction of triumph betrays a mediocre quality of psyche. We never speak of the 'successful' man or the 'successful' writer as a qualification of genius or true passion. There is also a facile temptation about success. Since it acts as a tonic, one soon seeks it for itself alone, by whatever means, the small-minded in rather stupid confidence, the conquerors of high calibre, with blind and tyrannical frenzy. In his hour of triumph man tends to believe, as popular wisdom has it, that 'he has arrived': he sees an end, he is bordering on retirement, he will live on his investments. His action is blocked, his ideas fixed, he wants to immobilise this moment of intoxicating equilibrium which was only given to him as a point of departure; he has arrived, he is aggressive to those who remind him of the rights of youth or of insecurity; he has transformed himself from an agent into a proprietor of life. The same evil threatens parties, revolutions, movements of all kinds at their apogee. This grossness of success as such, success trying not to be a joyful, elusive message for the future, is that which makes the success psychology to which we have alluded so pernicious.[37]

Freud has defined a type, which, on the other hand, is broken by success: Macbeth, Ibsen's Rosmersholm: the realisation of a long cherished idea suddenly reveals itself to them as being at a depressing distance from their dreams: they collapse into neurosis. The whole destiny of psychic equilibrium, perhaps the whole destiny of man, is played out between this tragic folly and the beatitude of the demented.

There are those, also, predestined to defeat: they recall only what they have lacked or suffered; they are perturbed by the difficulty of their enterprises even before they occur; if none occurs, they provoke them by a sort of affinity with misfortune, of active negativism: their constant rigidity thwarts the flow of events and unconsciously irritates other persons.

Whence comes this tendency to provoke misfortune? Sometimes it comes from some vital inadequacy. A strong person reacts in two ways to a setback; he starts again with fresh precautions, or he resigns himself and carries on. He can even draw new force from this setback. Kierkegaard found all his mystical and philosophic power after the painful breakdown of his engagement. And specialists in adolescence have noted that the decisive drives of puberty almost always start from a defeat: examination failure, disappointed love, a bereavement. Those who are not strong enough to transform their setbacks often deaden the shock by spontaneous, sometimes unconscious compensation. This may be the instantaneous transformation of the thwarted project into something easier of achievement, like those generals who suddenly switch their objective in the middle of a battle: this was the role of Mme Verdurin's salon for Swann, turned down by the *Faubourg*. The setback can also be digested by introversion, often accompanied by identification with the lost object (introjection), and often experienced as intensely as it is detested (Hamlet). Or, finally, a weak sublimation: the provincial academy for the misunderstood genius, religiosity or religious eroticism for those who have not found faith. But here defeat is still partially compensated by action, or semi-action. But with primary types, particularly with emotive and active natures, the pain of setback leaves as much trace as a stone falling into water. However it may be, a setback is initially depressing, heavy with all the disappointment of imposed renunciation, the sense of wasted energy, the apprehension of the effort that will have to start again from zero;

often complicated by a sense of guilt, particularly painful when it takes a collective form. These effects are all the more serious in that the psychological tension is already weaker. The first degree of weakness leads to withdrawal on the part of the unsuccessful agent: he reverts to his past, to his childhood, his native land, his memories; he withdraws from the conflicts of life and becomes fixed at an earlier phase of his action, as if he were trying to recover the warm and comfortable shelter of the pre-natal state.[38] Yet even this behaviour admits some acceptance of the given facts; the adjustment may be regressive, but it is adjustment. It only becomes morbid when it is systematised.[39] The really depressed do not succeed in getting free of their setback. When the grapes are inaccessible they do not say: 'They are sour', which, in Janet's opinion, was a really foxy way of warding off psychosis.[40] They wear themselves out by infinite renewal of their abortive act, either in action—like those patients who endlessly open and shut the same door, never being satisfied with the final gesture—or in rumination: he must at all costs cure this incurable evil, recover that impossible love, deny this bereavement, or perpetually elaborate all that he has not done, all that he should have done. There is only one thing to be said to those who are incompetent at liquidation: 'What is done, is done', and constrain them to seek a new destiny.

But there is more than a simple drawing back, a simple hold-up in the behaviour of defeat, at any rate when systematised into a dominant characteristic. Prone as we are to attribute values to all experience, the person who has experienced a humiliating defeat or series of defeats, welds together all their causes and projects them into a more or less precise belief that some avenging deity is punishing him, by defeat, for some fault (usually of a sexual character) for which he feels an obscure remorse. This complex of self-accusation becomes a complex of self-punishment which provokes fresh defeats. A sort of 'compulsive repetition' leads such persons always to make the same mistakes, always to bring down upon themselves the same calamities. This complex can be developed on a collective scale, in the event of an outstanding public misfortune, such as military defeat; or continuous misfortune, such as racial persecution. We then observe a mania for confession and humiliation, whose outwardly honourable aspect covers a strictly morbid reaction. This pathological formation might explain the facts to which we alluded earlier: the perfectly happy employee becomes neurotic the day he is made manager, other individuals react to success with criminal drives: they are punishing themselves unconsciously for their success. The need, which is felt as a moral obligation, to pursue their opposite explains why persons marry a partner the exact opposite of their ideal, or plunge into illness and accidents which were easily avoidable.[41]

GREATNESS AND MISERY OF THE WILL

*

  Pseudo-will-power appears . . . in its simpler forms as a phenomenon of rigidity lending an appearance of strength to a poor quality content. This content is not always habit, nor its rigidity always inertia: the narrowness of the field of consciousness may intervene and rivet obstinacy to a fixed idea, a fantasy, a craze, a passion: the 'strong-willed' man will carry it through to the end in spite of all obstacles, his so-called 'will' merely clears the path for his drives, shouldering away any obstacle on the line of least resistance for his particular tempera-ment. This is sometimes the least favourable aspect of secondarity, the inclination to systematise, which erects a rigid framework for the will: here we find that organised will-power that is less concerned with the objective than with maintaining an intact system. Thus we have the men of principle, ready to torture both reality, and those around them, in order to preserve their own imperatives: blind to the individuality of personal destinies, of the multiplicity of circumstance, they are, in spite of their pretentions, equally blind to what constitutes a true discipline of the intelligence, which is adjusted to that dual diversity. The systems to which they cling are usually somewhat naïve; a rich inner life would help them to unbend but we have seen that rigidity of psychic make-up also betokens its poverty.

  The driving force behind the will may again be harsh affirmation of the self. Paranoiacs are always talking of will-power, thus expressing their psycho-rigidity. Some 'strong-willed persons' whose career is quoted as an example of patient success, are only clever calculators, adapting their whole life, bending their relations, their friends, their very virtues to the service of their business or their ambition. With others, the pride of affirmation is found in its pure state: they enjoy the tension of their humour, as a wrestler the hardness of his muscles. With others, those to whom every gesture, the gesture from the heart as well as the decisions of the mind, is laborious, claim this sickly tension as a virtue and would willingly tame every natural grace in the world to their frenzied discipline. In its more degraded forms, the eloquence of word or gesture seems to be self-sufficient: these, the great majority of the 'strong-willed', prefer to watch and listen to themselves willing, instead of wishing to will heroically; a slight

---

* The abuse of the concept of will-power in earlier periods.

frown, an acid tone of voice is enough to reassure them against vague inner doubts whether they are acting without weakness.

In all such cases this pseudo-will-power appears not as mastery but as an autonomous mechanism. The content or origin of the so-called strong-willed behaviour has disappeared in the obstinacy which is sufficient to itself. 'I am thought energetic', said one of Janet's patients, 'because I never give way; I continue to pursue my own ends, even when it is clear that I shall achieve nothing.'[42] This dissimulation is irritating, for these strong-willed persons wear such a countenance of moral gravity, even when their manner covers nothing but a void. And there is also the most completely deceptive form of will-power, denounced by Spinoza, and abundantly illustrated by Freud, where obscure forces of the Unconscious beguile these solemn people into taking their veiled orders to be expression of their own sovereign decisions.

When an epoch has greatly abused a certain word or value, the danger of any negative criticism is that it will rally so many latent susceptibilities and rebellions as to become, against its intention, a purely destructive criticism. The crisis of the will-power of the strong-willed should not become a crisis of energy, as the contemporary novel has sometimes invited it to do. The field of personal action needed to be cleared of the psychological illusions which encumbered it, but we need now to restore the solid nucleus of a vital will, which excludes the compromises and the rigidities of fictitious will-power.

What the 'strong-willed' persons were unconsciously seeking in rigidity was a substitute for force of character. Should the will be reduced therefore to the application of effort, or, to use the language of the Schoolmen, to a *habitus* of effort? This sanctification of effort as such is perhaps at the very heart of their error. It is the concept of men of goodwill, but of little genius and less grace, and is founded on experience which it would be foolish to ignore. In man as he is conditioned, spiritual liberty is not acquired by a miracle. He must labour along the path of the simplest virtues as much as for the most elegant success. But this labour varies according to temperament and destiny: it is no measure of ultimate grace, which is the same for the last worker in the vineyard as for the first. We must therefore separate the idea of will from the idea of effort.[43] The will is wholly in resolution, which is an act coming from the heart of man. Effort is only the fairly constant expression of its practical application. But as it entails the action of our own body and the resistance of the object concerned, we, agents of flesh and blood, see, as Maine de Biran maintained, the very

source of our will in this application. This is what was meant by the
Aristotelian psychology, which laid down that self-possession was only
achieved by taking possession of the world. But effort is still only a
means. It may lead to merit, but is not merit, for it has no value in
itself: the value that we sometimes think to find in it, is a shadow
flickering between the intention and its purpose. Unconsecrated by
morality, effort finds no inner witness to sanctify it. The sense that
each of us has of his own power is not a function of the force he
exercises. The agitated and demented have a sense of overwhelming
power and of extraordinary facility. During the 1914–1918 war, a
patient considered himself Commander-in-Chief of the Allied armies,
and won as many battles as were required of him: a suggestion was
enough. Inversely, the melancholic does not think that he is incapable
of doing anything because he does nothing; he does nothing because
he thinks he is incapable.[44] The will, naturally, has its corporeal origin,
but even at this level it is not particularly linked with effort, but with
general vitality: the abulic are always found to be suffering from
devitalisation.[45] The capacity for effort is only one of the many
auxiliary factors that strengthen the will: activity, rapidity, resistance
to fatigue, resistance to discouragement, affective warmth, etc. Effort
is not even always at the service of the will's objectives: tests have
shown that the more we try to clarify an idea, the more it becomes
obscure; the more we try to remember something, the more it
escapes us.[46] Dr. Coué stated the rule that a forced effort of the will
was always, and without exception, less effective than free imagination.
Investigation into auto-suggestion and psychological efficacy have all
shown them to be centred in a state, correctly defined by Charles
Baudoin, as 'a particular equilibrium between relaxation and attention,
a rather stagnant attention, which remains fixed, without effort, in a
sort of torpor, on the ideas presented to it'.[47] If we wish to succeed in a
difficult or dangerous action, it is often good to isolate ourselves in this
way, passively concerned with the thing to be done, rather than
concentrating on it tensely: putting oneself, if one can say so, in a state
of attentive distraction. Without appealing to the will as effort, this
discipline (for it is one) educates the will as mastery, by destroying
rigidity and parasitical suggestions. Abramowsky's experiments have
shown that those who are most capable of such behaviour are also the
most energetic. The discipline of consciousness by effort is only one
little island in the discipline of the whole man, which also requires a
technique for training the Unconscious. Although such considerations
could be further pursued in the life of the spirit, it is not necessary to

step beyond psychology to discover the importance of relaxation and abandonment for the development of the psyche. The 'strong-willed person' . . . is a man who wishes to use his will the whole time, and thus paralyses himself by his projective activity, like an athlete trying to jump further by using only his agonistic muscles. We have indeed pointed out that there is a seriousness coming from total commitment, with the knowledge of the risks that it entails. But this other seriousness is often intolerable, since it expresses only a blind, abnormal tension. We all know, from our own experience, that the actions which have been the profoundest expression of ourselves have sometimes suddenly emerged, like flowers springing up silently at a smile from life itself.

The will is therefore none other than a person's act considered under its attacking rather than its creative aspect. But we should not equate one or the other of these aspects with attack and the qualities it entails: tenacity, consistency, resistance, aggressiveness are the expression of a creative energy. 'Effort', in James' admirable words, though he says 'effort' when he should have said 'will', 'appears to be the substantial reality of what we are, with regard to the other accidental realities which we only have and carry about with us.'[48] If we want a closer definition of the aspect of personal existence represented by the will, we can refer to the Christian moralists on force, that is, daring in the service of love: it brings all the powers of the individual to bear against the obstacle, resistance, endurance, aggressive zest and even the warmth of instinct, but in so doing it is animated neither by bravado, nor love of prowess, nor obstinacy, but by hope in God, which is the · most relaxed of all the virtues: its highest form is composure in the face of death: it is clear, therefore, that it is not a morose withdrawal but a function of personal gift. The pseudo-will-powers are closed wills, solitary labour of the self upon the self, sometimes ennobled by the desire for self-conquest or self-transcendence, but always with egocentric vision and method: it is this egocentricity which the Church finally condemned in the heroic eccentricities of the Desert Fathers. True will-power is an open force which takes man out of himself to centre him in an external and higher purpose, yet one deeply rooted in his soul. The tension of the pseudo-will-power is an attention to the self which confines action. A liberated will is a gathering of forces which expands action and locates it, crystallising every potentiality of a rich and complex environment for the pursuit of its end: it leaves in its wake a sense of the reality of agent and environment. It is an act of synthesis which gives unity, harmony and therefore penetration to an active Ego: 'an act is only voluntary in its novelty.'[49]

*

One might say that will-power begins when judgment appears, and that judgment is an act of authority as well as the recognition of a relationship. It is none the less true that to will it is first necessary to love, if each decision is, in principle, a sacrifice consented to for the sake of an attraction. In making the will the organ of the most impersonal abstractions the Kantian philosophy, or its substitute which governed the voluntarist philosophy of the nineteenth century, condemned it to sterility. 'Kantian philosophy has kept its hands clean', said Péguy. 'Yes, but it hasn't any hands.'

If we consider the power of resolution not at its source but in its effects, it frequently appears as an inhibitory force. It has, in fact, to contain all the particular or aberrant forces which are perpetually threatening to dislocate mental synthesis. In this sense it is the policeman of the personality and it is perhaps this that makes it unwelcome, even at its best, to the vagabonds of action. But even in this repressive form it does not produce rigidity. On the contrary, its task is to restrain aberrant rigidities.

It is, in its most simple form, resistance to automatism.

**

The will is also resistance to the impatience of instinct. The newly born infant . . . will not tolerate any delay in the satisfaction of its impulses. If this tendency is not rectified the child becomes capricious and tyrannical. The 'spoilt child' will always be an egoist, incapable of restraining his immediate interests in favour of more distant or more valuable ones, insufferable to those around him, insensitive to the difficulties of others. Education is largely a matter of learning how to confront and then to acquire a liking for what James has called 'the line of greatest resistance'. Privations which are understood and accepted, even blind obedience, provided the motive be neither stupid nor unjust, teach an adaptation to reality. But this restraint of instinct must be introduced according to the progress of the child's development. Every child passes through a distinctive phase, called a 'sadistic phase', quite incorrectly, since it transforms a means of exploration into a perverse deviation. Sexual development also displays its equivocal aspects at moments of crisis. If the child is disconcerted at such times by adult indignation which he does not understand, he may perhaps develop emotional complications or the more dangerous repressions. The training of instinct must be carried out with intelligent firmness and calm. Instinct must both be held in check and allowed to

---

* Discusses the experiments of Landowski, Shawran, Roracher.
** Reports on Kovarski's tests.

develop healthily. Coerced, it will cause trouble as surely as if it is allowed to run wild. Excessively protected, through fear of the accidents it may lead to, it withers and produces those hothouse plants who have certainly never broken a leg or burnt their fingers in any flame, but whose powers of living and creating are forever sterilised.

The widespread habit of inhibiting propriofective motor activity—the useless or excessive gesture—and of making these inhibitions one of the corner-stones of education, is particularly common in certain countries (England), and among certain classes (the wealthy). It is not without meaning, to the extent that gesticulation betrays an over-impulsiveness and a breach with reality, which both good taste and utility condemn. But the struggle with automatisms must not become another automatism, lest the child should learn to equate 'goodness with immobility and badness with activity' (Mme Montessori). The boy who touches everything has to be trained, but his curiosity must be retained. We should calm agitation but not kill spontaneity. 'Do be quiet' seems to be the supreme educational principle of most parents. It is true that they immediately reveal their interested motive: 'You make me tired.' Yet children are there to get to know the world by expending their energy, and parents are there to be tired. Here again one should only restrain by directing or bringing their multiple agitation into relation with reality, into devotion, or the like, according to the stage of instinctual development and attention to reality. No one can make the child profit from experience that, below a certain level of development, is not *his* experience. There is an age at which a child cannot be obedient or pay attention for a long time, just as there is an age at which he cannot walk: during this phase effort can only bring trouble. Progressive redirection should be accompanied by occasional and increasing exercises in silence and absolute tranquillity, as advised by Dr. Pichon: the child will accept them much more readily as exercises, which may acquire an affective interest, than as the perpetual repression of an activity which seems to him as natural as taking breath. Any other method will inevitably produce a series of affected young *poseurs*, whom most people quite sensibly ridicule, since with spontaneity of gesture they have also lost ease of manner and, what is more important, spontaneity of feeling and even the sense of reality.

Resistance to suggestion (and to its cousin, impulsiveness) can be trained like resistance to automatism.

*

* Further details of Kovarski's tests.

Finally the will is tested by resistance to both accidental and constitutional emotivity.

*

It would be completely illusory to believe that one can eradicate or forbid all painful effort in education. If some utopianists have thought so and even gained some credence, it is partly the fault of those who have made education solely a matter of training, restraints and prohibitions. Such servitude is necessary with wild, rebellious forces, but a man is not made solely by stakes and pruning knives. Give him an invigorating light and a horizon broad enough to make him stretch out with all his powers to reach it, and the tree will be strong and living and solid of structure. In this task the admixture of discipline and spontaneity must vary according to the individual: some, who listen only to force, must be strictly held; others can accomplish miracles through generosity and are depressed and irritated by meticulous exercises and would be stifled by authoritarian control. But it remains true to say as a general rule, look to the man, and the will-power will be added. As a general guide to the education of the will, spiritual experience reinforces the result of experimental study: too constrained an attention stifles action by narrowing the field of consciousness and twisting the spiritual drive into an egocentric drive. If the power of the will cannot be directly influenced by a kind of spasm at the appropriate moment, but only indirectly sustained by motivation, the principle of the education of the will is not to keep the subject in a state of high tension, but to enrich and expand the horizon of his values, as far as he allows, and in the direction of his main inclinations. 'To break the will' has no lasting effect if the psychological situation which led it astray is allowed to persist. Instead of a frontal attack on the relevant trend, it should firstly be subordinated as it is, and then progressively transformed by this subordination into a group of other corrective trends. These will not be chosen at random, but from those which have considerable influence on the individual concerned: the method suggested by every conclusion of experimental psychology is akin, in short, to the progressive absorption of a trend by sublimation which, we must remember, is an integration and not an idealisation. The operation will always be limited and carried out by specific means (Braunshausen) for, as the Schoolmen already knew, there is no general education of the will. But the trends aroused and the groupings brought into action will always have to be in keeping with the whole individual picture, from the instinctual roots to the world of values.

---

* Refers to Abramowski's tests, which have been suppressed.

As for the diversity of cases, a typology of will-power remains to be established.

*

THE TEMPERAMENTS OF ACTION

Every action requires a direction. But there is no single form of direction. It would seem that certain formulae of command separate men into two homogeneous and contrasting groups: those who command and those who are commanded. They overlook the fact that there is as much diversity, even incompatibility, in the capacity to command as in the category of 'leaders' and those who obey. This confusion leads, in practice, to repeated and unperceived errors; it ties people to places which are unsuited to them, breeds disorder and improvisation in organisations, and distrust and lack of confidence in those in authority. We have heard of the profession of leader: there are, in fact, several professions, since there are varying temperaments of leadership. The leader is not the administrator who, again, is not the animator nor the man who might be called the inspirer or adviser. Every organisation should see that each of these services is available to it and recruit its key executives on the principle that these types are hardly interchangeable.

The leader or 'chief' properly speaking is, if not the most complete —for each has his own perfection—at least the most complex of all. He is not distinguishable by his magnetic eye or his jutting chin, by the thinness of his lips or the cutting edge to his voice, nor by any of the stage effects only too well popularised by a colourful literature. There are chiefs with soft eyes, modest voices, insignificant features: there are some with classic profiles; some ugly or puny; and the greatest of them hate outward show. Authority is not for parade like the rulers of the barnyard. And if it is true that it is promoted by some show of ceremony, the wiser nations reduce this necessity to suitable proportions.

The chief is defined not by external signs but by dedication. He is above all the man who takes charge of others, assumes their hesitant or failing responsibilities. If humanity were perfect we should have mastered all the lethargies of automatism and disciplined the incoherent promptings of instinct. Each individual would be prompt to action and to responsibility, would have acquired the habit of decision and of taking risks. But humanity, in its current model, shows the passive triumph of inertia over initiative and automatism over the creative

* Refers varieties of positive will-power to Heymans' categories.

spirit, and the liking for tranquillity paralysing the vital sense of perilous adventure. The beatitude of passive obedience, deceiving itself as the result of some benign aspects of authoritarianism, is much more sought after than the joy of enterprise. If humanity were never to give way to this movement, it would perish by degrees. It is saved by its minorities. The temperament of chief is not only the vocation to assume one's share of risk and responsibility but the willingness and the gift of accepting the share that thousands are letting slide: the willingness and the gift of willing and deciding for others. His position is in the first place vicarious and sacrificial. Here perhaps lies the deep inner meaning of the mission assigned by Christians to Christ.

The chief is not therefore an animal tamer, a usurper who uses his subordinates as his property or instruments, a glorious prince who humiliates the multitude, a being sheltered from all combat. He is more alert than others, to be the first to perceive danger as opportunity; more perspicacious, the better to interpret the data of action; of better judgment, to utilise these data; swifter in decision, so that action is taken at the right moment; more audacious in the acceptance of necessary risks, in order to encourage others to accept their own; more courageous, to dominate the timidity around him; more persevering, to mitigate the usury of time or obstacles; more resistant finally to solitude yet richer in human warmth. His ascendance is due to the impulses transmitted by the active exercise of these qualities, and not by some external inflation of his prestige.

The virtue of leadership is therefore not solely a virtue of command. It is both a service performed and drive transmitted. Equally, the chief is a manager of men, not to be understood in the sense of a proprietor jealous of his privileges: the chief creates his equals. He propagates his breed, stimulating and inviting the humblest executive, without throwing him out of his orbit. Just as God affirms His omnipotence with regard to men by inviting men to become as gods, the true leader is only happy when he has aroused initiative, lucidity, decision, courage and audacity in the man who a short while ago was still a child in the affairs of life.

The chief is therefore not merely a good administrator endowed with some vague, mysterious aura. Nothing would better serve the restoration of authority than to strip the concept of leadership of its pseudo-mystical trappings which only betray a lack of analytic clarity. The qualities of leadership are concrete and decisive and acquire no force from obscurity and false mystery.

The *administrator* excels in the economy of things, or in the organisation of men, whenever men are capable of an exact pattern, or, by a provisional abstraction, of being considered as the elements of a complex and not as problems to be solved one by one. The best administrators are the unemotional, active types. The administrator may happen to be able to manage men, but this is not his real business and he is often clumsy. Yet wherever men are concerned, it is impossible to exclude the human factor entirely. If the administrator were to treat men as things, he would fail at his own function: it is more exact to say that he deals with them mainly in their relationship to things and in their functional capacities which can, up to a certain point, be objectified. This objectivisation is necessary to the good conduct of a business, even though it is partially inhuman. The drama of the technical direction of a business is that its purpose has its own claims, which are often in conflict with the human claims of the individuals concerned: in certain historical circumstances, which a single business man cannot himself reverse, the needs of production have been opposed to leisure and high salaries, and efficiency has opposed certain social demands. The administrator represents and controls the exigencies of things, and since things are not made productive by poetic and sensitive souls, he must be endowed with the inemotivity essential to his task. But he should nevertheless leave one window open on the side of man.

The *animator*, on the other hand, excels in dealing with the human apparatus of an enterprise. He is emotive and active: emotive, he is hypersensitive to the affective repercussions of decisions and to the reactions of his subordinates; active, he does not feel these reactions as compassion or inner irritation, but transforms them instantaneously by new orientations, reorganisations and modifications of tactics. He even feels the material structure of an enterprise as one senses the palpitations or the wishes of a human being; he may be ignorant of many of its details, but he often perceives what is needed, when it is needed, before the chief. Executives turn to him more readily than to the chief or to the administrator, because his enthusiasm or cordiality gives them confidence and, to some extent, suppresses distance. What is ossified by the administrator is restored by him to life. When the chief himself despairs, he is there with his youthful confidence. He makes the life blood circulate from top to bottom, down to the smallest cell of the business, from the heart to the head, and into every limb. In religion, he is the prophet or saint alongside the priest, the religious order alongside the clerical hierarchy. In parties, he is the propagandist; in nations, the hero or leader of men. He is not an institution in the smaller businesses; perhaps there he would lose his quality. The possibility should, however, be considered. But we should consider his negative side also, his excessive primarity. Do not put him in the pilot's seat: his thinking is too short-term, he is too unsystematic: without countercheck from others his impressions are of unequal value and, if of lively emotivity, he would proliferate in incoherent institutions, turn personnel and plans of action upside down every week, be sentimental in business and sow rancour by letting the preferences of his heart influence his dealings with men. But as second to the chief, responsible solely for creating enthusiasm, generating persuasion, human relationships and general circulation, he will work wonders. He is the born intermediary.

The excitement of action often leads to forgetfulness of the fact that every enterprise must continually re-think its sources, its spirit, its mystique, its future. There was the initial drive and then, for lack of time and detachment, absorbed by the daily round, one slips into automatism. The chief of a state or the audacious industrialist should maintain at his elbow a group of thoughtful men, relieved of all concern except continually to reconsider the basis of the work, and to maintain it in intelligence and spirit. This is the function of the *inspirer*. Like the preceding, it has fallen into disuse. Perhaps it is the effect of a withdrawal of intelligence, but also because modern leaders, as soon as they find an intelligent man, are tempted to overwhelm him with a command or an administration for which he is not necessarily cut out, and which deprives him of the means of developing his greatest asset, reflection. Thus the very thing that those in power wished to utilise, is dried up. Privy councillors, court philosophers and jesters were indeed corrupted by many immediate temptations, but they did satisfy, to some extent, this need. We should develop in every collective institution nowadays directors of study and directors of mission. The apparent sacrifices made to maintain them would, if they were given the means of remaining in vital contact with the organisation that employed them, be paid for in solidity and efficiency.

Finally we come to the *executive*.[50] But is there a pure executive type? A small number, normally, those whom a certain vital poverty and a passivity that has become habitual have deprived of the need for autonomy which is inborn in most. But in a well-constituted human enterprise there is, contrary to outdated beliefs, no cleavage between the chief and his executives, but a distribution, on a varying scale of application and degree, of the functions of chief, administrator, animator and inspirer. This should satisfy both the necessity of functional subordination and every man's innate desire to be, in at least one aspect of his activity, an initiator and a master man. This desire is more intense in some civilisations than in others, in some individuals than in others: a psychological and professional orientation is one of the elements in this attitude. If this desire is thwarted it is capable of a certain elasticity, but this elasticity ceases at a point beyond which all liking and capacity for initiative seem abolished. We have seen this happen when great masses of people, in high civilisations, have shown themselves capable of living for years in a passivity which one would have thought intolerable to any normal man.

6

THE SELF AMONGST OTHERS

ONE of the fundamental laws of conduct, according to Janet, is that we treat ourselves as we treat others. In more general terms, we treat ourselves as we treat reality. The human background, however, is for us a privileged universe, the only one in which we do not seem to be intruding. Fragile as glass, it is both the most natural of all backgrounds and, by its complexity and its incessant provocation, the most dangerous to our psychic equilibrium.
*

The awareness of others, like the awareness of reality, is . . . an intentional awareness, not punctual and centralised, like a spider at the centre of its web, but decentralised, prospective, penetrating, always shut in and always outward turning in a living universe.
**

. . . The apprenticeship to a human world is studded with crisis and ambush. Social life is an activity of high tension. It is sustained by aspiration, but there is no aspiration that is not subjected by life to a perpetual struggle. It must always overcome the resistances of egocentricity, the only resistances that never age, since they are reinforced by age. It must adapt itself to a multiple world, which disturbs the linear rigidity of instinct.[1] It must constantly respond to others' initiative, which is the essence of spontaneity and incalculability: they insist impatiently on responses, promise and forget their promise, resist when we thought they had agreed, upset our plans, wound our self-respect and keep us, finally, always on the alert. It is not astonishing that many refuse this invitation to humanity which, however guided by love, so strangely resembles a combat.

THE REFUSAL OF THE OTHER
***
In its mildest stage, the refusal of the other is expressed by mistrust, which may happen to pass as almost a virtue. It is not yet hostility, but

* Deals with the development of consciousness in early childhood.
** Continues the development of consciousness in childhood.
*** Refers to Heymans' categories and denies that there is any fundamental refusal to acknowledge the presence of others.

it reverses the natural movement of attention and sympathy. To the suspicious, the other is *a priori* synonymous not with a promise but with a threat. He is not even directly personalised: he is lost in the disquieting mass of the other, apprehended vaguely as a danger from without.

The heart reacts with mistrust just as the body reacts with disgust. It has been noted[2] that objects and odours which arouse disgust when coming from another, do so no longer when they come from ourselves, when they even arouse our interest, as if even the body loved itself organically and hated—because it feared—the body of another. A wound is not repulsive to a surgeon, because to him it is not *someone's* wound, but an abstract object of known lesions and movements. Disgust therefore seems to be attached to a threat not so much of danger as of violation: the animals that revolt us are not the most dangerous but the most capable of slipping into closest contact with our body without our knowledge. Disgust only disappears with primitive consciousness and is hypertrophied in patients suffering from a sense of possession.

But habitual mistrust is more of a danger signal than a simple protective reaction. It is no longer solely an instinctive spasm but already a form of human avarice. It refuses to others that credit from man to man which is a sort of anticipatory homage to the effects of generosity. In spite of its rather obvious sentimentality, the story of Jean Valjean develops the theme that generosity alone arouses generosity, and that to draw a cheque on this particular bank is to arouse in others the desire and the means to honour it.

To refuse one's confidence is not only to refuse a feeling, but to refuse effective help. Mistrust is not the lucidity it claims to be: it is the countenance of avarice. Frequent in the psychasthenic, it betrays their psychic penury more than their ill will. Elsewhere it is a lack of inner availability and, strictly speaking, an inhospitality of the heart. To the mistrustful individual, the man who approaches, be he visitor, passer-by, beggar, tradesman, stranger, is an enemy and a possible impostor. So he locks his door twice over rather than open it once to a nuisance. He counts his money with a sort of complacent insolence in front of the chauffeur who has just been driving him, he sets traps for his servants, he rebuffs all requests lest he be duped by one of them, he invites to his home only those of his own nation or particular circle, he accepts all human encounters as it were obliquely and with infinite calculation.

★   ★   ★

Maladjustment seems to indicate a more serious recoil than mistrust, which appears as still only a beginning of refusal. And yet the difference between them is similar to that between those slight, yet pernicious, infections which attack the heart of the organism and leave it permanently marked, and those more startling but less irreversible illnesses. Not all social maladjustments, incidentally, are equally significant. Some are accidents and rapidly readjusted. After a transplantation, or accidental loss or unwarranted increase of status, the process of social adaptation involves a rhythm so rapid that it calls in question every established action of normal life. We are concerned here with basic maladjustments which reveal a persistent structure of character.

These too have their slighter forms, that are mere suggestions of withdrawals. An animal hides itself after a defeat or misadventure. It is an elementary action on the part of schizophrenics or melancholics to hide themselves: they huddle up under their blankets and hide themselves from sight. It is the refuge of the scolded child, often also that of the adult who has suffered unhappiness, misfortune or bereavement. The presence of another reminds the vanquished of onlookers and conflict. The onlooker revolts him as an intrusion of external curiosity into his intimate personal feelings at the moment when these, in a state of crisis, are hyperconscious of themselves. Conflict does not appeal to his temporarily depleted energies. This strategic retreat may occur at very varying psychic levels. Amongst schizoids the search for isolation is brutal and expresses a decisive breach with the environment, followed by a retreat into the imaginary world of autistic reverie. The asthenic does not turn his back on others: he withdraws more or less deeply, without losing contact, 'in order to breathe', he says, both to restore his depleted strength and to establish a living space around him, which will fend off the approaches of the world which are a little too much for him. Without being, strictly speaking, subject to great fatigue, temperaments of the sentimental type need a period of solitude to quieten a sensitivity which is broadly active. Such withdrawals are more a positive pleasure than a rejection of society: such persons retire in order to enjoy pleasures which can only be tasted in detachment, rather than through a wish to break with others, who are intolerable not so much through being alien presences as by the noise they make in a mass, destroying the possibility of contemplation. Thus Maurice de Guérin said 'To leave solitude for the crowd, the green and lonely paths for the shrill, cluttered streets, where the only breeze is a current of warm, infected human breath; to pass from quietness to a turbulent life, from the vague mysteries of nature to harsh social reality, this has always been for me a terrible exchange, a return to evil and misfortune.' Between the quest for isolation, which is flight, and a positive liking for solitude as a rhythm necessary to personal life, a regaining of strength and of poise for the mind, there is an apparent continuity and many imperfect mixtures. But somewhere between the two lies the gulf which separates the behaviour which is refusal and the behaviour which is acceptance, a morbid rigidity and a vital rhythm.

The concept of privacy shares this ambiguous character. We can observe its fluctuations in attitudes related to modesty and secrecy. Modesty has the same relationship to disgust as detachment has to the refusal of contact. It is a recoil, mingled with some fear, but a gesture that protects more than it rebuffs. As against the natural tendency to display, it is the natural counterweight that keeps exteriorisation from becoming slackness, and communication from becoming promiscuity. To use an image from physics, it is a sort of surface tension of the personality. To see or to be seen, like touching or being touched, is a sacred act in all religions, because it transmits the transcendent. True modesty guards the portals of something sacred: to the believer it is the vigil before the 'temple of the Holy Spirit' or, from a more profane aspect, the custody of a poetry of the hidden yet available. 'An acute sense of the incommunicability of the soul', Dugas said of the timid, and the recoil of personal life. But modesty is a priestess, not a janitor, curt, surly and avaricious, as in aspects of puritanism: it does not refuse, but holds back: in the suppleness of the gesture there is as much acceptance as retreat, and not so much a warning as an invitation to greater respect. It can thus be distinguished from the arrogant, sickly prudishness, exaggerated compensation of a too vulnerable sensitivity, which betrays its own fragility by the rapidity with which, from time to time, it collapses like every artifice.

Secrecy may be regarded as modesty of thinking. To know how to keep a secret is the rarest thing in the world. Secrecy, in fact, is unaffected by social education, which for reasons which are partly traditional and partly utilitarian, protects modesty even in epochs where it is not highly prized. We say, quite correctly, that we 'respect' a secret. Someone who can hold a secret respects not only the privacy of the person who has confided in him, but also his own. We shall be dealing later with exhibitionism as both a common and primitive form of sociality. Secrecy weighs on us because it must resist this common trend for the sake of a higher sociality, which presupposes a certain quality of spiritual life. It weighs on us also because it leaves us alone, rigorously alone, with a knowledge that binds us, or a blistering experience. Few can endure this *tête-à-tête*: one never knows what it might suddenly lead to. If, however, we are accustomed to endure our own secrecy, we find it normal around us. It defines the distance between us and others, which, far from separating us, creates a connivance of secret understanding between persons who know that the infinite depths of life within them are not at their entire discretion. This feeling only disappears with a deadly simplification of personality: one sees it in the illness that gnaws at the heart of the paranoiac: he cannot endure secrecy around him, thus he perpetually suspects everyone. Respect, strictly speaking, only applies to the secrets of personal life, but it creates a habit of mind which extends to every form of secret. It represses a certain vulgar liking to relate and to reveal, to be the first man—or woman—to broadcast what is yet unknown, a sort of violation of which we are sometimes involuntarily the embarrassed accomplices. This sense of privacy is the sense of personal mystery. *Ego sum homo absconditus. Noli me tangere.* There is something of an imperfect symbol of transcendence in spatial distance, and in an acknowledgment of secrecy a recognition of metaphysical distance. Some patients with an enfeebled psyche complain at not being able to create the privacy they need. They cannot add to their experience that dimension of depth which gives them this inimitable quality.[3]

But there are secrets without secrecy, just as there are modesties without modesty. The sense of privacy is natural and simple: it fears neither the audacities of frankness nor of simplicity. Intolerant of vulgarity, it accepts with good humour the accidental intrusions which the hurly-burly of life throws against our most solid barriers. There is, however, a sickly, hypersensitivity of privacy; the man who moves house because he no longer feels at home after he has been burgled, another who makes a scene if someone comes into his dressing room, another who will not let anyone tidy his desk. All these are vulnerable persons who defend themselves spasmodically. Mystery-mongering is a similar deformation of the sense of secrecy. Some persons are perpetually on tenterhooks lest others should discover the turnover of their business, the amount of their income, where they are going, what they are planning or thinking, their illnesses, etc. It is not a question of that rather rare reserve which prevents us from assaulting other persons' indifference or soliciting their sympathy by a complacent display of our private affairs. Mystery-mongering is a much more active, even more industrious defence. Its real home is not in simplicity but in false mystery.

*

The social importance of such maladjustment can be more serious when it is not limited to withdrawal from the social environment, but intervenes, as J. Lefrancq says,[4] 'to destroy, transform or dislocate it according to the need of its inner resistances.'

**

Vetter[5] has studied experimentally the 'atypical' or dissident temperament. A born refractory, he always turns to the extreme, passing freely from one position to the other, provided it is always extreme. A typical behaviour seems to be not so much a congenital disposition as hypercompensation for an unhappy social experience. Vetter found it four times more frequent than the opposite disposition in only children, and a majority of cases amongst families of limited means. Emotional instability and originality of association are equally concerned here. It marks the frontier between hyperemotivity and the schizoid state. One shuts himself up in his study, the other in a desert. The prodigious adventures of explorers have more than once been due to the need to flee from men to pursue the secret of some inner dream. The great lovers of nature or the poetry of things are often of this breed. When he is not completely impersonal the schizoid only builds a slightly higher wall to separate him from the world. He requires of a strictly limited society that it should be a barrier between him and the universe. He loves sects, pseudo-communities, because they are made in his image, rigid, exclusive, intoxicated by abstractions. Or, in contempt for men, he adopts a superficial sociability, as glossy as that of high society, without real relationship to his surroundings. 'My life is, at bottom, nowhere except in myself', wrote Benjamin Constant in his *Journal*. 'I surrender its external forms to anyone who wishes. I am wrong, since it saps my time and energy, but my inner life is surrounded by a certain barrier, insurmountable to others. Sometimes they may make a breach, and cause me to suffer, but they can never master it entirely.' He disconcerts those around him. What is there behind this silence, this cold irony, this closed, withdrawn, impassible countenance? Suffering, indecision, hatred, contempt, indifference, the void? No one knows. Sometimes this rigidity adopts the plasticity of wax, frequent

* Quotes Janet and Dr. Ollier on cases of acute fear of intimacy.
** Quotes clinical examples of acute refusal.

in the 'model' schizoid child: it is only another way of evading a precise encounter.
*

Some psychiatrists maintain that a breach with the environment lies at the root of all mental disorders. According to Adler, the neurotic always tries to establish a distance, a protective zone between the larger or smaller society and himself. According to Charles Blondel, a morbidity of consciousness is grafted on to an incapacity to receive any social contribution: it is a liberation of what he calls, by a quirk of vocabulary, the 'pure psychology', that is to say, the purely individualist substratum, diverted from sociality and delivered to anarchy. Stripping this latter concept of its systematisation, we might say that every psychosis includes desocialisation as well as alienation. An isolated consciousness is a haggard consciousness which slips imperceptibly along the path to mania.

THE UTILISATION OF OTHERS

I may give the impression of accepting the existence of others and yet reduce this existence either to the service of my own personality or to some situation which is a practical negation of the privileges of personal existence.

The need to escape into the world is just as frequent as the need to escape from the world, 'the world', in the biblical sense of the word, is the 'other' dispossessed of his reality as a neighbour, and transformed into an object of entertainment. To a coquettish young mother, her child is one pretty bauble amongst others; to a complacent husband, his wife is a flattering embellishment, an element of his social prestige: if she is beautiful, he has acquired that rare and miraculous charm represented by a fragile luxury in the daily round.

How many men keep others thus, even their nearest, in a zone halfway between ignorance and indifference, where their right to an autonomy of existence vanishes completely. The noisy, variegated crowd is a vast fair in which it is the easiest thing in the world to lose oneself. Social contacts supply for some a vast alibi under cover of which they can seek fresh surprises for their desires, complicity for their weaknesses, nourishment for their gossip, the fever of partly consummated intrigues, near scandal, vague immodesties, nascent malice, excitement enough to provide a cold heart and empty head with the illusion of thinking. Proust has remarked that much of our love is, above all, the love of desperate flight, arising from the anguish

* Examples of active maladjustment.

of our solitude. It subsists on the more tolerable anguish caused by a fascinating object which evades one and which one pursues. The politician often seeks from other men a collective diversion of the same order. He requires an echo from his public, and emotions he would not be able to achieve himself: he is drunk with the swelling voice of the crowd and its capricious anxiety; it is not, however, sure that he always offers the commitment of a living faith and the experience of communion to those who march shoulder to shoulder with him.

The effervescence that the movement of others around us creates, provides a much sought-after excitement. Has one ever measured the role played by gossip in the affairs of the average individual? It creates that pseudo-community of daily tittle-tattle described by Heidegger, where the existence of the partners is nothing more than a gossip in common, and the interest in this gossip. In it we lose the will and even the capacity to understand others, as well as any deeper relationship with ourselves. Either our interest in others is only a superficial, uneasy curiosity, which prevents all penetration, or our attention is distracted between them and us, towards the current trend of fashion and appearance, feverishly seeking to know the opinion others hold of us, and the opinion we should hold of them, the agreed hierarchy of tastes and colours. Our attention pursues in others not their existence but what is 'interesting', that is, the picturesque. Some view this common death as social existence, this fall as an expansion, this whirl-pool of ever newer and more numerous relationships as openness of heart. The depressed are particularly satisfied by this fever: they are the first to exhaust themselves in social distractions and adventures: they are caught by their own fire, they vibrate, become inflamed with en-thusiasm, confusing the agitation of their temperament with communal zeal. The deceptive seriousness with which so many politicians seek to cover up their emptiness has always made them repugnant to lucid thinkers. It is the illusion of virtue, compared with true devotion, which sometimes makes the devotees of good works so irritating. One of Janet's neurotics declared: 'My only refuge is philanthropy, the refuge of the stupid, where there are most of them. I go in for good works because I am incapable of doing anything else; but I must admit that, for me, it is sometimes a useful remedy'.[6] This patient had more insight than most.

These waste lands which society sometimes maintains around our normal activities are, in addition, excellent repositories for a consciousness which wishes to remain peaceful and satisfied. We have already spoken of the semi-magical mechanism of *projection*. We

always think of ourselves as a closed box of wishes and desires, everything outside being literally foreign to us. But our psyche is much
more like a gas which diffuses itself into the surrounding atmosphere.
Thus we often think that we are going towards others when we are
only going to meet ourselves. This is a commonplace of moralists and
mystics, for which modern psychology provides startling examples.
Thus the habit of giving presents does not always prove the
generosity of the giver: in the 'narcissistic gift', recognisable because
it fits the personality of the giver rather than that of the recipient, one
is making a gift to oneself.[7] The same is often true of pity and of the
feelings, apparently communal but basically egocentric, which we may
devote to our family, our party, our country. But above all we project
on to others the feelings we do not wish to recognise in ourselves, our
unconscious complexes and particularly our self-accusations, legitimate
or not, our unadmitted faults. These projections, we must remember,
are unconscious. It all takes place in the Unconscious and impersonal.
Every man who casts a questioning glance upon me invokes a moral
responsibility on my part, either because the quality of his presence
invites me to an interesting conversation, or because through his
degradation he is, as it were, a living reproach to the inadequacy of
my own influence. The 'thou' is reserved, in English, to the dialogue
between man and his Judge. A moral consciousness meets this fraternal
judgment face to face, not the falsified, illegitimate judgment that men
pass the one *on* the other, but that which each man *is* for the other.
The satisfied consciousness, on the contrary, shuns this face to face, and
hastens to dissolve the reproach in the impersonality of the group,
behaving like the economic system of which it was said that it combined
the collectivisation of losses with the individualisation of profits. But
this sharing with the community of which one considers oneself a
member, although disclaiming its weaknesses, is still only a partial
reassurance for the satisfied consciousness, which is only completely
happy when completely detached from any contact with fault, when
this can be thrown on to a foreign collectivity, nation, class, race,
enemy group. Thus attention is distracted both from others and from
one's own sense of guilt. One of the most valuable sections of Marx'
work is where he describes the economic 'alienation' by which the
person of the worker is, as it were, voided of reality and assimilated to
a commodity, a thing amongst things. This happens. But the moral
alienation to which we have referred is still more fundamental, and
economic alienation is often in some way linked with it.

An unhappy link binds us to others throughout the network of unconscious projections. We do not see them as projections, and we pursue them with the hostility we feel, since they have been discharged by us. It is these feelings which we turn upon the persecuted paranoiac, in the form of omnipresent hostility. To some degree it is the same feelings which lead persons liable to self-accusation to see hidden reproaches in the intentions of others. They colour the universe of the inhibited with the colours of their inhibitions. The prudish see evil everywhere. This tendency to see the world uniformly in the image of what, consciously or unconsciously, we are ourselves, is all the stronger when egocentricity is powerful. Thus it explains the tendency, as common as egocentricity and proportionate to its strength, to depreciate others. We can only be delivered from this embarrassment of libido and from these living reproaches which we have expelled from the environment, if we devaluate them.[8] Those who feel inferior project their inferiority and consider their environment despicable. The suspicious feel surrounded by hostile intentions. The desire to put people on the right track, to save or to punish, is born of this unconscious phariseeism. One may refuse to save others, and yet be victim of the same aberration, like a character in the contemporary theatre who carried the system to its logical conclusion by proclaiming: 'Hell is the other people'.

*   *   *

Together with the use of others as diversion or alibi, comes the more common use of others as the mirror and reflector of an uncertain self. It satisfies a number of elementary needs which, as a whole, form what one may call passive sociality. A healthy consciousness is an expansive force which, with a single movement, makes us aware of the other, as it makes us aware of the object. But it includes a reflex, a tendency to return to the self, in opposition to this movement of exteriorisation. If vitality is normal, the reflex will be organically integrated in action, the reflexive *states* never asserting a usurped dominion over intentional *behaviour*. If, on the other hand, vitality is weakened, Klages[9] has shown that the faculty of exteriorisation is withdrawn and fixed on itself, becoming degraded into the need for representation; intervention or commitment is replaced by a love of show. The nearest and most docile spectator that one can find is oneself. This narcissism can be considered more as a failure than as a refusal of sociality, a failure even at the very outset. If vital weakness has not entirely impeded the movement of expression, then the spectators are sought in the world. But the underlying intention of such behaviour is an egocentric search for a mirror. It is still a narcissism, complicated by being routed through others.

*   *   *

The need to confide or the need to be known underlies the most elementary egocentric forms of sociality. We have already mentioned the burden of secrecy. Our deepest instincts seem to find secrecy intolerable. According to Freud, absolute secrecy is a factor in psychic disorders, absolute secrecy being that which becomes so by its relationship to our personal consciousness. Therapeutic treatment breaks up the nucleus of the complex it secretes around itself and restores the buried secret to circulation. At the beginning of *Deux Sources*, Bergson analysed the criminal's compulsion to make his crime known. All our inner states suffer this impatience. It is considerable in the psychasthenics who look for a strength on which to lean: in the normal person it is due more to a need for expression than for support. It is resolved in narration, which we elaborate whilst the experience is still alive, and are already relating under our breath to imaginary persons before we can pour it into an attentive ear. It is particularly strong when the experience involves value judgments: a bad conscience hopes for confession and pardon, the uneasy conscience for encounter and dialogue. Janet said of the confessional that 'it seems to have been invented by a mental specialist of genius, who was treating obsessional cases.' It is more than that to the believer, but it is at least this to a psychologist. When it is not a religious institution it reappears in multiple forms, sometimes in the most vulgar exhibitionism, sometimes as the sign of the rarest and highest trust.

The need to be seen or to appear, to 'be in public' as the Germans say, is already found in the animal kingdom (the peacock who always displays when he is observed). It appears at an early age, at about two, in the child. The exhibitionism of those adults who seek publicity and confidence at all costs, who are only happy in the limelight, is an infantile crystallisation of an instinctive phase imperfectly sublimated. Showing oneself, like narration, is an elementary gesture of social behaviour: to show oneself is to provoke the attention of others with a view to collaboration or exchange. But, like all stages of psychological development, ostentation may become fixed on itself: it then becomes a substitute for communication, just as words become a substitute for action. A parade before action, it may even be transformed into a parade against action: it is generally found in connection with inactivity and vital debility: the liking for effect overcomes any higher purpose in the scatter-brained types always pursuing some new spice for their uncertain or blasé palates; the sense of property becomes ostentatious when the zest of acquisition has faded: and sexual insolence often betrays, like emotive inflation, a falling-off of instinct.

*

The consciousness preoccupied with others is a rigid consciousness. Affectation destroys its naturalness, the quality of gesture which pays no more attention to itself than to the attention it attracts. The tone is forced, the style stressed, and something of a pose interrupts the vital rhythm and makes it mannered. There comes the moment when the attention of others is no longer desired, it is sought for: the behaviour takes on a disingenuous twist: haughty, complimentary, obsequious by turn. Such are the traits of vanity, disclosing its hollowness, arbitrary flourishes on a building. It is not, like pride, the overflow of power, but the inflammation of impotence: its successes are not an abuse of power, but a slight psychological swindle.

*   *   *

The desire to be seen creates a deceptive society of vague personages on the periphery of our character: one reflects a latent wish, another a futility, another a pretention or a regret: none of these is our real self, but each has the role of representing us, inside a particular social group, as we would wish to appear to be. Built out of our own material, with enough of our real selves not to be too improbable—and authentic to the extent that we wish them to exist—they borrow most of their texture, however, from the current taste that they wish to flatter, and vary accordingly. It is this social aspect that Rousseau attacked, his natural vehemence leading him to convert an intuition into a system. When he speaks of society as a corrupter he is, in fact, attacking opinion and prejudice which he accuses of transforming a normal, healthy love of self into egoism, and thus diverting us from the lessons of experience and defeat. A little more psychological precision would have prevented his pursuing an observation full of good sense to the point of stupidity.

**

Mozart used always to ask everyone: 'Do you really like me?' and

***

* Refers to Baudoin's 'complex of being seen' and Heymans' categories.
** Compares and contrasts the hysterical and mythomaniac character.

a hesitant reply would plunge him into despair. The need to be loved
or the need to please is, like the need to be seen, a sign of psychic
weakness when it occurs in a strongly egocentric obsessional form. It is
less immediately imperious and has wider repercussions than the need
for ostentation: thus, unlike the latter, it is more frequent with
secondary than with primary types. It is frequent in the depressed, who
seem to question their own existence, particularly since their very
primitive emotivity has led them to believe that to live is to live
emotionally.

*

This 'need for affection' is always grasping and jealous: to share an
affection is to admit that one shares attention. There are no more
fretful friendships than these avid friendships, no more stormy affections
than these parasitical, dominating affections: 'I want the first place, the
only one, I want things to be sacrificed for me . . . I am angry with
God, because He belongs to everyone.'[10]

**

In the same group we find the need to be approved. Like the two
former, it betrays weakness and passivity, as soon as it becomes
obsessional. 'If I need compliments, it is because only compliments can
make me resemble others, whereas anything that humbles me is bad
and throws me back into a morbid humour.[11] 'Kind words' have a
magical effect on such persons: inversely the slightest criticism
demolishes them. The horror of having enemies and the need to
obtain sympathy at any price, are often pushed to a slightly ridiculous
extreme: the woman, for instance who, on every railway journey,
would 'play up' until she had 'conquered the compartment'. External
circumstances may accentuate this need. Many persons who have
known no normal stability are always tortured by the feeling of being
useless or solitary. They have a perpetual need to be assured of
their contact with the general circuit of fruitful lives. But a basic trend
of temperament is more usually the cause.

***

In all the attitudes we have just considered the other is only
understood as an instrument. The very services which are required of
him are an admission that he is a source of affective possibilities: his
essential dignity may be misunderstood, but not his essential humanity.

---

* Gives clinical examples.
** Further clinical examples.
*** Discusses those who cannot bear to be approved, and certain morbid forms of
the need for approval.

But the instrument may turn from being a means into a pure object.
*

When the business man, the engineer, the priest, the statesman, are only concerned with problems, or interested in causes, without even beginning to pay attention to the individual mysteries that these problems affect, then the deadly process has started. Few men of action, few social figures escape it entirely. We often meet persons of infinite and devoted activity, who betray the onset of the disease by little details, for instance their contempt for the novel. Many intellectuals would be incapable of losing an idea in order to save a man. The evil must be noted in its slightest symptoms, or we shall perceive too late that death has insidiously taken possession where life seemed most animated. The most sociable man may be, by the very nature of his sociability, the most insensitive: Taine tells us of a courtier who, on his return from Versailles, stopped in the street to watch a dog gnawing a bone: he wanted for once to observe a real feeling.

THE PRESENCE OF THE OTHER

A behaviour of flight from the other, or of explicitly refusing to recognise his privilege of autonomy, reveals itself to us in very elementary forms. The presence of the other affects us also in a very simple way before becoming complicated by all the superstructures of sociality.

One of the most conscious and perhaps the most primitive forms of this interpsychology is the sensitivity we display simply to a look from another person. This is already quite clear in the newly born child, in whom it arouses a physical exhibition of pleasure.[12] A prolonged gaze usually intimidates or inhibits and produces a spasm of rage in the idiot.[13] Under its effect the timid lose countenance, factually and psychologically. Even the slightly asthenic are hypersensitive in this respect: there are many who find it much more exhausting to listen to a story in the company of others than alone, or even find it embarrassing to read in the presence of others. Very few, even the most confident, are entirely free: try coming late into a silent meeting, where every eye turns to meet you: the young girl who blushes as soon as she feels she is being looked at. Some find eyes in their back particularly intolerable; they cannot work with someone standing behind them, irrespective of the confidence and liking they may have for him. We

* Relates the tendency to use persons as instruments to Heymans' categories.

have stumbled on a very primitive dismay at the first advances of society.
*

The timid have been said to be 'ill with secrecy': they might equally well be called ill with the presence of others. In other words, we might term them hyperconscious of being seen; they react to the simple presence of another as to an indecent exhibition. They fear the judgment this single person may deliver: they fear they will wound or be wounded: rebuff or be rebuffed. The first effect of consciousness is always to disorganise an established order in order to promote a creative order: this is even why some are so desperately anxious that we should remain collectively stupid. The first social contact only disturbs a self-satisfied consciousness. The English use the word *self-conscious* to describe the timid. The word fits that abrupt hyper-trophied awareness of the weakness and isolation of the self in the vast universe: a hyperawareness, but hyperawareness of a fragility which reacts in physical and psychic disorder. This morbid inflammation of consciousness may pursue the timid even in their solitude: the acutely timid are incapable of action when they are alone.[14] Timidity is almost normal in adolescence: some very self-assured young men would be much astonished to be told that their excessive self-assurance, far from being an asset, is the sign of an infantile survival. One gets over timidity, as one gets over adolescence, sooner or later,[15] but some people never. Should timidity disappear altogether? If personal consciousness is inseparable from a certain modesty towards the perpetual mystery of man and the world, we should perhaps praise timidity or, at least, that minimum of inner uncertainty which, once glimpsed, gives depth to the most assured behaviour.
**

It we add together the exhausting effects of the presence of others: dispersal, distraction, intimidation and agitation, it is clear that periodical isolation is a vital necessity for everyone. Action recovers its breath, as in sleep, and renews its resources. But this need tends sometimes to exceed all measure, as in the schizoid. Adler classes as abnormal the refusal to choose one's own friends, when this continues up to the age of twenty; refusal to choose a profession, up to the age of thirty; refusal to marry, persisting up to forty. But we should not class anyone as schizoid simply on an unusual liking for solitude.
***

---

* The paranoiac reaction to the presence of others.
** The asthenic reaction and the factor of emulation.
*** The asthenic reaction, suggestibility and identification.

Everything has already been said about the illusions of one's inner feelings and the inadequacies of introspection. Not only do I deceive myself in a thousand ways as to what I am and what I think, but by living entirely with myself and my own thoughts I become partly blind to them. Thus in the very substance of moral activity germinates that spontaneous phariseeism from which it is never entirely free. Properly speaking, phariseeism is the sickness of isolated consciousness. However simplified the saying 'the eye sees everything except itself', it contains some truth. At least the eye can only see itself in a mirror, and the best mirror for man is another man. A child of two, trying to make his sister recognise his own property,[16] said: 'My yours' thus spontaneously describing a fundamental human journey. Consider the experience of the beginnings of a friendship, or better still the first stages of a life in common. A new being enters my immediate field, and everything is put in question by this single presence. Until this meeting I was located in a more or less coherent bundle of dispositions, beliefs, habits and ways of living. My judgment on all this was clouded by familiarity. I no longer saw the mediocrity of some, the grotesqueness of others. I had become used to myself, as others become used to their poverty or squalor. Furthermore, I reacted angrily when I ran across similar traits in others: if only there were as much generosity and nobility in the world as there are mouths to lament its egoism and depravity! The man who reproaches his political antagonists for subordinating religion or their country to political ends, is trying ingenuously to annex them to his own party on the pretext of saving them. But now a fresh pair of eyes is considering me. This disturbs the slumbering establishment. I become, but now in the most lucid sense of the word, *self-conscious*. Habits, tics, particularities, implicit beliefs, stand out as a result of this gaze alone, like a negative under the developer. Some looks act slowly, others strip you bare immediately. Some act at a distance, by letter, through a book. This revealing action is not the only one. Just as another's gaze lights up our inner contours, so our own gaze at another leads to a sense of proportion. These manias, these mediocrities, these cares and prejudices which I was taking so seriously, I see them in another for what they are, and how grotesque, or at least how psychologically picturesque they are! Malice is generally right in its diagnoses. Why is our judgment on ourselves not equally lucid and biting as it is for external use? There alone it recovers the true measure of man and sees his pettinesses for what they are. O *ridiculosissimo eroe*! Kohler has shown that in intellectual activity the quickest way from one point to another is often a detour, as if the physical world forced us to break the rigidity of action in the labyrinth it offers to the ingenuity of action. It would seem, by analogy, that the other is the quickest route between myself and my knowledge of myself. The isolated consciousness is blind, rigid, massive. The other is the question-mark on our path, the provider of salutary irony. Alone I am cluttered up with my sufficiency and my débris. Soon I become like a book that has been written, a harvest gathered. The other is the unexpected, coming to this stagnation with his reproaches or appeals, awakening my sleeping energy with his threats or promises. Under this acid irony, the profusion of these advances, I become aware that I am slightly ridiculous, and this is the beginning of wisdom. The sense of the ridiculous is a pleasant apprehension of our nothingness, just as boredom is its morose apprehension. It shatters the weak, the strong hit back with their own irony. The meeting of the two ironies make up that sturdy but modest humour, halfway between self-sufficiency and humiliation, which is the measure of mental health. It is not solely ironic: this 'delirious trouble at being concerned with an unknown life', of which Proust wrote, is one of the most overwhelming and disturbing of feelings.

ASCENDANCE AND DEPENDENCE

Before two men mutually agree to accept each other as men, a further temptation lies in store: that of trying to make the other submit, or to submit to him, by abdicating from, or restraining that freedom of association which is at the basis of human order.

The inclination to dependence takes on the quality of a real need in certain infirm natures. We can observe its infantile origin. The newly born child depends entirely on others, even for the satisfaction of his instincts. At first he distinguishes himself so little from the world around him that this total dependence is felt by him more as omnipotence, the care given to him appearing to be the immediate answer to his imperious needs. This primitive ambivalence can subsist in the need for dependence under the guise of tyrannical impulses. The child feels his dependence fully in the second stage when he encounters the world. This feeling disappears slowly in normal circumstances, up to the twelfth year. It should disappear at puberty, at least in its infantile, obsessive form, mingled with distress and diffused terror. The breach is made with violence in a reaction of opposition to the father's influence, and of rather irritable reserve to the affection of the mother. Parents do not always understand this crisis and hamper it in various ways; they rebuff this budding independence and turn it into revolt:

or they stifle it: incapable of renouncing the pleasures they received from the child's inferior situation, they prolong as long as they can, for their own satisfaction, his pre-pubertal mentality: they do not realise that once the right moment has passed some maturations become impossible and that by a puerile caprice they have turned their child into a permanently diminished being.

Every form of abnormal psychic dependence betrays a form of infantile attachment to one or the other parent. This is one of the best established discoveries of psychoanalysis. The subject, thus more or less fixated in a pre-pubertal mentality, projects on all sides, on to the faintest social authority, the paralysing feeling that the infant experienced when faced with the absolute power he attributed to his parents. When others look at him he feels, like a child, surrounded by concern and control, whereas the majority of men are thinking of something quite different from the person they are looking at. He lives in a chronic state of intimidation, not only by his superiors, whom he overrates, but by the first comer, the policeman at the crossing, the concierge, the ticket clerk, the social authorities. He is law-abiding in the special sense that fears more than respects the established order: for this reason he is often its most stubborn supporter. Excessively sensitive to public opinion, to 'what people will say', he makes this the receptacle for whatever capacity for intimidation he cannot localise elsewhere. Sometimes it is distributed amongst a hundred petty superstitions which he translates somewhat too quickly into providential warnings: a chance event, a mishap, a letter which does or does not arrive, are interpreted as messages from an invisible, unfavourable or protective authority. The intellectual who bites his nails jumps like a guilty child when his telephone bell rings whilst he is indulging in this harmless occupation—or a young girl will suddenly blush at a harmless question.

Such persons have to be supported in all their undertakings. They can start nothing themselves. They can never face authority, even the most imaginary authority, like that which they attribute to a simple shop assistant: they step aside. This practical timidity renders them so little combative of temperament that all initiative is lost and often even the happiest natures deprived of the audacity, courage and devotion which their instinctive generosity would otherwise inspire. Pondering over past actions, they blame themselves for unreflecting acts of cowardice which, at the time, appeared to be only insurmountable timidity, and their sense of inferiority is thereby aggravated.
*

* The effect of secondary on the complex of retreat.

More accentuated, their desire for dependence becomes a tyrannical demand similar to the need to be loved. The subject no longer finds pleasure only in 'being understood', mingled with a vague distress at not being understood. He suffers from an obsessional desire to be directed. This is a classic situation with depressed or weak and hysterical persons. 'Someone must take care of me, take an interest in me, no matter how', declared one.[17] They have an instinctive horror of solitude: women have even been known to take lovers not so much from physical need as from the terror of being alone. They can neither work nor amuse themselves alone. They have nothing that is not borrowed, their faith, their zeal, their ideas, their strength itself. They like to have a 'moral support' permanently attached to them; a doctor, friend, relative, confessor, whom they always idealise. Ever since adolescence they have been looking for this 'ideal' confessor or confidant, and when they have found him, they are obsessed with terror at the idea of losing him. They expect from him ready-made judgments and decisions for them to follow. They do nothing without consulting him, never questioning any view or decision that comes from him, and defend them more stubbornly against a third party than if they themselves had orginated them. Others are not attached to any single guide, but are always looking for someone to whom they can account for what they have done or are about to do, who must confirm even their most insignificant decisions. If this help is refused, they collapse, yet the whole strategy of such directors or friends should be to guide them progressively towards autonomous action. This infantile survival of abnormal passivity may inhibit puberty and then masculinity.[18] It is strongest in the phlegmatic and the amorphous.

*

Inversely, some temperaments cannot tolerate contact with their superiors or even their equals. The weak and the psychasthenic always seek their relationships amongst their inferiors, or persons, such as children or old people, whose age makes them docile or amenable. Except for the submissive we have just discussed, a too constant state of subordination afflicts a normal man, even if this subordination is due to gratitude or an overwhelming affection. Some are exhausted if compelled to pass half a day in a group which is clearly superior to them in intelligence or social standing. And if one is frequently

---

* A servile attitude as a product of over-compensation; false obedience not to be confused with the moral values of obedience and respect; attitudes of dependence in women; the spirit of juvenile revolt not to be confused with the development of personal autonomy.

irritated by the upright, it is not solely because they are so often insufferable, but also because mediocrity is unhappy in the presence of superiority. Intolerance of the superior type by the inferior is normal in primitive societies which, still uncertain of themselves, fear the disruptive effect of genius. The superior or original man is considered possessed of a devil and therefore suppressed: this was the misadventure of Socrates and Christ. The same feeling recurs in any society in crisis, that tries to find salvation in brutal conditions and uniform disciplines, when perhaps only the hardihood of the creator or the madness of a hero might save them.

This resentment of the superior by his inferior is neither as pure nor as impure as either would claim. When it is directed against usurped superiority, say the superiority of money, it often includes an authentic aspiration toward justice for all and dignity for everyone. But even then it is rare for it not to turn by infection against every form of superiority, even the most unchallengeable. If there is a basic equality amongst men, which challenges all empirical inequality, it is an equality of vocation, not of levelling: it should allot to all an equivalent destiny, given an equal effort from all. There must be a minimum of distributive justice. But distributive justice is only the substructure of the human order, whose guiding principle is generosity. When egalitarian feeling aims only at a mathematical regulation of distribution, its good intentions are really only instinctive avarice. Re-stating Bentham's utilitarianism, Freud derives social feeling from this captive instinct which, through a narrow concept of justice, he reduces to an egalitarian calculation. The individual is willing to sacrifice to the community some of the drives which his inborn jealousy would direct against social life, but only in the expectation of a strictly equivalent return. If this is not granted, he insists that the others shall, at least, be deprived of their dues: since I have a dead child, thought the mother who appeared before Solomon, the other mother should not have a living one. The passion for justice and the passion for equality would, in such a case, be only the transformation of primitive hostility into positive attachment by the identification of individual egoism with that of others.[19] Thus the abulic are always insisting on their 'rights' but this only means getting others to perform for them the actions they should undertake themselves.[20] On the same level, indignation at injustice is the feeling of being frustrated of the expected return. The revulsion of disappointment may lead to a fanatical desire for reparation, which breaks with social restraint and moral structures, seizing on any justification for the passions unleashed,[21] as an afterthought. As usual, Freud has built up the history of the psyche from its seamy side, but no one can deny that this process is still very active, so active that it has served, not without show of reason, as an argument to support the instinctive passions of anti-egalitarianism. The love of justice only ushers in a new world when it has passed from captation to oblation, from jealousy to a rivalry in generosity which has already been known to govern social intercourse, in such forms as the potlach, in societies said to be inferior. Then it can thrive on an inner abundance and lively collective interest, and not on an uneasy comparison with one's fellows. It tends not to the levelling but to the surpassing of the individual and the collective. The quest for this new man will be a long one, and no doubt is only just beginning.

To command is a higher form of behaviour, like obedience. . . .
*

But we should not confuse the vocation of chief with the desire to give orders. The first leads to a difficult situation without repose and often without glory. The second is the liking of the weak for an easy situation which substitutes words for actions, where authority multiplies the means at the disposal of their caprices, where others have to do what otherwise they would have to do for themselves, and where they hope to gain, by this fraudulent intimidation, the respect and esteem to which their weakness does not entitle them. Looking at both obedience and commandment, the behaviour of domination and the behaviour of submission appear as symmetrical figures, giving rise to analogous manias.[22] Consider, for instance, the mania for helping people. This is often not an excess of kindness, but the need to find a stimulus in another's action, through being unable to take sufficient interest in one's own. This mania for intervention is one of the most frequent forms of a woman's desire to dominate: through it she can express her devotion, her egocentricity and her dependent state (Heymans). It is the benign form taken by authoritarianism in the timid and uncertain, who project their own insecurity on to others: the travellers who exasperate their fellow-passengers with unwelcome courtesies, the parents who cannot leave their children alone to learn a game or discover a pleasure, the over-zealous helpers in a street accident, not omitting those overpowering women who do not appreciate how much a man likes to act on his own and have a little space to move in. An egocentric disregard for convention is a slightly aggressive form of this liking for intervention.

* Relates forms of command to Heymans' categories.

Authoritarianism is also the simulated energy of the weak. It is found usually on the borders of neurosis and it often alternates in the same family with a morbid scrupulousness. It has been rightly said of the authoritarian that, contrary to all appearances, he is a social abulic.[23] Sometimes he admits this by becoming the executive arm of a will that is stronger or more respected than his own. Without wishing to reflect on an honourable body of men, Janet calls this the 'N.C.O. mentality'.[24] One is nothing oneself, but one's employer or ally is important, and hallowed by the association one proceeds to make life miserable for others. Troubled epochs have thrown up thousands of such mediocre personalities, hurrying to submit their mediocrity to some power that will inflate it, and to forget it in some minor tyranny. The authoritarian suffers from a constant sense of incompleteness which he is eternally trying to compensate. In extreme cases he finds any initiative from others intolerable, resenting it both as a threat and as a theft of his own initiative. This impression, which he does not analyse, is due to anxiety and a sense of ascendency, and creates the impulse to lay hold on such insolent activity. Thus he will insist on an absolute conformity to his own behaviour. If he is talkative, everyone must be lively, if he cannot sleep, everyone must stay up. The least spontaneity on the part of others causes him dismay. He is also, as Dupuis has shown, irritable: his reaction to this dismay could be a passive imitation of the other, but his reaction is an angry, destructive mood. The true chief creates, develops, amplifies: *he* diminishes all he touches, everything around him tends to be parsimonious, meticulous, methodical: his malice is petty, his temper jealous, his behaviour narrowly egocentric. Listen to him: 'This is my house, and in my house it is right for me alone to give orders and nothing must be done without my orders.'[25] He knows no exception to his demands. Sometimes he seizes on a chosen victim, usually of his own family, like a beast of prey, and does not release his grip until he has drained his life-blood: he isolates his victims emotionally and sows discord amid them, so that they are exclusively his own. However paradoxical it may seem to those who witness these scenes, he loves his victim as the parasite loves its host, and between two outbursts may even speak of him to a third party with tenderness and gratitude. He is not to be imagined as always accompanied by flashes of lightning. Some try to secure submission by supplication and complaints, spoilt children, spoilt old men, who never give their families a moment of peace. Sometimes the same basic authoritarianism is complicated by the mania for being loved and guided: the result is a curious blend of hardness and submission, an iron mask to some of those around, a smile for others and for strangers. Sometimes the love of such persons cloaks a very primitive desire for domination: sometimes persons who undertake the most enterprising forms of philanthropy seem more inspired by the flame of battle than the zeal of an apostle: some mothers fondle their children in a way that is only an unconscious means of bringing them under more complete control: many love affairs, like those of Julien Sorel, are more inspired by an aggressive vanity than by love or desire. On the other hand, some women refuse love because it requires, they feel, too much passivity on their part, and the dessicated authoritarianism into which they harden is the cause more than the effect of their celibacy.

What the authoritarian kills is the very savour of human action, the excitement of its initiative, the lightness of its autonomy. 'They have got into the habit', complains one victim, 'of leading me by the nose. They are stupefied and furious if I do the least thing of my own accord, and that takes all the satisfaction and fun out of everything. . . . I have never had the pleasure of doing anything that was not ordered, and that is the chief reason we are all so inactive; you end up by getting a poor opinion of yourself . . . I would do things if I wasn't every minute being told to do them.' The authoritarian deprives those around him of that sphere of ease which is the living space necessary to all free beings to allow them to manoeuvre freely. Tyrannical kindness, a too pressing solicitude create the same feeling of suffocation in their recipients, and no doubt because they are not devoid of the desire for domination. This is a truth which should be remembered by those families of whom we said that they confused intimacy with promiscuity, by the friends whose affection is always presented in close-up, and by even the most legitimate collective authorities, who can only gain by discretion and are always ruined by excess of zeal.[26]

FROM THE ACCEPTANCE OF THE OTHER TO THE DRAMA OF THE OTHER

The imperialism of the individual is such that the most difficult thing of all for him to accept is the existence, side by side with him, of another man endowed with the same privileges as himself. Freud is wrong is saying that the self confronts every object with a single, primary, egoistic and narcissistic demand. But if this view is unilateral, we cannot ignore the existence of a very primitive intolerance of others at the very roots of personality. It is betrayed, passively, by the irritation provoked by differences of character in those we meet: when

two men detest each other, the opposition of their temperaments is usually a factor. Actively, this basic aggressiveness expresses itself in incessant criticism, envy and jealousy.
*

To accept the other is not merely to tolerate him through indifference, as is possible to the poorer, amorphous or apathetic temperament, who has not enough vigour to get outside the narrow circle of vegetative egocentricity. It is not merely to keep away from a desire for tranquillity. 'One must always', said Fontenelle, 'have a cold heart and a warm stomach.' He had neither wife nor child. He never quarrelled with anyone, says one of his biographers, to defend whomever or whatever it might be: he would throw pamphlets that attacked him into a big chest without reading or looking at them, and he was so fearful even of the surprises of life that he declared: 'If my hand were closed over a handful of truth, I would take very great care not to open it.' Bourgeois 'tolerance' springs from the same source. It does not suggest that the other is a mystery to be respected, understood and conquered, with an almost dramatic boldness, but reveals a half-sceptical, half-egoistic philosophy, as much as to say: 'Don't go to any trouble for so little.'
**

There is indeed, both in tolerance and idealisation, the beginning of a homage to the person of the other.
***

Idealisation mimics generosity and may, in the most favourable cases, catch a little of the same fire: we know the cheerful, pleasure-loving types, who are quite willing, between two bouts of dissipation, to help widows and orphans at some cost to themselves. But the inability to love seldom expresses itself in this way.

The sense of the other is conditioned by a general adaptability to the real. For the other is the experience, through a person, of something alien: the reaction to 'ragging' is a good test of this adaptability, and every collectivity has more or less spontaneously reinvented it. But the sense of the other, properly speaking, only begins with respect for the other, and what can we respect in the other if one does not first respect it in oneself? It is thus proportioned to the value one attributes to the mystery of man and to his very quality of mystery. There will be nothing to discover in the other, not that unfailing miracle of revelation

---

* The acceptance of others in early childhood.
** Relates indifference to and idealisation of others to Heymans' categories.
*** Relates to Heymans' categories.

experienced by saints and poets and the simple of heart, if I reduce myself to a mechanism without sequel, if I myself offer nothing unforeseen to anyone. Thus a taste for psychological analysis is by no means an unfailing criterion for this sense of the other. It may be only a liking for breaking down and building up again. It may be associated with the most implacable depersonalisation of the subject studied. The sense of mystery, which is its opposite, is not a fraudulent evasion of problems, but the direct recognition of an inexhaustible source of problems beneath all problems. The sense of the other is inseparable from a sense of inwardness. The other is *my fellow*, 'another self'.
*

Together with family influences, the structures of our outward life weigh heavily upon the formation of the sense of the other. In times of great public happiness or despair, every egocentricity seems to disappear. An enduring community of hope or misfortune may produce the same effect. On the other hand, existences built up of minor happiness and mediocre misfortune close in upon themselves. The style of profession plays a similar role, according to whether it tends to teamwork under conditions creating a community of interest, or whether it is exercised alone in single combat (liberal professions, skilled crafts, small businesses). Under such influences whole classes tend to have a very similar disposition.

If we now look for the inner structure of this sense of the other, we must be careful to avoid summary representations. Simple affective penetration (*Einfühlung*) is too capricious and uncertain to constitute an interpersonal relationship. Fools believe that it is the others who are mad, and many wise folk resemble them. The same can be said for introjection, and its particular form, identification, in which the subject feels as if he were the soul of another person or group ('I have a pain in your chest').
**

One would oversimplify the drama of living by not pointing out that spontaneous harmony is not the rule in the realm of values. A tragic conflict often occurs between creative needs and the concern for others. A creative person is so much absorbed in work that he often ceases to be interested in others: hence his appearance of inhumanity and indifference. This is not just a mediocre complaint which attacks persons plunged into objective studies. It can attack even the most

---

* The sense of the other related to Heymans' categories, and deals with Adler's theory of the influence of the family.

** Relates to Heymans' categories.

passionate. It would seem that man, with rare exceptions, cannot keep all his great capacities at high tension the whole time.

Hatred is a cumulative and tenacious feeling. It is thus the most appropriate to secondary types. But it must be fed by a living flame.
*

Hatred is generally a reaction of over-compensated impotence. But the hatred of the passionate is the redirection of a living fire. 'Toute entière à sa proie attachée', this hatred as burning as love often seems to mask the exasperation of a disappointed or wounded love. Hence its fury and ambiguity, which shows that it is in the nature of hatred to be not only a violence of feeling but also an active agent of destruction. We may note that we are not as careful to define our exact relationship of hate or love for another, as we are to classify our states of superiority or inferiority. Here we tolerate ambiguous feelings and false situations more easily.
**

Incidentally, there is always in hatred a disproportion of cause and effect, an element of delirium.

But over and above the influence of instinct, the environment, emotivity, activity, which all tend towards communion with others, the first place should be given to an irreducible feeling, the confidence of man in man. It is early in the field, in the unconditional confidence of the child in the adult, which precedes even primitive jealousy. If it is abused during childhood, which is so vulnerable to affective shock, the victim withdraws into a lifelong choice of egocentricity. A betrayal at this age has incalculable effects: the useless lie, the misleading example, the mocking laugh at an awkward gesture which slips out too quickly, may all, to a child, mean the betrayal of his confidence by an adult (Künkel).
*** 　　　　*　　*　　*

We have reached a point where interpsychology, the study of relationships between person and person ends, and collective psychology begins.

The primitive facts of collective psychology are: unison or affective contagion, conscious imitation, sympathy, approach, collaboration. We have already studied the first two. Sympathy, which we have called an openness to others, is not the same as an unconscious affective

---

* Hatred in the phlegmatic and nervous types.
** The nervous and sentimental types.
*** An indirect reference to French politics.

fusion (*Einfühlung*), or external imitation. It consists in reliving in ourselves the state of the other, as other, without thereby becoming what he is.[27]

There are a great many variations of approach. But running through them all is the great opposition between the schizoid approach, more or less abrupt and frigid, and the cycloid approach, considerate, engaging, generous, even if the generosity is a facile prodigality of the self.

The spirit of collaboration has been particularly studied in Hennings' tests, revealing three principal attitudes towards it.

Some do not know how to work with others. Sometimes these are secondary types hardened into their peculiarities and their crazes, those of whom one says that they treat as defects all the qualities they have not got, and as errors all the opinions they do not share. According to Gina Lombroso, this partiality is most prevalent in women, who are inclined to despise anything they find different: this is what makes it so difficult for women to collaborate. Sometimes this incapacity is also due to a kind of stubborn concentration of the worker on his work; he pounces on it like an animal on its prey, and refuses help even in the smallest detail, convinced, in the tenseness of his application, that no one can do it as well as he. Then there is the group of the anarchically minded, who have a systematic tendency to opposition without further motive. Their maladaptation may take an active form, as in the mischievous spirits who enjoy preventing other people from working.

Others, on the contrary, have an active need for help and are much better at collective work than alone. They may behave in two ways. Some dominate their partners: by an appearance of collaboration they satisfy a desire for control and intervention. In a simple intervention they behave like the fly on the paddle-wheel, with a great deal of sound and fury, but they manage to leave the most difficult work to their collaborators, satisfied by sharing the joys of triumph at cut price. If they are more active, they destroy the initiative of their collaborators. Their only interest in them is as subjects on whom to exercise their desire for mastery, to bend others' will to their own, but in fact they can no more be helped than those who refuse assistance.

Opposed to these are the passive who seek collaboration as a means of avoiding either initiative or trouble. Either they cannot take decisions and need someone who will take risks and decide for them: in such cases they make good and often energetic executives, provided they are covered by someone else. Or maybe they are completely parasitical on the work of others, busily preoccupied in doing nothing much, spending their time looking for someone who will pluck their chestnuts from the fire.

The whole of social psychology could be renewed and related to personal psychology by the Bergsonian distinction between closed societies and open societies. The man of habit finds the closed society his most harmonious background. All those whose psychic formula tends to the objectivisation of others, prefer it. Conservative and lover of routine, or doctrinaire of revolution, according to the environment and the principles which have shaped them, they fear human spontaneity as a force which, as they know from experience, escapes them: thus they are only interested in the apparatus which may enclose or control it. A man discouraged or thrown off balance by a long series of unfortunate experiences offers no resistance to the collective hypnoses which progressively reduce the social group to the crowd or mob: hungry for submission, he allows his personal conscience to be replaced by the strong will of a leader, strengthened by so many abdications.[28] Inversely, the resentful man, as Scheler has called him, tends to reject all social forms, because one form has injured him from childhood on. His suffering often cries aloud for vengeance, but its very excess prevents him from ever imagining a better, juster society: anarchists and libertarians are recruited from the highly strung temperaments of persons with shattered childhoods: as far as anything social is concerned they pass their lives as unadapted adolescents, who can only envisage the autonomy of the individual as a perpetual and uneasy opposition to all constituted society. The inner conflicts of many countries have clearly shown the division between these wild and unhappy children and the polytechnicians of the revolution.

The most revealing elementary form of open sociality is undoubtedly hospitality. The readiness to open one's door to friend and stranger, without regard to convention, compensation or prudence, has been carefully eliminated by a century of 'civilised' society, the clearest indication of the regulated barbarism by which we have been invaded. Hospitality is a much more selective criterion of openness to others than those used by Heymans. It not only characterises individual attitudes: it may be a family, a spontaneous group or a nation, but if it is concerned not to close in upon itself, and is aware of the oddities, the particularities, the ununderstandable ways that may arise from local and temporal conditions, then its members will show a freedom of outlook which is not exclusive of powerful communal feelings, but which introduces into the community a breath of fresh air without which it would suffocate.

7

THE AFFIRMATION OF THE SELF

THE self has for long been studied by psychologists as an object amongst others. Many laborious attempts have been made from outside to establish its identity, in order to confirm its existence through its incessant metamorphoses. Recourse was had to consciousness, to discover this identity, but following the method which was considered 'objective' because it reduced all experience to the conditions of sensory experience, particularly vision. Living consciousness was, as it were, withdrawn from the task by being transformed into an observatory, impersonally registering a film of states of consciousness. Now identity and impersonality are by definition the very properties of things. No addition of prestige, no dialectical virtuosity can lead one to discover personal reality, which is first of all affirmation, in an objective catalogue, such as that used by positive science to apprehend physical reality. The self is lived before it is seen, and is only adequately understood in its living activity. The prime merit of Freud and the first German personalist psychologists[1] is to have denounced this time-honoured illusion, common to both idealist and materialist psychologies, and to have shown that the highest 'mental' synthesis you can imagine could never turn a bundle of observations in the third person into an existence in the first person.

*

Now the most immediate datum of psychological consciousness is not a state, however unique, however subtle: it is an affirmation, understood as such by consciousness itself, first in its exercise and then in reflection on its activity. With this point of departure we are constrained to appeal to an irreplaceable experience: those who refuse to recognise it can only be classed by those who live it, as 'blind to the person' as Scheler says. Their blindness cannot be cured by demonstration but only by conversion.

These blind men are curious in that they think they are the only ones who can see. In fact they are content with seeing what must be first experienced in order to be known.†

* Criticises the idealist psychology of the last century.
† Quotes a pun of Claudel's: 'Connaître . . . c'est co-naître, naître avec . . . '

It is not that the affirmation of the self is a violent, irrational act at the beginning of knowledge. Like the experience of space and duration it has a depth unamenable to discursive rationalisation. But it also develops its empirical manifestations which give firmer and stronger bases for description as it moves from the centre to the periphery of living personality. Yet these manifestations never eliminate the necessity of reference to the fundamental affirmation of personal existence. Jung expresses a similar idea by the concept of three stages. The real object of self-knowledge is the numinous *Self*, a totality transcending consciousness, like Kant's 'thing in itself', and, in this sense, unconscious: in analysis, it is only an 'ultimate concept' which may be envisaged but not fully grasped. It is the phenomenal *Ego* that presents itself to the grasp of reason: this is none other than the conscious subject as he appears empirically to himself: this is open to description, but description tends, by its own activity, to disperse and materialise. So between the two Jung places the *phenomenology proper of the Self*, a sort of cast shadow, the projection of the Self on the Ego. It does not coincide with the whole of the empirical ego, but only with a very remarkable part of it, the process of individuation; the Ego organising itself in depth on a line with the Self; this phenomenology permits a 'depth psychology' which is a form of experimental metaphysics of the Self. We may add that it is extended into experimental ethics. We shall take this level as a starting point. We shall never lose contact with the living act of self-affirmation, which persists even in its most external manifestations. But we shall meet it in varying degrees of actuality, by covering the activity of the self from the periphery to the centre, from the self in extension, related to things, and the persons it has appropriated to itself, to the self in intention, the ruler and soul of this domain.

To become aware of oneself seems therefore far from being 'quite natural' but rather a progressive testing, a spiritual effort. Bergson and Heidegger, from different angles, have shown that we have an incorrigible tendency to interpret ourselves in the manner of the objects of our preoccupation. Like a congenital sickness, we secrete this tendency of dissolution into the surrounding world, into things and depersonalised beings. Action, daily gossip, even thought, each of the actions which should contribute to affirming our presence in the world, may also contribute to dissipating our existence. Certain temperaments are more exposed to this danger than others, and in their case we speak of extraversion or excessive adaptation. The affirmation of the self can therefore only operate through controlled ascesis. It is response—responsibility.

In addition, the manner of achieving self-awareness is closely dependent on social and historic conditions. Many classic psychological descriptions are unconsciously limited, as Ribot points out, not only to the civilised adult white man, but to the civilised, urban, bourgeois white man of the nineteenth and twentieth centuries. In social groups less educated to expression, interiorisation takes on more rudimentary forms.

*

Finally, individual differentiation is much more clearly marked in towns than in the country. Differences due to environment are, it has been shown, less accentuated in girls. It appears also, from many investigations, that self-awareness is generally less developed in the poorer groups, where all personal effort is concentrated on the struggle for existence, whereas introspective extravagances are reserved for the leisured classes. It would seem that balance and self-awareness require conditions sufficiently easy to banish real need, yet sufficiently disputed lest the mind be lost in reflections unproved by serious commitment.

Neither should we forget that our conscious attitudes and behaviour represent only a fraction of the total self. Behind them stands that elusive other self, that dreams and legends describe as the Shadow or the Double, the being that sometimes we would not wish to be, and yet are. Two threads are entwined: one from the unconscious deposits left in the course of each individual journey, the other spun by the collective Unconscious of humanity, containing, as Jung has shown, the permanent attitudes to life common both to the civilised and the primitive, to Twentieth century man and to the hero of legend. The fairly common desire to reduce the reality of the self to the sum of its conscious activities is the source of permanent disequilibrium. Unconscious life works both for good and ill (for Freudian pessimism simplifies the matter unduly), and provokes deep-lying states which conflict silently with conscious life. Even in calm waters it does not offer the limited and reassuring perspectives of conscious order. It opens everywhere upon the abyss, the infernal abysses of instinctive forces, the vertical abysses of spiritual aspiration; one might well say it *is* the abyss. It feeds the anguish underlying all our arrangements. The first conscious reaction towards it is one of terror and recoil. If we run away from it completely, as happens with the extravert, or the stupid,

* Reports an enquiry by Adolphe Busemann on introspection in young workers and peasants.

encouraged by the manuals of 'self-mastery', there is a gain in surface equilibrium and a certain facility of behaviour; but this is made up for by spiritual and aesthetic death, and this peripheral adaptation may not even succeed, for this refusal of inner conflict may even endanger psychic virility and turn into puerility and pusillanimity: this is a danger run by too outwardly directed education.[2] The man concerned only with the conscious creates a thousand difficulties for himself by projecting at random the desires and idealisations he cannot face on to individuals and collectivities that have enough of their own. Also the Unconscious, if scorned, takes a terrible revenge: a 'closing time panic' descends not only on individuals, to ravage in a few weeks a life as orderly as a garden: it erupts with no less violence in civilisations which believe they have, once and for all, neutralised both barbaric tastes and religious impulses by shutting them up in museums.

As against these hyperconscious types, living with insouciance over a volcano, some individuals are submerged by the dark torments of their unconscious life, women more than men, and whoever lives intensely poetically. Written work is the remedy for the madness which always looms ahead in such a subversion of equilibrium, but these persons are not always the most competent at describing and mastering the apparent workings of psychological life.

Between these two extremes the effort to create a self is an effort to collect around a centre and a project the dismembered portions of the psyche, unconscious stagnations, ill-placed projections, and conscious efforts. It is not only an attempt by consciousness to discipline the Unconscious. Equilibrium of the self demands the active participation of every zone of the self, and it then appears that unconscious life is not solely irrational and destructive. Jung has shown how unconscious drives are directed towards an end. It seems, in fact, that the Unconscious acts as a compensation for the conscious, so that attitudes which have atrophied in conscious life enter into the unconscious life, and inversely. Jung has also discovered in unconscious life a kind of permanent tropism towards the unity of the psyche, which continues by the means and material at the disposal of the Unconscious, even when the conscious being has abandoned the effort, and even against his errors. But these means are often very primitive: life's obscure effort should not be overrated or deified, even though it may suggest the higher vocation of the person. These discoveries support the idea which is being increasingly accepted, that even the psychoses are, contrary to all appearances, an effort at unification, but at the only level at which, in certain conditions, unification is still possible.

Every collective environment has its share in supporting or dislocating the structure of the self. If personal destiny is the highest form of organisation known to our experience it has, like all higher organisations, a fragility which in the majority of cases needs support. The framework of the group and the structures of the environment provide this support which is indispensable to the average man, and which no one can do without entirely. When they are not within his grasp, or have for some reason been lost, the man who is not quite certain of himself will provide himself with artificial ones. The mania for order and precision or meticulousness, when they take a marked or paroxystic form, betray an inner insecurity which is looking for protection. This insecurity is created, developed or dispersed in close relation with the conscious social situation. We have seen the importance of social grading, de-grading and supergrading. If it is true that strong men make a strong country, it is also true that a strong country makes strong men. Anyone deprived of certain natural supports, a normal family, a social atmosphere sufficiently stable to be slowly integrated, will always be vainly striving after a certain solidity of bearing, a minimum of vital assurance. The absence of professional training also tends to create an uncertain, utopian, insincere and rootless individual.

The environment always affects personal security in the measure we accept its influence on self-expression. Some are only interested in forms of expression approved by others. These are the majority: one can never overrate the importance of vanity, together with fear and sex, amongst human motives.

*

THE SELF IN EXTENSION: POSSESSIONS

The self is engaged in two adventures: the one in depth, towards the sources of time, the other in expansion, in the breadth of space. No coherence is possible unless one and the other are accepted, almost the one in the other—if the self neglects duration, there is the danger of dispersal into matter: if it neglects space, there is dispersal into dreams. It is quite right to speak of the eccentricity of the self. It is as naturally outside itself as it is essentially in itself. Therefore speech is as specific to personal living as reflection. One can only struggle against verbalism by returning to very simple observations. Man is a spirit that displaces itself: that must have some meaning. What need would a pure spirit have to displace itself? Would it not be, at will, either pure subjectivity or instantaneous ubiquity? Sometimes one speaks of the appeal of space, the appeal of things. Space is not just a receptable for man. Man

* Different ways of seeking authenticity of expression.

is called on to *take possession* of space, just as he is called on to take possession of himself. His vocation is shown by the position of his hands. If a painter wants to indicate the authority of his sitter, he shows him with his hand resting on a book, a sceptre, a globe, or simply closed, upon this knee or the arm of a chair. The lover of sensation, the juggler with ideas, has his hand hanging at his side. The eyes also are fixed steadily and attentively on objects or on other men's eyes, when he is confident in himself and in his place in the real world, or he yields, flees or deviates. The self has its dominion over space. It begins with the body, the perception of the situation of my body in space is an axis of personal consciousness. Thus possession can never be corrupted at its root. And grammar has its logic in placing the verb 'to have' with the verb 'to be', as a king pillar of human order.

However, just as we have found boredom, a sickness of living following like a shadow the good affirmed by our existence, so we shall find an even darker ill, a sickness of possession, which weighs on all our having, and works from within possession, if not at its very heart, to bedevil and dehumanise the possessor. Perhaps the psychology of possession may shed some light on this drama.

What is mine, that is, all the objects that in one way or another, I appropriate, covers an area of space that one might call the circle of possession. I form it by 'introjection' (Ferenczi) by incorporating into my personality the whole of the environment I experience: my body, privileged in that it is, at any rate in its central parts, the only property I cannot lose without losing myself, this body in which we believe so much that even the most irreligious persons are concerned to foresee how and where they shall be buried: my clothes, my flat and all it contains; my worldly goods, my family, my friends; my ideas, likings and hopes (which are not divorced either from spatial realisation and conditions): others, a captain for instance, will add: my men; an employer, my workers; a baron, my ancestors.
*

So possessions, in the form of inventory, form only a provisional slice of life taken from a process of conquest. Even when being grasped, they retain a sort of liberality. The conqueror is not indifferent to the solid fare provided for his ambition by his conquest, but he is concentrated on his progress, not on its results. As a soldier he despises the frontier makers who will follow him: as an apostle he does not count heads in his conversions, but tirelessly pursues the vision of his faith: an industrialist, he creates, like Ford, because he cannot stop

* Further details of the sense of possession.

creating, and not for the sake of piling up money; a collector, he enjoys the hunt and the discovery, not the display. What does he need for his happiness? A world that awaits him, not yet occupied (one of the elements of the complex charm of a young girl is this availability which is perceptible even to those who do not wish to claim it); a world, however, which resists him, and this brings him the astonishment and the renewal of a confirmation of strength: finally, a powerful desire, which gives him the physical and mental joy of expansion. Thus in the ages of youth, the peoples or classes still in process of formation, and adolescents who are not little old men, live by possession. A cadet at St. Cyr does not consult the pension scales (at least, we hope not). A bourgeois in the twelfth century was a man who cut loose from all protective ties in a dangerous world, to embark on the adventure of trade and money-making: from the fifteenth to the seventeenth century he was a man who aspired with all the growing energy of his class to conquer a centuries-old power. Since then he has become, all too often, a man sitting back on the conquests of his forefathers.

For in every victory there is a danger, in every culmination a despair. He who has conquered must maintain, and the fear of loss, already passive in tone, thwarts the reflux of the forward movement. The conqueror sought an obstacle, the victor is already irritated by resistance: he requires a passive submission to match his own growing passivity. The conqueror, rejoicing in the number of his rivals, provoked emulation, which acted as a spur to his covetousness, added value to the object pursued and prestige to his struggle: the victor succumbs to a deadly liking for exclusivity. The madness peculiar to power, ('Power drives men mad', wrote Alain), is the madness of the man who wishes to eliminate others, even including the resistance of things, which makes him nervous as a child. Henceforward he defends his conquests, and the defendant is in a bad position with regard to all the possible conquerors. Possessions remain living only under the urge of being. Henceforward his being is slowly stifled. It is the moment when a great country begins to falter in its greatness, when the class which has seized power begins to sink back upon its inheritance, when the successful man fattens into the small employer, when the young bourgeois who has acquired wife and position after a turbulent youth, takes his place in the ranks of prudent conservatism, and the conquerors give way to administrators, the prophets to apologists, the pioneers to those that inherit.

In the year, the age, or the generation that follows conquest the beneficiary replaces the victor. There is hardly any longer a question of struggle. By a series of withdrawals the possessor has left the great highways with their attendant risks. Modern industry has greatly facilitated this cushioning of possession by developing mechanical riches, which multiply themselves simply, are acquired without effort, and distribute automatic pleasures. It has produced a new type of man, the man of impersonal comfort. He is the armchair inheritor of a fortune which others put to work: an interior decorator provides his taste, Cook's look after his dreams, his lawyer looks after his quarrels, and when he turns a button, it is not to execute a mandarin, but to receive his daily dose of verbal or musical soporifics. Above all he wants not to have to conquer or struggle or organise. As for his possessions, he is just so far interested in them as is necessary to ward off boredom. Finally, by the weight of passivity he changes places with his goods and it is they who possess him and make him conform to their inertia. Sometimes he urges concern for his children as a justification, but the future he imagines for them is the image of his own abdication: it does not occur to him to develop their initiative by leaving them a sufficient margin of struggle, but only to insure them against the risks of life. Thus he propagates his own death from generation to generation.

In the final stage of this decadence of possession every form of ascendancy has vanished. The ostentatious are not concerned with possession but with having it known that they possess. The conqueror is sure of the vital link that binds him to his conquest and is not perpetually concerned with its official publication. The true writer, who loves the written word, tries to avoid the possessive pronoun when referring to his own work. But no one uses it more, makes it roll more lusciously off the tongue, than the man who in reality no longer possesses anything. He says 'my wife', 'my Cézanne', 'my castle', but this human being so close to him has never been welcomed into this stiffening heart which has never responded to the light creeping over three apples, nor to the freshness of a morning in the dew-covered meadows. He is no longer the incarnation of the primacy of having over being, but of the tyranny over both having and being of a purely declaratory form of possession. This is the moment of pettiness: the urge to possession is lost in disputation: if there is still some will to struggle involved in this final spasm, the battle has been displaced, the object of possession is no longer at stake, but only the title-deeds.[3] Thus possession has three ages, as Chateaubriand said of the aristocracy: the age of superiority, the age of privilege, the age of vanity.

*   * Morbid forms of the sense of possession.

We have spoken of the decadence of possession as a sort of inner sickness. In considering the crystallisation of the sense of possession in the adult, we should not underrate the influence of the reception he receives from his environment. We start with needs and desires which outstrip needs. If these are frustrated or disappointed, particularly in early childhood, the age of prehension, the sense of possession becomes uneasy and jealous, because it is demanding: it overflows into gourmandise and avidity, or withdraws into avarice and egocentricity. It is essential to note that an excess or too great a facility of satisfaction (the spoilt child) lead to the same result, making the subject exacting, impatient and insatiable.

Just as the pressure of my body, flexible yet precise enough amongst things, is due to the contraction and flexion of the muscles, so the mastery of the self over its spatial domain is assured by an equilibrium between the tendency to expand and the necessity of renunciation, far removed from the two frenzies of grandeur and annihilation. From time to time we are shaken by a stormy temptation to possess all that is possible. And yet, to grow and develop we have to repulse it. 'As soon as a single covetousness', wrote Nietzsche, 'or a general covetousness is predominant, as in the people, there is no such thing as a superior man.' The child must resign himself, between three and five, to no longer holding the whole world at his mercy; the little girl not to be able to command the masculine world as well as her own. Each stage of experience requires a fresh renunciation. And each reminds us of the presence of death in the fabric of life. But it is this harsh presence of death that gives life its form, its consciousness, and its sharp pleasure.

*

**   THE SELF IN TENSION: AFFIRMATION

[The affirmation of the self is] centripetal, marking a survival of infantile egocentricity, but now consolidated by a clear awareness of self. Vermeylen defines egocentricity as an exaggeration of primary individual tendencies (gourmandise, love of comfort, ease and an agreeable life), and also of secondary ones (self-love, and instinct of property, directed towards the satisfaction of the self rather than towards a consideration of the things possessed). Egocentricity is established, one might equally say, when the 'captive libido' of early childhood, with its tendency to assimilate everything to its own purposes, has

---

* Historical development of the instinct of possession, and the absence of the instinct of possession or prodigality.

** The development of the affirmation of the self in childhood.

failed to transform itself, by the discipline of successive weanings, into an 'oblative libido' adapted to others and to reality (Dr. Pichon). The 'pleasure principle' with its blind impervious impatience has survived imperfect repressions: camouflaged, it leads an underground existence, brutally pursuing its purposes in opposition to any social adaptation. Such definitions are liable to be too narrow in stressing the 'captative' aspect of egocentricity, whereas adult egocentricity often presents a more puerile aspect of impulsiveness and obstinacy.

*

In a passive personality, dominated by the need 'to be seen', the egocentric demand is always receptive: the egocentric are like children who want to see everything, hear everything, have a share in all that is said and done, always listened to and admired, and the first to be served; in a conversation they are impatient to produce their own reminiscences, their own experiences, the proofs that persuaded *them*; they interrupt, intervening indiscreetly when their presence is not required; they are fixed in their habits, their peculiarities, their beliefs, and as unreceptive as anyone to the habits, peculiarities and beliefs of others. Whatever the occasion they are impatient of any situation which has arisen independently of them. If a reflective consciousness has been developed to its extreme in a hothouse culture, a narcissistic element creeps into their lives, withdrawn into a voluptuous contemplation of the self. The self grips and absorbs the libido, which becomes more or less markedly diverted from normal sexual and social channels.[4] The emotive works up his emotions for the pleasure they give him: the introvert savours them at length. All the reproaches which some have felt it necessary to level at reflective or personal life, from the romantics to the present day, are only valid when an egocentric twist is imposed on the natural generosity of the person. Personalisation is the highest good in the universe. It is true, however, that by some secret channel there creeps in a sickness of the self, just as we suffer from a sickness of existence and a sickness of possession. To distinguish always means to separate, to break the universal unity. But personal life is founded precisely on vigilance with regard to egocentricity. The distinction between legitimate love of self and self-love, returning upon itself, and mainly due to social competition, is commonly attributed to Rousseau, but it was a commonplace of theologians and mystics. No one today is entitled to reproach Christianity, which has made the struggle against self the mainspring of moral life, for the misdeeds of individualism.

* Psychological deviations of the sense of affirmation in childhood.

In a more aggressive temperament egocentricity becomes a spirit of opposition. This, we have seen, sometimes has its earliest source in a psycho-motor inadaptability. But it is also frequently the product of a too harassing education, made up of ceaseless commands and prohibitions which the child cannot understand, since the majority come from outside his universe and many of the remainder only express the egocentricity of the educators who, in the pungent expression of Ezekiel, feed themselves and not their flock: in education even more than elsewhere like engenders its like. The knowledge of sin, said St. Paul, makes for sin. A barrier set up before a child inspires in him the desire to climb over it. The thousand 'Don't do this, don't do that' issuing in and out of season from the parents' lips do not create obedient children, even in the very egocentric sense which such parents attribute to the word, rather the contrary. Orders have been so abused that they lose all meaning and importance. Thwarted at every turn, the child reacts by negation. The forbidden takes on a marvellous glow of freedom and expansion. The poorest natures obey for the sake of peace and quiet and slip imperceptibly into emotional and intellectual obtuseness. The more lively natures turn to revolt. Hence come many refractory or socially delinquent types.[5] This is often the sole cause of stealing: 'All that is necessary to turn a child into a thief is to refuse him a coveted object without reasonable grounds.'[6] The child will also steal if he is deprived of affective satisfaction, to satisfy the captive instinct deprived of nourishment. Every theft, say the psychoanalysts, is psychologically a recovery. The revolt thus provoked may become a permanent trait, a liking for defiance. At other times the child obeys sullenly, but reshapes his thwarted actions and opinions in a world of his own, obstinate, narrow, entirely consecrated to the service of the protesting self. Then a hidebound conservatism, hostile to all change, replaces the anarchic explosion. One might say that there are two classes of men: the men who are *for* and the men who are *against*, for or against the world in general, for or against all that comes from outside, from men, from things, from events. The self rolled up into a hedgehog around its own conservatism makes the latter type, and their negativity is almost always due to the clumsiness of their education.[7]

*

Egoism is usually taken in a narrower sense than egocentricity. It is, if you like, an egocentricity hardened and fused into an essentially captive form.[8] Persons actively devoted to others, who could hardly

* Egocentric forms of the sense of affirmation.

be accused of egoism, may yet exercise the purest egocentricity in their devotion by the way in which they impose their will, their manner, their presence. True egoism is absent from devotion to others. It is not, as one might believe, a culmination of self-affirmation: the moralists who tried to make this the keystone of their ethics have perhaps fallen into this psychological error. It is frequently entirely foreign to the strongest personalities. On the contrary, it is the quickest road to the mental hospital. According to Adler, the final purpose of all neurosis is a fantastic exaltation of the sense of personality, which starts by an excessive attention to the self. Dr. Charles Blondel defines the morbid consciousness as a consciousness which has broken with socialisation. Künkel derives his four main infantile types from a psycho-sclerosis following on a victory of egocentricity.

*

Egoism is easily disguised by the aspect of a collective pseudo-disinterestedness: the egoism of married couples, family, clan, background, caste: these diverse forms do not express a broadening of the egoistic consciousness, but a detour adopted in order to acquire moral tranquillity, and a reinforcement of strength. A demanding attitude is the systematised, expanded form of the captive libido. It is generally the product of disappointment, mockery or frustration at the various 'weaning' periods which are spaced out over childhood: separation from the breast, from the mother, from the family, etc. Does this render suspect every form of demand? Let him who has never yielded to the claims of self-interest cast the first stone. The sacred flame of egoism is such that one cannot expect that others will abdicate from their own egoisms from a pure love of justice, and the aggressive rivalries of other egoisms are necessary to compel them to give way when they do not know how to abdicate spontaneously. But it is one thing for the sociologist to point out this necessity and another for the psychologist and the moralist to place it correctly in the moral picture. When it has crystallised by repetition into a demanding mentality, the 'justice' which is demanded by the injured interest is often degraded by a narrow, disquieting element, even if it still retains some traces of generosity. Justice is an admirable label for covering each individual's personal interests, resentments and ways of thinking. A preoccupation with equality often has the same foundation. It kindles in many hearts a sense of the original equivalence of man, and the legitimate hope for a better order, in which, in a diversity of function, opportunity and responsibility shall be better apportioned.

* Relates the sense of affirmation to the categories of Heymans.

But it also frequently tends to be but a jealous eye cast by the man who can do less on the man who can do more. A very simple criterion will enable us to distinguish a true sense of justice from the egoism that bears its name. The just man tries to reform his own manner of distributing justice at least as actively as he claims justice for himself: he feels that he is never entirely free from the evil he combats. The demanding person never suspects that he may have the slightest responsibility for any injustice, which he only remarks in other persons. The just man is happy at any increase in the level of justice around him: the demander takes any measure of justice granted to others as a personal injury, and calls it injustice if it favours his enemy. The just man hopes for the extension of an ever greater justice to an ever increasing number, not measuring it by a scale which is strict when it approaches his own interests and laxer as it departs from them: he does not even measure it, but the demander is always concerned with accounts and distribution, until his noble aspirations become pure quibbles. Köhler has greatly clarified this distinction by showing that the latter form of 'justice' already exists amongst chimpanzees. We must add that many of those who attack this demanding attitude, when it demands something from them, have no better concept of justice themselves but simply, having no superiors, make claims against their equals, and having means at their disposal to help themselves quietly, do not form coalitions.

The attitude of demand is so widespread that it creates perhaps the largest group of those constitutionally predisposed who live, amongst normal persons, on the margin of normality. We have all encountered those individuals with their little obsessions, full of themselves, regarding their fellow-men with contemptuous scorn, suspicious also, unadaptable, convinced that everyone is engaged in a conspiracy against them. They resemble, in milder form, the patients suffering from the delirium of systematised ideas of reference (persecution mania, megalomania). In 1909 Sérieux and Capgras described the constitutional basis of this delirium. It was designated a *paranoiac* constitution, from παρανοειν, to think wrongly.[9] Dr. Genil-Perrin distinguished the constitutional paranoiac from the delirious type by calling the former the 'lesser paranoiac'. They range from the bizarre to the demented: the actual boundary of the morbid states is nowhere more confused.

*

Basically it would seem that there is an inflation and a perversion of

* The aetiology of the paranoiac state.

the sense of personality due to a halt in the process of socialisation, which allows free rein to a primitive egocentricity. The paranoiac is always satisfied with himself: any pretext suffices to confirm his pride:[10] he admits neither his misdeeds nor his defects and no setback affects him. The hypertrophy of the self is present in varying degrees and manner, from gross and naïve vanity to discreet self-sufficiency, from arrogance to banal pretentiousness. An obsequious politeness, such as Marmontel describes in Rousseau, may cloak its aggressive arrogance. Sometimes it comes to the sound of trumpets, not unattractively, as with Don Quixote and Cyrano: the love of publicity makes men like Rousseau exhibitionist or histrionical, like so many little great men. They have nothing but contempt for anything that does not further their own distortion. 'The contempt', wrote Rousseau, 'which I have learnt by profound meditation to feel for the habits, the maxims, the prejudices of my century, made me insensitive to the raillery of those who share them, and I crushed their pretty little speeches with my sentences, just as I would crush an insect between my fingers.' The paranoiac advances, armed with his self-sufficiency and 'let the world perish rather than one of my principles'. Men are only walkers-on at his disposal on the stage. His bodily attitude expresses his character: he walks with shoulders back, his expression disdainful, quick with the shrug of the shoulders or the smile of pity which is sometimes almost engraved on his countenance. The whole picture betrays a profound disturbance of the faculty of self-criticism.

His distrust of his surroundings is the direct function of his touchy pride. It is a complex feeling, consisting of 'distrust, fear, rancour, hostile reserve, touchy susceptibility, uneasiness, suspicion, the painful feeling of being misunderstood by his fellows, of being isolated among men' (Montassert). Unlike the obsessional and melancholic, who attribute their trouble to themselves, he systematically accuses the bad intentions of others. We have already described how his sense of space is psychologically flattened out into one where everything concerns him and watches him. His universe, or that sector with which he is concerned, is nothing but an universe of concentric malice, a 'labyrinth of double meanings'. The whole attention of the world seems to converge upon his acts and gestures, he is alert for conspiracy, mockery, duplicity, interpreting everything, associating things that no one else would dream of, and the more his conclusion is paradoxical, the more triumphant he feels. It is interesting that this interpretation is always negative: it begins with a generalised anxiety which is finalised by suspicion. Then doubt is no longer possible. 'He is not accused,' said

Lesègue, 'he is condemned.' This distrust is multiform. There is a tendency to see a paranoiac in every sufferer from persecution mania, but many display only an unjustified but painful feeling of being misunderstood by everyone, or morally abandoned by them. Every child has experienced the beginning of such a feeling when upset by a scolding.[11] Others seek a refuge for their distrust in solitude (Tolstoy): they are akin to the schizoid, except that their retreat is broken by crises of fury, such as Balzac has described in the Count de Mortsauf in Le lys dans la vallée.

The paranoiac's bad judgment is very primitive and is found even in the mildest cases, owing to the interplay between vanity and a perplexed suspicion. The paranoiac is mistaken both as to himself and the external world: vanity and distrust are inextricably blended, expressing his fundamental discord with the environment in both its aspects. His paradoxes are often pointed and original, his argumentation subtle and sometimes brilliant. But it is always based on an error of judgment, an evasion of proof and a mistaken systematisation. His inadequate self-criticism and his systematising mentality are the two principal sources of his disorder. None is more reasoning, more careful to affirm that logic is his only guide, but no reasoning is more extravagant than his. The really demented push this extravagance to caricature, like the man who believed he was being treated as a 'blind husband' because cataract was being discussed in his presence. But even the normal interpretations are sometimes no less astonishing, when it comes to revealing hidden intentions or tortuous manoeuvres in others. Extravagant conclusions, perhaps, but rarely absurd, and always furnished with the maximum appearance of probability. The paranoiac, this Don Quixote of sophistry, endowed with a lively memory, is an attentive observer and often a skilful dialectician, who argues closely, quotes facts and dates, pursues shades of meaning, clears up dilemmas and pitfalls, like a prosecuting counsel. He projects an arid light on an extremely narrow field, the crude illumination picking out details to the detriment of perspective. He is therefore indignant if he is considered mad. There is no intellectual weakness, but, in Dugas' formula,[12] 'confiscation of the mind in favour of a fixed sentiment'. Some of them are scientists, others ministers. His way of thinking stands halfway between the rigours of the logician and the plastic symbolism of the poet or mythomaniac, an ideological symbolism, taking from the first its formal rigidity and from the second his ability to make the symbol reveal something quite different from its original content. This way of thinking brings the paranoiac not only close to the child, but

to primitive mentality, with its *a priori* outlook and contempt for experience: Tanzi considers the paranoiac a living anachronism.
*

There is some element of heredity and a large element of education in the paranoiac disposition. The child with paranoid tendencies is soon recognised by more or less distinctive traits. In the clearest cases he soon acquires a love of dominating or bullying his companions: he takes their toys, makes them obey his orders, assumes control over their games, in which he tries to make sure of the most favourable position. Intolerant of any resistance, jealous, suspicious, irritable, he has a precocious love of controversy: he 'answers back' and argues, is arrogant under punishment and a frequent truant. Such was Rimbaud's childhood. At school he is always complaining of the masters' injustice. No one must be as rich, as well-dressed, as intelligent as he. Certain embryonic forms produce a pathological timidity which is rendered furtive by ambition, as in Rousseau. At puberty he is noisy and rebellious.[13] He becomes cynically boastful and provocative, despising as idiots, or slaves, all those who do not share his convictions. Married, he becomes a domestic tyrant. He provides the majority of the recalcitrant and the deserters, and the least desirable recuits to sects and revolutionary movements.

The adored and spoilt child is given the most favourable conditions for the development of such dispositions. The only chance of avoiding them in a child who shows such tendencies is to deal with them in good time. He must first be led to know his own limitations by being given a chance of measuring himself against a competitive environment, against superior natures. Compliments should be sparingly administered. If a request has been refused on reasonable grounds, no concession should be made at any price, so that he becomes resigned to the limitation of his own power when it runs up against an absolute in the form of another's will. Then he must be taught to recognise first the rights, and then gradually the existence and value of others, by the practice of sacrificial renunciation.[14] His pride should not be openly humiliated or his temperament will be exacerbated and driven into rancorous dissimulation. It has to be sublimated, transformed, for instance, into a rigorous sense of honour, and heroic self-discipline. It would be utopian to believe that the child's anarchic instincts can be broken without the use of authority. In the middle of the eighteenth century, which was corrupted by such wishful thinking, Locke remarked, extremely appositely, that a child should be given only a

* Further details of the paranoiac constitution.

small number of prohibitions, so that authority should not be destroyed
by being tyrannical.

*   *   *   *

The affirmation of the self, in its centrifugal form, appears as
assurance which is, as it were, its public expression. It may be that
assurance expresses an inner solidity. It may also be a purely social *tic*,
a fact of education, a consciousness of social superiority inculcated
from early childhood, and the easy manner of an assured existence. It
is the typical expression of someone whose moral or financial credit
stands high. Its value depends on the value of the credit. It may lead
the way to presumption, but without presumption who would draw
near to the absolute? The quagmires of mediocrity are littered with
the falsely modest, the falsely prudent, always ready to point out the
'pride' and the 'temerity' of those who dare. But neither is it a proof of
audacity: how many young heroes have we seen flinch at the first
danger. Binet had two little daughters: one was very sure of herself
before attacking, but did not stand her ground: the other, uncertain of
herself, hesitated at the beginning, but persevered. Neither assurance
nor its absence can therefore define a man at first glance. Pretentious
assurance and morbid self-distrust have nothing to do with the serenity
of strength and true humility. A certain mental clarity, sustained by a
healthy body, leads to assurance. On the other hand, it seems that a
sense of the mystery of the world, and the magnitude of its secrets, is
inseparable from some disequilibrium which inevitably finds a visible
expression. The play of disguises is infinite.

A step further leads us to *aggressiveness*. It seems that no character
trait should be easier to note. Yet repressed—and like all powerful
instincts, it often is—it can be dissimulated in countless ways, even
appearing as its opposite. Thus a too stressed self-effacement is often
the product of an over-compensated aggressiveness towards superiors.
The painful scruple is both the work of a violent aggressiveness towards
oneself and a protection against its power by dissipating its energy in
a series of skirmishes.

Aggressiveness is rooted in the most elementary instinct. It is
proportionate to physical vigour: it increases at adolescence with the
sudden development of the muscular system. It is subject to the
influence of the endocrine glands, on which external agents (toxins,
foodstuffs, etc.) are not without effect. It follows the development of
virility. There is no manifestation of the sexual instinct, particularly of

* Details of the treatment of youthful paranoiacs.

the virile instinct, on which it does not exercise a latent irritation which takes, in men, the external form of a desire for domination.
*

We have spoken of a certain frenzy of the instincts, which tends to go beyond the objects assigned to them by their function, without, however, being able to depart from their nature. Aggressiveness is not yet such a frenzy of the power instinct, which would make it the least tameable of all: but it is the first stirring of vital irritation. It often happens that it develops its own brakes. It is often indicated by the habit of nail-biting, a symbol of aggression: thus it turns against itself and simulates a disarmament.

In the combative instinct as displayed by the child, this irritability seems to be, for the totality of the psyche, what cellular irritation is to the corporal organism, the expression of a vigilant, active tension which is the very tension of life.
**

It is . . . understandable that aggressiveness should be somewhat suspect in the world of values. Laden with the most savage instinctual drives, rich in more or less morbid deviations, it cuts rather a poor shape in the nobler regions of the psyche. It is not thereby in itself a vice, as some sensitive souls seem to believe. It is a normal form of instinct, and like instinct, both healthy in its source and dangerous in its frenzies or excesses. By trying to eliminate it, as dreamed of by a certain pacifism, which is not merely a political doctrine but a eunuch's way of life, one creates vaporised beings, who lose courage and even initiative with their violence. Moral courage and even self-assurance are as a rule partly dependent on a certain physical vigour. The man who feels his limbs at the mercy of another's audacity, lacks the robustness necessary to refuse to deliver him his thoughts and his heart also: even the best have difficulty in overcoming this weakness which is communicated from the muscles to the heart. Of this we have sufficient evidence today in the individual and collective defeats of a supine civilisation, of a childish and well-meaning educational system, which thought it could dilute the combative instinct, as well as the sexual instinct, by not talking to children of the fire in their veins. We are not attempting to deny that if the aggressive instinct is systematically encouraged from childhood on it will become uncontrollable, nor that individual and collective education should attempt to contain it

---

* Various expressions of the desire for domination, and the theories of Schaeffer, Havelock-Ellis, Groos, Stekel, Spaier, Adler and Stanley Hall.

** The combative instinct expressed in childhood and in various temperaments.

within acceptable limits. But simply because this is a commonplace amongst civilised peoples it is important to insist on the complementary necessities. The great virtues of self-renunciation and humility preached by most religions are not the idealisation of a vital weakness, but the free, generous, that is to say superabundant, gift of a self-reliant and healthy man to the men around him and to the duty that surpasses him. Thus man must be made proud and upright, so that on to his complete humanity may be grafted without mishap that higher destiny of renunciation which appears to be, as Pascal says, 'a reversal from for to against'. The reversal of for to against is not a watering down of for to nothing.

We have used the word pride: a susceptible virtue, shot through and through with the first stirrings of arrogance and aggressiveness. But by containing them and turning them inwards, their agitation is reduced to a slight, vital vibration, transfiguring their rigidity into uprightness. Abandoned without control it becomes degraded into a prickly sensitivity and false points of honour, whose mendacity is concealed by exaggeration. Dominated, it becomes the first step towards nobility and courage. To awaken it may be the first means of transforming hitherto unapproachable adolescents.

It is complicated by the sense of honour, which is also not entirely free from primitive combativity and arrogance. The age of chivalry placed it a little too close to sanctity. And yet, when one has dreamed that individuals or peoples might succeed in passing beyond it, and found them incapable even of achieving it, one must recognise that it constitutes an indispensable backbone to anyone who has not been able to adopt a more total disinterestedness, in truth and without illusion. As confusions go, it is better to confuse sanctity with honour, than with a cowardice clad in fine feelings.

*

One should add that, in its highest form, the affirmation of the self cannot be reduced to attitudes of egocentricity, demand or aggressiveness, movements which are more or less weakened by a direction and a meaning which is always marginal to the axis of a full personal life. They are too easily taken to be evidence of strength of mind. 'In humanity', writes Proust, 'the rule, with obvious exceptions, is that the hard are the weak who have not been accepted, and that the strong, who care little whether they are accepted or not, are the only ones to show that gentleness which the vulgar take for weakness.'[15]

The highest affirmation of the self is first of all, as its name suggests,

* Ambition and sternness as elements in the affirmation of the self.

a reinforcement of personal being by the deliberate assimilation of experience. By a movement arising from the depths, the person gives birth to itself by a series of choices. It chooses to be a person, in the light of a certain universe of values. It sets aside the easy but sterile profusion of all the available possibilities in favour of active resignation to one particular destiny. In a life where existence is, fatally, as much limitation as generous promise, it accepts limitation in order to be. The undecided and the dilettante never know the robust testing of choice, by which the psychic muscles acquire their tone. Here the narrow experience of aggressiveness is transformed into the essential experience of confrontation, the vital face to face, which always comes back by some detour, to a face to face with death.

It is not for its ugliness and depressive aspect, as some aesthetes protest, that suffering is an essential ingredient and as it were a revealer of personal life. It is because it is inseparable from an exacting choice out of a wealth of material, inseparable from greatness. It is also because it turns us inward, whereas sensation and knowledge turn us outward. 'Man has places in his poor heart which do not yet exist,' wrote Bloy, 'where suffering must enter so that they may do so.' So that we only know that which in some way makes us suffer. To eliminate suffering from this world would be to suppress both man and civilisation. That it should be the dream of those who have suffered too much is understandable. But looked at more coldly, only those entirely devoid of spiritual experience could consider it. Yet there is nothing less passive, less withdrawn, than the great movement towards the building up of the self. 'Inwardness', said Kierkegaard, 'is only achieved through action.' The phrase, which might also sum up Goethe's itinerary, is the crowning assurance of an adult life which has overcome, without extinguishing them, the banked fires of adolescence. The aspiration to the infinite reality which is at the heart of the person cannot stifle its periodical revolts against the limits of the self, nor altogether contain an instinct of violent negation of the constraints of personalisation. Yet these negations, unlike the morbid negation of the self, are only fruitful crises, already transfigured by an aspiration to fuller being.[16]

THE SELF IN INTENTION: THE THREE DIMENSIONS OF PERSONAL LIFE

The affirmation of the self, as the word implies, is not only the authoritarian attitude by which the individual self considers, confronts and confirms its will to intervention and self-preservation. It is the strengthening of a mobile and progressive reality which discovers and enriches itself and gains in inner authority. There is only personal affirmation on the basis of personal life.

This life goes on in the inner structure of the person. Personal man is not a massive existence, inwardly immobile or punctual, more or less blind to the world outside, the picture commonly put forward by materialist psychologies and individualist idealism. In its own way, like the atom, it has an inner articulation of form and movements, which are grouped according to three principal directions:

1.   *A movement of exteriorisation*, of adaptation to the totality of the world, through the environment. It corresponds to what Freud calls the *reality principle*. It consists of (a) a movement of extraversion towards things and towards others, which at this level of analysis may still be taken together in their common quality of objects or projects; (b) an effect of differentiation, the diversity of objects modifying the confused potentialities of the self in various ways, and shaping them into various aptitudes; (c) an effect of dispersal, which holds a permanent danger of depersonalisation; and finally (d) a reaction against this danger, a force of appropriation, which tends to strengthen the passage of the self amongst things.

We have already dealt with the characterological crystallisations of extraversion.[17]

*   *   *

*

Excessive differentiation creates the type of man who seems reduced to his technical or social functions. Differentiation is necessary to consolidate the traits of personal vocation. Carried too far it blocks potentialities and cuts off the margin of a free future. Thus we can distinguish and even contrast two undifferentiated types. The lower type is undifferentiated through lack of personality: a soul without frontiers or borders, which can only live in confusion, or change colours inconsistently like a chameleon. Such are the amorphous types whose very inconsistency inclines them to the changing roles of the theatre. Sometimes their basic amorphism is cloaked by a vehement, histrionic affirmation, in which eloquence of gesture endeavours to counterfeit inner assurance: we have pointed out this unconvincing compensation in the hysterical personality. At the other extreme of the psychological scale there is a higher undifferentiated type, which through the excess and breadth of creative power, retains a certain

* Gives further details of these crystallisations.

inner fluidity and a disconcerting range of possibilities. Graphology can distinguish the two types clearly. The 'thread' of the handwriting which is common to both (the dissolution of forms tending to a horizontal and hardly legible undulation) has marks of quality in the latter which are absent in the former.

*   *   *

We mentioned dispersal as a menace involved in exteriorisation, but it would be distortion of facts if one considered it inevitable. The slope which leads from one to the other should not make us forget the essential value of objectivisation as a means of personal culture. This touches on the element of living truth in materialism. The effects of the materialism of medicine at the beginning of the last century, then of positivism and historical materialism, have not been entirely negative. Without the brake that they applied European vitality might have disappeared in all the fashions of the period: the verbal rationalism of the 'enlightened', the languors of the romantics, the faded spirituality of the right-minded. An essential falsehood was vitiating the period, a sort of collective 'bovarysm'. Education was forming children to the model: scruple, religiosity, verbal facility, sentimentality, the fragile graces of distinction, instead of teaching them decision, faith, intellectual power, affective sincerity, complete virility and a feeling for ordinary virtues and for simple men. It is the function of the struggle with what we call, for simplicity's sake, matter, to develop not only muscle but moral and intellectual health. The man in a state of perpetual dialectical disequilibrium is sometimes reminded of this by materialist impulses. If, in their turn, they are overweighted in one direction, they are nearer than they seem to Christian, or at any rate to Catholic, theological tradition, which has always shown a preference for the view that a detour via matter is a necessary way of attaining not only a knowledge of the world but even of inner life and a knowledge of God. In any case the equilibrium of contemporary man requires that work, trade and techniques, the machine, the body, and sport, should be acquitted of the slur still cast upon them in certain circles. It is high time to stop equating the intellectual with the consumptive, the Christian with a tortured conscience, a sincere heart with weakness. What Montherlant wrote of the educative value of sport, the place where one cannot cheat, is true of every hand-to-hand struggle with the material of things, and should enter into general educational theory, for the health of what we call, for simplicity's sake, the mind. This hand-to-hand struggle brings man together. It helps to prevent intelligence becoming, as it almost inevitably does today, a force of indecision and dissolution; it prevents feeling from suffering baroque complications and refinements of bad faith: it would help to make religion popular and virile, and art essential. Yet a pedagogy of matter is ambivalent, like all tools destined to the use of man. We should not create a depreciation of mind parallel to the historic, yet even in Christianity relatively recent error, which attributed original sin exclusively to matter and the flesh.[18] The disease of the mind denounced by the materialists reappears in exactly similar form in our life with matter, for the good reason that 'mind' and 'matter' are identical abstractions from concrete man, both of them riveted to the same (and symmetrical) complexes of feeling. The use of and contact with things also engenders dispersal, evasion, alienation, if our personal authority over our experience does not promote the forces of association in material life over its force of dispersal. Here, as elsewhere, we cannot evade choice. One might even say that since, in all social circles, the things of the senses are more accessible to the greatest number than those of the spirit, the danger of alienation by external objects will always be more widespread, even in a better ordered society, than the danger of alienation by invisible illusions.

*   *   *

We do not need to dwell on the movement of appropriation which we have dealt with at length, except to recall that it is also fraught with ambivalence. Inseparable from the reinforcement of personality (this is the enduring part of the need for property), it is even, in childhood, one of its earliest manifestations. But, by an inner reversal, it may enslave the one it has once liberated. Here again matter shows itself a two-edged force.

2.   This movement of exteriorisation of the self is complemented by a *movement of interiorisation*. Here we have to add to the reality principle, so rightly stressed by Freud, a *principle of interiority*, which is totally absent from his psychology, an absence which incidentally throws all modern positivist psychology off balance. We have criticised these concepts of 'inner' and 'outer'. They are both penetrating and distorting. They express a valuable intuition as to the close liaison, verified clinically and by experience, between certain psychic realities and certain structures of space. But they fix attention on what is inevitably a crude projection of an infinitely more complex reality.

We should therefore maintain a certain reserve when analysing more closely the experience of interiority and its characterological forms.

It appears, first of all, as a retreat from contact with things (and persons taken as things), a withdrawal into more silent or more primitive zones in ourselves. But immediately ambivalence appears. The same movement may, in fact, have a varying significance. Flight is too poor a term in certain cases, self-recollection too rich in others.

Strictly speaking, the processes of flight from reality have nothing to do with interiorisation. In some cases they are as much a flight from inner as from outer reality. We have studied them under various heads: complexes of retreat, fear of action, narcissism, egocentricity, the refusal of others. In their pure essence, if there were pure psychological essences, they have all the dual quality of refusal and of fear. They are a fear of life and not a search for an increase of life. They impoverish and disarm the personality, and this is what materialist and activist critics reproach in all inner evasion.

In the variegated reality of things, the path which leads to the sanctuaries of the self is at its beginning the same as that taken by the refugees from life, and it is often difficult to distinguish, at least for a time, whether a step is taken in flight or in self-recollection. A great spiritual journey may start from a maladaptation to reality, and a concern for the inner life may develop into egoistic isolation. Such admixtures should not be allowed to devaluate this vital process of interiorisation in a fully human life. Ambivalence here is neither greater than, nor different from that found in our 'external' life. It does, however, produce a surface continuity which conceals a change of significance in the operation.

The key to the ambiguity is no doubt in the attitudes of refuge, which are less purely negative than attitudes of flight. They derive from a recoil, from a struggle, from a difficult adaptation (particularly sexual), from a setback or objective shock. But they strive to arrest the flight by resorting to some reserve of psychic life left intact by the battle in the front line of personality: and thus they result either in an impoverishment or in the enrichment of the total psyche according to whether they encountered dead zones, or forces which were still living, although regressive from the aspect of action. The researches of the psychoanalytic schools have established almost a geography of these zones of retreat. Here, they have pointed out a kind of symbolic and affective equivalence of mother, the past, tradition, and childhood, all centres of experience to which anabolic and vegetative life contribute more than the catabolic and active. The man who flees from the contemporary spiritual crisis into the facilities of comfort or the naïve cult of techniques (the materialist evasion), joins company with the scout who is equally evading it by naturalist puerilities, the disappointed politician becomes reactionary, the man shattered by life consoles himself by his memories of childhood, and the timorous adolescent clings to his mother. Collective symbolism places these sources of refuge on the left, the active gestures on the opposite side (an archetypal localisation which is imprinted on the handwriting). When the withdrawal ends in immobility there are no more stubborn and hardened complexes than those which develop around these zones of repose, whose frontiers are protected by the memory of painful anguish. A man who has been thus converted by recoil, and not by progress, to some opinion or faith, usually adopts its blindest and most unapproachable forms. But if the retreat has led to some inner oasis, which may be made the basis of a vast garden, he may begin to grow again in the very place where he was cut short. To such withdrawals we owe, no doubt, many of the artists of childhood, the writers of memoirs and perhaps also the thinkers who have been able later to link their meditations with reality.

But interiorisation proper only begins, even in the heart of the refuge, with the intervention of certain positive elements. The first is the recovery of the self. This is part of the normal regime of life for any temperament. Even the highest form of commitment must be balanced by an equal movement of detachment. But it is more or less urgent according to the greater or lesser degree to which the personality has been invaded and stupefied by the pressure of external things. Here we must appeal to an analogy with surface tension. Asthenics and emotives in particular are as it were overwhelmed and stupefied by the too prolonged presence of the noise of things and of people. It seems that instead of their dealing with the world, from a reasonable distance, it is always pressing up against them, bumping and bruising them. They need a periodic retreat more than anyone, and even a life which organises a permanent retreat which their own nature does not provide. The excitedly agitated are equally eaten up, particularly the extraverted emotive types. But the latter love their torture and only seek to cure their dizziness by further dizziness, being frightened of silence and solitude, and when this supervenes, it is extremely difficult to induce the relaxation which would be the beginning of recovery. Special movements to achieve this have been studied, both by the ascetics of every religion and by modern treatises on gymnastics. Here again the body is the beginning of spiritual life.

The recovery of the self is the step that leads to the deepening of the self. 'To recover oneself' is popular language. We have seen that it is not only a question of recovery from the mastery of things, but to recover the multiple projections of the self by which one has scattered oneself through the world. It is not, however, a simple balance sheet and recollection that is required. I am starting on an adventure of discovery, the limits and the drama of which I do not know, so indefinite seems the path and so unfathomable the abyss which contemporary psychology, from its profound experience, has opened beneath our feet. The quest is pursued through every layer of the personality, the thin strata of consciousness, which it can help to illuminate, and the bottomless pits of unconscious life. This quest only isolates us if we confine it to the narrow sphere of rationalisation of thought or feeling, to the play of ideas and the cult of the self. But we know today that the register of the visible and invisible waves of the personality is no less extensive that that of material waves. This exploration has only begun. From the shadows of the infraconscious to the lights of the supraconscious, passing through the subconscious and the various levels of the organised consciousness, we meet all the voices of heaven and earth, forces from the depth of the historic past and others, still almost unknown, coming from collective living. It is true indeed that we are encompassed by reality: it not only delegates to us the forms and signs which fall to our external understanding— senses, action, techniques—but also in the rear, the forces and the signs which animate the life of the psyche. We can only confront it in its totality, and find some opportunity of mastering it as far as this is possible, if we confront it on this inner line as directly and totally as in the field of external stimuli, to which alone many people accord the name of reality.

When dealing with introversion, which is not interiority, but the disposition most favourable to it, we saw what temperaments were inclined to it, and the reverse. The indication is maximum for the emotive and minimum for the primary types. The real inwardness of a man, whether he be a perfect man of action, or a purely contemplative nature, is revealed by certain physical signs. The clearest is, no doubt, a certain indefiniteness of gaze, in which can be read disquiet, self irony, enquiry as to what goes beyond persons and things, and the discreet yet urgent question which he puts at each encounter. Reserve, awkwardness, timidity even susceptibility, all signs of a certain lack of adaptation to the external, often take on a rare quality through an intense inwardness: even in the type of inward-turning man one sees too infrequently, who has acquired both social and athletic balance, they still leave a furtive trace, like a hardly visible signature at the foot of a painting. Psychically the ways of the man familiar with the inside world are not the same as those of a man absorbed by sense perceptions, or manufacture, or utilitarian relationships or the social game. An intuitive power constantly nourished by the subliminal zones of the self plays its part here, as much as any calculated operation of the mind. This is easily noted in women, usually closer than man to the subliminal life, and who are capable of so many correct intuitions without being able to justify them. The other side of the picture is an always dangerous tendency to subjectivity in matters which require objectivity, and connected with the permanent search for something beyond, a certain instability. No doubt this type may produce in its extreme form personalities ill-adapted to the rational techniques of manufacture or of action. But when it is a question of dealing with men, they will always be superior to the others. And when a man acts, he is always dealing with men.

*   *   *

3.   We have seen that exteriority and interiority may be crystallised into fixed behaviours and that both may even be dissolved into a process of depersonalisation. They only add to the fullness of man and contribute to his equilibrium when they appear as a *movement forward*, or of continual transcendence of the given. This *principle of forward movement* is as essential to personal life as the reality principle and the principle of interiority. Personal life is upheld, just like an aircraft or a bicycle, by this alone. Man is made to be surpassed: Nietzsche's formula has not only a moral value: it has, and no doubt had for Nietzsche, a functional meaning. Man does not stand upright except by constantly exceeding the given, the customary, the acquired. It is another way of saying that the force of gravity in personal life pulls towards the future. There is no need to insist further: all that we have already said about attitudes towards the future and the past is valid here.

*   *   *

It is not the least problem of personal life to create and maintain a cohesion and a balance between these three demands on the self. They are not the same for all.

Some persons are morbidly sensitive to the cleft or, if you prefer it, to the inner distance which allows the coming and going of the self in search of interiority and transcendence. All feelings of depersonalisation which have their incidence as much in the inner as in the outer world, arise from a sense of feeling lost in this inner space.

None of us can develop equally in every dimension of personal life. A complete humanity needs engineers as well as mystics. It even requires hybrids. It only rejects monsters, like the engineers of souls and the dreamers of action. There must therefore be a choice and a dominant. The danger is that one chooses an exclusive instead of a dominant. Man is then mutilated, for complete man is not someone who is psychically eclectic, but one in whom no essential dimension is radically repressed. The parts that lie fallow, as Jung has shown even more completely than Freud, remain rudimentary and archaic, liable to develop anarchically, sometimes with exuberance and always in a primitive key. Thus what one calls the pure intellectual, that is to say, the rationalist intellectual, or better still, the intellectually extraverted, who is cut off from all the obscure forces of instinct and affectivity, and all the resources of intuitive living, falls frequently victim to a *femme fatale*, or to a commonplace type of woman, or develops a rudimentary passion for certain peremptory beliefs (or lack of belief, and superstition). Inversely, a man intellectually thwarted, becomes embedded in abstract ideas he cannot handle. One could quote countless examples of such subversions due to exclusive exteriority or interiority, which explain many secrets of history as well as of the individual. Some brutal reactions would be explained by the neglect shown in previous periods. This would introduce a science of the future, a 'historical psychologism' which would not oust historical materialism from any field it has legitimately conquered, but would be able to replace some of its explanations by more essential ones. Half the understanding of history is closed to us if we attempt to explain the era of the world wars and totalitarian powers without reference to the European crisis of Christianity (the 'death of God' in many psyches), and the incontinence of organised, extraverted consciousness during the last two hundred years—industrial techniques, unilateral development of material sciences, rationalism, refinements of sentimental analysis, the intellectualisation of faith, the development of the utilitarian outlook, of riches, of economics, and so on.

We never complete this difficult task of the gathering together of the self. For better or worse we keep going with partial results, bundles of complexes, partial unities behind a hastily erected façade, 'part personalities', as Jung says, which lead us towards greater personalisation even while strewing our path with refractory obstacles. The way in which a certain unity of movement is maintained or relaxed in spite of so many ill-assorted components, is worth further study.

Some of Freud's disciples have admitted the inadequacy of reductive analysis in this respect. It understands life as movement, but it does not understand life *in* movement. It tends to reduce life to a system of immobile, stereotyped references: fixed in the past and the preconceived, however clever it may be in making us forget this reduction later. But what matters to a man questioning himself or another as to an existing psychic situation, is not why the situation arose, but to what purpose it was created. Where the professor of Vienna saw only more or less anarchic drives attracting and entangling all the energies of the libido, the doctor of Zürich[19] perceived a movement of unification struggling admittedly with dispersive forces, but which drove the subject, through conscious life, through dream or neurotic crisis, towards the uncertain victory of unity over inner division. What he grasps in this analysis is not only the mechanisms and the complexes behind the mechanisms, but an individual *movement* running the whole gamut of personality, from the conscious zones to the unconscious depths, in order to gather together and harmonise the forces that develop in relative autonomy over such a broad register. What else can one call this movement except a movement towards personalisation?

*

THE CONSTANCY OF THE SELF

Psychology in the third person was long tormented by the problem of the 'unity' and the 'identity' of the self. Once the self is posited as an object, empirically composite, granular like matter, but insisting on its precedence, then only impossibilities and contradictions could arise from such spiritual matter, or such mechanical spirit. If every moment of time modifies the self, how can we guarantee its permanence? And if its unity is absolutely immobile, how can we explain life? In fact, no solely objective representation of the self can grasp the secret of this changing coherence which can only be accounted for by the psychology of an act, a personal act. Absolute 'identity' is death: it is only found in the sterile uniformity of elementary energy, as the end process of the degradation of matter, or in the void of logical negation. The self is not identical in this sense, or only tends to be in the regions of greatest psychological poverty. The self is identical, just as one is constant, or faithful, by a continuous act of commitment. A flexible act, varying, sometimes attentive, sometimes combative, using the forces of the body like a massive flying-buttress,

* Refers to Jung's word association tests.

reaching out somewhere in prayer towards a greater possibility of being. In addition, the constancy of the self, even in its empirical permanence, would be quite erroneously depicted as a continuous line or thread of sound. It is incessant vibration, a perpetual movement, from repose to anguish, from defeat to victory, from faith to scandal. What is constant in the self is not the maintenance of identity but of a dialectic tension, and the mastery of the periodic crises whose erratic incidence is the outline of a destiny.

*

Freud has restored to our times what some would call the dionysiac consciousness, others the demoniac consciousness, or simply the consciousness of sin. If he has reduced it too exclusively to a lacerated consciousness, it is perhaps because his epoch offered only images of disorder. Psychology may correct certain traits in his pictures, but it cannot reject them as a whole on their own level. Through him it has recovered a sense of the drama of consciousness and a lucid vision of its depths. It needs now to pursue the same study into the field unexplored by Freud, into a zone even more central than that of the Freudian secrets, where the infernal forces are held and combined with the forces of creation. However much Freud believed he had detached his work from all considerations of values, no psychologist has ever so much revealed the point to which personal unity is linked with moral affirmation. Take his clinical interpretations. The mental automatism of Clérambault? The disaggregation of impressions revealing repressed tendencies. Paranoia? The external projection of a repressed tendency, which is turned against the self by a process of self-punishment accompanied by a transfer of responsibility. Melancholy? Once more a fury of self-punishment. Schizophrenia? The self-destruction of a personality which suppresses itself completely, as a punishment for not having resolved its Oedipus complex. Whatever one may think of each interpretation, there emerges, unknown to its author, the general idea that personal unity is an achievement of the moral character, where defeat is judged and severely punished by the self. Freud perceived a sort of moral magnetism in psychic structures. He regarded it with suspicion, like the physicists uneasy over the first research into electromagnetism because of its dubious association with animal magnetism. So he evaded the suggestion of jettisoning his preconceptions, although

---

* Refers to the psychology of Maine de Biran, and Janet's theory of mental synthesis. Also deals with clinical forms of dissociation and Freud's insistence on the primary importance of a psychology in the first person, and criticises Freud for not going far enough.

it arose from his own researches. In this he lacked imagination and audacity, but none the less he opened the door that he tried deliberately to keep closed.

Jung was the first disciple of a school that replaced the person as the centre of man, master of this turbulent kingdom. Just as God formed even the rebellious angels in His own image, so the person leaves its mark even on those forces which turn against its struggle for unity. Jung no longer speaks of impersonal complexes entirely detached from the subject. These so-called nuclei, although to him they do not possess the qualities that constitute a subject, are nevertheless true parasitical personalities which are produced by the person to express unconscious contents rising to the surface. Thus the Self [20] reigns as a feudal lord over more or less submissive vassals, but wields, by its own transcendence, the sole authority to concede to one or the other a directing function in the psyche. Deep in the Unconscious, yet eminently personal, it engages on the conquest of that personal synthesis, of which Jung has recently been studying the collective imagery (precious object to be detached, the search for a centre, for the subtle element, etc.). It is also a constant theme in Adler's psychology that conduct cannot be explained by blind drives, but that it is always animated by a directing, compelling force, intellectualised even when it deviates, like the 'directive fiction' of the nervous. The Unconscious, said Adler, is more the Ununderstood. The aim of education and of therapy is to introduce into it order, understanding and purpose. Some psychoanalysts more orthodox than Jung have already moved in this direction.

*

And again, the work of unification, if it is to come to fruit, assumes a preliminary acceptance of value: 'It is better that I should be one.' This will to constancy is only possible given an experience of a personal universe and its perfection, for no abstract idea of unity can contain the explosive tension of the forces of dissociation. This is not such a reversal of elementary psychic processes as the Freudian school would believe. Life confronts the forces of dislocation at their own level with an active power of regroupment (the *sineidesis* of Monakow and Mourgues), which in every case reconstructs the whole: from this angle a psychosis is not a form of stampede but, on the contrary, an attempt at synthesis, the only synthesis compatible with the given conditions. [21]

* Quotes four methods by which the later psychoanalysts try to re-establish the true energy of the self.

*
Whatever help personal constancy and coherence may receive from innate disposition, they are also the gradually maturing product of commitment and fidelity. Freud was right to seek the cohesive power of the self in a Superego, which through its commanding position could control the dispersal of consciousness in daily life. It is, as we have seen, through a movement towards the future, which is also a promise of expansion, that man can collect his strength and understand his frontiers. And yet this that-is-beyond-me must respond to my innermost need and offer me the entrancing image of what I can be. Bergson rightly said that nowhere in the world was there a more unifying quality than the appeal of a presence which is already a presence faithful to itself: in a word, to meet a man, or sometimes, a superman.
**

UNLIKE ALL OTHERS

There was a purpose in going so deeply into the study of the affirmation of the self before speaking of the desire for originality. This feeling and this wish to be irreducibly different from others are, in fact, must less important from the point of view of the psychology of the person, than its critics suppose. They occur under two aspects, of radically different origin.

In its most current form it is only a by-product of personal life, almost its parasite. The hero, when his energy is tensest, the lover when he gives himself, the creator at the moment of inspiration, are not concerned with differentiation or a comparison with others, but only to put forth their greatest strength. Completely absorbed in the movement of courage, love or creation, they see themselves at such moments not so much as exceptions, in some rare world, but as men who have achieved fulfilment, lifted up into a state of happy simplicity, which blossoms into a desire for communication. At the heart of the most personal creation, at the heart of the joy which is its mark, this desire for communication largely overwhelms the intoxication of being alone to achieve the summit. And if it is true that creative activity opens on to the unique, it soon discovers there a higher form of the commonplace. It is this commonplaceness which makes the monotony of great works, great lives and solemn oaths: it also creates such a lot of bad literature out of good feelings. A singularity bathed in banality, such is creative originality. The singularity vibrates in the success of its forms, the banality comes from the light that is the same

* Elementary forms of the constancy of the self in space and time.
** The physical expression in the care of the body of the affirmation of the self.

for all, which makes the miracle of a flower so simple, almost concealing it within its background, but illuminating it with a secret glow.

An object becomes bizarre when our attention is held solely by the singularity of its form, having shed its links with all around it that was destined to make it necessary or merely acceptable. It is the same with all originality which holds one's eyes without inviting one to look beyond it. It betrays some lowering, however slight, of value or reality. If a personality suggests first and foremost the idea of originality, we may be sure that person has renounced, however little, a fullness of being which would have given more substance to his genius. The man that seeks originality first, or too passionately, is no longer quite at the level of his art, but somewhat in retreat: he pursues its 'effect' as a detached spectator, and measures the intensity he can produce at the summit of his power less by an absolute in himself than by lateral or social judgments. He abandons greater being for the sake of being different. This quest for originality has nothing to do with a triumphant enjoyment of the unique, which is a gratuitous result of conquest. It is even less valuable than emulation which, at any rate in its higher forms, is centred on greater being: it only casts an occasional furtive glance sideways, which encourages its drive, without interrupting it. The root of a determined search for originality is a defence against those around one: and this basic rivalry makes it unfastidious in its choice of means. It is, in fact, of the same nature as the egalitarianism of the barbarians it deplores. Both for the one and the other it is first of all a question not of being, but of defending oneself against the being of others, either by levelling out their advantages, or by assuring oneself of some difference at any rate from them. These frontier operations have an accessory interest, but when they take precedence over personal drive they indicate an undeniable lowering of psychic level.

There is a vast difference in the act by which a higher consciousness becomes capable of savouring the absolute uniqueness of each moment of being. This is an act of high personal quality, for this uniqueness is only granted to an artistic and religious awareness, sensitive to all the harmonies of reality and its deepest perspectives. If any comparison were possible, it would be with the forward movement of the person, either because creative consciousness looks forward from its present state towards the inexhaustible generosity of being, avidly seeking for ever fresh power, or because it feels threatened from the rear by the dreariness of habit and flees from the deadly shadow of repetition. But this taste for the unique, even if conscious, is hardly premeditated: the creative mind has too much confidence in life to ask for pledges or guarantees: it receives life's fruits as a grace, seeking first of all the kingdom of truth or beauty, and the rest is added. The saint does not seek originality, as the Church quickly pointed out to those wonderful personages in the desert who, in order to feel closer to God, produced some remarkable singularities. The accomplished artist turns away from such things with all the more distaste.

There is, however, a time when the search for originality, even originality at any price, seems a normal phase of development in the person, and that is the 'crisis of juvenile originality',[22] the period that fosters 'the delicious bitterness of being, or feeling oneself alone in a hostile or uncomprehending universe'. It is the last and the most tempestuous of the crises of youth. It explodes at about fourteen in girls, about fifteen in boys, and is an essential element of that 'mental puberty' which Spranger opposes to the idea that puberty is exclusively sexual. Its onset is sudden and violent: the adolescent displays brusque irritation, rebels against both orders and an excess of affection: the family, school, the beliefs current in his circle, the father's generation, the monotony of daily life, are the principal objectives of his revolt. The budding personality, blinded by its youthful strength and fearing to lose it amongst so many ancestral traditions and solid conformities, tries itself out in extravaganzas in order not to be dissolved by hereditary habit. There are explosions of joy over the most futile scandal, fantastic apparel, love of gaudy colours and unsuitable cut, mannerisms, deliberate impoliteness, gratuitous actions, preciosity of language and pronunciation, a love of paradox, of extremism and the grotesque. It is important to astonish others and oneself. The instrument is new and is trying out all its stops, at the price of an occasional false note. Together with these eccentricities, and varying in proportion according to temperament, the self experiments in depth to see if it is unlike all others: it is the age of the intimate diary, long solitary walks, heroic efforts of discipline and thought, the aesthetic cult of the self and scorn for the philistines. One reads Barrès, Gide, Nietzsche and Stendhal and rushes madly in their footsteps. It is natural that this upsurge is much more marked in young people from circles that are cultured or bespattered with culture, than in working class youth whose harder lives divert them from fantasy and introspection. But even these do not always escape: a provocative cut to the Sunday suit, or workday shirt, daring opinions, fantasy in work; instinct will find a hundred cracks to slip through. The crisis is usually resolved at about twenty. The result is then achieved, the self has emerged from its

chrysalis. Henceforward the need to adapt to reality will be in competition with the need to be oneself.
*

EVALUATION

It was only through a kind of abstraction that we were able to speak of a pure and simple affirmation of the self. This affirmation is already a vote cast against nothingness or against death. The melancholic depreciates himself to the point of absurdity and finally kills himself. The paranoiac overestimates himself grotesquely and finally goes mad. The consciousness of sin is for the Christian the very basis of self-knowledge. This religious affirmation is part of a broader psychological truth. I cannot be aware of myself, in the most elementary act of consciousness, without according myself some value, either favourable or not. One might play at trying to discover neutral states here, as in affective matters, but they would only be abstractions within limited situations. This evaluation is supported by social references, which are the nearest scale of value in psychological matters, just as intelligence of being is supported by sense perceptions. But it cannot therefore be reduced to a pure social operation as P. Janet,[23] for instance, would have it. It is quite true that one man can seldom be in the presence of another without asking himself: 'What is he worth? Is he above or beneath me? In means, social standing, intelligence etc.?' But this social calculation refers to some scale of implicit values, varying with individuals and with civilisations and epochs. Some refer normally to a conventional scale, and in private, when they take themselves in hand, judge in their heart of hearts, by quite other criteria. Little light is shed on this operation by suggesting the analogy of some mechanical operation, such as 'the capillary attraction of society' which drives each individual to climb the ladder of social valuations rung by rung. If we must have a symbol, this 'movement to advance a little further' which, according to Pascal, we each carry in ourselves, would better describe the results of psychological observation.

*   *   *

The underestimation of the self is manifest in two ways, frequently combined: feelings of inferiority and feelings of guilt.

There is a normal sense of inferiority, a considered one, more or less accentuated according to the standards of the subject but which, even

* Examples in literature of the persistence of juvenile crisis in the adult; and the desire for conformity.

when appearing disproportionate, say, in the genius or the saint, always refers to some measure taken as an absolute. Each individual at the beginning of his life sets himself a standard of movement from less to more, according to his natural capacities or incapacities, and the first impressions he receives from his environment (Adler).[24] This standard varies in tempo, rhythm and direction. It is also a fact that each individual refers this movement to some inaccessible perfection, of whatever nature, enjoyment, power, virtue, etc. By this very fact every human life is in a sense vitiated at the start, or at least unbalanced and destined to a more or less vivid sense of inferiority. 'To be human', wrote Adler, 'is to feel oneself inferior.' This feeling, despite the suggestions of the word, is a positive feeling. Not only is it normal and healthy, its absence is a sign of debility: the really weak-minded do not possess it, and are the most satisfied of men with regard to themselves. But it takes on dramatic proportions in exceptional men, who no longer measure themselves by convenient social references, but by transcendent values to which they are acutely sensitive. The history of a man is a history of his sense of inferiority and his attempts to deal with it. Perhaps it is also the history of civilisations.

There is another, quite different feeling of inferiority, more or less vague, obsessive and paralysing, which torments the consciousness of the less assured. It is not the *result* of a standard or of a reflection, but a systematic disposition which inferiorises behaviour by the effect of *preliminary* intimidation. Even its uneasiness shows that it is closely connected with a disappointed desire for superiority: the two opposing feelings provoke and mutually exasperate each other. Its source is primarily in the fixations of childhood.[25] The child is always the weaker in its relationships with adults. Normally this perpetual defeat stimulates and incites him to surpass himself. But it is accompanied by an acute awareness of inferiority which may become fixed and aggravated under the effect of circumstances.

Some of these are organic: premature birth and the feeling of anguish which follows it for a certain number of days, may definitely create a disturbance of sensitivity. We know how Adler insisted on organ inferiority. Byron is a remarkable instance of this. He was obsessed from childhood by his club foot, for which his parents were constantly reproaching him. From childhood he had to stand up to ragging. So at school he would walk about with pistols in his pocket. He developed a precocious aversion to the society of men and fled from it.[26]

The real or imagined situation of the child in the family is no less important. When fathers crush their sons too brutally by their superiority, the sons become so aware of this superiority that they grow up with the paralysing feeling of never being able to surpass them: this childish idealisation will block their horizon for the rest of their lives.[27] The multiplication of futile advice about every action has much the same effect and makes life appear, very early, as quite intolerably difficult. Some psychoanalysts attribute inferiority feelings to self-punishment for excessive attachment to the mother. One has heard of 'younger son neurosis' when the younger children were made to feel inferior through having to make do with what was left by the eldest. All such humiliations set up in the child, as in the adult, a typical emotional shock, but it is more lasting, since his nerves are more fragile: he shrinks away from the injured zone, which will always remain a zone of insurmountable aversion. He will keep away from anything that reminds him of it, directly or indirectly. The humiliations may be numerous and daily, or a single one unfortunate enough to reach the living sources of sensitivity, and the inferiority feeling is established for ever. Of all humiliations, the one that is most deeply felt is guilt. It has been said that a conscious sense of inferiority generally covers an unconscious sense of guilt. But we have to establish whether such morbid guilt feelings are primary, or whether they are not themselves the way in which the individual disguises his refusal of action by self-paralysis. Quite apart from any specific humiliation, the child neglected by his family, or who feels himself neglected (psychologically the same thing) comes to the conclusion that he will be neglected all his life. The opposite extreme produces a similar effect, the child that is too protected or spoilt gets used to the idea that life is full of dangers and begins to fear it.

The feeling of inferiority is often insidiously introduced by collective situations and sensitivity. It is even part of the life of persecuted or repressed groups, the proletariat, national or ethnic minorities, etc.

*

Increasing with time, the feeling of inferiority gradually extends its systematisations into diverse zones of consciousness.[28]

**

It is this dual character, the systematisation of feeling and the unconscious nature of the directing process, which allows one to use, if necessary, the expression 'inferiority complex' which is often misleadingly used to describe simple feelings of inferiority, instead of a

---

* Künkel's theory of a predisposition to inferiority.
** Details of the expression of the sense of inferiority.

neurotic clinging to an infantile situation. The complex sets up a certain number of defensive or disordered reactions.

The simplest are the reactions of protection and security. The sufferer shelters his anxiety behind an excessive punctuality: he arrives at the station half an hour before the train starts and exacts a similar punctuality from others. He is often the most punctilious and meticulous of men: Salavin. This mannerism in behaviour shows inadaptation and the disquiet it causes. Model children, little saints, are often children of low calibre. In the adult, pedantry or fanatical erudition are a compensation similar to the studiousness of the over good pupil. Little obsessional tricks, like stepping on each division in the pavement, touching every lamp-post one passes, reaching a given point right foot first, are all ways by which the sufferer tries to make himself feel important, by creating something solid in the insipid texture of a banal life.

The sense of inferiority leads directly to dependent attitudes. Like a child the sufferer refers every action to real or fictitious authorities. He is haunted by scruples over imaginary faults. He creates for himself artificial obligations, endless duties towards indifferent or unknown persons, often to the extent of neglecting real duties. He has an imperious need to be loved, praised, reassured, and the least criticism demolishes him. He condemns himself to an absolutely passive life, to a systematic withdrawal, in order to avoid the risk of being judged.

But the reactions of emancipation from this feeling can be triumphant: a stammerer became Demosthenes, and according to Adler's statistics 70 per cent. of painters suffer from a defect of vision. In such cases, according to Adler's formula, he has redeemed his inferiority by qualities of an order superior to that whose absence he deplores. The stories of Cinderella and Tom Thumb are the expression in folklore of this universal wish. But such successes are rare. More frequently we find actions that are staccato, explosive and brittle, like an outburst of anger—the heroism of the timid, which amazes even themselves. The emancipation from inferiority is more usually weak and entirely inner. Something bubbles over inside, a turbulent and half-formed wish to break the spell. Sometimes this expresses itself in vindictive dreams in which the superior is outstripped and defeated, sometimes in daydreams in which manifold misfortunes befall the more lucky, and in which he himself acquires an audacious courage, performs marvellous exploits, enjoys privileged position. But governed as he is by an unconscious *a priori*, which whispers to him 'you are defeated before you start': these revolts are sterile and pointless, consuming the energy he could have devoted to action. He uses its last shreds to depreciate what he cannot overcome. Byron detested men, despised women and underlined his contempt by countless unworthy love affairs, going even as far as incest. The sufferer falls back into a sense of impotence until the next revival of protest, contenting himself, for the rest, with illusory compensations which disguise his defeat: the coward whistles loudly in the dark, the doubter swaggers, the impotent drives recklessly or expends himself in noisy threats. Sometimes the reaction of emancipation appears outwardly successful, but the sufferer has only freed himself from his enslavement to yield to another, like those who think they are taking liberties with time because they have unconsciously arranged to be always late: but they still have their eyes glued to their watch, and make excuses by throwing the blame on other people.[29]

Those who cannot conquer seek consolation in an equalisation of fortune in which their inferiority will disappear. As an equalisation of all psychological situations would be too heavy a task for their impaired vitality, they sometimes have recourse to a process similar to that which the psychiatrists call 'striking a balance'. They display a pathological intolerance of loss, whether of money, time or beauty. Not being able to overcome it in themselves, they insist on exacting compensation from others: as children they insist on equal shares in everything, as adults they show a morbid insistence on equality all around them. They are preoccupied with 'returning' everything and having everything strictly returned: visits, invitations, presents. Such behaviour is fairly commonplace, but a sense of inferiority gives it a rigid, strict and compulsive character. It may gain control of very powerful feelings. Charles du Bos points to Byron's lack of poise and self-confidence, which made him so aloof and insistent on the smallest prerogatives of his rank in a manner which suggests the parvenu rather than the aristocrat.

Finally, for lack of anything better, the sufferer exploits his inferiority, like the infant Cinderella. The infirm or the clumsy have to be waited on, the sick person sometimes prolongs his illness, to the extent of producing what Freud has called 'a refuge in illness'.

The reaction to feelings of inferiority engenders two spasmodic and distorted forms of evaluation, one a compensating overestimation and the other all the morbid forms of contempt for the self.

*

The sense of guilt often comes to strengthen the sense of inferiority.

* Morbid forms of a sense of emptiness.

A minimum of moral assurance is essential to the unity of the self, and moral uncertainty—not knowing whether one deserves love or hate—is one of the first things to cause a disturbance of the self. Self-development is often inhibited by the inner terror of a 'superego' which treats even the most modest affirmation of the self as presumptuous and inacceptable. There is a sort of morbid moral inflammation, without relation to rational consciousness, which makes the self violently intolerant of the idea of being at fault, of being wrong. This causes extreme susceptibility, an obsessive feeling of being always held responsible, accused or condemned or, on the contrary, there may be an irrepressible scrupulousness. But we shall return to this later.[30]

*   *   *

Overestimation of the self can be quite normal at certain stages of development. It characterises all the crises of growth of the personality. At the age of three, it is shown by the desire to be always first—to taste a dish, to finish a meal, to achieve some goal—and by the desire to outstrip others. These feelings are exacerbated in the nervous child (Adler), and in the young paranoiac. Overestimation reappears at puberty. It is the dominant trait of the paranoiac, whom it grips with the violence of tetanus. In the cycloid, who is less systematised, it contributes to a sort of general good humour, which embraces both the world and the self in a boundless optimism. In temperaments verging on mythomania, like Tartarin, it waxes and wanes and reappears at the whim of an unanchored imagination, and according to the needs of the audience, which conditions their behaviour: the cheery, talkative person is often depressed and doubtful without his public.

A feeling of superiority, like inferiority, may be concentrated and dominate a whole life, not in the false and rigidly systematic manner of the paranoiac, but like an active leaven which permeates and uplifts the whole personality. The study of this phenomenon is associated with the name of Adler. The will to power—an exaltation of the sense of personality and excessive affirmation of the will—fulfils the same role in the formation of personality as Freud attributes to the libido. It is contradicted in the child by a sense of weakness, increased by the great superiority attributed to adults. According to Adler, the child formulates this relationship of inferiority and superiority in the following manner:

weakness, inferiority, smallness, low = feminine
strength, superiority, largeness, high = masculine

Every boy tries to rise to masculinity. Every girl and every woman, though we do not necessarily have to suggest hermaphroditism, feels a general sense of inferiority through the fact that she is a woman. This general aspiration towards the virile, considered psychically (and not genitally) as a pole of superiority, constitutes the 'masculine protest'. The child aspires to what is 'high', to approach the adult, and more specifically, the father. At an early age he creates for himself an 'ideal self' a symbolic projection of the powers desired, which assumes the role of guiding fiction. All his efforts will henceforward be directed towards overcoming his inferiority in order to achieve these powers.

Some persons feel their inferiority more acutely than others, either because the inferiority, whether psychic or physical, is more marked, or because they are more sensitive to it. In childhood they have suffered from infantile inferiority, particularly organ inferiority. Ugly, sick, infirm or humiliated in some way, the child mobilises all the forces capable of strengthening his threatened security around this inferiority. The deformed, wrote Balzac, have only two possibilities: either to make themselves feared or to develop an exquisite goodness. He forgot a third. The desire to achieve omnipotence may be so violent that it leaves the sphere of reality and buries itself in clouds of fiction. This impatience and this drift towards the imaginary are the dominant traits of the temperament which Adler has defined, in this special sense, as the 'nervous' temperament.[31] This 'nervous' type, based on inferiority, is entirely dedicated to opposition. Opposition is his primitive manner of finding his way in the world. He does not attribute his inferiority to its specific cause, but to a more general and fictitious cause: heredity, environment, etc. He is, as a result, a prey to aggressive impulses against the environment. In the child it leads to insolence, in the adult to a tense, often cynical egoism (one thinks of Byron), to a demanding attitude, pretentiousness, authoritarianism, ambition, particularly in its vindictive and resentful forms.
*

Adler ascribes a considerable number of traits to this affective over-compensation. To mention a few: the tendency, in a woman, to command and protect (considered as masculine functions), shameless-ness and infidelity (considered as a means of equalling man), and coquettishness (a means of dominating man): more generally, a great deal of cruelty and perversion, sometimes hidden under a façade of anti-vivisectionism, vegetarianism and love of animals: the cynicism which, after every defeat, is followed by 'virtuous phases'; compensa-

* Further examples of over-compensation.

tions in which the subject is overwhelmed by scruples; the tendency to protect others and smother them with advice; self-aggression, designed to arouse sympathy and retain attention by a feigned inferiority which disguises a real inferiority; such as a violent asceticism, the effort of the weak to overcome their weakness, or flagellation or even some forms of suicide, of which Adler wrote that they constituted 'one of the most intense forms of the masculine protest, a final means of protection against humiliation, and a pact by which man takes revenge on life'; a certain, harsh, tense, ostentatious form of family feeling; finally the tendency to assert oneself as cheaply as possible, particularly by the arbitrary pleasure of disorganising everything around one, appointments, decisions and the position of objects. In this frenzied form of self-affirmation we have reached the very opposite of mastery; the first condition in the disciplining of our power is the exact measure of our acceptance of our own value.

*　　*　　*

It is Adler's merit to have shown both in the inferiority complex and the compensatory complexes of superiority, a precocious breach of the sense of community which, transposing Minkowski's description of adaptation to reality, might be called 'a breach of affective contact with the community'. The first creative act of the child is to find his position with regard to others: to help him to find his true position is the first duty of his teachers. If he is excessively spoilt, or, on the contrary, neglected and bullied, the relationship is falsified from the beginning. He develops an erroneous view of life, of men and of the use to be made of them, complexes of retreat or aggressiveness appear and his sensitivity is distorted for the rest of his life. Such errors must be guarded against very early. The child should live amongst others of the same age so that a relationship of equality is there to compensate for the relationship of constant inferiority with regard to adults. Our care and concern must be halfway between absence and excess. And if he suffers from some physical misfortune, persecution from other children must be carefully avoided or neutralised. Hothouse education, the pretentious indolence of a too liberal education and, of course, the effect of a broken home life, are the common sources of this inner maladjustment which mars the destiny of individuals and societies.

8

INTELLIGENCE IN ACTION

INTELLIGENCE is one of those concepts which circulate so readily that one believes that the evidence for them is almost statutory, whereas they are, in fact, inaccessible to analysis.

It is said that when someone asked Binet what this intelligence was that he was measuring all day long, he replied: 'It is what is measured by my tests.' This modest admission should be studied by all psychologists. They all speak of intelligence, but though they agree to distinguish it both from its external conditions, sense perceptions, resistance to fatigue, verbo-motor facility, etc. and from an accumulation of knowledge, they are not at all agreed on its limits and its connections. Let us examine some batteries of tests. Is it a question of memory? Half the tests include it in intelligence, the other half omit it. The same with sensation and imagination. It has been shown in turn that each was the basis of intelligence, and that they had no share in it. Here we are, said the American psychologist, Spearman[1] humorously, obliged to abandon the sovereignty of intelligence because we cannot find out who is the king. Is it a council of faculties? But nothing is more uncertain than the boundaries of these faculties and sometimes even their existence. We have seen the old concepts of affectivity and will scatter and dissolve with the progress of experimental research, into a plurality of new concepts, which will perhaps themselves be regrouped differently later. The old intellectual faculties have gone the same way. We shall be less concerned in the following pages with defining new faculties than with types of intelligence, intellectual syndromes derived from the study of correlations. In the present state of research we have much clearer ideas about these than about intelligence itself. Unfortunately, a person who belongs to one type in one class of activity may belong to another type in a different class. If we subjected intelligence to a galaxy of tests, and arranged the results in bulk under 'means' and 'levels', such a dispersion of research might have an advantage over verbal categories, but would betray a critical situation which should not be perpetuated as a method of explanation.

Such a crisis shows that intelligence can be defined neither by any isolated indication, nor by a horizontal grouping of faculties. Intelligence is personal movement itself, in so far as it is turned towards a disinterested knowledge of the universe and uses this knowledge to resolve new situations which can be handled neither by instinct nor by acquired automatisms. Whatever transcendence this may imply, the conditions under which intelligence is exercised never detach it from the totality of the human aggregate. It is only with the greatest difficulty that it can be detached from its links with the heavy weight of physical man. The powers that diversify general personality give it its first direction which can never be entirely neutralised by its attempt at disinterestedness. It is, however, the principal directions of the localised intelligence that we have to consider.

These are also partly determined by aptitudes. Capacities specialised in a certain direction of activity, skills of a technical character, these aptitudes were for long considered to be innate and independent of the rest of the personality, which only influenced them indirectly.
*

However, it appears today that even aptitudes may be aroused or inhibited by general reactions of character, to be found in affective impressions or training during childhood. By closing his mind to certain forms of study the child unconsciously rejects such and such a teacher. An attachment to a teacher may, on the other hand, permit forms of re-education that were unattainable by any other approach. Sexual taboos may shut out certain intellectual interests more or less accidentally connected with the taboo, and do so by liaisons that are very difficult to discover in the syncretic thinking of childhood. A love for geography is not divorced from the return to Mother Earth which obsesses the introvert, nor abstract sciences from the idealisation of reality. All depressed persons who have great difficulty in thinking of several things at a time, are weak in subjects which require a lively appreciation of relationships, such as mathematics. In other cases, adult authority has persuaded the child that one thing is true and the other false, this thing interesting and that boring, and this childish training leaves its mark throughout life. We shall meet these influences later. They are sufficient to warn us that a study of intelligence cannot be based solely on school reports, but must include the whole influence of the environment. As for the classification of aptitudes as such, this requires a special study which is outside our scope.

* Artistic aptitudes found in all types of character.

PHYSICAL INTELLIGENCE

*
  The close relationship between adaptation to reality and sexual adaptation means that intelligence, as the function which rationalises experience, must also suffer the vicissitudes of sex. The incapacity to opt conclusively for one's own sex leads to intellectual indecision, the concern to avoid taking sides at any price, and the desire to play several roles at once. Sexual maladjustment generally leads to introversion: an inordinate liking for pure ideas and cloudy utopias is a fairly frequent sign of impotence or at least of sexual inhibition. As for sexual excesses, their ill effect is not constant. They may deaden the faculties, but often seem to leave the finer qualities of mind unimpaired, as many a poet bears witness.

  It is still more difficult to distinguish scientifically between masculine and feminine intelligence. The problem is basically falsified if one starts off by trying to establish an overall superiority or inferiority between them. Intelligence is too complex to provide a simple answer to such a question. It is a fact that there are more great men than exceptional women. Inversely, mental hospitals hold more male imbeciles than female. Some conclude from this that women are on the average the equal of men, but tend less to extremes. This seems to be confirmed by Terman's graphs of general intelligence, which give relatively similar results for boys and girls, but a marked superiority for boys if confined to gifted children. Others object, though there is not yet enough evidence to decide, that such differences arise from different cultural conditions in the education of boys and girls. But if one considers the epochs in which this difference of condition tended to be non-existent, and in the fields where women were often more educated than men—art, religion, education—the proportion of exceptional men still remains markedly superior.
**

*   *   *

Intelligence is grafted on to instinct without the marks being always visible nor the influences assignable. We must abandon the idea that instinct is always a disturbing factor. It is an impetuous and dangerous friend, but if its influence is always alloyed, it is not radically bad. Instinct gives both individual thought and collective culture their

---

* Details of research into organic factors conditioning the intelligence.
** Further details of experimental research on differences in intelligence between men and women. The effect of health and illness on intelligence.

elementary directions. It lends flesh and blood to personal drives, and gives a robustness to the highest mental activity which keeps it from divagation and systematisation. Truth is also a passion. Thought turns in a void when instinct withers behind it.

*

One does not think with the blood, but when thought is drained of blood it becomes scattered and over-subtle, and develops cancerous growths. But it is not allowed much time in which to enjoy this profuse but debilitated vitality. The obscure and neglected forces concentrate and soon take their revenge, shattering the structures of clear thinking, provoking crises, establishing myths and sometimes individual and collective neuroses.

Intelligence may be grafted on instinct in diverse ways. Single-minded natures, controlled by a powerful and dominant instinct, show a robust intelligence but one closely bound up with massive objectives. Polyphonic natures, like Nietzsche, over-flowing with ideas 'that one may contradict but not destroy', have an intellectual life fraught with crises and conflicts: the register may be extensive but is continually and periodically enriched by the development of every possibility to its extreme. Symphonic natures, like Thomas Aquinas or Leibniz, are like buildings rising majestically step by step, growing gradually richer by the assimilation of all the material they encounter.

Instinct, however, only assumes this tonic function with regard to the higher forms of life: it is regulated by them and is subject to their overall purposes. Crude instinct, on the other hand, prevents reflection, without which there is no intelligence. Then, instead of *homo sapiens*, who delays his responses in order to compare stimuli, measure their scope and subordinate one to the other, we find the assertive personality,[2] in whom the perceptive stimuli are immediately transformed into representations accepted without criterion or elaboration, in the form of massive, irritable and obstinate assertions. These assertive beliefs[3] create a false appearance of solidity by their peremptory nature. These are the blind, deceptive certainties, whereby the subject deceives himself as to himself and becomes more and more riveted to his error. They are maintained by abnormally strong resistances, even in cultured and attentive minds, being based on some powerful vital interest (the inspiration of many political 'convictions'), such as a family prejudice (as to the value of a remedy, a recipe, a regime), an obscure preference of class or background: by the stupidity of their strength they betray that inertia of repetition which, as we have seen, characterises instinct

---

* Gives examples of thinkers who do not conform to romantic conceptions.

left to itself: 'enemies of truth', said Nietzsche, 'more dangerous than falsehood.'[4] They acquire authority through the pernicious belief that the more strongly we believe in something the more likely it is to be true. We should suspect the 'truths' that satisfy immediate feelings too easily: their reassuring 'evidence' only expresses the urgency of a need. And their stability is illusory: when instinct shifts into another quarter they change with it: not having been selected their only force of resistance is their inertia and the close support they often provide for each other. They are usually by nature egoist and are so many impediments to generosity, even when their contents appear insignificant: no idea, even a false one, is so ill-disposed to dialogue as these convictions, even when sensible. When they accumulate and become rebellious they destroy friendship and marriages more surely than infidelity.

Instinct, moreover, does not grow without defect in the heart of man. It becomes twisted and knotted at each defeat it suffers. Wrongly utilised, its sap turns into poison for the organism. The failures of instinct burden the sensitivity with affective complexes and, unlike the free moving instinct, are much more liable to create a sclerosis of thought by blocking the circulation of intellectual light with their nuclei of assertive beliefs.

These 'refuge' beliefs are fairly easily distinguished by the irritation displayed, ranging from simple vexation to anger or hatred, when they feel themselves questioned or compromised. Irritation may also accompany clear ideation, but then it takes the form of impatience or indignation that is aware of its cause and precise direction. An assertive belief provokes a diffuse, dull, ill-defined and therefore all the more convulsive irritation.[5] They are parasitical grafts on instinct, affecting the primary protective reflexes which cover the vital zones of the organism. The violence of our response deceives us as to its nature. What we take to be life are the stigmata of the wounds of life. If a man gets violently angry in a discussion, writes an American psychologist, his vehemence towards his questioner implies: 'Look at this wretched fellow: he is trying to pull off the scabs which were forming on my sores.'[6] Frantic, exclusive, irritable forms of admiration betray the same origin: this brings us to the impurity of certain passionate enthusiasms. Particularly of certain enthusiasms of collective character.
*

There is enough material to constitute a separate work on the complexes of fear, as important as that which the Freudian school has

* Gives details of more subtle expressions of assertive beliefs.

built up on the complexes of sexuality, for they are no less numerous nor less powerful. The fear of living is at the root of many beliefs tinged by a pessimistic view of life or man: it creates the protective doctrines employed by closed societies to justify their exclusiveness: it hollows out the vital depression which is filled by the whirlpool of scepticism. The majority of those passionate ideologies which are persecuting and vindictive are founded on a great fear which is trying to find reassurance, or is seeking release by exploding outwards. A nation which feels threatened by the uncertainty of its frontiers always finds an abundance of historic rights and ideological innovations to support its aggressive need for security. A slave nation employs the worst of sophistries to preserve its servile torpor and to avoid confronting the tyrant. The adoption of violently 'anti' opinions usually shows the site of an irresistible anxiety, which tries to spread the horror of its own fears in order to rally around it the tumult of disorder.

The passion for tranquillity is only the obverse of this vital anguish. Nietzsche was the first to denounce the stubborn reservations concealed behind the sectarianism of scientific or philosophic 'objectivity'. Exhausted and decadent minds seek 'the truth that leads to nothing',[7] because they do not want to embark on the disturbing quest for living truth, or adopt the partial views which alone open the way to the hidden truths, whose presence disquiets us and invites us to combat. This scientific scruple is often a beautiful name for intellectual cowardice.

An injured instinct is often more dangerous to firmness of thought than an instinct contradicted. The continuing sense of resentment keeps thought canalised in the blind rigidity of prejudice. One of the most powerful of such feelings of resentment is that directed by a newly acquired faith against the beliefs which formerly blocked its road. It is this that so often makes converts insufferable and such bad servants of their new faith, even if this is an intrepid scepticism. The rejection of past beliefs and the adoption of new ones has been for a long time a source of fear and desire, fear of the adventure and the breach with acquired comfort, and desire for a refuge. The final decision may come more to put an end to the anguish of crisis than as a denial of the past. It is no use for the unbeliever to reproach the believer, and the believer the unbeliever: atheism and religion and all the beliefs of the mind may exist in creative disquiet as well as in satisfied security. But converts who have been influenced by the need for security find it very difficult not to turn against this creative disquiet as well as against agitation of the spirit.

One should note the collective, or rather impersonal character of the processes which operate in the primary, instinctive zone of intelligence: identifications, blindness of contradiction, the affirmation of 'all or nothing', insistence on an eye for an eye, overestimation of defeat and success, and so on. This confirms the psychology of the person, which states that all thoughts without an 'I' fall into the primitive structures of assertive belief.

*   *   *

Should we speak of an instinct of knowledge? There are *some* instincts in knowledge, which is often misleading.
*

Without going so far as Klages as to say that the universe of mind is the personal enemy of instinct, it is undeniable that they live together in a sometimes balanced, sometimes unstable, sometimes hostile state of tension. It would be a distortion of the meaning of instinct to make it apply to a world which is qualitatively different.

*   *   *

Adult thinking shows the traces of its development, just as the body retains the stigmata of its illnesses and its good fortune.

Looking into the unconscious life of individuals and peoples, one discovers ever more clearly traces of the primitive thinking common to humanity, which is always reproducing itself in dreams, proverbs, folk-lore, etc. At this stage the mind is already impatient to embrace and unify what is complex, but does not yet dispose of the means of adequate analysis, and therefore relies on those first exciting and ambitious syntheses, the myth and symbol. They are formed by the associative work of feeling, which recalls the mechanism of dreams: juxtaposition of pictures within the same unity of thought, condensation of imagery, metaphorical associations. These supradetermined concrete symbols, very mobile (if you think of the fables of mythology), are inaccessible to contradiction. Primitive thought is quite capable of maintaining two contradictory propositions at the same time, provided both satisfy the requirements of the Unconscious, and is not concerned by passing from one to the other according to the needs of affectivity. It ignores the demands of reality, being, in fact, incapable of objective observation, and seeing things as it imagines or desires them. In this

* Argues that the intelligence works both to create order out of uncertainty and to prevent a fixation in certainty.

universe, governed by no laws of strict causality, everything is connected with everything else by the bond of magical participation. Before he can explain the world, primitive man feels the need to justify it, no matter how, to banish the anxiety of existence and of the unknown. He uses what lies to hand: drought ravages the crops, it is the fault of the curious headgear worn by missionaries: the village is decimated by an epidemic, and the blame falls on the unaccustomed presence of a portrait of Queen Victoria in the white administrator's office. Mysterious wills are at work in phenomena, affecting their appearance and disappearance.

We return to these ways of thinking far more often than we are aware.
*

THE INTELLECTUAL RESPONSE
**
Intellectual rhythms are subject to the general rhythm of the psyche.

The speed of intelligence is a special quality, independent of level. It is frequent in bilious, sanguine or emotional types. Landor classes it as 'one of the least of intellectual qualities and belonging to its lowest level'. It is often found in mental hospitals (particularly among the demented) and individuals can often impose themselves by exploiting it, to the paralysis of slower minds. This infertile virtuosity of the mind degrades the quality of thought as of action: at its highest in the inemotive and active types, it becomes a lively self-combustion, a display of fireworks often only illuminating a void.

Slow intelligences, as in the peasant or in certain peoples (Flemings, Nordics, etc.), are frequently and erroneously considered by quicker-witted groups or peoples as obtuse. This is a mistake. They function at their natural rhythm, and their capacities are only thereby diminished if they are hustled from outside, causing fortuitous inhibitions.
***

Intellectual rigidity can usually be ascribed to a spasm of a weak or temporarily weakened intelligence. It follows on all psychic weakness: the asthenic reacts excessively to ridicule, finds it difficult to pass from one subject to another, from one level of thought to another: he takes everything to heart with a sometimes exaggerated seriousness, which makes him little disposed to, and even irritated by the play of thought or even the play of words. This impoverishment affects his power of

---

* The growth of intelligence in childhood.
** Psychological debility and intellectual weakness.
*** Experimental research on the speed of intelligence.

retention and production, but not the content of his thoughts, which may be rich. Many dogmatic minds, on the other hand, may be poor in mental resources. The first idea that comes, provided it is introduced with authority, becomes sovereign and intractable for lack of counter-balance from neighbouring powers. This constitutes a primary type of mind, in the current sense of the word. A similar rigidity in the capacity to change ideas is found in minds that are not intellectually inferior, but whose ideation is rare and scattered instead of abundant as in others. Their thinking may gain in depth what it loses in variety, but although it does not lead to behaviour as stubborn as in less favoured minds, it lacks suppleness owing to the limitations of its scale. Such persons can change their point of view, but this needs a violent stimulus from external events or persons: they rarely do so of their own accord. Once they have changed, under the influence of some encounter, or some public upheaval, they feel happy, as if liberated by this transformation, which it is probably safe to say they would never have achieved from their own initiative. From then on they may take an active and intelligent part in this new movement. Finally, there will always be some rigidity in those whose education suffered in its early stages: they find it difficult to accept their inadequacies, and strengthen them by concealing them.

Intellectual activity is sometimes made more rigid, not only by inner poverty, but by a sort of propulsive tension of which the most typical example is the epileptoid way of thinking. Dominated by the ideo-motor adaptation of the moment, he is fascinated by his own activity. He is, as Wallon says, 'the slave of the film' realising each image of action one by one, in immutable order, incapable of grasping the whole, of omitting intermediaries, of considering potentialities, or of associating the richness of memory and reflection around the present impression. The least deflection of thought throws him up against the barrage of his own tension. He thinks like a brute. There are minds like his, which forge ahead the moment they start, giving the impression that they are knocking down ideas rather than receiving them. If they meet an obstacle, instead of going around it, they behave like the pike that hurls itself a hundred times against the glass that separates it from its prey, and continues to hurl itself against the site of the obstruction even when the glass is removed. Once they have adopted a train of thought they follow it, as if driven by some brute inertia, to the limits of its range, even to the absurd.[8] But intelligence can only see if it stops and looks back, in which it differs from elementary biological responses. The reflex, when stimulated, either appears or does not appear, it is complete or not at all. Instinct, without being as immovable as has been thought, only tolerates a slight margin of adaptation between failure and perfection. 'All or nothing' is the law of lower phenomena.

*

The true function of thought in behaviour as a whole is precisely to break the stupid entirety of instinct and the stereotyping of reflexes, by a greater and greater articulation of conduct. The trained mind is both a model and an instrument of flexibility. Its range of availability qualifies it for the immediate perception of the multiple relationships arising from a given impress: it rebounds like a rocket at each word, 'in a star-shaped explosion of perception, made up of a vast accumulation of symbols at each point of the intellectual field, of the intensity of this light and the rapidity of this communication' (Wallon).[9]

**

*   *   *

Thought and the experience of space are connected by deeper affinities than the purely symbolic. We have seen how it is impossible to describe the powers of the mind without using the words breadth and penetration: sometimes we speak of the 'open air' quality of a work of art, and Whitman liked to ask whether some work or other could stand comparison with the countryside or the sea. St. Paul speaks of the height, the breadth and the depth of the mysteries of faith. Intelligence, like life, appears surrounded by a field of varying breadth, itself as the centre of this field. Without being misled by the material nature of geometric images, one may feel that the persistence of the spatial symbolism in a diversity of thought and language expresses some very profound analogies.

Intelligence as it develops tries to centre itself upon a vital point, which assures it of the maximum range of movement. It seems that animals know only successive forms of behaviour, and that man alone tries to find a centre even at the sensori-motor level.[10] This attachment can be expressed in two different ways.

Some are like the lower marine species, who cling to the rough surfaces of the rocks to protect themselves from danger, avoiding experience by abandoning movement, and withdrawing from further evolutionary adventures under a protective carapace. These

---

* Forms of intellectual dogmatism.
** Janet and Burnett on the dual movement of thought. Also types of intelligence related to the categories of Heymans.

species are, or become blind. The life stream passes them by, abandoning them to a somnolent and restricted existence. This is the history of the mind of the man who at an early age became encrusted in some deadly simplification of himself and his vocation, which he calls principle, conviction, style of living, and which is only a socially acceptable way of refusing life. Such men have not chosen this centre of reference because it is necessary, but because it is convenient or helpful, either to their tranquillity or their interests. Perhaps at the start it was open to wider perspectives, but the laziness that dictated it allowed it to be invaded by an undergrowth of prejudice, and life withdraws little by little, leaving it to the minor death of fixed ideas. Others keep the place clear but, like children, are incapable of getting outside their point of view to compare their own measurement of things with some more comprehensive scale. Unable to renew themselves, they become a prey to rigidity and the degradation of repetition.

The free intelligence makes a quite different choice of its position in the world. A limited mind selects its footholds in order to become immobile; a located mind selects them for a take-off. The one obeys the 'death wish', the other the sense of incarnation in the service of the sense of transcendence. If the world were nothing but an indiscriminate flux, there would be no place for the eye to rest, no privileged spot from whence it could see further and better. To be, for me, is to be here and now, and in this place and time to take a certain measure of the universe, which I try to keep in a line with the measure of an universal consciousness. Leibniz gave solidity to the Cartesian world when he showed that this point of view and this effort towards the universal defined the personal consistency of man. The first movement of intelligence, at each stage of progress, is first to find out where it is, and then to shift from this point of view in order to lay hold on as vast a sphere of reality as it is capable of embracing. Thus located and locating intelligence hold the field in turn. The total intelligence is thus perpetually changing its centre, yet never ceases to be a centre and a measure. Solid, yet mobile, it is the very antithesis of the vagabond, disorientated intelligence, which flits from landscape to landscape and refuses to settle anywhere. Its various centres of measurement are no longer on one level. They are placed at varying degrees of height and are a measurement for each other. The gaze of this exacting intelligence, always outstripping its capacity, maintains a state of fertile disquiet. It is uncomfortable to be lucid enough to perceive the field of creation which is far above one, without being able to attain it by one's own creative powers. The sense of our limitations, usually somewhat tardy in appearance, comes then to complete our sense of location.

*   *   *

Just as there is a clear space and an obscure space, there is a clear and a nocturnal life of the intelligence. The first is that chiselled out by the facets of words and the analytic phrase. Stasheim has studied the influence of a verbalised rule on simple behaviour, such as finding the way out of more and more complicated mazes. Situations may be perfectly well resolved without the solution being formulated abstractly, just as the adult Frenchman frequently accords his participles by a sort of flair that he would be hard put to to justify. But the abstraction of a rule makes the operation much less hesitant and liable to error: it also facilitates the passage from simple to complex situations. All advance in knowledge seems to be bound up with the progressive clarification of the cognitive field.

Clear thought is often regarded as facile and superficial: this makes Germanic peoples constantly suspicious of the Latins. Yet the attempt at clear thinking is one of the most difficult that exist, through the complex associations that it arouses. It underlies sociality: a clear thought is a communicable thought: it reaches perfection in the cycloid, whereas the expression and the literature of the schizoid are the chosen domain of obscurity, neologism, allusion and reticence. The precious, the tortuous, both in manner and in style, are so many spontaneous methods of protecting oneself from dialogue. The cycloid feels almost guilty of an offence against hospitality if he allows the slightest ambiguity as to his intentions: for him simplicity is a form of courtesy or of charity. The schizoid feels guilty of a sin against the spirit if he abandons his sumptuous reality to the cruder light of clear concepts, which eat away the contours and the values of ideas. More confident in his wordless meditations than in the conversation of men, he is always afraid of exposing his reflections, for fear of allowing their inner quality to evaporate: a modesty of the spoken word, so customary in adolescence, explains all the byways he takes to banish the vulgarity of direct exposition. One such, Paul Valéry, spoke of the strange folly of trying to communicate. The attention of the schizoid writer or thinker is entirely concentrated on expression, an egocentric concern uncompromised by the desire for communication. But as one can only be renewed by getting outside oneself, schizoid thinking, even in the most eminent, retains a certain impotence. There is a stereotyping of themes and intentions, a slenderness of work: consider Mallarmé or Valéry. If one crosses the boundary of the normal, the feeling of wearing one's thoughts on one's sleeve without being able to protect them from the eyes of others, is an essential element in paranoiac irritability. We must go further: clear thinking, from this point of view, is connected not only with sociality, but with the sense of reality. The eighteenth century in France was not only the century of enlightenment, but the century of social living and the century of experiment. Yet consciousness dies from a too unilateral movement towards things and communication. A world of robots would be a lucid machine in the eyes of a possible observer, who would himself cease to think, invaded by its automatisms, its entire objectivity. Thought, like action, if too exteriorised, becomes immobilised in a dogmatic slumber, snoring away in increasingly rigid formulae, creating nothing but confusion, chatter or empty stupor. Conscious thought is therefore no less dependent on the attainment of privacy than on sociality and conversation. It is indeed true that psychically the artist remains something of a child. Myth and symbol are the transposition of the primitive forms of complexes at work, into the higher reaches of the mind. But it would be nonsense to talk, at this level, of 'regression'. If it be true that each achievement is a step towards death; if, as Nietzsche said in a tragic sense, 'to understand is an ending', an artist who keeps life and the world of thought unfinished, keeps the gates of life open towards thought, even if he does not pass through them himself.

A perfect balance at high level of lucid and obscure thinking, is rarely attained. To draw mystery into the light of day, without losing its strength and fascination, is the highest achievement either of art or of thought. Except for a few powerful characters who do achieve it, an ineradicable incomprehension will always divide the two families. The night thinkers will always accuse the clear-minded of yielding the universe to the superficial forces of consciousness, turning entirely outwards to limit, divide and dismember the unity of the world: contrasting it with a way of thinking plunged in myth, magnificent in strength, thinking that is power, magic, song, redemption as well as knowledge. And the clear thinkers retain an adamantine intolerance of the sketchy, the stammering, the obscure, the dogmatic rowdiness or tangled shadows in which the others delight, and of the mannerism which they seem to condone. Two families of poets, two families of thinkers, two families of scientists, two families of mystics: Jammes and

Claudel, Bergson and Heidegger, Descartes and Einstein, François de Sales and St. John of the Cross. Both may get lost in regions lower than thought, in the reflection of facile clarities or in the complacency of the unformed. Both may further the human adventure in the discovery of two superb universes which are only waiting to be united, even though one may doubt the capacity of man to achieve such unity except at some rare and miraculous moments.

⋆   ⋆   ⋆

Intellectual avarice appears in the shape of parsimony and in the desire to monopolise.

Even the decision to think out one's life is adventurous. The adolescent soon learns that thought, like love, is the daughter of grief as well as of joy. He feels it a torment as much as a way of growth, it leads him into disquiet and towards harassing or inaccessible problems. It would be so comfortable to hollow out an easy existence away from them. To wager on thinking, is to wager for every promise and also for every peril. Once the daemon has hold of us, no one knows in advance where he will lead, what renunciations he will suggest, and what demands he will put upon us, all incompatible with an agreeable, coherent life. 'The uncertainty of the final end', wrote Léon Brunschvicg, 'is the very condition of all spiritual reality.' There is certainly a madness in the 'fiat' of the man who from his earliest youth chooses consciousness instead of unconsciousness, the fever of truth instead of the soft lullaby of conformity. 'The most intellectual men, supposing they are the most courageous, are also those who suffer far the most painful tragedies: but they honour life, since it is to them that it shows the most hostility.'[11]

Avaricious hearts leave the serene territory of childhood for the coasts of choice, but refuse any such uncertain departure, particularly with thought as a companion. In so far as they have to use their intelligence, which may be lively, they do not devote it to action, but rather cast it upon things under their immediate control, a pleasant exercise with a fine, fortunate net which, with a little agility and some cruelty, will haul in valuable objects. Sometimes they have a way of clinging to details of the world, quite differently from the generous mind, overflowing with love for the least sparkle of reality. What they seek in these details is not superabundance, like the miniaturist whose heart spills over in the luxuriance of motif, but all that the detail suggests of the limited, restrained and separate. In argument they dwell on trifling points, split hairs, are defenders and conservers of doctrines; bilious critics who exhaust their strength in demolishing what is being built up; collectors, compilers, men of erudition, the chartered accountants of knowledge. This type of mind, in a Rorschach test, sees only what is peculiar or extraordinary in the shape of the ink-blots. Their constrained natures are often primarily due to an avaricious type of education, in which generosity has been repressed or even rebuffed, by a spiritually or materially sordid way of living. At other times this avaricious intelligence can be detected in the writer by a fixity of contour, a dryness of style, too brief, too immobile a clarity arising from the words, an absence of mystery and inner depth that no trick of style can replace. There is something of this in the writings of Fontenelle and Stendhal. In others, thought appears with circumspection, wearing a false countenance of peace, which is only the mask of a refusal of living. The liking for systems as a protection against the adventures of thought is one form of avaricious thinking. In this sense Brunschvicg was right to denounce the egoism of a certain too comfortable philosophic realism. Like any intellectual debility, avarice of mind is often accompanied by vanity.

These various forms of poverty may be concealed by an illusion of fervour and abundance. The mind hurls itself upon its objects and accumulates enormous reserves of learning. But this stock-piling is only a dead abundance. Just as the avarice of money is a compensation for a life which has refused all risks, the passion for accumulating knowledge in such quantities that the mind cannot circulate is the manoeuvre of an impotent intelligence trying to deceive itself. Compare the youthful, almost savage, turbulence of erudition in a springtime such as the first Renaissance, and the dust settling on the microscopic, uninspired researches of the epochs of decadence.

In the first flush of youth thought abandons itself generously to the drive that carries it ever forward towards an unknown god—and what god is not vastly unknown? It is never freer than at the moment when it has devoted itself entirely. But a jealous proprietor of his thoughts automatically turns them into slaves, like the Gallicans who acquired much greater spiritual power over conscience by refusing to accept any higher authority than that of the state. It takes only a trifle, we have seen, an imperceptible inner movement, for the very fibre of our behaviour to be corrupted by egocentricity. Objects may be blasted or exalted by thought according to its first intention. When thought is more eager to take, to record, to enjoy, to accumulate, rather than to discover and be astonished, to follow and to lend itself, then every object closes up at its approach and withers at its touch. The object covers up its inner resources, as it were, under a cloak of utilitarian form, which responds exactly to what was required of it. Thought has become an inert instrument, instead of a miracle of initiative. And from this moment it is at the mercy of the ambitions of temporal powers, for an implement is easily made into a docile weapon, and brute force, as it grows intelligent, takes its weapons where it can find them. Thus by devaluating thought the pettiness of the Alexandrine school directly prepared the way for the barbarian invasions which it regarded with horror. The catastrophic turn of mind which flourishes in similar epochs is often only another form of intellectual indigence, projecting its own disorder upon the world with a vindictive passion for annihilation, instead of attacking prejudice and listening, amongst the debris of the fallen idols, for the silent movement of tradition towards unknown worlds.

*   *   *

Generosity of mind lies not only in the initial wager. It is also the manner of its exercise, when it forgets acquisition in the communication of its unlimited fertility. Thus it is not astonishing that rationalism, a rationalism that is open and essentially available, from Descartes to Brunschvicg, should make it the chief virtue of the mind. There is indeed an element of mastery in the relationship between personal thought and its object. But this mastery is similar to that between the father and the child he has brought up, between the husband and the wife he has chosen, yet who is granted to him as a grace. The lively sense of revelation, a gift received, is inseparable from all authentic intellectual experience. And generosity is none other than the irrepressible response of gift for gift. There is no fear that the generosity of the world will one day be absent, the fear of the doctrinaire hallucinated by death and error. This metaphysical confidence may lead to a contempt for the limits of knowledge or the conditions of action: it must therefore be blended with a sense of incarnation, in order not to lose itself in the clouds: the purity of a face does not destroy its mystery, any more than the backbone of a word destroys its associations. But generosity is the force that jostles the sense of structure and limitation, so that it does not fall into dogmatic states. It is always reawakening the dialectic of the mind behind its decisions, the problems behind the solutions, and the mysteries behind the problems. By the same movement it holds the mind available for the still unknown revelations of an inexhaustible world, it keeps us open-minded towards the countless ways by which life and mind may surprise us in neighbouring consciences. It is always eager to discover being behind appearances, reality beneath the labels, the intention behind the words: pitiless towards faults of character but considerate towards awkwardness of expression and the detours of thought. Thus truth, without renouncing its thankless task, may by generosity become charity, that is to say, attention and respect.

*   *   *

The intellectual response is not reduced to the sum of the attitudes we have just described. It depends on a movement, on a creative tension, which ensures a firmness of direction and a flexibility of transition.
*

Intellectual effort is ineffective if it is solely the striving of an ungifted nature, or even the patient forcing of a sterile soil. Industrious persons are often pathetic in their goodwill and probity, but they cannot for all that display qualities they do not possess. But intelligence encounters a more insidious enemy than lack of aptitude, its own inertia. Thought that is not carried forward by a sufficient drive falls back on the poorest and least compromising of representations, turns spirit into letter, action into verbal gesture, creation into repetition. Thought therefore appears to be the culminating point of all the forces which, from the beginning of life, have struggled against the deadly relapse into habit. Most definitions of intelligence converge, more or less explicitly, on this central idea; an innate, polymorphous ability, manifested in the solution of problems (Ballard); capacity of conscious adaptation to the solution of new questions (W. Stern); capacity for solving new problems (Claparède); understanding of problems, direction towards an objective, invention of solutions and critical censure of imaginary solutions (Binet). Inventiveness is aided by various auxiliary factors;[12] interest, which awakens one to the problem, secondary, which adds the richness and diversity of experience; but we must admit the existence of a *caput mortuum* at the bottom of the well, a powerful spring of invention, without which mental operations are only repetition or combination. It is in virtue of this radical power that

---

* Organic disorders which compromise mental activity, and the dangerous aspect of extraversion. Quotes Webb's test of depth of apprehension and other tests dealing with the influence of intellectual effort on results.

intelligence is in contrast to instinct, which is a closed perfection, even a force of regression.

This power of invention is not an aptitude that can be isolated. It is part of the very quality of the person. It offers a more or less brilliant appearance according to the aptitudes at its disposal. But to those less endowed with special aptitudes it may grant such intelligence in living and in their daily actions as to make their minds of rare calibre, even though in current opinion their intelligence may only rank as average. Types of intelligence can be grouped most satisfactorily on the basis of inventiveness. After a considerable number of tests, Rossolimo divided intelligence into two categories, the creative and the assimilative, the one passing by degrees into the other. The truly creative intelligence is a superior type, that conceives and discovers fresh ideas. There is a lesser form, still considerably above average, in the elaborating intelligence, which also discovers fresh combinations, but makes use of what has been created by others; these are the minds that perfect, sometimes with genius, rather more than they create: they always re-think the ideas that reach them from outside. Rousseau in *Emile* was always aiming at the formation of this higher intellectual initiative: 'It is less a question of teaching him a truth than of teaching him to set about finding a truth.' Naturally Rousseau did not expect his pupil to produce it all out of his own mind, but he wanted him to assimilate what he acquired so well that he became almost the author. 'When understanding has made something its own, before handing it over to memory, then what it derives from it is its own.' Thus the formation of judgment is a direct contribution to the formation of character. As compared with these two levels of creative intelligence, the assimilative intelligence utilises and puts into practice what has been created and developed by the first two; it is the agent of exhibition and transmission. Of the same type, at its lowest level, is the purely receptive intelligence, unproductive, which receives and retains knowledge as it is handed out, repeating ready-made solutions and accepted opinions, settling down to routine and conversation. No doubt no one can be classed exclusively in one or the other category with regard to the whole of his intellectual activity, but each type of intelligence belongs fundamentally to one of them.

Given such distinctions, the various degrees of inventivity may take on scintillating forms—facility in some, a miracle in others—or follow the slower and more deliberate paths. The children of Heracles and the children of Prometheus, the ones laborious in their labours which

sometimes achieve grandeur, the others lighter of touch under the inspiration of divine fire, will always divide the field of creation.
*

THE DIALOGUE
**

Every experience leads us to the vital conclusion that thought only begins where there is a free passage for the mind between receptivity and initiative. Imagination unfortunately persists in placing thought in an immobile schema: the receptivity of the watchful eye, a recording disc, or inversely, as a purely autonomous creator which fabricates objects from its own substance. The inner dialectic of thought is a constant coming and going between perception and response, assimilation and invention, passivity and activity. The *capacity for reflection* indicates the mobility and penetration of which thought is capable in this dual activity.

Thus when we say that thought is dialogue, we mean this quite strictly. We never think alone. The unspoken thought is a dialogue with someone who questions, contradicts or spurs one on. This inner debate, however complicated and prolonged—it may last a lifetime—is quite different from rumination, which is a wandering around the same spot. Even if immobilised by crisis from time to time, the inner dialogue moves towards an aim. It is, in spite of its interiorisation, realistic thought. Its coherence is made of social encounters and solid experience. It has the same pattern as the elementary behaviour of thought, which is both *conversation* and *meditation*.

There are therefore two elements in the complex act of thought.

The first element of the dialogue is that of *opposition*. In opposition thought becomes aware of its limits and its aspirations. We have met it at each crisis in the growth of personality. It shapes practically the whole of adolescent thinking. Every great discovery of the mind, said Bergson, starts with a 'No'. Yet this 'no' is already framing the affirmations which will grow from it, like the plant from its seed; only those who have never experienced the dialectic of discovery will reproach young men of twenty for the negative character of their first statements of position.

They may perhaps settle down into an attitude of opposition. This egocentric fixation perpetuates some rebellious dissatisfaction of childhood; there is an excessive affectivity, sustained by the constant

---

* Gives an example from Paul Valéry.
** Discusses the effect of introversion and extraversion on thought, and the ambivalent meaning of the words 'inner' and 'outer' as shown by Jaensch. Also deals with egocentricity and exhibitionism.

need of all weak natures, to find, like the child, a sort of borrowed strength by opposition. There are persons who always need, to use one of de Maistre's favourite formulae, 'to fire their ideas point-blank' upon someone or upon another idea. 'Polemics are my natural style', declared Chateaubriand, 'I must have an adversary somewhere.' 'To think', said Alain, 'is to say no.' And we know how their common ancestor, Abelard, found it difficult to distinguish thinking from pugnacity.

But apart from this particular case, and the even rarer one of the perverse type, the refusals which the adolescent projects on every side are an explosive ascesis, already overflowing with the love of positive values, to which he is appealing in the midst of his inspired fury. For in living thought, opposition cannot exist in an isolated state, but only in relation to an actual or budding affirmation. A concrete thought consists of the confrontation of two ideas in a flexible antithesis, radically different from the 'all or nothing' of petrified thought. One dominates the other without eliminating it, for this inner adversary serves as a springboard from which it can surpass itself. Thus in the heart of affirmation lurks the questioning irony, to dislocate its narrowness, and the methodical doubt, which unsettles assurance, not to dissolve it, but to throw it forward towards wider understanding. If affirmation loses its hold, the latent antithesis gathers strength and compromises the established equilibrium. If the relaxation is temporary, this danger only stimulates the momentarily disconcerted affirmation to reassert its authority by a fresh test: then progress is made. Thus a living faith experiences, one after the other, without getting lost in any of them, all the doubts that might be put forward by its opponents, and often more lucidly than they do: this perpetual coming and going, in which each rhythmical return still moves a step forward, is the mental hygiene of faith. But in a mind without authority it creates a morbid oscillation between objection and affirmation. This weakness appears in its elementary form in the phenomenon of inversion of ideas.[13] A person is driven to an obsessive longing for something which is repugnant to him, even to an irresistible drive to realise it: blasphemous ideas invade the believer as he enters church or approaches the sacraments, a mother has an urge to drown the child she adores, an honest, prudish woman is attacked by obscene impulses. This affective ambivalence is always directed towards a preferred activity, which leads one to suspect that it is fear of action which throws them into such embarrassment.

We should not confuse these scrupulous, obsessional types with minds of a dialectic turn, like Plato, Hegel, Kierkegaard, Proudhon, who may, to a superficial glance, seem somewhat similar. Their acute sense of the journeyings of thought and their naturally great virtuosity give an astonishing quality to their work. But it develops a vast pattern instead of marking time or becoming immobilised in opposition. Yet even in them we find two poles of temperament, those for whom thought is a sword cutting off an alternative (Kierkegaard), and those for whom it is essentially synthesis.[14]

Affirmation without the rebellious seed which bursts through everything to make a way for life, the inner accomplice of disconcerting reality, will sooner or later drift towards the autistic circle. This extreme is represented by the paranoiac affirmation: it has become nothing but a compact block of opposition: since it has refused vital opposition, it has become opposition itself, an opposition without future, brutal and infertile like a lump of matter. The taste for paradox fluctuates on the edge of these two forms of opposition: sometimes a purely paranoiac aggressiveness, sometimes a lively awareness that truth, like life, uses a dialectic of dislocation in order to reproduce itself and make progress. The intelligence that has stiffened into contrariness withers. Systematic depreciation and negativism are embryonic forms of psychasthenia or paranoia, with a poor prognosis.

Intelligence which knows nothing of struggle dies another kind of death. Such are the irritating tribe of conciliatory spirits, the 'broad-minded' accepting peace at any price, always accepting the last opinion they have heard, respectful of everything because they respect nothing, ready to betray everything to enjoy the false truce of unison.

Living thought has also a factor of communication and, directly connected, a factor of expansion and conquest. The love of truth is a self-communicating love. A faith that is not missionary is a dead faith. The need for proof, for collective agreement, are basic components of thought: they are totally lacking in some madmen, and are obliterated in thoughts of a schizoid nature, which are intoxicated by their own affirmation. We rediscover the dual movement of thought in this fervour of communication: availability and affirmation. The effort at communication is constantly working on the forms of expression and stripping spontaneous thought of its false ideas, its utopias, its complications. This is the stumbling block of the schizoid, hence his defects of style, over-profusion, mannerism, obscurity.

But the forces of affirmation struggle ambiguously with the powers of response, for the disinterested zeal for truth is blended with an egocentric utilisation of thought. And instinct stands by waiting to take control of the operation. In convincing others, wrote Péguy,† lies the idea of victory, and in persuasion the desire to overcome may be stronger than the joy of communicating. Knowledge also fosters the instinct of possession and aggressiveness. In propaganda or in teaching some enjoy the sense of domination so much that they transform the service of truth into a temporal government of minds, an imperialism which is one of the most cruel in history.

The highest activity of thought, considered as a form of social life, is comprehension. It commits us, σὺν ὅλῃ τῇ ψυχῇ. It is, says Bleuler, something that happens 'between one whole and another whole'. It conciliates availability and affirmation. Doubly disinterested, for it opens twice upon the outer world, on a truth to be gained and on a neighbour to be discovered. Yet it mobilises all the forces of the mind to their highest power of concentration. Neither the acquisition of impersonal knowledge, nor the imposition of one's own views, requires such a skilful use of one's capacities nor such a strength of personal qualities. Like the sociologists, we consider that the social act is creative of the intellectual act, but to the materialist psycho-sociologist this act is a simple echo of the environment: in a personal psychology it is a highly organised response inseparable from a dialogue. In this response are found, one in the other, personal autonomy, the social link and the progressive universality of the mind.

THE DRAMA OF INTELLIGENCE

A vast offensive against the intelligence has been waged since the beginning of the century, and has now reached its culminating point. The prosecution has been opened in a hundred different ways. Let us take, for instance, the terms of Klages' indictment.

Character, according to Klages, comes into being through instinct. The healthy being is the instinctive being, in direct continuity with the universal cohesion of nature, in whom 'body' and 'soul' live a strong and indistinct life. On to this are grafted the parasites of will and intelligence. These two aberrant forces are forces of division, which dissociate vital syntheses, enervate creative dynamic, and distract us from virile action into imaginary paradises or dead abstractions. Therefore intelligence is not, as several centuries of Western civilisation have asserted, the crowning glory of humanity, but a kind of rare and pernicious disease which runs counter to the life stream. It is only a step from this to conclude that its exercise should be violently repressed

† 'Dans convaincre, il y a vaincre'.—Trs.

in order to create a regenerated man, and many have taken this step where psychologists have hesitated.

Let us examine the terms of the indictment one by one.

Romanticism has long been reproaching consciousness for having immobilised vital drives, and accuses thought, which articulates consciousness, of dividing and materialising the living unity of universal being. Can psychology shed any light on the debate? Let us recall certain primary truths. The function of consciousness is to suspend. We have seen that every primary action is explosive and therefore blind. The reflex appears instantaneously. Instinct precipitates itself on its object, requiring immediate satisfaction. Apart from delays of duration, it fastens on the objectives assigned to it by heredity. We see this precipitate, unreflecting character of action in the behaviour of hysterics (Janet). 'No sooner said than done' might be their motto. Their rapid and almost instantaneous gesticulation, their impulsive agitation, betray the convulsive discharge of intention. They may even do or say something they do not want, simply because the idea or the words occur to them. An image arising in the mind may also find its physical expression by this same sudden discharge. This rhythm is common to all impulsive, quick-tempered types of mind.

At this point reflection intervenes to suspend action, thus, and thus only, allowing a diversity and a control of behaviour. The fox who watches the hen *and* the movements of the farmer will be more successful than if he yielded to his voracity. Perception immediately stimulates the gestures which prolong it: all agnosis is accompanied by apraxia, and inversely. Suppose I am in a state of somewhat empty reverie, waiting vaguely for the news or for some music: the mere sight of my wireless set leads my fingers to the knob even before I have formulated any clear intention. If my intelligence at that moment shouts 'Stop!' it is not for the pleasure of opposing this drive, which may be only of very mediocre importance, but rather to ask of life whether there might not be something better to do: for the apparent spontaneity of the first movement is often only due to the inert pressure of instinct or habit. The halt imposed by reflection is therefore far from being the first step towards abstention from action and is, on the contrary, the prime condition for a superior action. So long as perception is tightly bound up with motor and postural reactions, as in the child and the epileptic, it remains global, servile and, as it were, clotted. Objectivisation, the doubling of subject and object, marked by the birth of verbal symbols, introduces the first flight of intelligence. In order to be human, action requires that I should be both an actor and the spectator of my actions.[15] This standstill of consciousness is a superior and difficult act, not to be invoked and sustained by everyone, the act of waiting. Thought remains in contact with action, it works on the messages supplied and prepares the way. The standstill of consciousness is an active intermediary between two actions.

It restrains the promptings of instinct, collects the forces of thought and allows for choice and maturation of decision. Socratic irony was intended to produce this effect on talkers who were carried away by the flow of appearances: sometimes it leaves the interlocutor in pieces, but stripped of false certainties, and ready and anxious to give birth to new truths. It is a vital halt, a generous irony, for without these truths blind consciousness would seize greedily upon its objects, incapable of broadening its activity, of bringing it into harmony with experience and enriching it with values which require time in which to be earned.

But if this standstill becomes detached from the movement of thought then this once living interval becomes a free field for external diversions and inner divagations. Cut off from the controlling influence of action thought is dissipated in reverie, in ideologies, utopias and uchronias wandering ever further from reality. The capacity for abstraction no longer serves to articulate the related realities of personal initiative and the external world, but becomes an immobile, infertile, parasitical activity. Consciousness always covers its errors with noble pretexts. There is an eloquent way of asserting, in spite of one's defeats, one's confidence in 'the power of ideas' which is often the meagre consolation of poor soldiers of thought, who have not been able to employ their strength in the paths of reality. Weaker minds like to justify their resignations by a complacent anxiety not to sully the 'purity' of their ideas by the compromises of life, as if the first purity of a located, incarnated mind did not consist in sticking to its allotted post and using the means at its disposal. John Stuart Mill relates in his autobiography how one day, when he was possessed by the desire to reform the world, he asked himself:[16] ' "Suppose that all your objects in life were realised; that all the changes in institutions and opinions which you are looking forward to, could be completely effected at this very instant: would this be a great joy and happiness to you?" And an irrepressible self-consciousness distinctly answered, "No!" ' Thus, even when it has originally chosen the goal of action, intelligence may of its own accord slip towards a void and refuse action. The zeal that first kindled the passion for the goal may subsist, but lose itself on the confines of the intellectual operations which should prepare the way for realisation. This explains why so many persons, with audacious ideas and projects, become so pusillanimous as soon as they are confronted with the consequences of their affirmation. This uncentred activity of the intelligence robs intellectual life of as many men as the mechanisms of administrative life which deprive them of a gift for leadership and a liking for responsibility.

This disharmony of consciousness appears in all its impotence in the obsessional researchers, who have given rise to the term 'metaphysical madmen'. They too, like Socrates, are fond of questions but questions without root, without inspiration, without future: sticking to one spot and blocking the movement of thought. 'Why are the trees green?' 'Why are men not taller?' The question invades the whole field of consciousness like a jungle weed, stifling any sensible movement at birth. We met this overgrowth of regressive questions in the schizoid, when action is required: each question retreats upon another, multiplying in a turmoil of impotence whilst the action disappears.

All intellectual activity may thus totally disappear at the impact of reality or, even worse, be utilised as a way of escape or a protection against action. The word 'thought' covers many different realities. When we defend thought against the attacks of the new barbarians, we envisage a sovereign power, which completes life, confirms our humanity and plunges into reality in order to transfigure it. The psychically weak have a different thought in mind, and a different reality within them. The psychasthenic, who are incapable of performing successful actions in reality, become capable of the same actions if allowed to carry them out in an absent-minded way, or in a state of diffused consciousness, without having to adapt them too strictly to the environment, or having to co-ordinate their tendencies to match their actions, or to formulate definite certainties of possibilities of enjoyment. This state of dreamy action is moving towards schizoid thinking.[17] We have seen how a love of abstractions develops in the narcissistic child: it may acquire a contentious quality (particularly when there is a passion for reading), which shows its affective origin: some wound was received in the struggle for reality, some defeat has to be consolidated and compensated. Thus, in many adults, thought serves as a protective system against the mysteries and ambiguities of immediate experience.

*

The most constant effect of this retreat is intellectual indecision. Sometimes, as in the abulic, there is a perpetual oscillation on the

* Various ways of creating intellectual systems of defence.

feeble theme of for and against. They are incapable of forming a project which, like a projectile, might deliver them from these morbid antitheses and drag them out of their impotent hesitancy. Sometimes they are overburdened by the competing attractions of disjointed parcels of knowledge, none of which is sufficiently strong to pull them into action.

Sometimes the general stampede of intelligence is affected by the savage violence of a destructive aggressiveness of psychological origin. This intellectual nihilism does not always show its true face. Epochs where culture is agreeable and highly social dissimulate it in light-hearted games, decked with the charms of innocence, but it is no less lethal.

In such cases, the act of reflection instead of being an athletic meditation, a gathering of strength before plunging once more into the fray, becomes a narcissistic contemplation of its own forms. Intelligence observes itself instead of being and acting: an agreeable occupation, for its gestures are beautiful. The failure lies in preferring its own image to its own function. But this is too flattering. Once it has withdrawn from the fertility of life into this shadow play, it can no longer devote itself to its own direct image, but to reflections that are indefinitely withdrawn and impoverished. It has become perpetual suspension, without density, without inclination, without love. *Amor meus, pondus meus*, said St. Augustine. It would have been equally Augustinian to say *intellectus meus, pondus meus*. When intelligence has no inner weight, reflection, instead of concentrating attention, exhausts it. It dissipates the assurance of the mind and deprives it of a base. In the obsessional and hysterical we met those ambiguous certainties in which professed belief contradicted belief as experienced, and even then yielded like shifting sand under any critical enquiry. All minds that have lost the invigorating contact with reality yield to this inconsistency. Not that the normal mind always moves forward in clear and tranquil certainty. Take Prince Andrei Bolkonsi's profession of agnosticism on his death bed, in *War and Peace*: 'Nothing, there is nothing certain except the nothing of all that I understand, and the majesty of something, which I do not understand, but which is much more important.' The weight of experience behind such a total confession of ignorance is worth a hundred of the most peremptory assertions of intellectual dilettantes.

Just as dissociation of consciousness operates in depth, so the abuse of analytic thought may cover the whole surface of intellectual operation. Here again we meet two different types of analysis. One is part of the discipline of intellectual activity. Observed facts present themselves spontaneously as individual incidents, heavily charged with affectivity. Analysis removes this precipitate, whilst allowing an outlet to the energies unleashed by a purely affective perception of the object. This analytic function of separation, far from impeding action, is closely correlated with it (Heymans); it neutralises emotivity, which is its most constant embarrassment; it fosters optimism; it has a positive correlation with activity, whereas inactivity leads to undifferentiated attitudes: cacatony, intellectual rigidity, mental confusion. It is easy to make fun of hair-splitters. They are, in fact, fools with razor blades. But if physical truth can be measured to a hundred-thousandth of an inch, it is also true that psychological or moral truth may sometimes walk on a razor's edge. So the critical faculty, confronted by the rapture of emotion, and the dullness of brute instinct, seems one of the principal techniques of self-mastery. This provokes the enmity of an unanimous chorus of satisfied imbecility.

But if it is no longer sustained by a strong mind, attentive to reality, it turns into an obsession with distinctions, and to a mannerism characteristic of attitudes out of touch with reality. There is a primary stupidity, which confuses ideas in order to compromise them, and a meticulous stupidity, decked with the appearance of intellectuality, which divides in order to rule. Such is the spectacle provided in the modern world by the hypercritical. Break up a religion, in which each gesture has a meaning only in relation to others and to the common aim, misconceive its intentions, disarticulate its internal solidarities, and all that is left is a series of petty contortions and bizarre concepts which resemble a freak of nature. Take the idea of a nation, and show that neither race nor language nor soil nor history nor political regime nor industry nor even independence is either necessary or sufficient to create it, and you reduce it to an illusion of instinct. Take a living text, a living person, and put them through the sieve of an erudition without perspective, and you will destroy them in less time than it takes to learn the method.[18] Historically speaking, periods of scepticism are always grafted on to epochs in which spiritual drives, apparently exhausted by some vast effort of creative thought, have crumbled away to leave society maladjusted, without enthusiasm and without a sense of reality. 'Perhaps one is an atheist', said Renan, 'for not seeing far enough.' One is always sceptical for lack of breadth of vision. Just now we were justifying analysis. One must add, with Goethe, that often one does not see something through looking at it too closely, and that one can only know something properly at an angle of

45 degrees. There is a lethal quality about analytical explanation. 'Something explained', said Nietzsche, 'ceases to interest us.'[19] Objective minds always push their explanations beyond the point which allows for the movement of spirit and for problematical uncertainty. Others cannot live if the problem has been destroyed in them. Nietzsche, noted Lou Andréas Salomé, had to have a problem that was eternally insoluble, which perpetually tormented his soul and finally shattered his reason. The intelligence which, by day, is precision, clarity, mastery, cannot live unless by night, solitary and tireless, it can wrestle with the angel.

Lacking this, it introduces innumerable mystifications into its own workings.

One of the most common is the dialectic of twin frenzy, described by Bergson. When thought encounters a problem, it divides like water meeting a rock. The two currents thus formed may retain the fluidity of the water which eventually encircles the rock. They may also each follow their own course in a straight line, creating two torrents of hostile and uncontrollable absurdities. Mediocre minds are pleased by the turbulent extremism to which this leads; its paroxysm creates an illusion of the absolute. The hurly-burly of competing 'isms' which replaces dialogue in so many false debates, is fostered by this cold folly: individualism and communism, authoritarianism and liberalism, clericalism and anti-clericalism, nationalism and internationalism. The pairs stretch end-to-end interminably. They occupy too much place in history, and commentators exaggerate them further to fill up their paragraphs.

But some minds, by dint of understanding everything, lose the ability to judge and to choose. We should note that in spite of its fine sound, this is not always comprehension. The weakness is often due to forms of thought still bathed in infantile magic, where all is in all, where oppositions break down and frontiers are wiped out by a pathological dialysis of ideas. But a subtle temptation is still there, even when there is comprehension: what error does not contain a grain of truth? What disposition of ideas is not presented to us in the guise of a living man, working out his own drama, begging us not to reduce its moving terms to abstract schemata? As comprehension ripens, it sees more grounds for peace than for war in the obscure intentions, groping towards each other beneath the quarrels of principle. Is it not the function of intelligence to understand, as it should be that of religion to unite? And yet truth is jealous and if its framework does not always correspond with the frontiers of intellectual parties, it still has

its destiny, its exigency, its exclusiveness. The systematically con-
ciliating spirit refuses these, as it refuses all strict engagement with
reality. The inexhaustible and moralising indulgence which it accords
to all 'sincerely held opinions', the terror of any too harsh affirmation,
of any hard argument, the passion for sweeping aside divergencies and
emasculating discussion, is often due to the amiability of a weak
character: sometimes it is due to a slightly schizoid withdrawal and
betrays a fear of conflict and an indifference to external determinations:
sometimes, however, it can be found in depressed cycloid types, who
feel the need for harmony at any price and can only achieve it at a low
level. 'The instinct of wanting to know everything *indifferently*', wrote
Nietzsche,[20] 'is on the same level as an undifferentiated sexual instinct:
a sign of *vulgarity*.' 'To understand everything', he added, 'is to despise
everything.' This weak toleration is also often found in the highly
sensitive and unstable person, to whom the least opposition is a
torture. We should add that their benevolence is so comfortable and
their reputation so high that one cannot always avoid the suspicion that
self-interest also plays a part.

Verbal facility is one of the most frequent instruments of this
contempt for intellectual commitment. The agitation of words without
consequences in reality seems to have become the principal objective of
some types of mind. In the mental hospitals are patients who talk
interminably, without bothering about the significance of what they
say or whether they are understood. This level of inconsistent language[21]
in parallel to the 'collective monologue' of the child. It is superior to
that in which the word is closely linked with a need: in this the
mentally deficient are superior to imbeciles, in their intoxication by
this new facility of performing actions just by moving the tongue. Thus
the psychologist cannot rate very highly a trifling intellectual chatter,
however cleverly an intact brain may be able to disguise it.

*   *   *

These analyses are always bringing us to the verge of ethical conclusions which it is finally impossible to avoid. There are so many
subtleties, overlappings, somersaults, such a refinement of ambiguity,
evasion, optical illusion, confusion and obscurity, which are so useful
to us that we have to suspect their hidden influence everywhere. If
certain constitutional weaknesses and certain educational errors
explain at least partially the inhibitions, the clumsiness and the
withdrawals of intelligence, which those affected regret themselves; if

the complexity of reality sometimes throws us into desperate uncertainties, contemporary thinking must still be debited with many a bitter reproach. These divisions, these detours, these feints and shades of meaning which it has used and abused, are so many occasions granted to cowardice. The recent trials of strength have shown that the distribution of intelligence was not always the same as the distribution of character.

To accuse intelligence for this is an abuse of language. None of the aberrations of intelligence has the right to represent free intelligence in the prosecution we have just examined. Authentic thinking, the active intermediary between two actions, starts from commitment and ends with commitment.

But commitment is neither alienation nor blindness. Intellectual commitment has its own dialectic: far from dissolving character, it is perhaps the strongest discipline of character we can find.

Firstly, it entails an asceticism of lucidity, which will sweep away assertive beliefs, always messengers of egoism, and confusions of dead habits and affective tyrannies. To dissociate words, disrupt partisan positions, disentangle the pattern of ideas and reality: such work is long and hard. All the forces of the mind have to struggle against the laziness of thought, which is always lagging behind, asking for blinkers. This is never finally overcome.

This preliminary work is directed towards an affirmation. Affirmation is the central act of thought, and not suspension, as the critics of intelligence claim. Thus activity helps to give intelligence to thought, whereas inactivity compromises and sometimes degrades it.

*

As W. Stern writes:[22] 'It is not the fact that a man *can think* which makes him intelligent, but the fact that he *can dispose of his thought* as a means of fulfilling his tasks in life, and particularly that he can dispose of it where it is most useful, and that he uses it in a way most effective for his purpose.

'Two quite different elements are included in intelligence.

'First, the psychological element, represented by the possession of a certain thought content (concepts, judgments), and then by a capacity for accomplishing the operations of thought (abstractions, continuations, comparisons, even relationships).

'Then the personal element (and this is really decisive), that is to say, the placing of contents and operations wherever the chosen goal of the personality suggests the necessity.'

* The inactivity of thought as a form of indifference, and affirmation as a means of engaging thought in reality.

A thought which does not lead to a decision is an incomplete thought. As opposed to the complacent fluctuations of an indolent mind, life presents each minute a to be or not to be which is the force of gravity of reflection. Even in its elementary operations thought must have the power of attack, as it had with the Stoics and Aristotle, which constitutes its essence, far more than the mechanical combinations to which static psychology, formal criticism and ideological practice reduce it. This power, which is decisive in the shaping of judgment, requires the whole work of man. The abulic are even incapable of registering their perceptions correctly.[23] Webb found astonishingly high correlations for good sense, which is the habitual capacity for forming good judgments, with depth, which implies several moral and social qualities, and each of its psychological correlations was remarkably parallel with these same qualities. This daring turn of thought, so attractive in a Lucretius, reappears in a Descartes. Descartes, said Péguy, 'this knight errant who set out so bravely', the philosopher 'who deployed his intelligence like cavalry'. He only introduces doubt in bulk at the beginning of his meditation, because he wants none of that unhealthy doubt stagnating along his route, envenoming every step: if one must doubt, then doubt properly, once and for all, to the point of absurdity, until one liberates the decisive intuition whose ever present energy will break the inertia of the powers of suspension. The *cogito* is the absolute affirmation, which expels the poison in thought. Although there must be perpetual presence of mind to bring affirmation back from intuition to intuition through all the pitfalls set by reason on its path, Descartes may perhaps be reproached for not having anchored this affirmation sufficiently in the very flesh and bone of personality. Judgment attains its choices in a dramatic struggle involving the whole of the human aggregate, from unconscious instinct to the fine edge of the intelligence. An imperceptible slackening of any one of the forces involved and this nascent truth hardens, is deformed, voided of its soul, displaying falsehoods in the garments of truth. The trouble has risen from those depths within me, where responsibility and irresponsibility are blended in an inextricable formula, unknown to me: for if my irresponsibility sinks its roots into the obscure night of heredity and collective ill-fortune, my responsibility is laden with all the irresponsibilities that I have allowed to settle by unconscious weakness. No doubt 'invincible ignorance' exists. But it is a far cry from that natural innocence the Greeks attributed to thought. Its mysterious formula is a secret in each of us, that can only be read by an infinite generosity.

Commitment requires sacrifices and a choice. It is never possible at the same time to save all the aspects and all the possibilities of a truth, without abandoning it to impotence. This is the disease of too finely-shaded minds, who, by idolising truth, immobilise it, and by trying to save every detail, kill it as much as the bad painter kills expression by trying to reproduce all the subtleties of sensation. This intellectual puritanism has its psychological root in the manias for precision and perfection we have already studied. It is all the more necessary to be aware of its faint morbidity in that it appears so alluring to a mind enamoured of the absolute. Action must become resigned to truncated truths and impure truths. It must also resign itself to fighting captive truth, though never truth itself: evil and error are always built around a partial truth: to let them pass because they hold something dear to us as hostage is a result of stupidity. This 'truth' in their power has become a poison, and the worst of poisons, for it appears with a borrowed halo: the confusion of mind has made it dangerous and it is better to leave it temporarily in the shadow, since it is temporarily impossible to evoke its true visage, and an unintelligent loyalty may easily become the involuntary accomplice of its exploitation. On the other hand, it may perhaps be necessary to the salvation of some vaster truth to ally truth, conditionally, with a temporary evil, if history has stacked the cards that way. It is very difficult to make absolutists admit how much affective rigidity underlies their spiritual intransigence.

The absolute appears to us as part of the unfolding of history: it is both incarnate and transcendent, and does not always wear the same face or appear under the same light. We always overlook the historical situation of the precedents we demand from the past, as if it were an abstract pharmacopoeia. St. Augustine only linked Church and State so closely because *at that time* the support of the Church alone seemed capable of bolstering up the tottering Roman state. The men of 1791, proclaiming a liberty and equality that today we find very abstract, had *in front of them* a forest of privileges and abuses and petty regulations which frustrated talent and initiative. It was important for a contemporary of St. Augustine, or of the Declaration of the Rights of Man, to know whether the happier side of history was represented by Christianity and the French Revolution, and if so, then to co-operate with history in spite of its detours and not to refuse one's contribution to contemporary thought from some reservation of conscience. It is such practical wisdom that shows the marriage of intelligence with the sense of reality.

It is true that men are more frequently prepared to come to terms with reality than to swim against its stream, preferring to attack the most obvious adversaries than to save difficult positions. The temptations we are considering attack only the elite. They are peculiar to intellectuals and to the most exacting of them. The least betrayal of truth is painful to them like the slightest breach of tact to the highly sensitive. Does this mean they must either renounce action or the service of truth? Neither the one nor the other. On either side a comfortable position awaits them. And in the course of history they have not failed to slip either to one side or the other. On the pretext of realism they have flattered power, justified success, or simply renounced their duty of vigilance within the parties they have adopted: on the pretext of integrity they have fled from the effort of historical creation to the more facile requirements of discarnate principles. In both cases there is a defect of character although the second, less profitable, sometimes engenders a heroic perseverance worthy of greater lucidity. He who chooses the part of intelligence has no easy life. He has a duty to bear witness to a transcendental truth and, pursuing it, must combat the passions and limitations of his own friends: he must be committed to an activity which at every step infringes on his most cherished loyalties: he can refuse neither the one nor the other, nor hope ever to reconcile them in perfect harmony. He must move perpetually from one to the other, here accused of a breach of combat discipline, there of tampering with truth, and always struggling with his own conscience in each of his decisions. But he must hold unwearyingly to each end of the rope: on the one side ceaselessly recalling the requirements of truth, fighting at daggers drawn against falsehood and the utilitarian exploitation of spiritual truths: rescuing, rescuing, and rescuing again, at a time when the struggle is only to confound, to hate and to destroy: and at the same time choosing and sacrificing. There is a perpetual commitment and detachment in order to build up, the one through the other, the one in spite of the other, the freedom and effectiveness of the mind.

*

We should overlook an essential aspect of our experience of thought if by talking of commitment we forgot the no less passionate need for detachment which it reveals. Thought perceives itself confusedly as transcending the objects it must explain, the terms it must relate, and the collective needs to which it must respond. Objects are always threatening to impose their impersonality, concepts to imprison it in their forms, the collectivities to enslave it in their interest. By evading

* Gives the example of Erasmus as a typical case of intellectual hesitation.

its commitments on the pretext of the dangers incurred, thought betrays its mission and loses value for lack of sap. But if it must be in the world, it must also be there as if it were not there. Like the knights of the Grail, it must protect its transcendence from all the attachments of the earth. This is something practical, political minds will never understand, taken up as they are by the interests of the moment and without mental reservations as to the future. Luck will have it that resistances from the past and egocentric complacency look, to the narrow view of the man of action, the same as the independence of the devoted mind, and he includes both under the same ban. He will never admit that the man who has answered the call of living spirit rejects, as much as he, the hesitant and the evasive, whilst refusing to mistake domestication for commitment. One must needs conclude that the mind that follows the dictates of its own integrity to the limit will always be destined to crucifixion in the outer world and to be torn apart by its own inner commitments. Nothing is more difficult than to maintain the commitment and detachment essential to the vocation of intelligence. Few indeed have found this equilibrium: perhaps it has never been achieved. An Erasmus slips perhaps too far towards evasion, a Pascal becomes perhaps too stubborn in the quarrels of an epoch. In the light of these difficulties we understand the paradox of those thinkers who have been able to attain in thought a heart-stirring experience of which they were incapable in daily life: none spoke more profoundly than Kierkegaard of existence, choice or marriage, whereas a form of negativism completely paralysed him in front of concrete options. And the philosophers of carnal enjoyment sometimes have hardly enough flesh on their bones even to live.

*   *   *

In discussing forms of intellectual behaviour we seem to have covered tracks which are already too many and too complicated. Yet we have only sketched in the main features. To interpret experience correctly we should never forget that most minds are composed of extremely heterogeneous material, in which puerilities co-exist with the most elaborate maturations, sometimes quite unknown to the subject. The most exteriorised characters, the minds which are most dependent on social expression or objective determinations, suffer least from their inner inequalities. Intellectual effort is like spiritual effort in that it is a ceaseless aspiration to resolve these discrepancies in one comprehensive and passionate unity.

9

SPIRITUAL LIFE WITHIN THE LIMITS OF CHARACTER

THE CHARACTEROLOGY OF THE MORAL ACT

*

THE moral sense has a modest and fragile history.[1] It is formed at the same time as instinct, social life and reason, mingled with these primitive shapes from which it is difficult to distinguish it.

We have seen the child at first dominated by captative forms of instinct. Broadly speaking, his first estimation is that what he can eat and keep is good, and what has to be rejected or expelled is bad. The baby's consciousness is largely digestive. Perhaps at this period there forms in some a tendency always to attach a positive moral value to the virtues of acquisition and economy, and a negative moral coefficient to losses and misfortune: this underlies the prestige of riches and the widespread belief that the poor have always fallen into poverty through their own fault. But apart from his earliest months, the child is not the perverse and brutal primitive described by Freud. His life is, rather, divided between a kind of avidity and a kind of grace, both still foreign to morality. The external prohibitions of his parents are his moral law. His submission is not, however, always due to external constraint alone. It is also inspired by affection and by that first attempt at co-ordinating values which Monakow and Mourgues were to discover in every behaviour of life. But this morality is very undecided until about the seventh year, a period of 'dual morality' to use Anna Freud's term. The child has difficulty in adjusting a diffused moral consciousness to the extrinsic authority of parents or social pressure. The former is gradually moulded by the successive renunciations which lead from captation to oblation, from the first bowel training, passing through the acceptance of weaning, the victory over the crisis of possessiveness and personality in the third year, and the repression of egocentricity through the companionship of other children in the family or at school. But this consciousness is only faintly aware of itself. The young child seems to be still dominated by a social concep-

---

* Although spiritual life is not within the direct competence of the psychologist, it is not separate from life.

tion of fault.[2] He is solely, or almost solely, concerned with its publicity. An unperceived fault seems to him infinitely less serious than one which is known, and a lie which is believed is not, for him, a lie. Shame, which he feels very early, is above all social. It is a fine point to decide the proportion of the two moralities. The second is a necessary support for the first tendrils of inner morality, which can only grow with the age of reason, but it must be discreet enough not to stifle it entirely: an abuse of intimidation may even at this age lead to deviations towards a morality of fear which may produce a permanent miscarriage of the morality of love. It has reasonably been suggested that the moral instruction of children, either at school or in the confessional, should be entrusted to those who understand the workings of this particular age group.

Towards the seventh year the child passes from a puerile to a reflecting state. The sense of guilt grows stronger, together with the sense of inner law. This latter develops very strongly in the child fortunate in his religious education, which presents God as an object of love, a friend who asks him to surpass himself, rather than as an invisible but well-informed replica of social authority. This maturation is not solely inner. By adapting to the reality principle, the child learns to accept renunciation, to accept others and to accept struggle. In school-work, in meeting other children, in apprenticeship to life, he is constantly meeting with setbacks. Care must be taken to see that he can 'terminate' these setbacks, that he can live and consciously endorse the renunciation required by the order of things, or the happiness of others, learning to dominate the passing defeat and to start again with fresh vigour and assurance. Otherwise the tests that are not accepted will leave as many scars, to push him into separation, opposition, and protestation all the rest of his life. It is such lack of adaptation that gives birth to moral anarchism, attitudes of defiance, the pseudo-perversities and all forms of egocentricity.

The pre-pubertal period from twelve to fifteen is one of crisis. Apparent morality is somewhat precarious: it is the 'graceless' age. According to Stanley Hall, children are twice as incorrigible as at other periods. According to Marro, the figure for bad behaviour is twice as high for pre-puberty as for earlier periods. But this 'bad behaviour' is largely due to a great need for independence, and for an opposition which is temporarily necessary to psychological development. Generally speaking it disappears without trace if tactfully handled.

The morality of puberty is a chaos of contradictions. It is an age in which every string of personality is strung to its highest pitch. Goodwill and benevolence towards others are now greater than they will ever be (Stanley Hall), yet the need for independence sometimes rouses the adolescent to fury against those around him. Instinct is brutal, perversity cynical, but introspection and scruple complicate beyond measure the simplest duties. Independence rebels against the slightest pressure, yet no age is more sensitive to the influence of a teacher or to the persuasion of example.

This crisis is resolved towards the twentieth year. Either egoism has won the day against spiritual feeling, and is beginning to establish the comfort which will surround the grown man, or moral consciousness has frayed its way through successive resistances and, at the age at which formerly one received knighthood, has adopted a world of values which will henceforward be the sovereign guide to behaviour. This transcendence grafted on to the very core of the person now finally yokes the tendency to autonomy with the tendency to heteronomy in a creative conflict, in which solitary heroism and unconditional devotion try to achieve sufficient strength to avoid slipping back into the quagmires of egocentricity and conformity.

Moral education must allow for the moral structure of each period of life, if it is to be understood and effective. This is the acceptable interpretation of the discretion recommended by 'negative' education. A moral concept explained too soon or too badly for the age concerned, remarked Rousseau, either is not heeded or creates fantastic notions which can never afterwards be effaced.

The moral equilibrium or disequilibrium that results from this laborious process concerns both the psychologist and the moralist. We have seen that an evaluating consciousness is of first importance in the affirmation of the self. Our possessions escape our usage, our frontiers fade away over the abysses of the heart and the shores of the universe. But 'he that is spiritual judgeth all things'. First of all we apply this judgment of order and esteem to ourselves, and thereby find our greatest inner assurance. Even more than a minimum of physical assurance a minimum of moral assurance is essential to the most elementary personal equilibrium. Moral uncertainty, on the other hand, the inability to decide whether one deserves love or hate, is the cause of countless psychological difficulties. Not that an excessive attention to our own view of our worth or unworthiness is good tactics either in spiritual life or in mental health. But however anxious we may be not to impede the flight of spirit by too much application, we must, even as it carries us away, try to hold together this entangled pattern of muscle and thought, desire and inertia, memory and innocence, which tries to represent our inner countenance in a physical, historical and social environment. Our movement forward is a movement in equilibrium, and there must be equilibrium.

Characterology is not competent to pass judgment on the ultimate value of a moral imperative. Good intention or malice can never be shown experimentally. All we have to ask ourselves here is whether a moral preoccupation is a structure of character amongst others and is at least related to certain constant psychological proportions. Or is it fostered by certain character traits whilst others obstruct it? And finally, do differences of temperament differentiate moral behaviour to the point of creating groups of moral attitudes which endanger the unity of morality?

It may indeed be possible to define an ideal moral attitude, provided we admit that experience would rarely offer it to us in its full richness. It has for long been customary to stress the sense of external pressure, whether due to transcendent law or social authority. But although it usually accompanies moral action, producing correlations of intimidation and submission, the least that may be said of this feeling is that it is considerably reduced in the higher forms of morality. Bergson has shown that behind it lies the appeal of some moral figure, hero or saint, which is echoed by the aspirations of emotion, generating liberating concepts and reactions. There is a third term which Bergson has somewhat vaporised, between the two preceding ones, thereby tending to split moral action between training and mysticism, and that is personal affirmation. This resists the impersonal thrust of instinctive emotion and social conformity, yet allows them whatever is required by adaptation to reality: it is opposed to the dissolving force of sentimental ecstasy and moral idealism, yet is able to follow an absolute belief or loyalty. Moral temperaments can be grouped according to the predominance of one of three fundamental attitudes; affirmation, submission and forward movement.
*

* * *

At every step I am confronted by a situation which is for me, now, however enlightened I may be as to my specifiable duties, a leap into the unknown. At every move there is an effort to maintain a pattern of data which is liable to fall apart in every direction. To wrestle with

* Develops the theory of James that moral action is action along the line of greatest resistance.

the angel whilst one's legs are struggling against the clutches of
spectres. No form of life requires greater strength, a strength not
necessarily to be found in bodily health. The rather partial equilibrium
which health contributes to the spiritual and physiological may, on the
contrary, promote moral indifference or spiritual sloth. Moral power is
rather the union of qualities of breadth and attack.

*

Hardly has one understood morality as affirmation than, in the heart
of affirmation, arises the mortal danger of egocentricity. Why did
Nietzsche stop halfway? He could have compared the mystification of
passive mind by resentment, with the correlative mystifications of
avarice and the narrow aggressiveness of the self. The adherents of the
spiritual have always made self-love the first and most rebellious
adversary of moral effort. But what is self-love? The pleasure of living?
It derives from instinct and has as yet no access to morality. The exact
understanding of our powers as of our limitations? The natural love of
self which, as it were, is spontaneous homage to the beauty of man?
Who shall condemn it, when the most exigent morality, that of the
Gospels, takes it as measure for the love of one's neighbour? Yet there
is a sickness of the ego as there is a sickness of existence and a sickness
of having. It mingles with the affirmation of the self, as the two others
share in life and possession, and all three so intimately that only a fine
spiritual awareness can discover them with certainty, and we can never
finally isolate them. No need to recall the aspects of egocentricity,
which have already been discussed at length. We have seen that they
are as numerous as the aspects of character and that, normally, no
gesture of the self escapes entirely from their influence. Egocentricity
fastens the life of the self to the image of the self, an arrested image,
already dead, deprived of the perspective contributed by contact with
others and a reference to higher values;[3] we cannot help being silently
irritated by this enforced immobilisation, which arouses a compensatory overestimation of the image of the self and a depreciation of all
values which arise outside ourselves. Such is the normal process of
pride.

**

'The power† of the Highest shall overshadow thee', said the angel
to Mary (Luke i. 35). Virtue belongs to no one. This magnificent
anonymity is the supreme lucidity of personal life. Without virtue the
self offends everything. And it is because virtue almost always presents

* Refers to the categories of Heymans.   ** The egocentricity of virtue.
† In French: 'La vertu du Très-Haut vous couvre de son ombre'.—Trs.

itself with a strange cargo of tics and particularities that shock the particularities of others, that it often offends rather than assists.

In powerful natures of a passionate type, in whom one may expect the most striking examples of morality, the insertion of self is violent and daring; hence those lives in two parts, which attain the heights of spirituality after having achieved a summit of disorder, like St. Augustine; or lives which are a closely woven blend of extreme disinterestedness and human pride, like a Bloy or a Péguy; or those who hestitate between the force of their spiritual drive and the equal strength of their instinct, like a Chateaubriand for ambition, a Verlaine for the flesh and a Jacques Rivière for intellectual possessiveness.

No doubt these savage expressions of the self, these sacred possessions, were necessary so that moral life might tear itself away from the collective slumber of an epoch which still held it captive. The cult of heroism is the first myth to inspire man on his quest for individuation. It still retains certain traits of a jealous passion: but if our virtues have not the hard edge of instinct, how will they be able to shake off decadence?

Alongside this powerfully muscled egocentricity, the moralism of moral gentry shows its more banal forms. They have their own way of hatching their virtues, like their comforts, their ailments and their tics. Their seriousness, instead of confirming their virtue, shows up their inadequacy, their application betrays awkwardness, and in their attention to self which mars their noblest actions one perceives an intolerable pedantry. This profitable morality serves as an outlet for the exuberance of the sense of property. Their virtues are accountable funds which can be invested, protected by all the play of vanity, mysteriousness and calculation of interest. But in order to have one must keep, and morality dies when it is put in the bank. To count, one must have a measure, and the quality of moral life is that the scale of good and evil grows at each progress, and a moment of pardon and of love outweighs years of parsimonious hoarding.
*

*　　*　　*

The discredit attached to morality by expansive and powerful characters is due to that morose obedience which it often seems to impose on life, and the states of more or less morbid contention to which it seems to lead. Here Nietzsche and Freud have swept out many

* Describes the influence of typical forms of character mentioned earlier in the book on moral expression.

obscure crannies in the contemporary mind and this spring-cleaning, after an initial dismay, should make a fresh departure possible.

The dependence which we feel with regard to moral law may include a very crude desire for passivity. Then it is no longer a spiritual element of deference and devotion which dominates this moral homage, but a much grosser attitude of fear and submission which goes back very far in our psychic history. Before there are any distinct moral attitudes, the child perceives a tension between the urge of the egoistic and asocial tendencies of the instinctive zone, and social pressure. This is represented in his world by the authority of the parents, particularly of the more sharply defined authority of the father, to which he assimilates all external authority. One can imagine the power he attributes to this being, so close to him, who produces every moment, just by raising his finger, the appearance of a miracle. So overwhelming an authority must inevitably appear to him as violent, however just the father may try to be. And it is all the more so, when it is divorced from affection and reason to become capricious and arbitrary. An inordinate affection for the mother, largely egoistic and possessive, may create the same spell-binding effect as the father's severity.

Weighing heavily upon the child, these external pressures build up an intimidating pressure within him. This development, which is foreign to his moral life, is closely blended with the relationship of dependence which is formed at a higher level between values and aspirations, with the difference that it is blind, ponderous and sterile. But the concrete unity of the individual often introduces these contradictory aspects into the liberating activity of values. How can one work out the details of this fascinating whole! Extrinsic pressure may simply augment the inner pressure of duty, and there is no morality so distilled as to be free from the weight of some external constraint. It may also completely pulverise the spirituality of transcendence, or spirituality itself. 'Their moral skin', said Péguy of such moral persons, 'makes them impermeable by grace.' We recognise here the workings of the Freudian Superego.[4] Even if it may sometimes aid moral values in the training of instinct, it is not entitled to represent them, for it has no aim and sometimes exceeds all measure. It is the delegate of social order on the frontiers of instinctual tumult, more or less accepted by the deeper moral consciousness. It expresses throughout life, beneath the direct spiritual experiences of the individual, the concept of authority as practised in early education. It tends, in fact, to behave towards the self as the parents behaved towards the child. More precisely speaking, it seems to be formed, not so much on the image of the parents, but on the image of their own Superego, with its appreciations and attitudes.[5] Thus, throughout the generations, it represents an element of conservatism and inertia, opposed to the anarchy of instinct and the initiative of morality. It is like an Upper House of moral deliberation. It constitutes, in fact, the sole moral instance in many people who have a strong physical memory and not much metaphysics: thus, when they lose respect for their real father and mother, or for the real persons who constitute social authority, they generally lose their moral sense also.

The immense majority of men can be more or less strictly classed as falling within this category, in its higher or lower forms. But not all are inclined to it by nature. Alongside the sons of Abel, their moral life submissive and fairly harmonious, we find the small, dark band of the sons of Cain, in revolt even against the harmony of good. In so far as there is at least a partial psychological explanation, their moral attitude is often derived from a more general attitude of opposition, of which we know the source, particularly the infantile source. But like submission, it may be of very diverse quality. Some are simply primary rebellious types, unadjusted, whose sarcasm produces nothing, carries nothing. But others belong to that audacious breed which, from Lucifer to the Titans, from Prometheus to Nietzsche, seek their fortune in a struggle against the gods themselves, and seem vowed to a demoniac witness, in the paroxysm of scandal, to moral freedom.

The element of intimidation, which is an undertone to the sense of moral obligation, should normally disappear as the subject discovers his autonomy and the nature of true spiritual homage.[6] There is a primitive, incomplete type, in whom drives demanding a brutal realisation coexist with a severe, persecutory moral judgment. This is often due to a harsh education. When such a person comes from a happy-go-lucky family it seems due to a delayed aggressiveness, long inactive for lack of provocation.[7] The combination is extremely common. Puritan strictness is nearly always allied to a strong repression of instinct and a strong reaction on the part of instinct to this punishment: a coldness of the senses does not generate such passion. Exalted moral sentiments are not always the strongest. The very extravagance of prudishness, indignation, peremptory nobility, headstrong idealism, betrays the tension of inner conflict, the hypercompensation for a strong feeling of guilt. This is why they are neither solid nor productive.

This type of moral structure suffers from so many misshapen forms, commonly confused with the true shape of morality, that they should be shown in their right proportions.

In this type of man fault leaves more than a deeply serious, yet passing regret, to be carried forward by a creative movement towards the future. Ponderous, fixed to the past as such, complicated by excessive secondarity, it is driven by remorse into a moral hypochondria. Such a man clings to his fault as others to a defeat or a bereavement. Perhaps unwittingly a 'slave of sin' as much as those who abandon themselves to it, in spite of his frantic efforts to set himself free. 'Deliver us from evil' is more than contrition, it is a prayer to be delivered from the obsession of guilt, after having been a means of struggling against temptation. This obsession may indeed, in some way, serve the interests of life or a moral future. Thus it is particularly fixed to the perverse impulses which refuse to be integrated in the self, as Freud remarks (all sexual aberrations and particularly the most common, onanism). It then appears to be a reaction of the species, clumsy but purposeful, and behind this biological concern it expresses perhaps a deeper intention of unity and generosity. But it can easily become, by autonomous development, a morbid and unconscious insistence on guilt. Luther calls to mind those who are always discovering trivial faults in themselves for fear of living for a few minutes without a morose awareness of sin. A conscience of this kind may appear exacting, but in fact it keeps them on the surface with a simulacrum of drama, a commentary on action, whilst sterilising the sources of spiritual generosity by its inhibitions and preoccupations. It absorbs them in an observed self instead of in a creative self. Instead of leading directly to the eradication of the faulty intention and its effects, it frustrates this salutary drive by a sterile rumination over the past. It establishes a sort of oedema of moral life.

This virtuous taste for sin by the intermediary of self-reproach is not without relationship to exhibitionist or mythomaniac drives. To humiliate oneself in public, when the fault is frequent, is a way of attracting interest, of arousing moral pity and of simulating virtue without changing one's way of life. 'Me a sinner' is a key to success, if one has enough talent to awaken complacency behind the curiosity, and aggressiveness behind the complacency, keeping all these feelings alive without pushing any to extremes. Half convinced, half inventing, these public sinners, like all those who are principally devoted to the spectacular, usually lack the capacity to commit the terrible sins they boast of, or to undertake a radical conversion when they humiliate themselves. Behind their cynical vaunting the former quickly betray the poverty of their temperament, and the latter, behind their specious, noisy and indiscreet humility, a lack of docility, little compatible with the protestations of repentance.[8] A remarkable aspect of this moral exhibitionism is an aggressive dirtiness, or a vulgarity of speech—a demonstration by skin, clothing or language of the inner sense of guilt.[9]

But this spectacular agitation, however common, eliminates more frequently than it encourages the sense of moral dependence with regard to fault and to the law. A morose bad conscience increases it, however, to the point of oppression and allows it to invade the whole psyche. We have already noted the cancerous nature of this morose sense of guilt. It kills, as cancer does, little by little. By its obstructive power it aids the refusal of action: 'Obedience to duty', said Tarde, 'has two great advantages: it usually obviates the need for foresight, and always the need for success.' A fanatical asceticism is not always a violent reaction against an excess of temperament, or a sickly liking for suffering: the person who appears to deprive himself is not always depriving himself of something pleasant; he may prefer to avoid the torment, the agitation, the sociability induced by pleasure.[10] An obsessional self-accusation shelters us in the same way by discouraging effort in advance, or rather, it rationalises an already settled discouragement. It is understandable that a sense of guilt should be one of the principal causes of lying, of the lie to ward off a difficulty, a vital anxiety, and the initiative they might suggest. A morose conscience, by its permanent impotence, betrays a trend towards psychasthenia. It is difficult to conceive the zeal with which it finds fuel for its flame, particularly in childhood. Thus the child accuses itself bitterly for its instinctive resistance to a difficult weaning, for its embarrassment by the greedy, egoistic and possessive affection of certain mothers, or for the suffering it feels over a state of conflict between the parents.

The invasion of consciousness by this endogenous evil is all the more sinister in that guilt develops unconsciously without giving its name. Once repressed, it is transformed into a different feeling, an obscure discomfort, anonymous, intolerable, and intolerable because it is anonymous. It freezes action by a generalised phobia which overflows from situations requiring moral responsibility into all those that call upon the individual. Every social presence appears to the man with a load of guilt as a possibility of judgment, every misfortune a chastisement, which he relates to the whole of his life or to any absurd fixation, through failure to perceive its reason. The sense of inferiority is often only an attenuated variant of this anguish of guilt. A load of guilt is a form of persecution mania, but a moral persecution: the sufferer does not transform the world into a vast conspiracy, but into an immense tribunal. A morbid sense of unworthiness—which so often taints the sense of sin in Russian literature—mars most of his actions and feelings from within: he feels remorse for everything, the profession he has chosen, and those he has not chosen, his defeats, even his physical blemishes. We perceive the very relative value of this apparent moral sensitivity when we find it again in the true psychasthenics, who display the same general obsession with remorse: obsession of the missed vocation, obsession of self-contempt overflowing into general behaviour, from frantic doubt to moral scruple, and a sense of shame at eating or fulfilling normal physiological functions. They torture their imaginations to find extreme or hideous actions for which to blame themselves.[11]

*

We should never understand the liking for punishment if we did not pay attention to the fact that it provides agreeable relief from the anguish of guilt and is therefore necessary to the subject, just as we enjoy the slight pain of tapping an aching tooth as a momentary relief from its continuous dull ache. A pleasure of relaxation, no doubt, but then only a negative pleasure. The stubborn, ill-humoured fury with which self-punishment goes to work reveals more violent drives: an aggressiveness which enjoys destruction, exacting amends for a fear or a regret. It is the intrusion of this morbid flavour which makes the Church very suspicious of ascetic excesses. Nothing is more suspect as to its quality and nothing less just in its application than this 'immanent psychic justice' as some, by a flight of vocabulary, have called it.[12] Most of the illustrations we have quoted are due to a mechanism of reversal: the subject tempted to commit a fault turns his aggression against himself. But this auto-aggression, becoming obsessional, is launched at random, affecting the most just of actions as much as any perverse intentions. Psychologists have said of this self-punishment that displacement is its most normal proceeding, the sense of guilt and punishment being fixed on a banal action in order to direct consciousness away from the centre of guilt. Can one all the same justify the justice of the Unconscious? The sense of justice, says Allendy, knows no isolated fault, limited in time and space. This remark might have far-reaching consequences if self-punishment, with disciplinary and curative virtue, attained the heart of the self where particular faults are formed and unformed, and whose general moral

* Describes various forms of masochism.

state is more important than symptomatic delinquencies. But to strike aslant is not to strike at the heart, and to spread a disease is not to circulate a remedy. Unconscious self-punishment is like a peculiar doctor scratching and envenoming the surroundings of a sore on the pretext that he was not obsessed by it. It is doubly immoral: it deforms a bad conscience by making it malicious and it destroys the clairvoyance of moral consciousness which is held up and poured back upon the past action instead of being carried forward towards a salutary action.

In addition, as admitted even by those who have studied it, it is the means chosen by the sick self to throw off a burdensome weight of guilt. This is a reversal of its mission. We must note that, if everything takes place as has been said, what the self is seeking in this morose guilt is not to get rid of something disagreeable, since it develops and aggravates its suffering, but to escape seeing guilt as guilt, not to know it any more, even in disguised form, at the sole point at which it was originally felt as guilt. This is the true shape of the morose conscience: it seemed at first sight to be a barbarous but zealous excess of the moral sense: now it appears that it works, beneath a show of urgency, towards the stifling of morality itself. It is, ultimately, an attempt to throw off Nessus' shirt, to reject the painful responsibilities of the flesh, by brutal repression, and to obstruct spiritual consciousness by the demoralisation of the affective and penal consequences of fault. We conceal this desertion by plaguing ourselves with lofty concern for apparent virtue: but we have none the less laid down the arms we should have devoted to the virile activities of a healthy heart.

If we incur such tribulation in order to avoid tribulation this frenzied mystification can only be explained by some very deep interest. Freud attributes it to the sexual instinct and the Oedipus situation. This is not sufficient. By its universality and rebellious persistence, the feeling of guilt manifests the intervention of the deepest and most central aspects of life. Professor de Greeff seems to come to closer grips with the phenomenon when he sees in it the effect of every violation of our affection liaison with others (or with the world); also every violation of our inner integrity, of that unlimited richness of childhood which is progressively compromised by the adult world. The feeling of guilt is an ambivalent expression of these vital losses. Both an instinctive effort to halt them by sounding the alarm, and also a danger: we may aggravate them by trying to justify them against an inner accusation, or reinforce them in order to affirm their innocence. It is both a disease endemic to the species and a spiritual sign, which should not be purely and simply eradicated by a mental treatment which would diminish its significance.

This is confirmed by the mechanisms of alienation in the satisfied conscience. The parallelism should be stressed. For if the modern world, devout and moralising, has made itself hideous with the grimaces of morose guilt, some of its adversaries sterilise an equal amount of energy by eradicating a virile awareness of fault from the contemporary conscience. If in such matters psychoanalysis offers lasting results, this is because there is a poison of moral forgetfulness as potent as the poison of obsessive guilt. The former is less obvious, more long-term, and its first effects are exhilarating. But the initial outbursts of twentieth century man allow us to doubt whether its results are less deadly.

The most common procedure of the satisfied conscience is to project the guilt it has rejected upon an external object, against which the self can unleash its aggressiveness in conscientious rage.[13] The ambivalence of all our actions, all in varying degrees heavy with guilt or light with innocence, is intolerable to us. It is a commonplace that we suspect others of doing what our inner impulses, behind our conscious admissions, would so eagerly have us do. Jealousy bears witness to a vague desire for adultery. We cheerfully ascribe our moral stagnation to our teachers, the difficulties of the times, the perversities of circumstance, when our own ill will is almost solely in question. Thus collectivities, suffering in times of crisis from an inner guilt, soon find a scapegoat on whom to unload their misfortune. Even our indignations are rarely pure. The mob howling with rage outside the law-courts is demanding a stone age sacrifice: it vomits its inner self-reproaches over an expiatory victim, using a case of apparently obvious guilt as a means of self-liberation and of creating a sense of innocence. On the other side of this moral barricade, the prisoner employs precisely the same manoeuvre. After, and no doubt before his crime, he throws the responsibility on to some vaguely defined moral entity, resembling in its essence the society or the judicial administration of the moment.[14] One often meets, particularly in politics, men with quite mediocre personal standards, who suffer from a chronic need for indignation: their furies sound hollow, for it is clear that they serve only as a stimulant to a weak faith. Profound indignation has a different note, and yet it is always partially distorted by the need to serve as a justification for ourselves.

Phariseeism begins with this distortion, the ethical projection of egocentric distortion: that is to say, it insinuates itself, perhaps imperceptibly, into all our moral professions. If it is thus attached to virtue, like a shadow, it is the result of the projective nature of moral consciousness. Outstretched towards the image of the good to be attained, it forgets the reality of the subject that pursues it. One is not entirely mistaken in believing that, in one sense, one *is* one's aspirations more essentially than one is one's weaknesses, and this semi-illusion is a spur to doing better. But one identifies too quickly with this future ideal: it is the unawareness of this projection which adds so much bad faith to virtue, and makes the virtuous so absent-minded as to the real quality of the methods they employ. It may be added that when the amoralists attack virtue, they are just as pharisaical as the virtuous attacking vice. Primary types, with a narrow field of consciousness, are more liable to this than secondaries, who are more able to embrace the different levels of understanding.

Phariseeism is complicated by the fact that none of our actions can be reduced to a simple motivation. Usually an action is a convergence of instinctive or self-interested drives and an aspiration towards a value. Some bitter moralists, like La Rochefoucauld and Nietzsche, have like the immoralists a common propensity to detect the first element, which is most often unconscious. No doubt they also yield to an impulse, to a reaction of 'resentment against the high' as opposed to the 'reaction against the low' of utopian moralists. If they happen to misunderstand the 'noble' element, it is none the less true that one cannot do it justice without reservations unless one has understood the nature of the so-called lower elements. Phariseeism is the refusal of such clarity.

*   *   *   *

We too often confuse these parasitical formations with a living, balanced, moral consciousness in order to compromise or reject them together. A true moral consciousness has as its mainspring an acute sense of fault, but although this is central it does not obliterate moral life like the iron mask of morose guilt. We should consider what happens in higher moral natures. More significant than any other is the behaviour, Christian in its inspiration, which has been particularly accused of being a direct encouragement to a slave morality.[15] Christianity has far too deep and therefore too realistic a sense of the Incarnation not to allow, in the transfigurations it proposes to us, for

---

* The paranoiac as the extreme form of the pharisaical type, and the repressions of the satisfied conscience. Stresses the dangers of trying to remove all expressions of a sense of guilt.

the rule that constrains and sometimes breaks in order to liberate; it even consecrates the impurities we have described, preferring to lead them, if possible, into something else rather than to crush them; to Christianity they seem inevitable in a subject of mixed composition, wounded in its nature by a radical predisposition to every aberration, even in the zeal for good. With the concept of sin, it gives a sharp edge to fault, making it offend an order superior to man, and more than an order, an abounding goodness. It is often even called on to insist on the sense of sin in an epoch which finds so many stratagems to get rid of it. But it is not the attention to sin, as a persistent Jansenism suggests, that is at the centre of moral Christian life, but the Μετανοια, the change of heart and the life of grace, its cause and its crowning glory. Even this vocabulary should show how its realities are foreign to morose obsession and the dead weight of the past.[16] Spiritual writers often speak of the goad of sin. An ideal awareness of sin should, in the Christian, have the thrust and rapidity of a dart. It is as strict, for instance, as the Freudian consciousness of the omnipresence of egoistic drives. It even largely exceeds it. 'Lord', said the Psalmist, 'cleanse me of my secret faults, and pardon thy servant for the sins of others.' † But it refuses to devote to sin the prolonged attention that it reserves to recovery. 'Your trouble', wrote St. Francis of Sales to Madame de la Croix d' Antherin, 'is that you are more afraid of vice than you are in love with virtue.'[17] To concentrate too long on the evil done is to confirm and prolong it. 'Sufficient unto the day is the evil thereof: the evil of each day may become a good if we leave it to God.'[18] Otherwise the morose conscience breeds a world of phantoms which obscure the purity of spiritual vision. These pseudo-aridities, morbid aversion to fault, fear of imaginary derelictions, tormented ruminations, solitary cruelties, are unhesitatingly classified by theologians as anomalies of the spiritual life;[19] in this they follow the great tradition of Gerson and St. John of the Cross, who suspected any of the faithful who attached too much importance to their inner state, whether of compunction or scruple, in temptation and in moral joy. 'None of these monsters is real', wrote Fénelon. 'To make them disappear, the thing is neither to see them nor to listen to them voluntarily: simple non-resistance will dissipate them.'[20] Or again, Father Surin: 'As soon as one becomes aware of a movement of one's faculties even slightly disorderly and displeasing to God, one should try to bring everything to order, with a heart as tranquil as if one had not slipped, without worrying about

† Vulgate. Psalm 18, 13, 14 'Quis delicta intelligit? Ab occultis meis munda me, Et ab alienis parce servo tuo.'—Trs.

reflections of self-love which suggest distress at the fault, or a greater contrition. Such feelings can only hinder the advancement of virtue: for whilst the soul entertains itself by caressing its chagrin and fathoming its past faults, this useless return upon itself paralyses its actions and disposes it to fresh lapses. A peaceful regret for badly employed time, combined with a very attentive application to making good use of the present moment, such is the true character of a love of God.'

A very attentive application to making good use of the present moment: this is the proper point of moral application, that of a present laden with possibilities: the concern of the Christian is the point whence hope springs: his abasement is the humility which stimulates and not the humiliation which overwhelms.

Far from warping man's structure under an oppressive subordination, this open sense of moral life expands it into a spiritual life, 'so that we may have life and have it more abundantly.' In this, sacrifice and ascesis may effect real and painful mutilations, but their meaning does not lie in the pleasure of mutilation: they prune in order to enlarge, annihilate to resuscitate. Constraint is obvious and astringent, but it never expresses the arbitrary will of a power determined to hold man in a state of dependence: it merely supports him, in his ignorance and weakness, in view of the liberation which is its true purpose, the outcome of love and the creator of love. 'Now I say, That the heir, as long as he is a child, differeth nothing from a servant, though he be lord of all: But is under tutors and governors until the time appointed of the father. Even so we, when we were children, were in bondage under the elements of the world: But when the fulness of the time was come, God sent forth his Son, made of a woman, made under the law, to redeem them that were under the law, that we might receive the adoption of sons. And because ye are sons, God hath sent forth the Spirit of his Son into your hearts, crying, Abba, Father. Wherefore thou art no more a servant, but a son; and if a son, then an heir of God through Christ.'[21]

According to whether one uses a religious or profane vocabulary, one can say that such a moral attitude is inspired by a sense of grace or a sense of generosity. Neither the moralist nor the theologian will, indeed, assimilate the two formulae. But in so far as our subject is concerned, they agree with common structures of attitude and behaviour. Moralism, understood as the predominance of the morose conscience, often allied with an utilitarian conscience, expresses a lower world, hardly detached from puerile terrors and convulsed by all the diseases of a primitive humanity which has only partly succeeded in

silencing its clumsily repressed instincts: its highest achievement is the
rationalisation of social conventions. Madame de Staël, remarking that
the legends and dramas of ancient times were rarely imbued with a
purpose of moral exhortation or edifying example, noted that the
moderns acquired this moralist concern, so unlike a spiritual concern,
from the habit, in business, of always moving towards a specific end.
Quite the reverse for the moralities of grace and generosity, which
with a heaven of exacting values above them, and a strictness of
present action, move towards an ever open future.

They are perpetually struggling to free the moral world of the
morose conscience. This inner 'non-resistance' of which Fénélon
spoke, provided one does not confuse it with the facile quietism of
indifference, has the additional advantage of not creating aggressiveness
around it. Harshness towards others is often a simple prolongation of a
moralising, masochistic aggressiveness. Neither the one nor the other
represents true spiritual firmness. When the rigorous critic allows his
morbid bitterness or his self-interested rigidity to appear, he does not
set the guilty person free, but provides him with a justification for his
faults by the injustice with which they are received. In return, if pardon
liberates, it is because it cuts through this vicious circle of aggression.

THE CHARACTEROLOGY OF MORALITY, OR VOCATION
WITHIN THE LIMITS OF CHARACTER

Moral life is not separable from spiritual life. It is its heaviest and
most organised layer, where the freedom of the spirit comes to terms
with the disciplines of the body, of reason and of society, in order to
find its way through a corporeal, causally determined and public
world. To isolate it is to reduce it to terms of mental hygiene, science,
good manners, or the utility which covers all three, so many ways by
which moralism can destroy morality.

The sole end of morality is spirituality, for which it does the
housework. If it knows how to simplify its preoccupation and respect
the freedom of the heart, it serves our vocations without restraint,
through the concrete diversities of time and place and temperament. It
runs riot as soon as it tries to play the queen and arrogate to itself the
pure intuition of spirit, which it will not find in the solitary revelations
of conscience, for morality is presence in the world and an effort
towards the world; nor in the logical universality of Kantian law, for
it is concrete vocation and perpetual incarnation in conditions that are
always particular. Every moral law tends to universality, but can never
be formulated in terms that are automatically and universally applicable.

It is the universalising principle in an infinity of particular behaviours, which never strictly imitate each other, but which permit, where there is creative fervour, a spiritual induction to which each responds according to the structures of his personal sphere. Each moral situation confronts us with a situation which is partly unprecedented and incomparable. In the time-space in which it advances towards me, there never has been, and never will be, a spiritual nexus precisely identical with the one I am to resolve by my act, this act, here, at this moment. Nothing is less capable of being made logically universal than the highest action of man. Some such actions, in a personality of great breadth, and stripped of their particular temporal significance, would even become a danger in the hands of ordinary men: such are the audacities and follies of saints. Others lose their nature if they are not exceptional, and in large doses would poison a society which they honour in their rarity: thus some suicides for the honour of a group, or some paradoxes of behaviour maintaining a precarious balance in lives one can neither justify nor condemn. Moral laws, and the psycho-physiological laws they bring into play, are more or less close approximations where only cross-checking can guide us: they will never replace the experience and the inner initiative in each moral decision, which provide the total response of an autonomous person to the total question of a prevenient world.

But law has a vital role in protecting personal experience from the infiltration of egocentricity. The dialogue between an incommunicable moral experience and the diverse forms of rule and common experience, does not impersonalise responsibility but makes virtue less of a possession.

The promptings of character occupy a peculiar position. In so far as a character approaches the general norm, then this character is the legal formula of a personal being, the most closely adapted to his inner vocation, but leading it towards an attempt at universality where it might prefer to remain in solitary complacency.

In so far as character defies analysis and disconcerts its own formula by resources springing from the heart of the person, then the characterological formula is, in regard to moral law, the first conceptually understandable form of the principle of differentiation and personalisation. The most universalised laws of behaviour must yield to possibilities and be applied in accordance with the resources offered by each formula.

In this sense the first duty of all morality is the knowledge and mastery, by the moral being, of his own character. In our moral treatises a chapter on moral characterology should precede the examination of the incidence of morality in our various spheres of action.

The first of its rules is: *Know yourself and accept yourself, because you will never be effective outside the paths and the limitations that have been assigned to you.* In other words, *Don't try to jump out of your skin.*

One hopes that this book has been modestly successful in showing that this knowledge is long and difficult to acquire, and is never final. Each of us presents a very summary view of himself to himself, and one that will not stand up to examination. The manner in which it is formed, the illusions it creates, and the way it defends itself against criticism are in themselves a criterion of character, and a simplification of oneself, like one's account of an experience immediately after it has happened which, growing gradually poorer year by year, finally blocks direct access to its recall. Thus I misrepresent all the secondary personalities I maintain around my main personality. It is often a social presentation of myself to others, varying according to the ideas of the day and the circles frequented. At other times it is a survival or an anticipation of myself, the obstinate expression of what I was and am no longer or the deceptive formulation of what I would like to be and am not able to be. It may finally express my reaction against myself, a system of protection against my deeper anxieties, a verbal compensation for my weaknesses, a consoling idealisation or a morbid depreciation of my ambiguities. These mirages reflect each other in a thousand ways. Only the robust simplicity of a committed life and great purity of vision can counteract their reflections, which science alone cannot decipher.

Strictly speaking, one should even say that to know one's character is always to react to one's character. One could start an interesting chapter of experimental characterology on the subject's reaction to his own character. Through these reactions passes the invisible suture between the moral aspect and the psychological aspect of our problem. The knowledge of oneself is always knowledge acquired by action and by the option for oneself.

At this point a new difficulty arises. Meditation and effort are necessary to carry out this admixture of self-discovery and self-education. But an excessive attention, a too sustained effort, may lead to the opposite result and clamp us down into moulds which may deform us instead of liberating us. The danger is visible even in childhood, more sensitively and flexibly receptive than ever again. If a child shows some tendency to gourmandise, to stubbornness, to vanity, if you keep on telling him he is greedy, or headstrong or conceited, you will probably, by the magic power of suggestion, stabilise the very fault you are trying to disparage and eliminate. It would have been cleverer to remove opportunities for such faults and distract the attention of the offender from them. Massive inhibitions, the abuse of authoritarian vetoes, often have the same effect: sometimes even the most affectionate goodwill towards the child, when it turns him too continually towards a diligent search for himself and his perfection. One must know how to mingle grace with discipline, relaxation with effort. Here we meet again the difficult dialectic of the will, which we have already discussed. Will, as it is still generally understood, this consciously applied pressure of the self upon the self, has to admit to being sometimes incompetent and inconvenient. It is incompetent to reach the whole (very considerable) unconscious area of our psyche. It often stabilises the tendencies it wishes to combat by attracting too much attention to them. It develops resistances which reinforce them, whereas a technique of distraction would have reduced them. More than once, finally, it is encouraged by the diffused sadism which is blended with the parental exercise of authority or by the masochistic tendencies of the person concerned. This narrow, tense morose will should not be confused with self-mastery, which is a broad strategy, rich in resources, which may, if necessary, employ direct attack, fierce passion, a straitness of the gate: if necessary, also indirect means; it needs real mastery to utilise an automatism, to clear the ground for a profound, vital rhythm, to organise a healthy distraction, to open up possibilities for a deviationary or exclusive tendency, and to lead it into a sublimation without direct repression: as much mastery and more as we often employ to bump our heads and wear out our fingers against the obstacle.

The inability to accept oneself is an ambiguous reaction: on the negative side it is a flight from reality, a pretext for inaction: on the positive, a bitter sense of our limitations, the will to pass beyond the frontiers of the individual and to answer the call of unknown lands beyond our customary landscapes. In this latter aspect there is no one with an intense personal life who has never felt tormented by the repetition of the too familiar gestures trammelling our freshest inspiration, and the desire to shatter a visage on which life has marked each of its stopping places. Expression liberates us if it stays with us, but enslaves us if it remains immobile. One day, perhaps by accident, we adopted an attitude. We formulated it, and the formula thenceforward holds us captive. The same with our opinions, our customs, our way of dealing with people, all our creations. This besieging of ourselves by ourselves, most accentuated in secondary types, irritates our profoundest sensitivity, lyricism and spiritual drive.

Age and temperament lend diversity to this common revolt. It is crude in many and is the basis of the bad temper and bitterness which ruin the joy of living. The vision of adolescence becomes attenuated between an exasperated affirmation of the self and an exasperated impatience with its limitations. This lack of acceptance may take on aggressive forms, self-destructive, as far as suicide or the systematic accusations of morbid melancholia. Sometimes it is disguised by a compensation which pins a moral appearance to the real personality, for instance, prudishness, preciousness, overlaying a foundation of savage instincts: moral conversion is then side-stepped by the mystification of outward show. The same result, more or less unconsciously desired, is obtained by all forms of evasion. One of the most common is a hopeless desire for perfection. All moral drives depend on the pursuit of some absolute. But the sense of the absolute is only moral if it is always incarnating definite, effective acts, whilst pursuing the ideal before it. The fear of action, however, leads the abstracting imagination towards an obsession with an absolute without content and without effect, which burdens us with a vague nostalgia. We have already met the illusion of all forms of swollen thinking, in which a repugnance to particular actions disguises itself as an aspiration towards the infinite. Speaking of Tolstoy,[22] Ossipond remarks that the concern for universal perfection, far from revealing an exceptional breadth of personality, indicates a narcissistic origin, whenever it results in anxious inactivity. It is much simpler to be fanatical than to be both human and exacting, to play at highmindedness in a circle of the highminded, embellishing a sheltered life by conventional language, than to live as a man of flesh and blood, sociable where necessary, moderate where necessary, intransigent where necessary.

'Consider that all desires are suspect,' wrote St. Francis of Sales to Mlle de Sulfour,[23] 'if, by the general agreement of good people, they cannot be followed by their effects: such are the desires for a certain Christian perfection which can be imagined but not practised, and which many persons turn into admonition but not action.

'Know that the virtue of patience is that which assures us the most perfection, and if we must be patient with others, we must also be patient with ourselves. We must endure our own imperfection to attain perfection.' And to the same recipient:[24] 'It is good to desire greatly, but we must order our desires and produce them each according to its season and our capacity. . . . It is good to prevent this multiplication of desire lest our soul should take pleasure in it, and neglect the effect, where the smallest execution is generally more useful than the majestic settings of things remote from our control, since God requires of us rather a fidelity to the little things which He has set within our power, than a fervour for great things which do not depend on us.'

Impatience with our limitations comes largely from the fact that we consider them too frequently from their negative side. These limitations are both the pattern, the evident surface and even the beauty of personality. Like the silhouette of our body they are the outer modelling of the forces which work within us. Usually, to refuse them is not to lift ourselves above them, but to opt for inconsistency. All grace excludes incompatible graces. The intellectual rarely knows the joy of the athlete and it is unlikely that one single life could add the tragic ardour of a Pascal to the sublime serenity of a Francis of Sales. There is a muddle-headed thinking, a petty impatience of limitations, found in those who cannot succeed in locating their personal lives by a definite choice and like to bedeck themselves with internationalism and all the religions of the world through an inability to live fully an openhearted concept of nationality or a universal concept of religion.

Let us be clear, however, that the choice of a dominant direction is not necessarily the choice of an exclusive direction. Jung, the psychologist who insists the most strongly today on the therapeutic value of spiritual unification, also describes this unity of the self as a pyramid of subordinated personalities rather than the monarchy of a principle. Man unifies himself by orchestration and not by impoverishment, and even our discords may contribute to the purpose of the symphony.

*   *   *

The rule of self-acceptance should not, in any case, be interpreted in a static manner. If character is a play of forces in movement, it can only be validated in connection with a correlated principle of self-surpassing. *You will never discover what you are (prospectively) except by perpetually denying what you are (statically).* But what concrete policy should result from the combined operation of these two rules?

We know by experience that to press too heavily on the lines of our character hardens them, develops parasitical expressions, constrains them to the point of cramping and stifling personality. In addition, we aspire to being more than we are, whilst being to the fullest extent what we are. We want to force our boundaries beyond their natural elasticity in order to become more fully human. 'All that is perfect of its type', said Goethe, 'should surpass its type.' And to illustrate this rather abstract formula: 'In many of its notes the nightingale is still a bird, and then it surpasses its species and seems to be wanting to show all the other birds what singing really means.' To counteract possible hardening, to achieve this enlargement, we need to treat our temperament by contraries, as the old hippocratic medicine said. But how to combine the two methods?

We find the answer in the very structure of our disposition. Temperament itself does not know morality. But, considered here from a moral angle, its inclinations move in two directions, one towards virtue, the other to a corresponding absence: the man who tends to be courageous is seldom merciful, he who loves gentleness usually lacks force, the generous are not prudent and the prudent not always generous. 'Follow nature' is therefore no certain guide to action, since nature is ambiguous. What is moral is the choice I make to push my natural inclination towards its virtue or its weakness or, better still, to enlarge it, without hope of complete success, in the direction of simultaneous realisation of the two complementary virtues which lie hidden within it and its opposite. One cannot therefore speak of nature, either from the aspect of force or value, as a uniform and constricting field of action. Natural inclination includes in itself an option for an ascending or descending movement: it is an enigmatic propulsion. I can let it pass into summary, explosive expression of low level and quality, or carry it to a high degree of sublimation,[25] raising the greatest area of the self to the greatest possible richness of values. This endeavour towards the highest potential of value may have an incomparably salutary effect even on the most elementary psychic equilibrium. Weakness and illness are almost always due to dissociations, and no force of assembly has such cohesive power as the high choice of values which integrates a vast area of personality. There is still much to be done to extend psychotherapy in the direction of an agiotherapy, or treatment of personality disorders by commitments of an ethical nature. There has been talk of a 'religious psychotherapy';[26] there is also occasion for an aesthetic and a philosophic psychotherapy. The resources of each realm of values would be applied according to the temperaments concerned. The curative value of these options of value is strictly independent of their value as truth. One might consider that an unstable and rather hypochondriac nature would profit greatly from the discipline and strong sense of incarnation afforded by

Catholicism: that an incurable schizoid would find a relative balance and a safety valve for his systematised reveries in a small, mystic sect: this does not mean that one is passing any judgment of truth, independently of such an individual, on the metaphysical value of Catholicism or the sect chosen.

Such building up should above all obviate the deformations entailed by a unilateral development of character. It encourages the virtues complementary to our natural virtues, and rarely removes their privilege of origin, but humanises them and amplifies them by a play of simultaneous and successive contrasts. It is one of the elementary principles of education: this choleric type should practise gentleness; this mystic, action; this extravert should be initiated into his inner life. The practical problem is to know how, and to what extent, this medicine should be administered. If it is too brusque it may break the resilience of certain natures. A sensitive, introverted child, brutally thrust into surroundings of games and laughter, may beat an even more frantic retreat into dreams. It is a mistake made by many parents to think that to be on the right track it is enough to weigh heavily in the opposite direction to any weakness. And yet it is always good to treat such weakness with a little violence.

Another error is to adjust the freedom allowed to inclination and the counter-thrust given to the opposing forces so exactly, with the idea of creating a 'balanced' individual, that they are neutralised in an ungolden mean, in which each of the conflicting elements has blunted the edge of the other's attack, and become immobilised against it. One should rather say that virtue and the summit of human quality are to be found, not in a mean, but on the summit of a ridge dominating two watersheds: goodness and lucidity, gentleness and virility, openness and reserve, discretion and audacity, wisdom and generosity, simplicity and penetration. Or, if we speak of a mean, we must specify that it is a mean of reason and not of situation, so that the 'golden mean' may sometimes be on the side of moderation but sometimes also on the side of passion.[27]

If this effort to create a balanced character is not to be harmful, it must try both to find a harmony of counter-values and to establish a solid central direction. To choose a point of attack, to choose it well and to bring all one's forces to bear on it, is the fundamental principle of tactical genius. Too many desires at once, or a nonchalance of action, and we are dispersed without any accumulation of knowing, or having, or knowing-how. Wanting to live on all our possible levels, or experience to the limit our incompatible contradictions, prevents us from living one life, our own. For each of us there is a line of character, as of intelligence, along which we can best utilise our strength and extract the maximum from our potentialities. Some techniques of spiritual life, based on the struggle against a principal defect, have understood this: they sometimes make the mistake, in practice, of systematically paying too little attention to resources and too much to a struggle against limitations. The whole policy of life rests on being able to single out in good time the two ridges of character, and to decide in time on the necessary sacrifices. It is not static equilibrium that we are trying to achieve, but a forward looking, dialectic tension between the axial drive of character, its lateral thrusts and the counter-thrust we bring to bear on it ourselves, in order to enrich and stimulate it. From one crisis to another, weighing first of all on the positive side of character even to the point of rigidity, then to the opposite side to the point of intolerance, then let our temperament take the reins again, and so on. To sum up the policy of flexibility: *Push each of your inclinations in the direction in which it will bring you the greatest richness and openness: disarm rigidity and exclusiveness: try to harmonise your character by its contrary dispositions, but keep it firmly organised along one master line.*

This dual attention can bring the characterological structure we are given to its highest degree of effectiveness. Can we go further, break with it, or at least distend its shape? After we have accepted our character and composed its counterpoints, can we surpass it? Or must we, in the name of science, allot to each individual a little card of strict directions and forbid him to exceed its formulae? Here we meet again, on a practical level, the problem we stated theoretically at the end of the first chapter. Modern psycho-physiology teaches us that though there are fixed connections between regions of the brain and certain psychological functions, alternative pathways are possible by which a healthy region can take over the role of a damaged region. These alternative pathways have sometimes shown themselves to be of astonishing breadth and disconcerting suddenness. What is possible in the relatively highly systematised and non-plastic material of elementary functions and their related nerve systems, cannot surely be suddenly impossible in the most mobile zones of the higher psyche. Experience teaches us no doubt that the highest sublimations of character still retain a certain form, or at any rate certain traits in common with their elementary expressions. But the psychology of conversion also offers us examples of such radical reversals, showing that at any rate some men, perhaps at the furthest possible limits of humanity, have proved the possibility of victory over the impossible. Without prejudice to what we have said about habitual behaviours, we should not confuse vocation with a determinism of dominant characteristics. Vocation is transpsychological. It must begin by accepting its data, but it may struggle against them to break their spell. Just as the framework of the species and of our personality will restrain most of our development within two limits, upper and lower, we are always more or less unaware of our coefficient of elasticity. Neither do we know that of humanity as a whole, nor the final direction of the road which has covered so much ground in the minor geological epoch since Neanderthal man. But what rules of mental health, what police force, or what morality will dare to forbid Icarus to break his wings so that twenty centuries later night pilots and war pilots may take their powerful flight?

*　　*　　*

Corresponding to the rules which govern our behaviour with regard to our own character, are the rules which direct our behaviour toward the character of others. They can be summed up in one basic principle: *Understand and accept the character of the other, for it is the only way to lead you to his mystery, to break down your own egocentricity and establish the working foundations of a life in common.*

The reaction we present to the character of others is indivisible from our attention to others, which we have already studied.

Our egocentricity projects all around us our ways of being and seeing. Just as the primitive diffuses his soul into his surroundings and peoples the world with gods and spirits in his own image, we easily believe that the world shares our tastes, our feelings, our judgments, our perspectives, and the more our egocentricity is strong and our inner vigilance relaxed, the more we believe it. In order to know ourselves we must first of all sweep away this projection of ourselves which conceals the face of others and our own.

Characters of unemotional type and especially those who are inactive, little vulnerable to their surroundings and little inclined to provoke or struggle with them, can easily protect themselves from contacts by a withdrawal into egocentric indifference, but not into aggression. Their own dynamic thereby loses its power of stimulation and appeal which comes from the presence of others.

A pharisaical harshness is still more common than indifference. It is indeed significant that a spiritual indifference to others is very often accompanied by violent moral bias, always of the critical sense. The reason is that indifference is a precarious equilibrium that few persons can maintain under the pressure of instincts, resentments and the bad conscience that arises from them. The child is already ferocious towards the faults or even the differences of others. A community of children eliminates without pity anyone who is noticeable for an accent, unusual clothes, or infirmity. Anything that separates or arouses comment is punished by ragging. This is, of course, the projective mechanism of the satisfied conscience with its counterfeit indignations, destined to divert bad conscience from enquiry into personal matters. Resemblance irritates as much as difference: the difference, particularly if it is in favour of the other, demoralises the unconscious feeling we have of our limitations, and when we respond to it without generosity it embitters instead of stimulating us: an obscurely perceived resemblance to a fault or vice reminds our weakness of that deep remorse we do not want to admit, and forces us to look upon an image of ourselves which we prefer to deny to consciousness. Even a resemblance to what is good is irritating, for although our own virtue is tinged with our inner warmth, virtue looked at from outside admits its poverty too flatly. This pharisaical harshness of reception does not ennoble us. We know the part played by that social occupation known as backbiting, but perhaps we do not always appreciate the way in which it slowly sterilises the moral sense. It has often a cruel lucidity, but this lucidity, paradoxically, seems to have no other effect than to increase our blindness towards ourselves, so true is it that knowledge is never a morally neutral activity.

The over-estimation of others and the burdening of personal consciousness by this systematic illusion is connected with the morose-ness of conscience and psychic weakness: such persons are either shattered by the presence of others, or feel compelled to make their admiration absolute in order to bolster up their own uncertainty. This idealisation of others reinforces inactive tendencies and inhibits moral life by chronic discouragement.

Another sign of psychic weakness is irritation by another's character. It occurs in the asthenic, unless he has made a personal effort to correct it, and is increased by the fatigue of adaptation, or the mere presence of others, and by the narrowing of consciousness. It is at its least in the well-adjusted. One should not confuse this elementary conditioning with openness or lack of openness. It does, however, facilitate or thwart the desire for communication of which it is a part.

A lucid attention to others is, on the contrary, the greatest aid to the knowledge and the perfecting of the self. As a neighbour, in a moral universe, the other is both approach and reproach: a means of approach and expansion by the attraction of his moral qualities: a moral reproach simply by the silent witness of his fidelity or infidelity to the values I have neglected. An accessibility to human reality and diversity provides both the greatest solvent of egocentricity and the greatest insight into my own inner diversity. A lucid indulgence (and not the lazy indulgence of indifference or the amorphous indulgence of idealisation) is the chosen weapon of comprehension: by awakening in others all that my generosity has first attributed to them, I kindle in myself the superabundance that generosity returns to generosity, a universe of unhoped-for resources.

Our reaction to others' reactions to our character is no less revealing. (With a little detachment, we could study them in the way others respond to our reactions to *their* character.) They are almost universally concerned, except in persons of a rare freedom of mind, with valuations and counter-valuations. Here again we find some, either inemotive or phlegmatic, who are indifferent to the judgment of others. The adapted type, with his vital need for approval, gives his friendship and his confidence without reserve to all who accept him as he is, ready, for the sake of maintaining affective unanimity, to blind himself completely to the partner, and to accept every illusion about himself. The maladapted, on the contrary, irritated by approval, react by a violent withdrawal or an aggressive twist: the passively maladapted underestimate the consideration available to them, and withdraw into their shell: the actively maladjusted snaps back and disconcerts the goodwill he does not desire: one observes him actively breaking friendships, rebuffing disciples, discouraging devotion. Opposition, on the other hand, calms them, but discourages the adapted, whom it throws like the inactive into a crisis of depression. It excites the emotive, if it does not disconcert them, particularly if, by a strongly marked secondarity, their inner dialectic enjoys this opposition, or if they are sufficiently active to appreciate rivalry and combat.

This play of actions and reactions continues without a halt when two characters are together over a length of time. They develop phenomena of sympathetic vibration which may have a considerable influence on their development in flexibility and lucidity. If inclined to a slight rigidity which, isolated, might dissipate its effects, they may eventually inhibit each other to the point of lethargy and lifelessness. Incomprehension invites incomprehension, and generosity, generosity. Thus we have the consolidation of collective atmospheres, in the family, society, marriage, etc. which are governed by indifference, sufficiency, phariseeism, irritation, indulgence and other moral attitudes.

*   *   *

The whole substance of character falls under the authority of moral life.

Is there an irresponsibility derived from certain irrepressible states? It is an idea that has been much abused by the supine indulgence of recent decades. One of the most common errors is to confuse unconsciousness with irresponsibility. Now the best and the worst of ourselves may emerge in an actual semi-conscious state: 'As far as we can judge,' wrote, at the height of determinist belief, the novelist of our ambiguities, Herman Melville,[28] 'blind moles that we are, the life of men seems only to move by mysterious suggestions: it is somehow suggested to us to do this or that. Truly any ordinary mortal who has somewhat considered himself, will never claim that even the least of his deeds or thoughts has its sole origin in his own well defined identity.' Must we admit that the best and the worst in us escape our knowledge, leaving us to a sordid housekeeping with our mediocrities? But the obscure voices of inspiration are only heard by those who have made their hearts available to them: thus, in the last resort, it depends on us whether we hear them or not. Similarly a slave mentality or a sophisticated intelligence can no longer find a dividing line between the good and the bad in instinct. Jean-Jacques Rousseau, who can hardly be accused of moral severity, wrote of this irresponsibility: 'No doubt they are no longer responsible for being bad or feeble, but they are responsible for becoming what they are.'[29] A somnolent consciousness likes profitable distractions, and knows how to confuse the arguments in order to avoid the trenchant clarity of decision: it excels at settling down to a false state of grace, by suppressing all the adjacent zones that might recall it to duty.[30] But it cannot thereby suppress responsibility, which has merely been displaced from the unfavoured clarity to the preferred nonchalance.

It is argued that, however rare they may be, there are cases showing a complete and invincible obliteration of the moral sense. The study of perversity seems to lead us to such a conclusion. In 1889 the International Congress of Medicine bestowed on it the name of 'moral insanity'. In some recidivist delinquents there had for some time been observed an almost total obliteration of every higher feeling, and even of the faculty of assimilating elementary moral concepts. Neither reason nor education nor affection had the least effect on their moral indifference. This deficiency allows extraordinary power to crude instinct. As a result there are deviations, usually interconnected, which have allowed Dupré to classify them as the syndrome of the perverse constitution.[31]

The perverse are obvious even in childhood (Arnaud). Even at this early age they seem to take pleasure only in evil. Neither force nor gentleness can touch them. Radically vicious, they spread vice around them, just as others radiate calm or energy. A precocious instinct of destruction expresses itself physically in the breaking, tearing to pieces or slashing of objects. They show no sincere emotion, although often simulating it for ulterior motives. They do not interpret their surroundings, like the paranoiac, but simply exclude them and oppose them without grounds. Their sexuality is usually precocious and already delinquent: they cannot be kept anywhere, expelled from every school, then a juvenile alcoholic, and delinquent, they evade or desert from military service, and if women, soon give way to prostitution. Their physiognomy is closed, scornful, the shifty gaze evades others in a sort of 'moral strabism' as if they wished to deny their presence which might entail a clear response and responsibility.
*

All the perverse . . . are not necessarily constitutionally perverse. Etienne Martin and Mouret considered that out of three hundred juvenile delinquents studied, only one or two showed instinctive perversity so great that their case history seemed inevitable. The Italian criminologists of the school of Lombroso stress the 'born criminal', but Lacassagne and the Lyons school emphasise in addition to constitutional weakness the decisive role of background. Freud saw the majority of perversions, apart from homosexuality, as an acquired regression to be attributed to excessive sexual repression.[32] More recently, dealing with difficult children, there was a stress on distinguishing between the perverse, the *false pervert* and the perverted.[33] The only true perversity is a prolonged, rebellious, moral indifference: thus the perverse should not be confused with the impulsive or morally careless. In the first the instincts are not so much deviated as exigent and turbulent: the moral sense is intact but is not used: the foundations are sound, without basic malice, as in the perverse: the disorder is in the power of inhibition, in behaviour rather than at the root of character. In the second we should speak more of the debility than of the obtusion of the moral sense, of slackness rather than of moral

* Clinical details of perversions and moral blindness.

indifference: there is a lack of tone, often predominantly physiological. But above all many cases of authentic perversity are acquired perversities, as we learn from the increasing number of cures. They are due to disappointments, rancours, infantile hatreds, unconscious affective shocks, or even from living as a child in an immoral background. They are often more a revolt than a true perversion: such as the bad feeling and coarseness induced by poverty. These many cases of acquired perversions are curable. Methods of treatment are being elaborated in many countries, whilst at the present moment France still throws the slightly contaminated into the promiscuity and abandonment of prison. It is essential, first of all, to rescue them from the immoral surroundings in which they usually live, and give them an atmosphere of confidence, work and strict control, which can be relaxed according to the progress of the cure. At the same time there should be attention to and encouragement for the faintest appearance of moral feeling which can also be stimulated (for instance, entrusting a habitual wanderer with an errand at a distance, a thief with important purchases). Complexes should be unravelled and sublimated. Cure is not indicated by an exceptional action, often followed by relapse, but by the persistence of rehabilitation.

The margin of perversity which eludes personal and educational effort seems therefore slender. Some authors have extended the sphere of freedom yet more audaciously and seen a kind of moral option at the root of all neuroses and psychoses. For Adler every neurosis is a form of falsehood, *Unechtheit*, a more or less unconscious counterfeit produced by the patient to cover up an incapacity. For Prinzhorn, psychosis is a reaction of self-esteem which grafts a lie on to a vital weakness to which the subject will not resign himself. Dr. Pichon, for his part, writes:[34] 'The key to all purely psychiatric syndromes of childhood is a moral key. The lack of self-mastery, leading to a failure on the part of the child to control his appetites, to sacrifice certain desires on the altars of others, is always the origin of purely psychiatric disorders, however diverse they may be.' We know also that a constitutional predisposition is in no sense an inevitable cause of psychosis. Naturally in the majority of cases it is impossible to distinguish amongst the obscure sources of mental disorder, the ounce of responsibility which has finally swung over a vast weight of predisposition. But psychiatric fatalism appears more and more to be an over-simplification of problems.

In the light of these modern findings it is less surprising therefore to find theologians, to whom communal life has given a great experience of men, introducing moral considerations where we do not naturally expect to find them. Thus they considered sadness a sin, at least that 'sadness of the world' which Cassian opposed to the 'sadness of God', and which he contrasts with St. Paul's portrait of Charity, as 'harsh, impatient, hard, full of rancour and chagrin and painful despair'; the same for *accidie*, the general vague disgust with the place where one is and the persons one meets, which Cassian identifies with a 'spirit of laziness', product of idleness and an uneasy mind.[35] And also for the agitation of mind which introduces tumult where faith and hope require an unoccupied conscience available and abandoned.

Alongside the theologians we find, unexpectedly, psychologists who also admit the introduction of moral determinations after a sustained effort to banish them from psychology and psychiatry. Few psychologies have been as systematic in this as the Freudian, and the part Freud attributes to sexual prohibitions in the genesis of neurosis would seem directly counter to any moral determination. But, unlike his disciple Reich, the apologist of integral sexual liberty, Freud did not venture to pronounce judgment. And Ernest Jones, who owes so much to psychoanalysis, asserts that the reduction of sexual constraints would be followed by a considerable loss in the values we attribute to life and love.[36] Quite recently an independent disciple of the school, M. de Saussure, with a Freudian outlook full of good sense, tried to establish some moral directives: to know oneself, so that one's unconscious complexes do not undermine one's personality, to allow a healthy satisfaction to one's instincts, which avoids the ill effects of repression and substitutes sublimation for clumsy inhibition: to encourage the priority of reality and of altruism which save us from becoming schizoid: and to free the path for the expansion and the inventivity of the person.[37] We are not discussing the content of these instructions. What is interesting about them is that it is an effort to find a common ground between science and morality. It is never science that can provide an imperative.[38] But as it explores the heart of man, each of its findings, without changing its nature, can become part of a picture which enlightens the subject, even if it has not the authority to decide. When psychoanalysis has replaced an unconscious neurotic conflict by a human and conscious one it has not, as Dalbiez points out, provided a solution to the conflict, which can only be resolved by the patient. But it has raised the level of the conditions of action, and dealt a better hand to the autonomy of the self against the tyranny of the Superego.

A number of facts therefore induce us to ask whether a spiritual attitude, I would not say always fully deliberate and conscious, does not often underlie the determinations of character: thus, for instance, the Pascalian 'diversion' seems to play an important role in the genesis of schizoid states or of extraverted excesses, a flight from commitment and a flight from oneself.

*   *   *

Though the moral point of view may have authority over the whole range of characterological facts, this does not authorise it to exceed its competence by intervening without discretion in the fragile mechanisms of psychological processes. The imperialism of objective science is sometimes confronted by an imperialism of morality, or at least of moralism, which is often deadly to personal balance. We have alluded to the imponderable responsibilities which can be found even in neurosis and psychosis. But they are not, under any hypothesis, introduced by a clear understanding. Bearing this in mind, it is possible to reconcile all we have said with the no less energetic assertion of Dr. Forel that no neurosis was ever due to lack of will-power, or was ever cured by will-power. We have said how useless it was to preach effort to the depressed. Dalbiez[39] quotes the case of a young girl who tried to cure herself of a morbid masturbation by a simple attempt at religious fervour: she achieved a tension so intolerable that she nearly lost her reason. There has been an attempt to outline a psychology and a therapy of the seven cardinal sins.[40] Elsewhere a distinction has been drawn between cases where laziness is a fault and where it is an illness.[41] This attack on moral over-simplification is as necessary as the attack on medical over-simplification. Just as it is not the deliberate choice of a religious subject which gives a religious quality to a poem or a painting, so it is not by the application of moral commonplaces, often based on prejudice and routine, that personal effort can master delicate psycho-physiological mechanisms. For the benefit of ethics we should leave the word to doctors and psychologists for a long while yet, though preventing them from shackling our sphere with a pseudo-scientific pessimism.

We must equally avoid attaching a coefficient of praise or blame to any particular structure of character. We generally tend spontaneously to erect our own character as a norm of morality. This meticulous person, to whom disorder is anguish more intolerable than any other, against which he protects himself by his fastidiousness, sees disorder as *the* cardinal sin, which begins wherever a little liberty or fantasy disrupts the immutable arrangement of his time and his possessions. The bohemian despises as the servility of a bourgeois spirit any method in education, restraint in expenditure or cleanliness of appearance. The floridly well balanced suspects the asthenic of slackness and ill will. The emotive, who experiences in himself the attraction of emotional vibration, accuses the phlegmatic person of indifference and mediocrity, without asking whether still waters may not run deep, and if his own fevers are not sometimes more an agitation of temperament than spiritual warmth. The same phlegmatic person, in revenge, does not fail to consider the highly strung as superficial creatures, incapable of serious plans or lasting fidelity. The majority of the handbooks which call themselves so erroneously handbooks of psychological training, take it for granted that we want to be nothing but men of action, energetic, of regular habits, meticulous, slightly plethoric, entirely directed towards success and bourgeois happiness. We should once and for all cure ourselves of this moral myopia, which is one of the numerous forms of egocentricity. It is no more healthy when it reverses the appreciation and confronts the self, discouraged at being what it is, with the over-estimation of a type of character whose chief attraction lies in its being unachievable. Apart from a very limited number of exceptional graces and definitive disgraces, *there are no good or bad data of character*. There are poor temperaments and rich temperaments, there are combinations more difficult than others, but even the most thankless are capable of sublimation and even of transfiguration by heroism and by sanctity. Even petty bourgeois mediocrity found its Jacob's ladder in the little Sister of Lisieux.

Not everything that passes for sin is sin, nor everything that passes for virtue, virtue. The century of comfortable morality was scandalised by Nietzsche's criticism. It was already there in La Rochefoucauld. And before him, in Pascal. And before Pascal, the sharp mediaeval moralists had never ceased to denounce the lies of false virtue. But there comes a moment when a too uniform note is no longer heard, and one has to shout to attract attention. Re-read, for instance, Cassian's *Institutiones* with its attacks on the vanity that apes virtue. Re-read the mystics, speaking of the apparently highest states of spiritual ascesis. 'Dryness', wrote St. John of the Cross, 'is not always due to the passive purification of the senses: it may often accompany sin, lack of energy, lukewarmness, even a disordered mood or bodily indisposition.' As we see, the same apparently virtuous state may be due to three possible and radically different sources; supernatural origin, a psycho-physiological origin, or a moralising mystification. We have already met a hundred times this ambivalence of virtue, the rigidly punctual meticulousness of the nervous, the false chastity of the repressed, the false piety of the sentimental, the false love of the mania for protection and egocentric devotion, the false goodness of the weak, the false mercy of the inactive, the false generosity of the prodigal, the false obedience of the inferiority feeling, the false ingenuousness of the puerile, the false indignation of the envious, the false autonomy of the anarchist, the false serenity of the lymphatic, the false moderation of the mediocre, the false strictness of the rigid, the false spontaneity of the impulsive, the false gravity of the satisfied, the false nobility of the eloquent, the false contrition of the guilt complex, and so on. It is difficult to stop: there is no virtue that is not followed, like a shadow, by an ambiguous double, which turns and devours it as soon as it contemplates itself with any complacency. A good conscience is on the watch for these profitable weaknesses in order to build up a bargain price morality. The first modern criticisms of morality played havoc with this confused virtue, but in the long run it helps us to distinguish a morality in spirit and in truth. Not a discarnate morality and 'pure' with an impossible purity, but a morality moving dialectically between an immense benevolence and a high severity, its purity lying in measuring neither the one nor the other.

RELIGIOUS EXPRESSION AND CHARACTER

Since we are here judging attitudes and not directly the values which inform them, we cannot take as criterion of religious man his adherence to a positive religion. This adherence may be pure sociological conformity, whilst there is a religious way of being atheist. Whether positive or negative, religion from the angle of man, which covers only a portion of its field, always proposes to some degree to bring man into touch with the most intimate part of himself, to bring him into communion with a social, moral, cosmic or supernatural reality greater than his own individuality, and to lead towards an aspiration to surpass himself. Religious life is thus a general mobilisation of human forces. There is no aspect of the human condition into which it does not claim to introduce its influence. . . . Practised by men of flesh and blood, it is mingled with their flesh and blood in the empirical existence it has in them. However great its effort to maintain its transcendence, it always offers to the observer, and even to the uneasy heart that seeks it, this deceptive admixture. Much confusion in religious and anti-religious polemics arises from the fact that one is normally too inclined to accept the appearances reflected by a diversity of temperaments and historical conditions[42] as the authentic expression of a religion. Religions are constantly threatened with dissociation through these refractions, and their dislocating activity would suffice to justify the existence of a Church through the need for religious integrity. Characterology is not qualified to speak of the basis of the religious problem. But it can be of considerable help in disentangling the ambiguities of the arguments which claim to deal with the essence of religion but only touch its adulterations or its psycho-physiological substitutes.

The religion of the adult is rarely free from affective weaknesses and survivals coming from his childhood and, beyond childhood, from the primitive mythological stores of humanity.[43] It would be useful both in religious training and, as it were, to a geological study of the religious attitudes of the adult, to formulate the various ages of religious awareness, from birth to puberty. Such a study has not yet been carried very far.[44] Up to almost the third year, the discovery of the self and of the external world is enough to occupy the infant's mind. Nothing could surpass in majesty the image formed by the omnipotence of the father. We should follow, from this age onwards, the formation or absence of religious feeling in the child who receives a religious initiation and in the one left to himself. The first representations of religion are grafted on to the sense of dependence the child feels towards the parents who instruct him, and are blended with fear and affection according to the composition of their own feelings.

In authoritarian families there is a unilateral development of the attitude of fear-laden reverence, which lasts a lifetime, particularly if it has been engraved on the imagination by terrifying or fantastic pictures: the adult thus formed cannot conceive of any other attitude on the part of the faithful except of passive submission, and God Himself as a strict father, or vengeful judge, always spying and punishing. This state of mind is not solely to be found, as one might think, in the adherents of the transcendental religions. Irreligious minds brought up in the same atmosphere easily find equivalents of this sacred terror. Some are as much intimidated by science as by the most jealous of deities. Humanity, the Progress of Enlightenment, Race, the Revolution, have produced no less fanaticism and no fewer hecatombs than the passions of the Church. One sees 'emancipated' minds clinging to a hundred minor superstitions. Bernard Shaw relates how, one day, in a mixed gathering of believers and sceptics he told the story of the atheist[45] who pulled out his watch and challenged God, if He existed, to strike him down within five minutes. He wanted to show his audience that no one had anything to fear from such an act of defiance, neither the atheists, for whom God does not exist, nor the believers, who would not accept that the God of Justice and of Truth should be at the mercy of a parlour trick. Having explained all this, he said he was going to repeat the atheist's challenge. But, he adds, no doubt there were no true believers nor true atheists in the hall, for everyone left before the five minutes were up. Bernard Shaw was no doubt neither a true believer nor a true atheist himself, or he would have seen the bad taste of the joke. It is none the less probable that a vague terror, both more primitive and less profound than a religious feeling, took possession of his audience, a feeling they would not have been able to rationalise. The 'fear of God' of the higher religions is part of this overwhelming sense of majesty and infinity inseparable from the religious feeling, which, however, avoids cherishing the flavour of morbid terror which obstructs the way of religion of love and truth.

The filial confidence which the child displays towards supernatural presences includes both an attitude that is more abandoned and more generous, and therefore often more truly religious than that of the adult, and an infantile element of passive submission, irresponsibility, and naïve tenderness which should last only for a time. When it persists it gives a puerile and mawkish tone to religious behaviour, falsely confused with a 'childlike spirit' and spiritual humility. It infests pious literature, cloys the piety of the adolescent and undoes the virility of the adult. We have to thank these failures of spiritual puberty for one of the aspects of the religious world which is most repellent to modern minds trained to a certain vital simplicity, even to a certain hardness. In addition, numerous cases of semi-neurotic hostility to religion are only the transference to God of a hostility to the father of flesh and blood.

The child's imagination imposes his store of myth and all his prelogical faculty of symbolisation on the first religious ideas presented to him. This is no cause for scandal: our deepest convictions employ many different successive languages in the course of our lives, and each of them appears later intolerably crude as compared with the new, although each was used to express, beneath its provisional terms, the same veiled truth. We should go further and adapt elementary religious instruction more closely to the mentality of this early age, burdening it with fewer indigestible abstractions and proofs without effect on a childish mind. But we should also see to the replacement of these fantasies, not by the elimination of the marvellous, which springs from nature and the destiny of man, but by the substitution of metaphysical marvels for imaginary marvels or, if we wish to keep in touch with this first poetry, by deepening the imaginary marvel into the metaphysical marvel. Hume remarked that there was as much astonishment at hand over the germination of a grain of wheat as in any authenticated miracle: he might also have spoken of the heart of man. Not that to believers the miracle is imaginary. But they have often a way of accepting it which is more appropriate to the magic of childish imagination than to faith. If it has not shed these early precipitates of the imagination, the religion of the adult is laden with assertive beliefs, a lazy resort to a crude 'supernatural' and animistic and pantheistic explanations which discredit faith in the eyes of the intelligent.

The next phase of childhood, from seven to twelve, is the age when, under the influence of a realistic discovery of the world, and of objective relationships, there should be a springcleaning of this childish sense of religion. Puberty brings a renewal of mystical and introspective fervour: it is the period of great conversions and great vocations. The drive towards the absolute is indispensable to give life at its outset sufficient living energy to withstand the deadening influence of maturity. But it must come to terms with reality or it will soon be lost in chimaeras, in utopias, in a diffused, disincarnate religiosity. This age is also the age of revolt. Frequently it turns against the exteriorised forms of religion, against the too authoritarian, or too indiscreet pressure with which religious beliefs have been inculcated, or against the automatism of a practice in which habit has killed life very early; sometimes the religious feeling is swept away indirectly with the social or family authority with which it was associated. When this revolt is perpetuated, instead of calming down and coming to terms with life, or inspiring a stronger or purer religion, then it develops into an aggressive religiosity, swollen by years of accumulated resentment, and sometimes stricken by the lockjaw of interminable negation.

Social adaptation, success, the acquisition of a definite framework of life, all this offers a powerful resistance to the religious feeling in adult life. Old age will either crystallise this resistance or encourage the renewal of religious meditation at a time when the problem of death becomes more pressing and instincts less impulsive.

This is only the outline of a history which needs much further study. It shows the first origins of what we might call corporeal religion. If the very movement of religion is to burn up and little by little transfigure this body of clay lent to it by man, one cannot conceive of any humanly incarnate religion not being subject to its laws, unless it perishes and man with it. The 'impurity' of which the great religions are accused on this point, far from speaking against them, is a proof of their clarity as to the condition of man.

*   *   *

The spontaneous religiosity which inspires primitive religions is much more dependent on climate, soil, race and social status than the great revealed religions, with their powerful spiritual forces. It seems, however, that even in more advanced and relatively homogeneous civilisations, the unease and almost physical mobility of the Germanic peoples, or the savage independence of the Anglo-Saxon populations, encouraged a reaction against the rational architecture and the strongly centralised power of the Roman Church. Breton mysticism, somewhat sharp and inconvenient but imbued with tenderness, may equally well produce an orthodox St. Colomban, or a rebellious Lamennais or Renan. Western religions, in varying degrees, are juridical, rational, individualist and realist in their forms of expression: many Eastern religions, in spite of considerable differences between them, are plunged in a vast, mystic dream, immobilised in a common recoil from temporal action. Nietzsche contrasted Northern Christianity, active, anti-pessimist, with an ascetic, Asiatic Christianity, saying no to life, which he attributed to Jewish influences. In religious matters as elsewhere, the countryside is the home of more loyalties and more fanaticisms and encourages a mystic sense of nature and meditation: the towns promote creativity and heresy, a liking for works and an uneasy fervour. A country in which authority is strongly organised, as in the France of Louis XIV, supports a strict and disciplined religion, whilst at the same time provoking the revolt of libertinism and a Jansenist *Fronde*. The political and philosophic liberalism of the last two centuries has automatically brought in its wake a religious liberalism: political forms are not entirely divorced from the destiny of the spiritual. The passion of irreligion also obeys the winds of history. For over two centuries the West has seemed to be invaded by a slow death of God: perhaps it is only a twilight of the idols with which we have obscured the face of God, a second Golgotha necessary to a second Easter. But psychology must take into account that one is more and more likely to be born an atheist just as in earlier periods one was naturally born a Christian. Forms of behaviour take shape little by little around this attitude to life: here carefree utilitarianisms, a total blunting of the sense of interiority: there, on the other hand, an atheism lived as an inner experience and a spiritual combat: experienced here as a desperate hardness in a voiceless universe, there by the intense, somewhat egoistic serenity of the disciples of Epicurus; elsewhere by the attentive coldness of a composed mind, or inversely, by a despairing pity for the destiny of men.

The structure of our religious mentality is most often that we have received from our family: which we preserve as we have known and loved it, cherishing it with the warmth born of childhood memories, or which we have formed in reaction against the family religion, and thus still under its influence: a badly controlled resentment may then as much explain the narrowness of perspective as a docilely accepted routine. The mentality of the day, the circles frequented, add their mark to the background of tradition. As a minority, submerged in a persecution or dominant environment, religion becomes fanatical, prickly with defences, stifling the discovery and the radiance of its riches by uneasy apologetics: or, if its blood runs thin, becomes shamefaced, begging for indulgence, toning down its dogma. Decadence abounds in conciliations but, at the same time, produces the great reforming movements, and sees a flowering of sects of initiates, savouring amongst themselves the last spices of a banquet which is ending. One should add that the Spirit bloweth where it listeth, and can cause as many exceptions as can be wished to these categories of influence.

* * *

Instinct closed in upon itself, with its double taint of egoism and automatism, senses the religious mind as a too direct menace and tries to reduce it by cunning and domestication where it cannot be eliminated. The mysteries and the dynamic of eroticism contrive to associate in uneasy partnership with the more uncouth forms of religious sentiment. Sometimes the adolescent baptises his tumult and mingles the exaltation of his senses with the fervours of his faith, if he does not simply take the one for the other. Sometimes the confusion is already canalised in a process nearer to sublimation: in a young man, the cult of the Blessed Virgin; in a girl, the love of Christ or attachment to a young priest: both a part of a search for sexual balance and may contribute to it, just as they may go astray under the influence of too unco-ordinated drives. Religiosity often replaces religion in frail adolescent boys, and if they fail to achieve virility it prolongs their feminine sensitivity and their vague disquiet into adult life, producing a compromise of religious feeling with a gentle sensitivity, happy to find itself thus idealised without the sacrifice of its gourmandise. . . . Primitive religions are usually much more crudely and overtly sexualised. But the higher religions struggle against such *quid pro quos*. When St. John of the Cross met them on the confines of mystic states, he accused them of arising from 'a certain weakness of sensuality' and refused them any status in the city of the spirit. It is not only the strength of the sexual instinct which enables it to slip into religious feeling, but sometimes its weakness which adopts religiosity as a form of compromise, as in those women who, neither entirely women nor entirely nuns, too little feminine to give themselves to love, too irresolute to give themselves to the cloister, pursue a vague, unrealised ideal of their youth through the course of an uneventful life.

Other instinctive elements may enter into the composition of certain forms of religious feeling: the masochistic element, for instance, is strongly marked in all forms of puritanism.

Good health, that enemy of disquiet, may for long maintain religious indifference, in so far as it offers at each instant a plenitude of satisfactions and settles down into a somewhat plethoric egoism. A superabundance of vitality seeks for outlets, and soon finds a substitute for religious fervour in social satisfactions suitable to the easy conscience: a playfulness of human intercourse and a devoted agitation, both occupations for soul and body which can sometimes be enhanced by very fine qualities. The diversionary effects of good health are then rather like habit, which makes belief or unbelief automatic and which stifles metaphysical drives under its cushioning mechanisms. Every religion suffers from this, as, in the course of its life, it extends its apparatus. The prophetic outbursts which occur throughout the history of Churches attack the religion of habit as much as their corruption. Individually speaking, temperaments subject to perseveration are more exposed than others to this slow decay of religious life.

God evident to the heart, such is the dominant need of the emotive. His burning faith consumes as it approaches and one might say that his true mission—*ignis ardens*—is to maintain this sacred fire against all the chill winds that menace it. He produces the most impetuous of apostles and martyrs. If he is active his faith is militant and headstrong: intrepid and authoritarian with regard to unbelievers, he represents an ardent fanaticism compared with the dogmatic fanaticism of abstract thinkers: if incredulous, he is so with enthusiasm: the born persecutor.

St. Paul is the patron saint of both types. But emotivity is also at the source of many religious aberrations. It fosters all exaltation, from collective hysterical delirium, a ritual amongst certain sects, to the unhealthy fever of some forms of piety. It tends to subjectivise religious feeling to the point of reducing it to a sentimental glow, happy in its own feelings, producing either a state of trance or a pious purr: of such is the parish of the *Vicaire Savoyard*. It creates heretics, who cling to a divergence like a child to its anger, and fanatics in whom intolerance is a fever in the blood. It sustains both the best and the worst in religious anguish: the deep concern without which formalism triumphs, but also diffused and childish terrors, feverish perplexity and, in the Jewish people, that nameless anxiety, that mobility of heart, mind and body, which flickers like a flame in their eyes.
*

*   *   *

Christianity has often been accused, from Nietzsche onwards, of serving to defend the vanquished and of deifying the needs of the weak. This criticism is based on certain parasitical facts which develop in times of failing religion. Some go to seek in religion a consolation for an unrooted heart, others an audience for their laments, others an insurance against the anguish of a purposeless life and the risks of an adventure with uncertain outcome, others a means of not having to struggle with the urgent problems of life. And faith is, indeed, a powerful rampart for weak natures. It produces a synthesis which is the strongest possible support for the neurasthenic, as a specialist, Dr. Vittoz[46] has declared. But those who have experienced a more virile and attacking religion will deny that it can be reduced to a mental hygiene. Weakness of vitality has so little to do with religious fact that it leads away from faith as much as towards it. Many 'lose their faith' in the way the neurotic successively 'lose' their relatives, their friends, the objects around them. They have no longer the strength to hold it. Such are the nervous and the inactive, whose fervour is always lapsing (Vigny). An attempt has been made to link mystics with neurotics. Janet suggests that they may be those who, fearing action, seek ecstasy as a perfect immobility of the will. This explanation sounds somewhat strange when applied to a St. Augustine, a St. Theresa, a John of the Cross, whose lives speak to the contrary. As Dr. Laignel-Lavastine writes: 'the psychism of the mystics is different from that of the neurotic, in that it denotes an increase and

* Religious expression related to Heymans' categories.

not a decrease of psychic energy. It can be distinguished by this criterion, on which St. Theresa insisted most strongly, and is important as a means of eliminating the false mystics who have abounded at all times.'[47] The great centuries of religion knew faith as a rugged strength, a healthy sapling, taking deep root and its sap pushing its boughs towards all the winds of heaven. The faithful, when they sinned, sinned with energy, but then plunged into the solitude of the cloister. Western Christianity was not built by lawyers and scholiasts, but by somewhat savage knights, men of honour, passing from the battlefield to the monastery, shaping men before they shaped out their pastures, and then, as monks, standing firm against the powerful and, undergoing a savage self-discipline, still finding time to care for the wayfarer.

Man cannot be thrown into the mystery of the world without support from his unconscious forces. Primitive religions rely almost exclusively upon them. Romantic religion restored them to a place of honour and we see their unbridled activity in some contemporary 'mysticisms'. Roman Catholicism keeps them more under control by providing the safety valve of the confessional and collective ritual. In puritan countries, they explode in little, violent sects, or overflow into a sentimentality of the whole religious life. The more a religion is socialised and intellectualised, the more it tries to be conscious and develops a cult of consciousness. But the psyche within us is not entirely at our disposal. The enlightened, conscious religion (or irreligion) which we have built up is constantly battered by the waves of unconscious life, much vaster than the conscious, much broader than individuality. Jung[48] has analysed at length the way in which universal religious themes returned by devious routes—particularly in dreams—to the Unconscious of an intellectual young man, who was otherwise extremely sceptical, lucid and self-controlled, until he was overcome by neurosis. Beneath religious attitudes, whose conscious pattern was particularly clear, one would no doubt often hear disturbing echoes from the great deep. Little superstitions, designed to ward off the avenging presences around one, reveal the repression of complexes of guilt.

*   ★   ★   ★

We have already established the relationship between a certain religiosity and psychic weakness. The fear of action, derived from it, shows a similar picture. Religion frequently serves as a support for the

---

* Religious life related both to Heymans' categories, to introversion and extraversion and to the cycloid and schizoid types.

fear of living, in times of spiritual debility. One has only to observe the high peaks of religion, at their greatest historical effectiveness, in order to see that their main destiny lies elsewhere than in this vital depression. However, the fear of living does lead to several religious deviations. When obsessional, it fosters scruple, particularly in the introverted, and with this, childish terrors. Or, the exact contrary, it quenches religious concern and converts religious feeling into a security system which guarantees a man against the dialectic impulses of his warring, unsatisfied nature. A belief in the supernatural, divorced from its true meaning, is an easy shelter for sloth in action.[49] This attitude characterises weak religiosities in particular: don't believe too much, was the gist of Emerson's teaching, you will save yourselves trouble: when you meet a difficulty, let yourself go, for the soul which always refuses a fight is always victorious, and lulls you to sleep with its gentle soothing authorities. Harshness of social or family pressure may also create in the very centre of religious feeling a behaviour of passive obedience, obsequious towards authority, directing worship towards the Father, the omnipotent judge, rather than towards Christ as a brother. Constant persecution and perhaps a psychological awareness of circumcision have developed the same feeling in the Jews.[50] Strictness of doctrine and jurisdiction tend to promote it in many Catholics; incapable of living the full life of a disciplined community, they place their own initiative in their hands, and thus materialise the authority they are trying to honour.

The promise that divinisation and the presence of the Kingdom of God may begin, if we wish, in this world, is, however, a powerful stimulus to action: it even offers a temptation to the instinct of power: Nietzsche could only admire, in Christianity, the fighting Princes of the Church, the great nobles and conquerors of the Renaissance, the rulers of peoples, who, we might argue, hardly represent the highest ideals of Christianity. In some phlegmatic types the love of action invades religion to such an extent that it becomes the optimism of the business man, or at best, a philanthropy. Such was Channing, the founder of Unitarianism, who has been called the Babbit of Christianity, he had a terror of mysticism, enthusiasm, dogma and authority: his deliberate altruism situated faith somewhere between benevolence and civic virtue.

Although they invite man to seek God in the depths of his own heart, the great religions wage open warfare against egocentricity, which encourages the aggressive powers of instinct, hinders spiritual communication, destroys the sense of neighbourliness and dislocates the sense of community. The believer is always praying like Claudel, 'Lord, deliver me from myself'. But egocentricity sometimes takes its revenge by developing religious individualism, of which there have been many sudden explosions in history, when the pressure of the Church has been too heavy. It leaves the sinner alone, alone with his sin, alone with the uncertainty of his destination in eternity: sometimes his life gains thereby in grandeur, but it may also be overwhelmed by anguish and try to defend itself by reflexes of puritanical rigidity. Religious individualism, when it does not run to the absolute autonomy of 'inner religion', also develops that secret enjoyment, that mystic sensuality, that domestication of religious feeling to the service of peace of mind or practical enjoyment which St. John of the Cross outlawed so violently from religious life.

Every variety of communal feeling finds expression in religious states, from collective exaltation of a hysterical character in primitive religious assemblies, to a reasoned tolerance or to a sense of mystical communion in the same spiritual body. The sense of religious community is so powerful that it is only extended with difficulty to the unbeliever. This difficulty is particularly great when the religious community is identified with the physical community, which colours it with its own jealous strength (tribal and national religions). But the difficulty may also occur through individual psychological factors. Thus schizoids are happiest in sects which allow them to distinguish themselves from mass religions and quietly to introduce, between their own frontiers and the vast world of the uninitiated, that abrupt cleavage which is their favourite protection. Those who do not go so far as the adoption of bizarre cults, turn religion into a protective zone, outside which lurks the anguish they have once and for all expelled. Contrary to the beliefs of a timid liberalism, intolerance appears therefore to be the product of a weak or inverted religion: it yields, on the other hand, to a depth and quality of faith which can also maintain the strictness of its spiritual loyalties.

When a believer depreciates intelligence, one should consider whether he is not in this way liquidating some personal defeat in the understanding of his faith, or whether he is not cherishing an atmosphere of childish and unreflecting belief in the warm shelter of childish fixations, in order to escape the conflicts it would otherwise involve. The phenomenon is fairly common, particularly in women, to the extent that some have equated religious feeling with prelogical thinking, or a taste for intellectual obscurantism. Pleasure in intelligence is, however, the sign of a robust faith, *fides quaerens intellectum*, a faith seeking intelligence, seeking light even more than warmth, knowing that no heat is enduring if not nourished by light. It is, however, in the nature of faith that no intelligence can free it from concern, dispense with the risk of the generous action which is the primary condition of religious activity. No system of dogma, no ritual discipline, no warmth of collective communion can root out of man's heart the original spiritual anguish, the experience, at first disquieting, and then overwhelming, of the meeting with spiritual fact. It is a hard experience, and no one can undergo it, whether the final response be yes or no, without his life being changed. A great many of the attitudes which men call religious are, in fact, systems of defence against the religious attitude. Many persons use for this purpose the means devised by religion to enumerate, canalise and construct religious experience, not to stifle it. They lull it to sleep to the murmur of ritual cycles, they barricade it with blind belief, narrow reasoning, systems that are sometimes accommodating and sometimes aggressive but always protective. The dogma dispenses with the need for thought, providence with the need for risk, reason with the need for awe. These defensive attitudes, most frequent in the emotive and the anxious, are not exclusive to believers. Unbelief has as many barricades against the fundamental religious alternative as the religious conformities have refuges.

Like ordinary life, therefore, religious life may be invaded by the sombre, viscous vegetation of moral repressions and masochistic rigidity. This danger is greatest where there is no safety valve for the turbulent strength of powerful, even shattering feelings, such as the sense of sin, or the sense of the eternal responsibility of action. We know the benefit of confession and prayer from this psychological angle alone. Perhaps Protestant societies seek a substitute for the confessional and the release it offers, in their extensive utilitarian and philanthropic activities. Sometimes, as in the Oxford Groups, they attempt a direct substitution. We know that psychological analysis in all its forms, Freudian, Adlerian, Jungian, has developed much more in Protestant than in Catholic countries. It is certainly an important psychological function of religion to act as a release for the obscure zones of the self.[51] 'Casting all your care upon Him, for He careth for you' (1 Peter v, 7). This release is of tremendous importance in the Christian religion in which, with God, the communion of the Saints takes over the burden of man. A healthy religious life thus makes for free and liberal minds: only unhealthy expressions encouraged by a too inhibited or solitary religious life lead to uneasy religiosities.

Indefinitely many are the visages of men to walk the stage of religious life. But this shadow play leaves us still only at the gates of the religious universe, properly speaking. Nowhere do we find such a striking, almost scandalous ambiguity of the psychological person: this heady, indissociable blend of a vocation in which religious action, seen from the aspect of man, is nothing but creative detachment and a bundle of particularities, so many obstacles to oblation and the surpassing of the self, to the unification of consciousness in a universal totality. It seems that when it approaches religious experience, psychological experience touches on a fire in which every singularity is volatilised, whilst the person emerges in a form radically different from that known to a limited and possessive consciousness. In any case, the constant teaching of the mystics speaks of this link between the search for the *nada*, the psychological nothing, and a progress towards perfect spiritual fulfilment. Perhaps there are no words in our language to define it, and very few states, in our present experience, to contain it.

If, from the common ground on which we stand, we look at the very diverse faces of the spiritual masters, in whom each temperament finds its transfiguration, we must indeed conclude that, even to the conscious gaze of psychologist or poet, there is nothing less banal than this combustion at high temperature. Perhaps, as in the potter's craft, it is the necessity for the warmest and most lasting colours. There is a moment, however, when this 'prayer of simple attention' shedding its light on man, discourages the attention of the psychologist. It does not make nothing of his long labour of preparation. It consecrates it, summoning from the very heart of his knowledge, the high wisdom of the prayer that one day slipped through a crack in the composed mind of M. Teste:

'Remove all things so that I may see.'

APPENDIX I

THE CHARACTEROLOGY OF HEYMANS AND WIERSMA

IT was decided to omit detailed reference to Heymans' characterology, although Mounier uses it to a large extent as a basis to his work, in order not to compel English-speaking readers, accustomed to other typologies, to familiarise themselves with a completely new set of types. But for those interested a brief outline of the Heymans and Wiersma characterology is now given.

The types are based on a study of the biographies of historical personalities, ninety-four men and sixteen women, of Dutch, German, French, English, American and other nationalities. Certain fundamental traits in these characters were worked out, and then tested in relation to living subjects, in a carefully worked out questionnaire. From these investigations certain correlations were established, from which the authors claim to have discovered three fundamental properties of character:

emotivity, which consists in being more agitated by trifles than others are;

activity, or the quantity of action expended on a given purpose, all other conditions being equal;

persistence, of representation, which in primary types does not outlast the present, but persists for longer periods in the secondary types.

Between the emotive and the inemotive, the active and the inactive, the primary and the secondary types, there is a difference of degree and not of nature.

The various combinations of these three properties give eight typical structures of behaviour, which can be listed, in the order of their strength, as follows:

1. amorphous (inemotive, inactive, primary)
2. apathetic (inemotive, inactive, secondary)
3. sanguine (inemotive, active, primary)
4. phlegmatic (inemotive, active, secondary)
5. nervous (emotive, inactive, primary)
6. sentimental (emotive, inactive, secondary)
7. choleric (emotive, active, primary)
8. passionate (emotive, active, secondary)

'The method', says Emmanuel Mounier, 'requires a fairly lengthy experience of the intuitive perception of types and their properties. Diagnosis is facilitated when cases are clearly marked, but in others some hesitation will occur before a final choice is made. According to M. Le Senne, in his introduction to this method (see his preface to Heymans' *Psychologie des Femmes*, and in *Nouvelle Revue Théologique*, Louvain, June, August, 1938), this hesitation is due to subjective reasons: a phlegmatic type tends to reduce the method to statistical processes, looking at man from outside: an emotive relies on introspection. Thus when making a diagnosis we must also criticise our own standpoint. But our hesitation may also come from the fact that the subject is halfway between two characters; one can only then locate him by placing him between the types which he suggests in turn.

'It is obvious that this classification can no more be applied with strict rigidity than any other. The three factors, emotivity, activity and primarity–secondarity, give the overall structure of behaviour; emotivity provides spontaneity as well as the physical roots of character, activity denotes the contact with reality, primarity–secondarity, the rhythm that unites both. But the frontiers of each function are not well established and it is an open question whether other basic factors should not be added.'

APPENDIX II

TABLE OF CONTENTS OF THE ORIGINAL
TRAITÉ DU CARACTÈRE

APPENDIX III

TRANSLATION OF MOUNIER'S NOTES FROM THE ORIGINAL *TRAITÉ DU CARACTÈRE*

The bibliographical details are in the main given as printed in Mounier's original French edition. An asterisk * by the side of a note indicates that it has been abridged.

CHAPTER I

1. Pierre Janet: *L'état mental des hystériques.*
2. Minkowski: *Le temps vécu*, 207 et seq., et passim.
3. See Ch. Baudoin: *Introduction à la science du caractère*, Journal de Psychologie, 1935.*
4. G. Poyer: *Les problèmes généraux de l'hérédité psychologique*, Alcan, 1921. In 1880 Dégerine and Charcot stated that the sphere attributed to heredity would continually increase.
5. Ziehen, Haecker, Peters.
6. It should be remembered that Mendel defines several types of heredity. A brief outline of the Mendelian theory is given.*
7. Pfahler: *System der Typenlehren*, 1929.
8. Kroh: *Gesetzmässigkeit der seelischen Entwicklung Z. für pädagogische*, Psychologie, 1936.
9. Jaensch: *Grundformen seelischen Seins*, 1929.
10. Jung: *Les formes et les métamorphoses de la Libido.*
11. Cf. Marcel Nathan: *Des psychoses évitables*, Flammarion, 1929.
12. Monakow and Mourgues: *Introduction biologique à l'étude de la neurologie et de la psychiatrie.*
13. Cf. Maurice Nédoncelle: *La Réciprocité des Consciences*, Aubier, 1943, p. 154. This book, written after *The Character of Man*, confirms what the author has written.*
14. Spranger: *Lebensformen*, 1927 edition.
15. Each type has superior and inferior varieties. This point of view confirmed by Vernon and Allport: *A Test for Personal Values.* Journ. of Abnorm. and Soc. Psychology, 1931.*
16. Paul Valéry: *Introduction à la méthode de Léonard de Vinci.*
17. Dessoir: *Types caractérologiques*, Journal de Psychologie, 1935.
18. Cf. Ravier: *L'éducation de l'homme nouveau*, Spes, 1941, II, 436 et seq.
19. Reich: *Charakteranalyse*, Vienna, 1933.
20. André Breton: *L'amour fou.*
21. Hawthorne & May: *Studies in Deceit*, 1928. With regard to moral attitudes, someone who is fraudulent on one occasion may be a perfect citizen in other circumstances.

22. Cf. Minkowski: *L'Encéphale*, 1921, and *Société de Philosophie*, 1927.
23. Klages: *La loi de rivalité des mobiles.**
24. Alexander & Staub: *Le criminel et ses juges*, Gallimard.
25. Green: *Psychoanalysis in the Classroom.*
26. Cf. Janet: *De l'angoisse à l'extase*, II, 633, in which he distinguishes 'inverted feelings' from true ambivalence, by the fact that the subject has a painful awareness of ambiguity.
27. Alexander & Staub: op. cit. *Un possédé du voyage en auto.*
28. Kierkegaard presents one of the most striking examples of this generalised ambiguity.*
29. The myths of Prometheus and the Titans have been interpreted as myths of men struggling with the Gods, and turning their aggression against themselves.
30. The same abuse of words is Freud's use of 'perversity' to describe infantile sexual ambivalence. Sartre (*L'Etre et le Néant*) describes bad faith as a sort of slumber or dream, but which is nevertheless a position adopted.
31. So far only published in outline in two series of articles in *Esprit*, 1937 and 1939.

CHAPTER 2

1. Dupré: *Pathologie de l'émotion et de l'imagination*, p. 245.
2. Cf. a case quoted by Janet: *Obsessions et psychasthénie* I, 519 et seq.
3. Cf. Janet's changing views on emotivity: *Rapport sur les problèmes psychologiques de l'émotion*, paper read to the Société de Neurologie. Revue de Neurologie, 30th Dec., 1909. *Obsessions et psychasthénie* p. 519 et seq. *De l'angoisse à l'extase*, II, 449–495.*
4. Cf. case quoted by Janet: *Névroses et idées fixes*, II, 43.
5. Refers to Wallon's stress on the primacy of psychogenesis over organogenesis of the emotions.*
6. Cf. Devaux & Logre: *Les anxieux*, Masson, 1917; Freud: *Introduction à la psychanalyse*, ch. XXV, and Jones: *Traité de psychanalyse*, Ch. XXVI; Hartenberg: *La névrose d'angoisse*, 1901.
7. According to Freud, anxiety covers all the primitive anxieties of childish origin.*
8. Cf. Freud: *Nouvelles conférences sur la psychanalyse*, 1936: 'Sur diverses instances de la personnalité psychique.' Compares the psychological view of anxiety with Heidegger's philosophy.*
9. Kierkegaard: *Journal*, 12th May, 1839.
10. The psychosis of anxiety may be grafted on to a constitutional anxiety. Freud calls it 'anxiety neurosis'; the passage from one to the other is neither inevitable nor even frequent.
11. Janet (*Obsession et psychasthénie*, I, 232) stresses the intellectual elements of anxiety. See also ibid. 517–535.*
12. The anger of the emotive type, futile, of short duration, soon forgotten, is different from the anger of the paranoiac, rare, but strong and organised, and from the anger of the perverse, which is the most violent and primitive.
13. Wallon: *Troubles du développement psychomoteur*, p. 67.
14. Le Senne: *Mensonge et caractère.*

15. Le Senne: op. cit. p. 108.
16. Alexander & Schäffer had revolver shots fired during the execution of memory tests. The memory of emotives suffered considerably. Emotion has also an effect on the mental operations of animals.
17. Janet: *Névroses et idées fixes*, I, 143, 474. 'Emotion', says Janet, 'makes people absent-minded.'
18. Heymans' figures are confused here. The emotive are good, even exceptionally good observers of things that interest them, bad in other circumstances.*
19. Anxiety neurosis is the most direct result of the emotive constitution, but it may also facilitate the onset of acute melancholia, hypochondria, neurasthenia and hysteria. Dupré has defined an emotive psychoneurosis.
20. Nietzsche: *Will to Power*.
21. Cf. Gilbert Robin: *L'enfant sans défauts*, Flammarion, 1930, II. Special attention should be paid to nocturnal terrors, which are sometimes due to organic trouble, but also simple indications of constitutional emotivity.
22. In the most difficult cases doctors will prescribe, with due caution, sedatives for the sympathetic nervous symptom, such as opium.
23. Cf. Abramowski: *Recherches experimentales sur la volonté*, Journal de Psychologie, 1913 and 1915.

CHAPTER 3

1. Criticises Janet's definition of force as being purely conventional.*
2. The means of transmission of this heredity by no means clear. Special structure of the protoplasm? Variations of wave-length at atomic level? Glandular insufficiency is often observed.
3. Janet: *Force et faiblesse psychologiques* p. 269. Cours du Collège de France, M. Miron, Enstein, 1930.
4. Cf. Dr. G. Robin: *La paresse est-elle un défaut ou une maladie?*
5. Cf. Dr. A. Deschamps: *Les maladies de l'énergie*, Alcan, 1908, and *Les maladies de l'esprit et les asthénies*.
6. Cf. Dr. Deschamps: op. cit.*
7. Cf. P. Janet: *Les médications psychologiques*, III, p. 18 et seq.
8. The latter is still described as mental level. Cf. P. Janet, *L'automatisme psychologique*, p. 451 et seq. *Obsession et psychasthénie*, p. 445 et seq. *Les médications psychologiques*, I, p. 94 et seq., p. 292 et seq., p. 301. *Force et faiblesse psychologiques*, p. 67 et seq. *De l'angoisse à l'extase*, p. 38 et seq. With the concept of psychological tension, of indefinite degrees, Janet improves on his first early distinction between automatism and mental synthesis, which can only properly be applied to hysteria.
9. In his later publications (*De l'angoisse à l'extase*, p. 207), Janet was obliged to make it clear that tension means not so much the absolute complexity of the reality in question, as its apparent complexity to the subject.
10. Janet: *Force et faiblesse psychologiques*, p. 28 et seq. . . . Boredom . . . appears to derive from a perpetual restarting of preparatory actions which collapse almost immediately by a kind of inability to find an outcome.*
11. Janet: *De l'angoisse à l'extase*, II, 142 et seq. On boredom see also: Le Savoureux: *Le Spleen*, Steinheil, 1913.

12. Janet: *La pensée intérieure*, p. 365 et seq. The state also found in dreams and in religious revivalism.*

13. Janet: *Force et faiblesse psychologiques*, p. 104.

14. Janet: *Evolution de la personnalité*, Cours du Collège de France, p. 163.

15. No individual can clearly perceive more than five or six objects at a time, about ten sounds and certainly fewer ideas. . . . Spearman was astonished that so little attention had been paid to this fact, since perception disposes of some three to six million retinal cones, and the cerebral processes of some ninety-two million nerve cells.*

16. Binet: *Etude expérimentale de l'intelligence*, p. 256.

17. Gilbert Robin: *L'enfant sans défauts* and *La paresse est-elle un défaut ou une maladie?* Both books are a warning against a too quick diagnosis of laziness, which is often only the child's defence against surroundings.*

18. As example of the second type, see Phellion in Balzac's *Petits Bourgeois*.

19. Minkowski: *Le temps vécu*, p. 260 et seq.

20. Janet: *De l'angoisse à l'extase*, II, 641 et seq.

21. Otto Gross: *Die Zerebrale Sekundärfunktion*, 1902.*

22. The observations that follow are based solely on correlations established statistically by Heymans and Wiersma.

23. Kroh: *Experimentelle Beiträge zur Typenkunde*, 1929. Pfahler: *System der Typenlehren*, 1929. Sensation itself is of shorter duration in primary types.

24. Describes Wiersma's test for persistence.*

25. Cf. Proust: *Le temps retrouvé*, II, 22.

26. Related in a certain sense to the concept extraversion–introversion, it also recalls the concept objectivity–subjectivity put forward by Binet.

27. See Minkowski: *Le Temps vécu*, pp. 74 et seq., 366 et passim., in the series *L'Evolution psychiatrique*, Artrey, 17, rue de la Rochefoucauld, Paris 9e, and the analyses of Heidegger and Jaspers.

28. Janet: *Obsessions et psychasthénie*, I, 268.

29. In Freudian symbolism the house symbolises the mother and a pre-occupation with a house betrays a mother fixation.

30. The question asked by Saint-Exupéry (*Pilote de Guerre*, p. 105) on observing a poor bedridden woman cloistered in a little silent town.

31. Minkowski, op. cit. p. 163 et seq.

32. Dr. Dide: *Variations de l'intuition étendue-durée*, Journal de Psychologie, June, 1929.

33. There is a parallel lack of orientation both in time and space in mental pathology.

34. Guyau: *Genèse de l'idée de temps*, 1890.

35. G. Klossowski: *Temps et aggressivité*, Recherches Philosophiques, V. 1935–1936.

36. The concept of duration depends on the cortex, particularly the frontal area. If sub-cortical reactions predominate, the concept weakens.

37. Minkowski, op. cit., p. 72 et seq.

38. Mlle Morand (Année psychologique 1914–1919). See also Janet: *Evolution de la mémoire et la notion du temps*, p. 133 et seq.

39. Gabriel Marcel: *Etre et Avoir*, p. 148.

40. See Péguy: *Mystères* and Marcel, op. cit. p. 110 et seq., 135 et seq.

41. Minkowski, op. cit. p. 290 et seq.

42. Minkowski, op. cit. p. 233 et seq.
43. Relates an anecdote told by de Greeff.*
44. Janet: *Obsessions et psychasthénie*, I, p. 481 et seq., and *L'Evolution de la mémoire et la notion de temps*, Ch. III.
45. Minkowski, op. cit. p. 142.
46. Kierkegaard has provided the modern metaphysics of this living repetition, this perpetual reaffirmation of the eternal in time. The theme of recommencement is central with Péguy, and even affects the rhythm of his prose.
47. Jankélévitch: *L'alternative*, Alcan, 1939, p. 126. See also Tardieu: *L'ennui*, Alcan, 1913.
48. Le Savoureux: *Ennui normal et ennui morbide*, Journal de Psychologie, 1914.
49. Janet: *La pensée intérieure*, p. 324.
50. Illustrated by a quotation from Balzac.*
51. Cf. Jean Guitton: *La justification du temps*, Alcan, 1941.
52. M. Proust: *Le temps retrouvé*, II, 16.
53. Rogues de Fursac: *L'avarice*, Alcan, insists on distinguishing between a basic avarice of money and a radically different 'pusillanimous pseudo-avarice'.
54. J. Toulemonde: *Les parcimonieux*, Journal de Psychologie, 1930. Toulemonde distinguishes parsimony from avarice, since he restricts the meaning of avarice to a greed for money for personal use. One should, however, say that parsimony is the ordinary expression of basic avarice, of which avarice of money is a special case.

CHAPTER 4

1. J.-P. Sartre: Nouvelle Revue Française, 1st Jan., 1939.
2. Jung: *L'Inconscient*, Payot, p. 73.
3. Ralph: *Connais-toi toi-même par la psychanalyse*, p. 209.
4. Pfänder: *Seele des Menschen*, 1933, gives an analysis similar to that of Jung.*
5. Dugas & Moutier: *La dépersonnalisation*, Alcan.
6. Mosso: *Education physique de la jeunesse*.
7. In their defeats as in their successes. In *Métamorphoses et symboles de la Libido*, p. 128 et seq., he no longer identifies Bleuler's 'autism' with Freud's 'autoeroticism': in the schizoid there is not only autoeroticism, but the construction of a psychic equivalent of reality.
8. It is important to remember the role of sexuality in this adaptation to reality: from adolescence onwards, sexual adaptation is probably the key and the point of departure of all later adaptations: the least false step here leads to a weakening of general behaviour.
9. *La structure du corps et le caractère*, Payot. There is a slight ambiguity in his vocabulary. He employs the word 'cyclothymic' to describe the general disposition, which will be given later, whether the picture presented is normal or paranormal. When he wishes to distinguish between the two latter, he reserves the word 'cyclothymic' for ordinary variations of humour, and 'cycloid' for the crystallisation of the tendency. But this distinction has not been followed.*

10. See p. 63 of this book. The cycloid constitution can be a basis for the manic-depressive psychosis (or 'circular madness' identified, named and described by Kraepelin in 1899): the alternation of wild excitement and melancholic depression. The first is a way of approaching the external world with a frenzied eagerness (Bleuler), so rapidly that contact is reduced to an instantaneous contact, without outer penetration or inner duration (Minkowski). The second is an almost total servitude to the past.*

11. H. Bouyer & Martin Sisteron: *L'Hygiène mentale et nerveuse individuelle*, Maloine, 1928.

12. This seems to favour the view of those who, like Bleuler and Kretschmer, include paranoia under schizophrenia, and constitutional paranoiac states in the schizoid sphere, as against those who, by reaction, have tried to separate the two too sharply.

13. Minkowski: *La schizophrénie*, Payot. The term 'dementia praecox' which was for long used to describe this state, is doubly incorrect: there is no intellectual collapse, hence no dementia, and the state may occur at any age.*

14. See Rogues de Fursac & Minkowski: *Contribution à l'étude de la pensée et de l'attitude autistes*, Encéphale, April, 1923.

15. There are degrees in this breach with reality. Janet (*La pensée intérieure*, p. 364 et seq.) noticed that many schizoids were dissatisfied with dreams, and made efforts to achieve contact with reality, which explains their false recognitions. A morbid sense of beatitude reveals an acceptance of an illusory world.

16. Mannerisms, 'a series of variations on propriofective themes' (Wallon) short circuit reactions to postural functions.*

17. Sérieux & Capgras: *Les interpétateurs familiaux*, Encéphale, 1900.

18. Jules de Gaultier: *Le Bovarysme;* Lévy Valensi: *Bovarysme et constitutions mentales*, Journal de Psychologie, 1930. Dr. Gentil Perron observed, apart from the imaginative excrescences of 'bovarysme' an undeniably paranoiac element of false judgment.

19. On these disguises see Freud and his disciple Silderer, particularly an earlier work of Freud, *Lois psychologiques du symbolisme*, Alcan, 1895.

20. Janet, *De l'angoisse à l'exstase*, I, 254 et seq.

21. Proust, in *A l'ombre des jeunes filles en fleur*, II, p. 130, gives a good, if somewhat exaggerated account of such treatment.*

22. See particularly Albert Béguin: *L'âme romantique et le rêve*, Vol. 2, Cahiers du Sud, 1939.

CHAPTER 5

1. Piaget: *La représentation du monde chez l'enfant*, p. 123 et seq.*

2. For pathological examples of inconsistency of language, see Janet, *De l'angoisse à l'extase*, I, p. 220 et seq.: e.g. the sleepwalker who was told he had no head, and looking in the mirror, remarked 'It's rather sad and ugly not to have a head.'

3. Heuyer & La Manche: *Le mentisme*, Encéphale, 1929.

4. Janet: *Médications psychologiques*, III, p. 405. For examples of the 'morose inaction' of the depressed, see also *De l'angoisse à l'extase*, II, p. 216 et seq.

5. Janet: *Obsessions et psychasthénie* and for the later revision of the views expressed, *La pensée intérieure et ses troubles*, p. 319, and *Force et faiblesse psychologiques*, p. 282 et seq.

6. Janet: *Force et faiblesse psychologiques*, pp. 30, 93.

7. For instance, the old lady quoted by Janet: *Médications psychologiques*, II, p. 128, who was perpetually interrupting those present in order to forbid their doing something.*

8. The timid are vagotonic. The term 'crises of intimidation' has been employed, in a medical sense.

9. Janet: *L'évolution psychologique de la personnalité*, p. 345 et seq.; Jean Lacroix: *Timidité et adolescence*, Aubier, 1936; Hartenberg: *Les timides et la timidité*; Yoritomo Tashi: *La timidité et les moyens de la combattre*; L. Dupuis: *Les stigmates fondamentaux de la timidité constitutionnelle*, Revue Philosophique, 1915.

10. Janet: *La peur de l'action*, Revue Philosophique, 1927.

11. Just as in the course of evolution the tusks of certain mammoths curved in upon themselves so much as to lose their maximum efficiency, so depression can lead to the inversion of action and even of desire, like the cyclist riding into the tree he wishes to avoid.*

12. Bernard Grasset: *Remarques sur l'action*, Gallimard, 1928.

13. Janet: *Médications psychologiques*, II, p. 104.

14. Such as the profound anxiety covered by the brilliance of the psalms in *Nourritures terrestres* (Gide).

15. Janet: *Névroses et idées fixes*, I, p. 48.

16. Janet: *Médications psychologiques*, II, p. 104.

17. The treatment of the over-scrupulous is a special branch of the training of the irresolute. Many suggestions can be found in A. Eymieux: *Scrupuleux et obsédés*, Perrin.*

18. Abramson: *L'enfant et l'adolescent instables*, Alcan, 1940.

19. Ch. Baudoin: *L'âme et l'action*, Ed. du Mont Blanc, Geneva, 1944.

20. Even in a muscle detached from the organism the contraction is as violent as the resistance to it is strong.

21. See Mlle Morand's study of waiting, in Année Psychologique, 1914–1919, and Janet: *L'évolution de la mémoire*, p. 133 et seq.

22. Hans Fallada: *The Tin Bowl*, the study of a man who has been several years in prison.*

23. Janet: *De l'angoisse à l'extase*, II, p. 127 et seq., particularly p. 154 et seq., showing that effort does not simply consist in doing something 'more strongly'.

24. Ibid. II, p. 137 et seq., on the sense and behaviour of enthusiasm.

25. Bremond: *Les passions et la santé*, p. 121.

26. Janet: *Médications psychologiques*, II, p. 77; *Force et faiblesse psychologiques*, p. 88.

27. Abramson: *L'enfant instable*, Alcan, 1939.

28. Janet: *Etat mental des hystériques*, p. 684.

29. Janet: *Médications psychologiques*, I, p. 276 et seq.

30. Janet: *La peur de l'action*, Revue Philosophique, 1927.

31. Studied by Freud in his *Metapsychologie*, Payot, 1939.

32. Janet: *La peur de l'action*, art. cit.

33. Janet: *Médications psychologiques*, III, p. 255.
34. Eymieux: *L'obsession et le scrupule*, Perrin, 1910, p. 60.
35. Eymieux, op. cit., quotes the case of the woman who from time to time bought 60 litres of eau-de-cologne for her charwoman to wash the mouldings of her ceiling.*
36. See Janet: *De l'angoisse à l'extase*, II, p. 380 et seq.*
37. The attitude has even been found in religious literature.*
38. Gives details of Freud's theory of return to the womb, and suggests that this would partly explain the theme of return to the soil which was found in French propaganda after the defeat of 1940.*
39. Arnold Meyer (Baltimore) suggests that dementia praecox is provoked by a complete absence of success in adolescence.*
40. Janet: *Médications psychologiques*, II, p. 80.
41. Dr. R. Laforgue gives several such cases in *Psychopathologie de l'échec*, Cahiers du Sud (undated), a work of otherwise doubtful value.
42. Janet: *Médications psychologiques*, III, p. 199.
43. See the distinction made by Aveling between 'conation' and 'resolving' in British Journal of Psychology, 1926, and at the International Congress of Psychology of the same year.
44. Janet: *La pensée intérieure*, p. 187 et seq.
45. Janet: *Névroses et idées fixes*, I, p. 55.
46. Abramowsky: *Etudes expérimentales sur la volonté*, Journal de Psychologie, 1915.
47. Ch. Baudoin: *Suggestion et autosuggestion*, Delachaux & Nestlé, 1924, p. 16. Baudoin speaks of self-hypnosis where Americans use the term concentration.
48. James: Précis de Psychologie, p. 610.
49. Janet: *Névroses et idées fixes*, I, 2, 55.
50. The word executive is used throughout in the English meaning of an employee who takes no administrative responsibility. [Trs.]

Chapter 6

1. Janet has noted that a dog to whom several balls are thrown at once runs after each in turn in confusion, becomes angry and fails to decide on a line of action.
2. Wallon: *Stades et troubles du développement psychomoteur*, 271. According to Sartre, the sticky, object of physical and ontological horror in nausea, is also a force which stifles liberty, the other being then perceived as a form of dominance.
3. One should consider the metaphysical and spiritual extensions of this sense of the secret in Kierkegaard, and the significance of modesty in Jaspers and Soloviev.
4. Art. cit.
5. Journal of Abnormal and Social Psychology, 1930–1931.
6. Janet: *Médications psychologiques*, III, p. 189.
7. There is also a tendency to give presents particularly to those one dislikes, for instance the husband to the wife he is deceiving: a rite of appeasement for one's conscience. Similarly there are those whose presents are always misplaced, because they are not really directed to the recipient.

8. Jung: *Modern man in search of his soul.*
9. Klages: *Principes de caractérologie,* p. 142 et seq.
10. Janet: *Médications psychologiques,* II, p. 152.
11. Janet: op. cit., III, p. 180.
12. Wallon: *Les origines du caractère chez l'enfant.*
13. The arrival of others frequently produces agitation in the demented, who only recover after a period of rest.
14. Janet: *Médications psychologiques,* III, p. 239.
15. Treatment consists in a precise, progressive habituation to overcoming intimidation: this saleswoman to be spoken to confidently, a protest to be made in public, etc.*
16. Reported by H. Bouchet: *L'individualisation de l'enseignement,* p. 140.
17. Janet: *Névroses et idées fixes,* I, p. 456 et seq; *Obsessions et psychasthénie,* I, p. 382.
18. It is at the origin of some abnormal forms of behaviour, such as a man wanting to be kept by a woman.
19. Freud: *Psychologie collective et analyse du Moi,* p. 79 et seq.
20. Janet: *Médications psychologiques,* II, p. 143.
21. On the role of this process in the psychology of some criminals, see Alexander & Staub: *Le criminel et ses juges,* Ch. II, Gallimard, 1934.
22. Janet: *Médications psychologiques,* II, p. 128 et seq.
23. L. Dupuis: *L'autoritarisme comme aboulie sociale,* Journal de Psychologie, 1927. See also Janet: *Obsessions et psychasthénie,* I, p. 193 et seq.
24. Janet: *Evolution psychologique de la personnalité,* p. 370 et seq.
25. Janet: *Médications psychologiques,* II, p. 152.
26. Here, as always, one must guard against the temptation, when using these bi-polar descriptions, to force individuals into one exclusive sector. Allport observed experimentally that the majority of persons are neither markedly dominant nor markedly submissive.
27. Max Scheler: *Nature et formes de la sympathie.*
28. The process has been well described, particularly by Freud, discussing Le Bon, in *Psychologie collective et analyse du Moi.*

CHAPTER 7

1. Cf. Politzer: *Introduction à la psychologie,* Rieder.
2. For instance, what we have discussed elsewhere, 'scouticism' a parasite on the Scout movement.
3. I have tried to analyse various consequences of this state of mind in *De la propriété capitaliste à la propriété humaine.* Desclée de Brouwer, 1936, republished in *Liberté sous conditions,* Ed. du Seuil, 1946.
4. The theme of the double is frequent in literature and has been studied recently by Otto Rank: *Une étude sur le double,* Denoel, 1932; Ch. Baudoin, *Découverte de la personne,* Alcan, 1940. The heroes of these stories are always more or less attached to their double, but as they defend themselves at the same time against the narcissism which he expresses, they hate him as a persecutor. The doubles are defeated by a woman, symbolising the triumph of sexual love over narcissism.*
5. Alexander and Staub: op. cit., p. 110 et seq.

6.   G. Robin: *L'enfant sans défauts*, p. 146.

7.   Chavigny: *L'esprit de contradiction*, Rivière.

8.   Freud similarly distinguishes between narcissism, an inversion of the libido, and egoism, a calculation of self-interest, alien to sexuality. But he admits that the first, in practice, results in closing the subject in upon himself.

9.   Montassut: *La constitution paranoiaque*, thesis, Paris, 1924; Dr. Genil-Perrin: *Les paranoiaques*; Hyvert: *Les tendances psychopathiques constitutionelles*, thesis, Valence, 1924, and on the mania of interpretation, the articles of Dromard in Journal de Psychologie, 1910.

10. The 'pride' of the moralists may be based on very varying psychological pictures: a paranoiac tendency; a 'protest' compensating a weakness (Adler); a narcissistic regression; a hysterical exhibitionist drive; a love of domination, etc.

11. For analysis of the feeling of 'being excluded' see Baudoin: *L'âme enfantine et la psychanalyse*, p. 220 et seq.

12. Dugas: *Le soupçon*.

13. See Jules Vallès: *Le bachelier*.

14. Starting with the most humble subjects, early bowel training, avoidance of oral hedonism, by not encouraging sucking of extraneous objects, etc. (Dr. Pichon).*

15. Proust: *Sodome et Gomorrhe*, II, 122.

16. St. John of the Cross had already noted the difference of this mystic state from the states of loss of the self. In the mystic there is joy at the union with God, whereas the others are only the sign of 'a sort of paralysis, or melancholy or other natural mood of the brain or heart, which invades the senses and produces a suspension of life'. *Ascent of Mount Carmel*, Honnaert edition, I, 104.

17. See Chap. IV.

18. An ambiguous use of the word *flesh*, incidentally, persists. In St. Paul, as in the great spiritual tradition, it means not the body, but the whole of the forces which, in the body, oppose spiritual movement.

19. See Jung: *Essai de psychologie analytique*, Stock, 1931; *La théorie analytique*, Aubier, 1932; *L'homme à la découverte de son âme*, Ed. du Mont Blanc, 1944.

20. When the author is using the word 'self' in the popular sense, it is printed with a small 's'. When he is using it in the Jungian sense, the transcendent and personal self, it is printed with a capital. [Trs.]

21. Mignard: *L'unité psychologique et les troubles mentaux*, 1928.

22. Debesse: *La crise d'originalité juvénile*, Alcan.

23. Janet: *L'évolution psychologique de l'individualité*, p. 342 et seq.

24. Adler: *Der Sinn des Lebens*, Vienna-Leipzig, 1933; *Menschenkenntnis*, Leipzig, 1931; *Praxis und Theorie der Individualpsychologie*, Munich, 1930; *The Education of Children*, New York, 1930.

25. Claparède: *Le sentiment d'infériorité chez l'enfant*, Cahiers de pédagogie expérimentale et de psychologie de l'enfant, Geneva.

26. See Maurois' study of *Byron*.*

27. See, for instance, the evidence of Benjamin Constant and Kierkegaard. It seems, on the other hand, that an authoritarian climate does not have any profound effect if it is introduced after the twelfth year.

28. Dr. Charles Ollier: *Egalité et psychologie individuelle*, a special number of Etudes Carmélitaines, 1939. The collection is published under the general title: *Les hommes sont-ils égaux?*

29. See the case quoted by Wexberg: in l'Encéphale, 1926.

30. See Chap. IX.

31. Adler: *Le tempérament nerveux*, Payot. (Translation.)

CHAPTER 8

1. Spearman: *The Abilities of Man*, Macmillan, 1927.

2. Cf. Janet: *De l'angoisse à l'extase*, I, 224, 245 et seq., 370 et seq., 426 et seq.

3. The word 'belief' is ambiguous. It could be reserved to these primary credulities, since loyalty to transcendental values can be expressed by the word 'faith'.

4. Nietzsche: *Human, all too human*, aph. 383.

5. Freud has shown that intelligence tests are falsified when they introduce words associated with disturbing complexes.

6. Ralph: *Connais-toi toi-même avec la psychanalyse*, 213.

7. Nietzsche: *Thoughts out of season*.

8. To be compared with certain morbid states. For instance, the obsessional quoted by Janet (*Obsessions et psychasthénie*, I, 136) who declared: 'I would prefer not to pass water rather than not do it perfectly.'

9. Wallon: *Stades et troubles . . .*, Flammarion, 1935.

10. Janet: *Les débuts de l'intelligence*, Flammarion, 1935, pp. 155–159.

11. Nietzsche: *Twilight of the Idols*.

12. Heymans: *Psychologie des femmes*.

13. Janet: *De l'angoisse à l'extase*, I, p. 330 et seq.

14. Kierkegaard's principal work is entitled '*Of two things, one*' badly translated as 'Either/Or': the key word in Hegel is *aufheben*, which means to suppress, or carry forward or outstrip.

15. Wallon: *Stades et troubles . . .*, p. 146.

16. Quoted by Paulhan: *Esprits logiques et esprits faux*, Alcan, 1896.

17. Janet, describing this state in *Obsessions et psychasthénie*, p. 482, represents it simply as a step towards thinking. The psychological concept of thought in Janet's work is influenced by the special sector in which he worked.

18. The English have a word for this process of elimination by explanation—to explain away. Péguy said that when one begins to explain, one begins to betray.

19. Nietzsche: *Beyond Good and Evil*, aph. 80.

20. Nietzsche: *The Will to Power*, Gallimard ed., Vol. 3, aph. 153.

21. Janet: *La pensée intérieure et ses troubles*, Chabine, 1926–1927.

22. W. Stern: *Die Intelligenz der Kinder und der Jugendlichen*.

23. Janet: *Névroses et idées fixes*, p. 152, quotes a case of a woman abulic who saw nothing, grasped nothing, and found her perceptions so peculiar that she even doubted their reality.

Chapter 9

1. All methods of investigation have been tried. The categories chosen by Heymans are too exclusively practical and social. Tests of morality were inaugurated by Fernald, 1912 (classify crimes and offences according to their gravity). May & Hawthorne published sixty-eight similar tests in 1925, a further one hundred and ninety-six in 1926. The tests were of three types, reactions to moral situations, to professional or scholastic situations, to actual situations in the subject's life. Hermsmeier (Leipzig) extended this type of investigation in 1931. Various objections raised to this type of investigation, particularly the difference between knowing what one ought to do, and actually doing it. Psycho-analysis, in spite of its claim to amorality, has done great service in clearing the lower reaches of morality of many parasitical growths. The phenomenology of moral attitudes has hardly started. For a typical example, see Max Scheler: *L'homme du ressentiment.**

2. Piaget: *Le jugement moral chez l'enfant*, Delachaux & Nestlé.

3. One of the dominant themes of St. John of the Cross is the clouding *even of natural understanding* by the indiscretion of the self. *Ascent of Mount Carmel*, III, ch. 19.

4. This leaves to one side the role attributed by Freud to the liquidation of the Oedipus complex in the formation of the Superego. The theory can be disputed. When Freud writes that 'social anxiety is the basis of moral conscience' he leaves the door open to a wider interpretation of this origin. See Dr. Odier: *Contribution à l'étude du surmoi et du phénomène moral*, Revue Française de Psychanalyse, 1927. Also same author, confirming our analysis, *Les deux sources consciente et inconsciente de la vie morale*, Ed. La Baconnière, Neuchâtel, 1943.*

5. Freud: *Neue Folge der Vorlesungen zur Einführung*. Discord between the parents sets up a division in the Superego and moral uncertainty.

6. It often subsists in a fragmentary manner, weighing on certain zones of the conscience, and not others.

7. Freud: *Nouvelles conférences sur la psychologie*. 'Sur diverses instances de la personne psychique.'

8. Reik: *Geständniszwang und Strafebedürfnis*, Internat. Psychan. Verlag, 1925.*

9. Inversely, and by over-compensation, an excessive cleanliness (common amongst homosexuals, particularly at moments when they give way to their passion) may be designed to cover a sense of profound guilt.

10. See, for instance, Janet: *De l'angoisse à l'extase*, I, p. 408.

11. Janet: *Obsessions et psychasthénie* ch. I. Baruk: *Psychiatrie morale*, notes the profound, irrepressible and debilitating character of remorse in the neurotic and lunatic.

12. Dr. Allendy has even spoken on this question of 'the divine in us'.

13. To be compared with the Freudian mechanisms of displacement and resistance to interpretation.

14. It was curious to note in French prisons, between 1940–1941, how the majority of common law prisoners identified their cause with that of the Allies, as if offences against social order were a national duty. Alexander

& Staub, op. cit., p. 93, show the criminal's desire to provoke authority to injustice in order to justify his own crimes. Similarly children provoke their parents to extremes.*

15. It is impossible entirely to overlook the theological aspect. It is important to know that Catholic theology equally condemned Calvin's conception of repentance as an obsessional inner feeling (Council of Trent, *De pœnitentia*, Canon 43) and Luther's view of it as a simple change of living, without active distress over the fault (do. Session XIV, ch. IV).

16. The Freudian universe is more likely to weigh us down with a systematic obsession of guilt. See E. Borne, *Le rationalisme freudien*, in *L'homme et le péché*, Plon.

17. St. Francis of Sales: *Letters* 16, III, 1643.

18. Fénélon: *Lettres spirituelles*, No. 235.

19. See Etudes Carmélitaines, Dec., 1937. *Aridité et processus psychophysiologique*.

20. Fénélon: *Lettres spirituelles*, No. 382.

21. Gal. IV, 1-7.

22. Ossipond: *Tolstoi Kindheitserrinnerungen*.

23. 22nd July, 1603.

24. April–May, 1603.

25. Sublimation, according to Freud, is the mechanism by which tendencies (sexual or others) 'exchange their sexual purpose for a distant aim and a greater social value', which gives a considerable increase in psychic productivity. Although Pfister speaks of 'a derivation leading to results of high moral quality', he, like Freud, gives morality a purely social significance.

26. See A. Lortsch: *La psychothérapie réligieuse; ses résultats, sa nature*, Paris, Jouve, 1925.

27. St. Thomas: *De virtutibus*, q. I. a 13 ad 13.*

28. Herman Melville: *Pierre or the Ambiguities*

29. Rousseau: *Emile*, Vol. 1, ch. V.

30. Cf. Rousseau in the *Dialogues*: 'Here am I alone on the earth, having neither brother, nor neighbour, nor friend nor society except myself. The most sociable and loving of men has been banished by unanimous agreement . . . '*

31. Dupré: *Pathologie de l'imagination et de l'émotion*.

32. Psychoanalysts admit other causes of delinquency, the spoilt or neglected child . . . Alexander & Staub (op. cit.) follow the orthodox Freudian view in saying, 'Everyone is born criminal', and that criminality is repressed in most persons, but persists in the criminal.

33. G. Robin: *L'éducation des enfants difficiles*, Presses universitaires, 1942. Ch. on the perverse child.

34. Dr. Pichon: op. cit., p. 228.

35. Cassian: *Monastic Institutions*. Book IX, ch. X.

36. Jones: *Traité de psychanalyse*, p. 733.

37. R. de Saussure: *Etude des normes en psychothérapie*, Hygiène mentale, Jan., 1935.

38. 'We do not compel any patient to get better' (Freud).

39. Dalbiez: op. cit., II, p. 420.

40. Dr. Lemonnier: *Thérapeutique des péchés capitaux*.

41. Dr. G. Robin: *La paresse est-elle un défaut ou une maladie?*
42. What we say of religion is also true for all choices of values. There could be characterologies of political, national, aesthetic feeling, etc.
43. On this last point, see the work of Jung.
44. There are isolated works, such as those of Bovet, in Protestant circles, and Spranger: *Psychologie des Jugendlichen.*
45. Said to have been Mussolini, during a lecture at Neuchâtel.
46. Similarly Dr. Laignel-Lavastine: *La méthode concentrique dans le traitement des psychonévroses.* He sets faith in the first place as a cure for neurosis. See Dr. Lortsch, op. cit.
47. Laignel-Lavastine: op. cit., p. 152. It is true, as Fr. de Sinéty has said (*Psycho-pathologie et direction*, 1934) that one can only recognise the true mystic by making a large allowance for the false. Fr. Poulain considers that three-quarters of those who consider themselves favoured by mystic states are deceived. Fr. de Sinéty considers this is still too generous. He distinguishes four groups: those in mental hospitals (Janet's Madeleine), spiritual psychopaths (Marie des Vallées, Fr. Surin) in whom an authentic spiritual life has met with real pathological accidents, just as it might suffer from neuralgia or rheumatism ... 'If anyone claims to attain union with the divine without losing his health', said Tauler, 'let him declare himself': authentic mystics with slight psychopathic tendencies, and authentic mystics without trace of psychopathic or neurotic tendencies. See also the Etudes Carmélitaines, on *Sécheresse et Inhibition*, Desclée de Brouwer.
48. Jung: *Psychology and Religion*, American lectures.
49. As in psychopaths also. See Janet: *De l'angoisse à l'extase*, I, 373.
50. See, for instance, Dr. Leuba: *La famille névrotique et les névroses familiales*, Revue Française de Psychanalyse, 1936.
51. A point of view stressed by Jung: *Formes et métamorphoses de la Libido*, p. 61.

INDEX